D1450594

Learning Disorders:
An Integration of
Neuropsychological and
Psychoanalytic Considerations

Learning Disorders:
An Integration of
Neuropsychological and
Psychoanalytic Considerations

Arden Rothstein, Ph.D.; Lawrence Benjamin, Ph.D.
Melvin Crosby, Ph.D. and Katie Eisenstadt, Ph.D.

International Universities Press, Inc.
Madison   Connecticut

Special thanks go to Iona Aibel for preparing the illustrations in this volume

Library of Congress Cataloging-in Publication Data

Learning disorders.

    Includes bibliographies and index.
    1. Learning disorders. 2. Neuropsychology. 3. Psychoanalysis. 4. Learning disorders–Case studies. 5. Neuropsychology–Case studies. 6. Psychoanalysis–Case studies. I. Rothstein, Arden. [DNLM: 1. Learning Disorders–psychology. 2. Neuropsychology. 3. Psychoanalytic Theory. WS 110 L4383]
RF506.L4L435   1988   616.89   87-2857
ISBN 0-8236-2956-2

Manufactured in the United States of America

Table of Contents

Introduction to the
Integrative Perspective and
to Major Clinical Cases

Despite the burgeoning development of the field of learning disorders, an unfortunate polemical atmosphere continues to pervade its study and treatment. Many clinicians evidence at least a subtle preference for either a psychodynamic or neuropsychological[1] explanation of etiology. This state of affairs may originally have reflected an inevitable trend in the development of science as the concept of minimal brain dysfunction was advanced in an area previously dominated by psychoanalytic approaches. Kuhn (1962) suggests that discoveries necessarily involve "noncumulative developmental episodes in which an older paradigm is replaced in whole or in part by an incompatible new one" (p. 92). In a different vein, Rangell (1972) interprets polemical argument as an expression of aggression: "It is impressive to me, in a negative sense, even among analysts, how surely one can expect in any scientific presentation for a discussant to bring up and 'protect' some other factor than the one presented by the author. It is as if dichotomies are needed for aggression to be discharged" (pp. 5–6). Whatever its etiology, the time seems ripe to abandon such conflict for the sake of the patient's clinical realities. *The major premise of this book is that children and adolescents who manifest learning disorders will best*

---

[1]A "neuropsychological" etiology refers to some form of brain dysfunction, but not necessarily damage, in the context of average or better overall intelligence and intact sensory equipment. See chapter 2 for a more detailed discussion of definitions.

be served by an unbiased, extensive, and, when the data argue for it, integrative formulation of etiology. Oversights and/or inaccuracies in treatment planning can thus be avoided. This is in contrast to an "attempt to force nature into the preformed and relatively inflexible box that the clinician's paradigm supplies . . . [which results in] . . . those that will not fit the box . . . often not [being] seen at all (Kuhn, 1962, p. 24).

This book is primarily addressed to the clinician who is conversant with psychoanalytic concepts and principles. The authors have taught for years in psychoanalytically oriented departments of child psychiatry within medical schools in which we have had the task of conveying to colleagues (many of whom are seasoned child and adult analysts) and trainees in a spectrum of disciplines (fellows in child psychiatry, pediatrics, and neurology, psychology interns, social work and medical students) the nuances and complexities of disorders in learning. We hope that we have succeeded in augmenting the scope of the perspectives they bring to the evaluation and treatment of children, adolescents, and adults with these disorders and thus to their ability to unravel the confusion inherent in this work.

Having become acquainted with the issues which were typically perplexing to our colleagues and students, and the areas in which they had not appreciated the existence and nature of controversies, we felt it was time to give more systematic exposition to basic principles and techniques with the use of illustrative case material they, and of course our own patients, have brought to us. We are especially concerned with forwarding an integrative perspective in a field in which polarized debates surround all aspects: etiology, diagnosis, and treatment.

In our efforts to communicate with the particular audience we have selected, it may at first glance appear that we have replicated one of the central problems we address: a biased view of these disorders. Since we assume a high level of sophistication in understanding psychodynamic considerations, we focus more heavily upon the neuropsychological factors which may interact with other sectors of the patient's personality in parallel or interweaving fashion. However, this emphasis is by no means intended as an alternative view since psychoanalytic concepts serve as major organizers of our own clinical thinking. Instead, we are trying to convey a more complex rendering of the assessment and treatment of patients with learning disorders.

A related goal derives from teaching and clinical experience as consultants on cases in which the best interests of the patient seemed previously to have been overlooked or not fully met due to subtle polemical leanings. Sometimes this reflected failure—on the part of the original evaluating professional or the one from whom a second opinion was requested—to appreciate what constitutes an adequate evaluation. At other times, clinicians were unaware of controversies within the neuropsychological and remedial fields, and thus were unable to assess the validity of a previous treatment effort or the advisability of varying future treatment possibilities. We hope to acquaint our readers with the parameters and controversies of a burgeoning field with which they are not likely to be familiar since these contributions are not published in the journals and other publications they customarily read. We will suggest some questions with which they might approach professionals within the neuropsychological and remedial fields rather than having to accept their methods on faith or, conversely, to reject them out of hand. A secondary goal is to foster better communication with these professionals, to the ultimate benefit of the learning disordered patient for many of whom we feel the child guidance model of division of functions among various disciplines is particularly ill-suited.

To facilitate our goals we will extensively explore several clinical cases. We hope you will accompany us in our thinking about three children, Noah, Daniel, and Matthew, each of whom presented a diagnostic challenge which argued against facile, preformed conclusions. We will begin by presenting them as they appeared to us,[2] without the benefit of a completed diagnostic formulation. We will describe the way in which diagnostic thinking and treatment planning evolved, including mistakes we felt were

---

[2] "We" refers to the major authors whose views are reflected in this book. However, two of the cases were treated by other clinicians, Drs. Daniel Feinberg and Lee Gardner, and the third case by Dr. Melvin Crosby. The cases were written by Drs. Feinberg, Gardner, and Crosby after consultation with Dr. Rothstein about the aspects of evaluation and treatment especially pertinent to this book. In some instances, the sex of the clinician, as well as other identifying data, was disguised for purposes of preserving the patient's confidentiality.

committed, and the process and data which led to their revision. These children's case histories, as well as those of several others to appear later, will aid in conveying what we consider to be a balanced approach to diagnosis and treatment, rather than a single school of thought that is applied to all patients. When a balanced outlook is maintained, it is likely that the richness and complexity of each child's clinical presentation will not be overlooked and, most importantly, that treatment will not be misdirected.

The wish to demonstrate model clinical management was only one factor in the choice of these cases—several other factors were equally salient. We hope to illustrate an array of types of learning disorders, as we conceptualize them. We also want to communicate the realities of the diagnostic dilemmas and the sometimes ambiguous nature of the data with which the clinician must struggle; this includes the experience of being at least temporarily misled and the need to raise and revise hypotheses, sometimes over a substantial time period. This is especially characteristic of work with children in the earliest school years, since the fact of ongoing development may render clinical findings ambiguous. Thus, age considerations in part governed our selection of cases. Insofar as these children presented for early diagnosis, they are model cases; years of mismanagement due to misconceived notions of etiology had not resulted in significant psychological sequelae.

After introducing these clinical cases, in chapter 1 we will elucidate the major principles and theoretical framework that describe our clinical approach to learning disordered patients of any age.

In chapter 2, a spectrum of diagnostic possibilities within this manifest symptom picture is presented. Related to this, we clarify our use of terms, since the failure to do so is responsible for much of the overall confusion in this field.

In chapter 3 we review the literature on diagnosis and treatment from the perspectives of the theoretical framework presented in chapter 1 and the question of whether—and if so in what manner—various contributions kindle polemical debate rather than integrative thinking. It is also intended to acquaint our readers with the central controversies of the neuropsychological and remedial fields, with which they are in all likelihood less familiar. This ought to aid in establishing guidelines for gauging the efficacy of previous evaluation and treatment efforts.

Chapter 4 describes assessment procedures which are for the most part complementary to standard clinical interviews. However, this in no way diminishes our regard for them as essential to successful diagnostic and therapeutic work with learning disordered patients. Special emphasis is given to an exploration of adequacy in psychological testing to aid the clinician (whether or not he or she is a psychologist) in evaluating the aptness of previous efforts or in making successful referrals.

This phase of the work with our three major cases will be presented in detail in chapter 5. Other patients for whom an adequate evaluation was not performed until later in life will be the subject of a section of this chapter entitled "Pitfalls of a Partial Evaluation."

Chapter 6 discusses common neuropsychologically based disorders of learning which may emerge from the careful diagnostic assessment recommended in chapter 4.

Chapter 7 explores the multiple treatment possibilities which exist and the essential nature of flexibly and specifically tailoring interventions to the type of learning disorder manifested by an individual patient. Not only the initial, but the continued, detailed diagnostic assessment will guide decisions about the relative emphasis in treatment upon the following: (1) interpretation and resolution of dynamic conflict which interferes with learning; (2) ego structuring based in part on the interference of neuropsychological dysfunction with the development of ego functions and object relations; or (3) construction of alternative pathways for learning in the context of cognitive dysfunction. Combinations of psychoanalytic psychotherapy preceded by, concurrent with, followed by, or without remediation are illustrated by our major cases as well as several others. Original remedial approaches[3] are thoroughly explicated.

Finally, in chapter 8 the above material is summarized and questions for further consideration and research are proposed.

---

[3] These were developed primarily by Dr. Benjamin.

MAJOR CLINICAL CASES

Case 1: Noah, A Learning Disorder of
Primary Psychogenic Etiology

Noah was a fairly tall, thin, 8-year-old boy, whose great concern
about his eyes was expressed immediately upon entering the
psychologist's office. He was the eldest of three children born to
professional parents. Noah's parents sought consultation with
Dr. Meyers, a clinical psychologist with expertise in neuropsychological dysfunction, because teachers reported that their son
had a short attention span and distractibility. They had taken
their son a week before to a well-known pediatric neurologist
who detected some difficulties on the Bender-Gestalt. In addition, Noah had had a decided eye tic for several months. There
had been a two-year history of severe discord between Noah and
his parents centering around academic attitudes and performance. This was characterized by mutual frustration, irritability,
and hostility. Noah's parents treated him as if his avoidance of
homework were misbehavior in need of corrective punitive
measures, while the boy grew increasingly angry, negativistic,
and depressed. Noah also evidenced nightmares and phobias.

From Noah's perspective the eye tic was his major problem.
He asked Dr. Meyers questions about it in each testing session,
and, at the time of the last meeting, it became clear that he
ruminated about his tic in the school situation. He also wanted to
know why he became dizzy and nauseous during car trips. He
felt the tic was influenced by people with "yucky eyeballs" who
looked at him and made his lids feel heavy. He added, "I want to
make sure there's nothing wrong with my eyes because my
daddy doesn't know everything and he might be wrong. I want
to see if my daddy's right. He says I'm tired. I don't know if that's
right. And I want somebody who will make me so I don't get
dizzy in the car." Noah's somatic complaints were plaintive and
fraught with anxiety. As far as schoolwork was concerned he felt
his reading and spelling were "all right" but that he had trouble
memorizing the multiplication tables.

Noah was a very tense little boy who seemed to experience
pleasure only rarely. He was very diligent about working in the
testing situation and certainly did not present in a way that could

be interpreted as "lazy"; nor was there clinical evidence of hyperkinesis or distractibility. He tried to do well and constantly enquired if he were succeeding. While concerned about his performance, he was not ostensibly gratified by success; nor was he overwhelmed by failure. Yet his tic seemed to be a barometer of his sense of effectiveness: during more relaxed moments, the tic-ing was reduced. As he began to do poorly on more difficult items, it increased once again.

Case 2: Daniel, A Learning Disorder of Mixed Neuropsychological and Psychogenic Etiology

Daniel was a lean, alert-looking 7-year-old boy with expressive but intense brown eyes and disheveled straight black hair. His fine-featured face was simultaneously serious, animated, and reflective of many moods, including humor and pleasure. He anxiously expressed his need for his mother to be in the office with him but then came in bouncily, playing and conversing spontaneously. While he was not hyperactive, there was a constant impression of inner and outer tension manifested in Daniel's facial motor activity and tendency to jump around, frequently clutching at his penis.

Although both his mother and father were well aware of Daniel's periods of acute separation anxiety, jagged maturation, and painfully disruptive behavior patterns, there was a "conspiracy" of inaction and a wish that time and denial would heal all. Some aspects of his behavior were especially confusing. His outwardly sophisticated appearance and social ease were in marked contrast to the infantile clinging he manifested in relation to his mother when they went out together and his whiny, anxious preoccupation with where she was and when she would return if she were to leave him at home. He could handle himself with calm and poise in his father's office or at a large, primarily adult social function, but was withdrawn and frozen with anxious immobility when expected to play casually with several children his own age. His outbursts, which occurred by and large in his parents' presence, were characterized by panicky wails, facial tautness, thrashing, kicking, and helpless but resolute obstinacy as he fastened himself unyieldingly to a stair railing.

The excellent private school he attended duplicated his parents' inertia in dealing with these problems. Suddenly, in June of the first grade, the school called a parent–teacher conference to share their startled realization that Daniel was not learning, not participating in activities, and not developing peer skills and relationships. In the summary prepared for that conference, his teacher stated: "Daniel is an eager and friendly 7-year-old who is very, very anxious to please adults. With adults he appears outgoing and trusting and continually seeks all kinds of involvement. He wants them to help tie his shoes, do his project, or answer his questions. When asked if he would like to share his ideas with a peer he refuses, saying 'he might not understand.'"

Although he always engaged in deceptively mature conversations, he would, after verbalizing facilely what he would like to do, demand a great deal of help, praise, and supervision in order to carry out the simplest task. His attention span was short and he rarely accomplished a project. Unable to participate in group situations, he would stride around the room, look out of the window or door, or sit "dreamily" sucking two fingers of one hand, while rubbing his ear with his other hand. Daniel had more or less alienated the other children by shadow boxing around them, poking and teasing them to get their attention. The school report's final category, "suggestions made to parents and notes for next year" stated simply, "It has been our feeling that Daniel should have another year with this age group."

His parents immediately sought professional advice. They consulted with a psychoanalyst, Dr. Marks, who referred them to Dr. Loni, another psychoanalyst, for consideration for psychoanalysis. In the first session with Dr. Loni, Daniel needed to have his mother sit in a corner of the room reading a magazine for the first quarter of an hour but then tolerated her departure. It was striking that when calling his mother, he used her first name, "Rose, stay with me." He chose to sit close to the analyst, looking at her (the analyst) timidly and guardedly, but also sweetly and appealingly. While his body positioning, gaze, and voice quality were poignantly intense—indeed somewhat like a scared little rabbit—he evidenced an undeniably active, thoughtful, and refreshing spontaneity. He moved sometimes with a commanding, jaunty stride and at other times with an "old-man"-like, depressive slouch. He was undoubtedly alert to his environment, often in a frightfully guarded manner, and less often, manifested a hungry receptiveness to new experiences and ideas. While he typically seemed constrained by his apprehension and anxiety, he was nevertheless affectively warm and had an unusual capacity for wit. With gentle exploration he spoke of his troubles: not wanting to go to school because of stomachaches, not liking most of the kids "cause they tease," and "sad and scary feelings last year that have all gone away."

Daniel attempted to differentiate tasks with the current analyst from those with Dr. Marks, the original consultant. He stated that he liked Dr. Loni better than Dr. Marks because Dr. Marks "didn't say we could do whatever we wanted to here." Dr. Loni explained, "Part of the difference was because we had different jobs. Dr. Marks had to answer the question, 'Does Daniel need help with his troubles and, if so, what kind of help does he need?'" Daniel interrupted this explanation by asking the analyst, "Why did he want me to see you, Mommy?" He perceived his own slip and said, "What's your name?" At this point the analyst chose not to address the slip and replied simply, "Dr. Loni." Daniel then went on, "Mrs. Loni, what troubles?" When the question was reflected back, he snapped, obviously recalling an incident in Dr. Marks' office, "Well, I didn't want to stay in the waiting room alone . . . 25 minutes! You don't like being alone so many minutes do you?" The first session was ended with Dr. Loni's suggestion that maybe he was wondering if she could understand that painful feeling.

Daniel's thrust for a relationship with Dr. Loni was pungent. Slowly studying the office, he was most curious about her and her other patients: "Who gave you that desk? Who sleeps on the couch? Do other children draw? Can I see their work?" His interest in the history and meaning of what he observed was promptly exemplified by his response to a clear glass paperweight with a large flower inside. He took it off a shelf and returned to his perch near Dr. Loni's feet to study it. He then began to talk about how the flower got into the glass, what the colors meant, and under what circumstances the flower could come out.

Daniel presented the paradoxical picture of a little fellow who was so painfully anxious and easily overwhelmed by his rage and fear that he could not separate from his mother, relate to peers, or learn in school. Yet he was able to engage in a relationship with Dr. Loni with unusual swiftness, warmth, perceptivity, and genuine affectivity. Other features of his functioning, however, were less clear. The psychological protocol and clinical picture of school difficulties indicated the need for further exploration of possible neuropsychological difficulties through specific psychological tests, discussion with professionals in his school, and the development of a more detailed developmental history.

Case 3: Matthew, A Depressive Reaction to an Undiagnosed Learning Disorder of Neuropsychological Etiology

Matthew typically presented as a boisterous, talkative, and energetic child. He was the kind of boy who would be considered classically hyperactive by some clinicians in that his behavior was sometimes fragmented as he jumped from one task to another without finishing the preceding one. He sometimes missed the fine or not so fine social cues in dealing with others. For example, during his second day in a new first grade he slipped and said "shit" as he had trouble reading a word; he realized his social error only later. His activity and energy levels were extremely high such that all adults and many children had difficulty keeping up with him. At the same time, however, Matthew was quite charming. He was clearly able to calm himself and become involved in work and with people. Therefore, he was something of a puzzle. He often seemed to be a very typical energetic 5-and-a-half-year-old; yet at other times it was clear that he was a boy for whom everything was not quite right.

His parents requested an evaluation because his teachers in kindergarten said Matthew was a "blank wall" to them. He "misbehaved" in school and was making no progress in academic learning. They were enamored of him but yet felt mystified. Matthew's parents were puzzled as well. He was "mean" at home, refusing to do what he was told. Struggles over eating, dressing, bathing, and bedtime were a daily experience. One of the activities in which both parents and teachers could always count on Matthew being interested, and one to which he often turned himself, was drawing. The first call for help followed Matthew's drawing of a house burning down with the mother left inside, about which both teachers and parents were upset. Other common drawings represented a huge pit of fire or Matthew being chased by a shark about to kill him. He was also considered by.both parents and teachers to be a leader "but in the wrong direction." Matthew incited other children to commit mischievous acts, for example, to sneak up on the teacher and frighten her. He was seen as a boy who, because of his physical prowess, despite his diminutive size, simply awed children his age and even older. He could do acrobatics, jumping, swimming, and most other sports activities at a level way beyond that expected for his age. Yet his ability to get along with other children was poor. Fights were frequent since he was unable to let another child have his way. Girls were rarely involved since he "hated girls and women." Everyone reported that he got along better with and responded more readily to men and other boys. These were all long-standing difficulties, changing only somewhat over the previous few years of his life.

The confusion people felt in dealing with this boy and the intensity of the feelings he aroused were striking. It was as if everyone wanted desperately to find some way of understanding and helping him but was nevertheless left feeling angry. Matthew's parents and teachers concurred in simultaneously perceiving him as delightful and "bad." Only once was an alternative suggested; his mother wondered whether he might be "brain damaged," by which she meant hyperactive, an explanation previously dismissed by Matthew's pediatrician.

We will later rejoin Noah, Daniel, and Matthew after having explored the theoretical principles that govern our approach to learning disorders, as well as central controversies of the field, and the nature of the diagnostic process we recommend. The diagnostic work done with these three patients will be elaborated in chapter 5 and the varying treatment approaches resulting from this work will be presented in chapter 7.

Chapter 1

Theoretical Foundations

This chapter will present the basic theoretical constructs, which inform the clinical investigative and treatment processes with learning disordered patients explicated in chapters 4, 5, and 7: the developmental framework with its reliance upon the principle of multiple function, the task analytic approach, and the law of parsimony. These constructs also serve as organizers of the classification scheme proposed in chapter 2 and the critical review of major contributions and central controversies in the field which comprises chapter 3.

The first of these constructs is the developmental framework, by which we mean to convey the complex and inherent enmeshment of physiological maturational forces and psychological development. Intimately related to this is the second construct, Waelder's (1930) "principle of multiple function;" in his ego psychological expansion of Freud's earlier concept of "overdetermination" (Breuer and Freud, 1893–1895), Waelder simultaneously considers the multiple vectors that constitute the scaffolding of any psychological production. He maintains that all significant behavior is multi-determined; that is, it reflects the influence of all psychic structures (id, ego, and superego), the compulsion to repeat, and the ego's attempt to "assimilate" these factors. Related also are A. Freud's (1970) views on the symptomatology of childhood, which emphasize the multiple routes, both genetic and structural, to seemingly

similar surface manifestations of psychopathology. Her classic
paper on this subject highlights the necessity of attending to the
individual's uniqueness in discovering how each child's problems
weave their own pattern.

In a very different realm, the task analytic approach to diagnosis of neuropsychological dysfunction similarly maintains a broad
perspective on all possible contributions to a disorder in complex
higher cortical functions. That is, all the individual building blocks
which comprise any one task must be identified and examined to
precisely determine the nature of the difficulty. For example,
diverse neuropsychological etiologies may eventuate in the same
degree of academic disorder in arithmetic.

A final principle may seem, at first glance, to stand as a contradiction to those already mentioned; however, the conflict is only
apparent. While being sensitive to the overdetermination and complexities of symptoms, we wish simultaneously to keep in mind the
concept of "parsimony" in scientific conceptualization. The best
hypothesis is the simplest one that is capable of encompassing the
data and is reliant upon the fewest untestable assumptions. Invoca-
tion of more general or abstract concepts is unnecessary when a
simpler explanation suffices, and indeed may result in "stretching"
the data to fit the concept. Conclusions should be generated by the
data rather than by some aesthetic or scientific preference either for
complexity or simplicity.

Since the principle of multiple function and the law of parsimony are part of the basic working vocabulary of psychoanalytically oriented clinicians, we need not further explore their bearing
upon learning disorders at this point. We will return to their clinical
application in the course of our case presentations. However, some
aspects of the developmental framework and task analytic approach
require a more in-depth look, the former to clarify and elaborate
upon some already familiar contributions, and the latter to propose
a neuropsychological orientation to learning with which readers
may not be wholly conversant. The task analytic approach will be
presented first to better elucidate the subsequent discussion of
neuropsychological functions as they impact upon psychological
development.

THE TASK ANALYTIC APPROACH

Prior to explicating the task analytic approach we will briefly
review the underlying cortical mechanisms, structure, and func-

tions in adults that serve as its foundation. The clinical applications of this perspective in the context of assessment and treatment of children and adolescents will be amplified in chapters 4 through 7. Practically all of the work in brain localization has been done on adults with already developed skills. The problem with applying these findings to children is that most who suffer real injury to the brain recover, if they are young enough at the time of trauma and if the damage is localized. Some children with massive disturbances as a result of viral disorders or toxicity show few sequelae and others remain grossly disturbed or retarded in intellectual development. Still others with no history of illness, poor pre-, para-, or postnatal care or injury manifest a cluster of dysfunctions which correspond to patterns of brain localization. However, substantive evidence of damage is absent on electroencephalogram, X ray, pneumoencephalogram, clinical examination, or history.

The cortex of each hemisphere of the brain is divided into four main areas: the occipital, parietal, frontal, and temporal lobes. When one sees something, light, stimulating the retina, is transformed into electrical energy which is transmitted to a central projection area of the occipital lobe. Each eye transmits information to a central projection area of the occipital lobe of both hemispheres, the information from the right side of both eyes going to the left hemisphere and the information from the left side of both eyes to the right hemisphere. If the central projection area is damaged, depending on the extent of the damage, the patient either is totally blind or experiences field cuts; that is, part of the visual field remains unrepresented in the brain.

When one is tactually stimulated, the representation for that stimulation is somewhere posterior to the sensorimotor strip in the parietal lobe. There is a fairly clear point-to-point relationship between the part of the body stimulated and the area of the brain in which that body part is represented. The greatest amount of cortex in this area is responsive to the hands, represented in the parietal lobe adjacent to the temporal area. Sensations from the left side of the body are represented in the right hemisphere and vice versa for sensations on the right; motor acts are similarly contralaterally controlled. Thus, a lesion involving the motor side of the sensory motor strip results in paralysis or poor control of that part of the body on the contralateral side.

When one hears, sounds are transmitted from each ear to the temporal lobe of both hemispheres. If the central projection area of both hemispheres is damaged, cortical deafness exists. An interesting developmental phenomenon occurs with hearing. In most people language becomes localized in the left temporal area and the other aspects of sound—timbre, rhythm, inflection, tone, pitch, and the like—become localized in the right temporal area. It is the left hemisphere that has come to be known as the dominant hemisphere in most individuals, probably because it controls language, a distinguishing characteristic of humans. Lesions in the left temporal area will affect language functioning, leading to conditions such as aphasia and other impairments in auditory memory. Lesions in the right temporal area may lead to difficulties in recognition of tonal qualities of speech and amusia, a difficulty recognizing familiar tunes, as well as visual memory. One can think of the temporal areas as controlling memory functions, the left controlling verbal memory and the right visual memory.

The frontal lobes control highly complex functions such as planning, foresight, and intentional actions. Our main concern here is with the other three areas, the intactness of which is required for imagery, although the conversion of an image into an act involves the frontal lobes.

The remainder of the cortex, the association cortex, serves a transmission function; that is, information received in one part of the brain is transmitted to all other parts of the cortex. It is because fibers connect these sensory receptive areas that one can learn that the word "cup" refers to a particular stimulus which feels a certain way (i.e., the sound representation from the temporal lobe becomes represented also in the parietal lobe) and looks a certain way (i.e., the word becomes represented somewhere in the occipital area). Similarly, a visual stimulus of a cup excites temporal areas producing a word image which can get transmitted to the verbal motor area informing it to have the mouth move in a particular fashion to make the sound "cup." To the extent that auditory memory is intact, if the word that emerges does not sound exactly like "cup" the individual will make an adjustment in what he has just said through the process of auditory feedback.

There are various names for specific disorders related to lesions in adults involving specific association areas. Some common left hemisphere disorders include agraphia (inability to write), alexia (inability to read), anomia (inability to name things), and acalculia (inability to calculate). Several right hemisphere disorders are inattention to visual stimuli, dressing and constructional apraxias (inability to voluntarily execute coordinated movements).

In addition to fibers connecting the central projection areas there are fibers connecting the two hemispheres. Some very interesting work in brain function has involved the study of the two hemispheres after they have been disconnected surgically in a procedure called a commisurotomy. Geschwind (Geschwind, 1968; Geschwind & Kaplan, 1962) and Bogen (1969) have demonstrated that patients with a dysconnection syndrome show some rather startling behaviors.

Of interest here is the following phenomenon: after commisurotomy their left-handed patients had great difficulty writing from dictation or spontaneously with the left hand even though they could draw perfectly adequate geometric designs with this hand. Alternately, all right-handed patients could not draw geometric designs with their right hand but could write quite intelligibly with this hand. It will be remembered that words and letters (i.e., language images) are left hemisphere functions in right-handed persons. They become unavailable as information to the right hemisphere because there is no way for that information to cross over and instruct the left hand to write words. Geometric patterns, initially represented in the right hemisphere, needed no contralateral transmission, and thus the left hand could copy these figures. The right hand, controlled by the same hemisphere as language and its skills, could easily write. But the difficulty lay in the fact that visual–spatial information had to be transmitted to the left hemisphere for instruction to the right hand. When the patients were taught to associate language to these geometric figures they performed better. Thus, words could instruct a hand to perform when it could not perform by simply using visual information.

Similar interesting phenomena occurred on tests for tactile agnosia. When presented with an unseen object in the right hand the patient could name it but could not simply pick it out in a visual multiple-choice situation. When the object was presented in the left hand, he could pick it out from among others but could not name it.

This series of studies of adults points to the general finding that in right-handed persons, left hemispheric lesions result in language disturbance and right hemispheric lesions result in visual–spatial disturbances. As noted above, findings with children and adolescents are by no means as conclusive or clear-cut. Nonetheless, one can proceed with a neuropsychological investigation in the same way one would if there were a specific localized lesion, testing for its effects as well as for intact functions. That is, it can be assumed that something is awry in either the receptive, discriminatory, or associative functions of the brain, *as if* one were dealing with an adult with a specific lesion. Thus, one can trace those pathways which are more disrupted than others. The ultimate intention is that of defining a profile of strengths and weaknesses for clarification of the nature and extent of the patient's difficulties. In some instances this is preparatory to the development of a remedial plan in which the area of dysfunction would need to be bypassed by using pathways that are intact (see chapter 7).

For either or both purposes, a fine-grained analysis must be performed to determine which of the multiple routes to the noted disorder may be held responsible. Only by examining them all may some be ruled in and others ruled out in a reliable manner. It is this process that has been designated as "the task analytic approach." An analysis of the numerous tasks required for several basic academic acquisitions will best convey the nature of this process.

What must a child learn in order to read? What is meant here by "able to read" is the ability to decipher a word not previously seen, in contrast to the ability to recognize a set of lines which signify some concept. That is, if a child learns that when he sees "D-O-G" he is to say "dog" and when he sees "C-A-T" he is to say "cat," this will not in and of itself be called reading. Although the functions that go into the task "D-O-G" equals "dog" and "C-A-T" equals "cat" are important functions for learning to read, they are not of a much higher order than those of the rat learning to discriminate between a circle and a triangle. True reading involves behavior that demonstrates recognition of the fact that letters or combinations of letters signify sounds, and that these sounds when put together in a certain order and in a certain manner happen to make a word that one has already spoken or heard. True reading requires conditional learning, that is, that some stimuli presented in one context signify one form of behavior and the same stimuli presented in another context signify a different form of behavior. An example of this in reading is the difference between the sound one makes for a vowel when there is an "e" at the end of a word and the sound one makes when it is absent, for example, "tap" versus "tape."

The multiplicity of functions that are called upon for reading will now be described (the way in which they are assessed will be a subject of chapter 4). The first and most obvious function is perceptual discrimination; of particular interest are two perceptual modalities, visual and auditory. Even more specifically, reading demands discrimination of shape, as opposed to color and size, in the visual modality, and sound discrimination as opposed to concept discrimination in the auditory modality. Stated simply, one wants to know if the child can recognize whether or not two stimuli are the same or different.

The second function necessary for reading, assuming intact perceptual discrimination, is both short-term and long-term memory. Although the details of memory are still under investigation, this distinction is a simple and important one. When one asks the information operator the telephone number of a department store, that number is usually transiently retained in short-term memory. If one has not recorded the number and a busy signal occurs, one will typically have failed to commit the number to memory. In contrast, should one move one's residence and thus obtain a new telephone number, that number is committed to long-term memory.

A third function necessary for reading is smooth vocal–motor production which enables the child to imitate all speech sounds heard. This function assumes intact auditory perceptual discrimination and short-term auditory memory.

A fourth function is sound blending. Independent of visual stimuli, the child must put together (synthesize) two or more sounds. The function assumes intact auditory discrimination of speech sounds, short-term auditory memory, and smooth vocal–motor praxis.

A fifth function involves left to right orientation, especially as it applies to letters as stimuli. A sixth and most crucial function is the ability to make transmodal associations. The function assumes intact auditory and visual discrimination, short- and long-term memory, and may, depending upon the task, require a left to right set. The question asked here is whether the child can learn that an arbitrary pattern of lines reliably signifies a certain sound. That is, can he associate arbitrary visual and auditory patterns? If all other functions are intact except this one, one can speak of an association disorder.

A seventh function involves conditional learning. Can the child learn that a triangle and circle on a red background require a response to the triangle, whereas the same stimuli on a white background require a response to the circle? In reading, for example, he has to learn that an "A" is pronounced /ă/ except when it is presented after an "O" in which case the "O" is responded to and the "A" ignored.

An eighth function involves attention shifting between sensory modalities. In the reading process one must transform letters into sounds, stop attending to the printed letters, blend the sounds, and produce the word as a gestalt. In the continual presence of visual stimuli the child must shift his attention from them to the sounds they represent. Obviously, for smooth reading one is constantly engaged in rapid shifts of attention, and the inability to do this can truly be called an attention disorder.

Some of the same functions that are required for reading obviously apply to the acquisition of arithmetic skills: auditory and visual discrimination, memory, directional orientation (here a bit more complicated and involving conditional learning), transmodal associations, and attention shifting.

The first additional function is the ability to count, that is, to learn a one-to-one correspondence between a rote set of words— "one," "two," "three," and the like—and a series of usually visually presented stimuli such as blocks. That is, only one word is applied to each stimulus in the counting process. Regardless of the spatial orientation of the set of stimuli or the characteristics of the components of the set of stimuli, the verbal sequence is applied one word to each until all are accounted for. The child must also understand that the last word he has said, "seven", for example, denotes not only the end of the chain of sounds but represents the entire class of objects he has just counted. Adequate visual spatial organizational abilities, and usually coordinated hand movements, are necessary for just the simple task of answering the question, "How many?"

The child must also learn that each of these number words has visual counterparts called numerals, that these numerals placed in different juxtapositions represent different numbers, and that the clue to number reading is embedded in a left to right orientation, a task not unlike reading. A specific difference from reading, however, involves the teen numbers. With these numbers, "17," for example, the first sound one is supposed to say is indicated by the number on the right; one is supposed to ignore the number on the left except for the contingency implications it carries. The number "17" means "seven-teen," not "seven." Yet when one reads "71" he is supposed to proceed in a left to right direction. Children with difficulty reading or writing numbers frequently manifest a specific impairment with the teen numbers suggestive of left–right disorientation.

Most children learn to do their sums in the first grade by reference to the most available and constant set of objects: their fingers. They, therefore, need good finger discrimination and recognition for their use as primitive calculators.

The child must learn to shift set from left-to-right to right-to-left in doing operations with numbers of more than one digit. His spatial organization must be good enough to organize numbers in columns and rows and he must attend to the significance of operation signs.

He must learn which numbers are larger and smaller, more and less, which come before and after other numbers. Therefore, his language must be sufficiently intact to understand these concepts both in terms of their spatial referents ("bigger" and "smaller") and their temporal referents ("before" and "after"). Children with arithmetic difficulties often demonstrate language problems that are not manifest in reading skills because the language used to teach these skills is different.

And lastly, the building blocks essential to reading a clock will briefly be considered. A host of spatial, language, and conceptual elements must be grasped, for example, counting by 5s ignoring number values, part–whole concepts, and vocabulary (e.g., 60 minutes = 1 hour, 15 minutes = a quarter after, 30 minutes = half past), spatial and numerical before and after concepts, right–left discrimination (e.g., the right side of the clock is "after" and the left side "before"), and size discrimination (the difference between the small and large hands).

THE DEVELOPMENTAL FRAMEWORK

There is an inseparable interplay between constitutional and psychological features of the developing child. Only with careful recognition and exploration of these trends can the complexities of their emerging relationships be grasped. More than three decades ago Hartmann (1950) published a fundamental paper calling for investigation of the impact of the child's ego equipment upon his intrapsychic and ego development. However, it has spawned surprisingly few psychoanalytic investigative efforts in the field of learning disorders. He wrote:

We come to see ego development as a result of three sets of factors: inherited ego characteristics (and their interaction), influences of the instinctual drives, and influences of outer reality. Concerning the development and the growth of the autonomous characteristics of the ego we may make the assumption that they take place as a result of experience (learning), but partly also of maturation. . . [pp. 120–121].

We have to assume that differences in the timing or intensity of their growth enter into the picture of ego development as a partly independent variable, e.g., the timing of the appearance of grasping, of walking, of the motor aspect of speech. Neither does it seem unlikely that *the congenital motor equipment is among the factors which right from birth on tend to modify certain attitudes of the developing ego (Fries and Lewi, 1938). The presence of such factors in all aspects of the child's behavior makes them also an essential element in the development of his self-experience* [p. 121, emphasis added].

So far we have in analysis mainly been dealing with the intervention of conflict in [the autonomous ego apparatus's] development. *But it is of considerable interest not only for developmental psychology but also for clinical problems to study the converse influence too: that is, the influences which a child's intelligence, his perceptual and motor equipment, his special gifts, and the development of all these factors have on the timing, intensity and mode of expression of these conflicts.* We know infinitely more, in a systematic way, about the other aspect, the ego's development in consequence of its conflicts with the instinctual drives and with reality [p. 123, emphasis added].

The major exception is Weil (1961, 1970, 1971, 1977, 1978) who has made a number of masterful contributions to our understanding of how the neuropsychologically based deviations that affect learning simultaneously interact with the psychological sphere in the development of a neurotic personality organization. Weil's work, as well as that of De Hirsch (1975) in the area of language, will be drawn upon extensively in the following sections. Parallel, although less in-depth studies of the relationship between minimal brain dysfunction (MBD) and disturbances of ego functions in schizophrenic, borderline, and neurotic conditions in adulthood have been made by Hartocollis (1968, 1979), Bellak (1979), and Greenspan (1979).

There are two aspects of the interdependence between neuropsychological and psychological development. One, a nonspecific effect, is the greater likelihood of pathology when highly varying rates of development exist in different personality sectors, to which A. Freud (1963) has alerted us in her comparison of developmental lines in a diagnostic profile. In this realm fall disturbances in such areas as the regulation of self-esteem and the sense of competence. The other aspect is the more particularized impact that specific forms of neuropsychological dysfunction have upon the development of particular ego functions and/or facets of object relations. This is a corollary to what has just been described with regard to delimited aspects of learning.

Among the latter—those dysfunctions which pose more particular interferences—there is variability as to the scope and time of onset of the deficit's impact. This will depend upon the severity of the deficit and the degree to which the affected apparatus is critical to basic early ego acquisitions. When multiple and/or central ego apparatuses are involved, the impact upon psychic structuralization will tend to be more profound. This is in contrast to the more delimited deficits (e.g., in visual sequencing only) affecting functions which do not take on central importance until academic requirements are imposed on the child. Deviations in these functions are not likely to have the same import for the development of the ego and object relations, assuming several conditions: they are identified in the earliest school years, they are mild in degree, they do not exist in the context of other more fundamental dysfunctions, and they do not dovetail with special parental investments.

We will now explore the first aspect of interdependence with special emphasis upon how the neuropsychologically impaired child's uneven abilities impact upon his emerging sense of competence; then we will proceed to the second aspect. In the service of conveying the overdetermination of any one aspect of psychic development, we will delineate the multiple ego apparatuses and their functions which contribute to a central aspect of psychological development: the formation of integrated self- and object-representations. In so doing we will explore how various forms of neuropsychological dysfunction might serve as anlage for pro-

found deviations in this process. Subsequently, individual neuropsychological functions will be examined with regard to their
implications for various ego developments. The division of these
functions is for heuristic purposes. Like most classifications this one
necessarily fragments what are in reality inextricably interwoven
phenomena.

Nonspecific Developmental Effects of
Neuropsychological Dysfunction

In the development from birth to maturity there are at least four
major trends that rely upon a combination of neuropsychological
and environmental factors:[1] (1) increasing facility in and control
over physical and other neuropsychological skills; (2) gradual mastery over and adaptive integration and channelization of affects
and impulses; (3) steady growth in cognitive development from a
predominance of primary to secondary process thinking, the
former being concrete and egocentric and the latter being logical,
conceptual, and symbolic; and (4) increasing development of the
sense of self as separate—first from mother and eventually from the
family—with a consequent move away from the influence of home
toward a concomitantly greater influence of peers and internalized
standards and goals.[2] The individual and interdependent paths
taken by these trends are further complicated by the fact that
development follows a pattern in which there are states of equilibrium (periods during which the child seems more organized, not
as easily ruffled or moody, more in control, more integrated) and
states of disequilibrium in which quite the opposite is true. However, some children seem to live a bit more than others on the side of
breakup or disequilibrium. Even at so-called calm stages, they have
difficulties such as disorientation, disorganization, problems with
integration, impulsivity, frustration tolerance, affect modulation,
and the like. The neuropsychologically impaired learning disordered child often fits into this category.

Children with neuropsychological dysfunction are by no
means uniform in their clinical presentation, but rather each is

---

[1] These are only some of numerous possibilities for conceptualizing the complex interactions between all sectors of the personality and the environment.

[2] This section draws upon the work of Ames (1968), D. H. Cohen (1972), and Smith
(1979).

immature in some aspect(s) of his development. He may, for example, stand in contrast to the normal nursery school child who has come from a state of complete physical dependency at birth to one of sufficient agility and bodily control to allow him a great deal of latitude in coping with the physical tasks set before him. The typical child's feelings of competency are heavily based on solid achievement of a physical character, gained by trial and error, and ending in mastery. As he matures, he also evidences increased facility with words which may lead the adult to mistake adultlike language for a comparable level of thought and affect modulation. Despite his flow of language, the 5- and 6-year-old is still subject to the demands of the body for movement; emotions frequently carry greater force than does logic. Mastery of the body and its senses in the service of coping with the environment is too basic to selfhood to be ignored and too intertwined with learning in the early years to be bypassed without consequence. The normally developing child learns to control his body and to concentrate in a progressive fashion, each new stage laying a foundation for the next. Random and undirected behavior and thinking become focused and efficient.

Not so for some children whose physical, neuropsychological, linguistic, and/or conceptual development is delayed. This impinges on their development of a sense of competence or mastery. They may manifest one or a combination of the following: distractibility (indiscriminate reactions to everything going on around them), disorganization (an inability to integrate doing two or more things at once), impulsivity (a rapid switch of attention and behavioral response from one stimulus to another), egocentricity in thought and feeling (an incapacity to grasp the other's perspective and an expectation of being the center of attention of parents or teachers at all times). Such a child has more trouble defining who he is and depends on the adults around him for a longer period of time. Many such youngsters draw superheroes as reparative self-representations long after others of their age group have ceased to do so; their immaturity and/or deficits prolong their search for ways to shore up insufficient feelings of power and competence.

Development of complex language—the hallmark of the movement from concrete thinking to abstract conceptualization—may also be impaired, contributing to egocentric thought and behavior. Dependency needs and feelings of helplessness may be exaggerated. The thrust from attachment to parents toward greater involvement with peers, while difficult for many so-called "normal children," often becomes perilous for children with neuropsychological dysfunction. First the world may be experienced as confusing due to their lesser ability to sort things out and to discriminate. A natural tendency is to be reluctant to let go, with a concomitant hesitancy to let go on the part of parents. By the time a child is 8 years old, a measure of separation from parents and movement toward autonomy of thought and action is a normal phenomenon. The tug-of-war between independence and dependence exists for all children, but manifests itself in a particular fashion for the child with neuropsychological dysfunction. While he must acquire skills and techniques necessary for independence, the people, parents and teachers, who can best help him attain these skills and techniques are the very ones from whom he is struggling to free himself emotionally.

It is often helpful to view resistance to help, remedial and otherwise, from this perspective. Peer pressures for conformity become increasingly strong as the child enters latency. Minor differences (e.g., red hair and freckles) are regarded with disdain. Likewise, the need to conform to the demands of learning skills is great; learning to read, write, and do arithmetic at the same rate as one's peers, becomes essential to one's acceptance in the pack. The neuropsychologically impaired child stands out from the beginning—physically, motorically, linguistically, conceptually, and/ or socially—precisely at a time of life when differences are intolerable to him and to others. The frustration related to obstacles in one's quest for conformity remains terribly painful throughout the school years. Therefore, the school environment with its myriad of demands—physical, cognitive, social, and emotional—can be experienced as an assault on the neuropsychologically deficient child's already shaky feelings of competence.

Specific Developmental Effects of Neuropsychological Dysfunction

Object Relations: A Task Analytic Analogy.   We will now explore the numerous neuropsychological functions involved in one developmental line—object relations—and the multiple deviations to which they may contribute in the event of dysfunction. This is an analogue to the task analysis of problems in academic acquisitions described earlier. Both fine and gross motor functioning relate to the process of self–object differentiation. For example, in fine motor grasping those stimuli with which there is only the sensation of touching versus those that elicit both sensations of touching and being touched, come to be differentiated, the former as the other and the latter as part of the self (Hoffer, 1952). Gross motor awkwardness typically eventuates in especially prolonged support by mother and may interfere with appropriate experiences of brief separation. The same may be said for difficulties in spatial orientation and organization. On the other hand, premature gross motor capacities may present the child with experiences of separation which he is psychologically unable to manage.

In the sphere of perception, special hypersensitivities interfere with attention to outside stimuli and thus discrimination of inner and outer (Greenacre, 1941). That which is new may create panic and lead to withdrawal, rather than exploration and curiosity. In terms of expressive capacities, the child who emits indistinct or unclear cues demands special sensitivity from mother. This may result in an attenuated sense of impact upon and consistency of the external world as opposed to the self. In addition, the poorly endowed child may be less able to draw mother into attachment.

Shifting sensitivities, as in an undiagnosed or uncontrolled seizure disorder, make for a very specific obstacle to developing firm body boundaries and a stable sense of the self versus the outside world (see case 8, that of Brad, in chapter 7). Serious visual–perceptual discrimination deficits will confuse and hinder mastery of figure–ground distinctions and boundaries. Tactile processing, which is related to the above-mentioned fine motor problems, involves more than just coordination. Tactile agnosias may not permit registration of differences between various stimuli. Such deficits may stimulate clinging and impetuous wishes to be constantly in contact with the environment (Weil, 1971).

In the absence of intact language, the child may be deprived of the contribution of language to self–object differentiation in underlining the distinction between inner and outer stimuli, in highlighting relationships, and facilitating distancing from the immediate situation.

Memory functions are extremely significant as well. The child must be able to retain in memory those experiences of differentiated stimuli and affective experiences in order to integrate them into a meaningful whole. Retention of the quality of mother's voice and the image of mother's face assumes intact auditory and visual memory functions in general. A very rare condition of facial agnosia—an inability to recognize the physiognomy of a familiar face—has been reported by Benton (1980). The contribution of this deficit or other more frequent and less dramatic perceptual, memory, or integrative disorders to deviations in the development of object constancy is an interesting area worthy of investigation.

Thus we can see that all of the above input and output functions, as well as the abilities to organize and integrate them, have relevance for the development of stable self and object representations. When many such functions are compromised by constitutionally based deviations, this line of development is likely to find interference, even in the context of sensitive parenting. This might contribute not only to splitting as an active, regressive, defensive process (Kernberg, 1975) but to an initial defect in welding together disparate visual, spatial, auditory, kinesthetic, and affective stimuli which are different perspectives on the same object.

Individual Neuropsychological Functions.   We will now delineate some of the developmental implications of specific neuropsychological functions just as we earlier examined their import for learning.

Motor inhibition.   The progressive ability to curb impulsivity and hyperactivity, beginning in the toddler period, has important implications for the way in which the world is perceived and processed, for self-esteem formation and regulation, and, later, for successful learning and peer relations. Many features of the visual, auditory, and interpersonal world will elude the child who is constantly in motion. In a fundamental infant study Fries (1944) demonstrated that an excessive need to move intrudes not only upon fine motor competence but also upon good perceptual registration and, therefore, upon reality testing. Anthony (1973) creatively exemplified similar trends much later in life, among latency age children. Comparison of descriptions by a hyperactive and a hypoactive 7-year-old, each of whom was asked to take a walk around the same block and then to report what he saw, conveyed the richer and more subtle texture of affective and interpersonal observations of which the latter child was capable. Not only were the impressions of the hyperactive child characterized less by nuance, but they were also more disorganized and unpredictable and, therefore, less likely to be assimilated and internalized.

Excessive motor disinhibition affects the development of self-esteem from early on. As the toddler's mother introduces demands upon him for control of motility, he is painfully confronted with an area in which he cannot fulfill her expectations. This eventuates, Weil (1961) has written, in a vulnerability to neurotic development since there is a "gap between some degree of ego and superego formation and a physiological inability to live up to it" (p. 88). Furthermore, "because of the wish to be good and to please in association with the greater dependency, the organic child often, despite impulsive urges, will hold in aggressive, hostile thoughts and feelings which then emerge in fantasy, fantasy play, but are also projected outward in phobic tendencies (not rarely amalgamated with difficulties from other sources)" (Weil, 1977, pp. 60–61). Furthermore, such difficulties with controlled drive discharge interfere with the development of sublimations. With the onset of latency, the demands of peers for conformity and those of teachers for self-restraint create additional arenas in which a discrepancy between what is possible and what is aspired to will be experienced.

Attention. In a similar vein, the child who is incapable of voluntarily monitoring his attention is prone to have associated difficulties in processing stimuli. He cannot respond selectively to stimuli, for example, in sorting out the relevant from the irrelevant and his memory of what he has seen is likely to be global and unfocused at best, or inaccurate at worst. Such a neuropsychologically determined cognitive style may serve as a nidus for the later development of defenses such as dissociation or denial.

Sensory processing. Hyper- or hyposensitivities irrespective of modality. The child who has a low threshold for sensory stimuli, regardless of the modality, tends to experience difficulty in maintaining attention to the external world and thus with the emerging differentiation between self and other. He will evidence a proclivity for anxiety—even panic in some instances—in the face of stimulation and, concomitantly, an avoidance of that which is novel, thus posing a serious obstacle to learning. The smooth and effective functioning of signal anxiety will be precluded by this more global disposition to be easily flooded and overwhelmed. Instead there are likely to be massive efforts to prevent such a state of unpleasure (Bergman and Escalona, 1949). Weil (1978) has suggested several forms they may take: ritualistic behavior, vigilant control of the self and the environment, or the turning of passivity into activity by joining in or instigating external chaos which affords a projection of inner turmoil. In contrast, the child with an unusually high threshold for registering stimuli may present a manifest picture similar to the hyperactive child but for different underlying reasons. Bender (1945) has described the manner in which many such children evidence hyperkinesis:

> [It] may be understood as an effort continually to contact the physical and social environment and to re-experience and integrate the perceptual experiences in a continuous effort to gain some sense of orientation to the world. The asocial behavior may be understood as the result of the lack of capacity to live out certain infantile drives and build up some understanding of one's place in the world in a temporal pattern . . . and inability to learn from past experiences and build up a concept of aims for future satisfactions [p. 165].

Tactile. Excessive sensitivity to tactile stimuli in particular presents an especially early threat to the normal developmental process as it seriously interferes with pleasure in the mother–infant matrix which is so heavily colored by tactile experience. The infant unable to be comfortably held may at the same time crave this form of contact. Weil (1978) has additionally observed that such an infant may "require distance and is prone to a greater wish for and fear of melting" (p. 468), especially if boundary problems exist.

A more delimited deficit, in the direction of a failure of sensory registration—and one not diagnosed until the early latency period—is finger agnosia, as studied by Gerstmann (1940) in adults and later by Kinsbourne and Warrington (1963) and Kinsbourne (1968) in children. This disorder has implications for a disturbance in the development of a fully intact and well-differentiated body image.

Visual. Failures of visual discrimination range from those of a more pervasive and basic nature to those which are more delimited. Profound difficulties in figure–ground distinctions and in visual discrimination will pose a serious obstacle to the recognition of familiar, as compared with unfamiliar, animate, and inanimate objects. While the construction of such object concepts relies upon a complex interplay of auditory, tactile, and kinesthetic qualities with the visual, the latter is centrally and increasingly important, as Fraiberg's (1968) work with the blind suggests. She found a delay in the attainment of object permanence which ultimately relied upon compensatory sensory stimuli. Figure–ground discriminations are also necessary for the development of notions of causality and spatial relations studied by Piaget (1954), for which the ability to follow trajectories in space and to find hidden objects in view are essential components. Implicit also is the necessity of such discriminations as a beacon for the elicitation of sensorimotor behaviors.

The less pervasive difficulties in visual discrimination—those involving a failure to distinguish between similar although different stimuli, for example, "b" and "d"—are typically not diagnosed until the early school years since they are neither demanded nor expected of the child and are likely to be much less disruptive in their developmental impact in the preschool years. Their most likely psychological effect would be in the form of interference with the establishment of competence in the early school years.

Auditory. As with the other modalities, disorders in the auditory realm vary in pervasiveness and thus in their possible psychological impact. Severe failures in the ability to make gross discriminations between individual voices and between sounds produced by inanimate objects will interfere with the construction of object representations. If such development has taken place, the child with auditory discrimination problems will nevertheless have more difficulty in object recognition in situations in which cues from other sensory modalities are not available.

Difficulty in finer auditory discriminations will affect communication in that acquisition of new vocabulary and comprehension of what others say will be more difficult. Closely related sounds will be confused, for example, words like "choose" and "shoes." Similarly, failure to recognize these nuances will interfere with written communication in that spelling efforts will be compromised.

Spatial orientation and organization. Disturbances or delays
in spatial orientation will serve to inhibit the child's exploration of
his environment and foster a greater reliance upon mother and
other significant adults. Such a pattern once established may outlive
the resolution of a lag. A disorder of this sort, especially if combined
with memory and/or visual perceptual difficulties, may render
frightening exposure to new physical settings, or even what ought
to become familiar settings outside of the home (e.g., that of a
neighbor or a local store).

More delimited spatial difficulties with right–left orientation
or with analyzing and synthesizing part–whole relationships in
space, as in assembling a puzzle, may complicate the mastery of
routes to new environments. They may also intrude upon enjoy-
ment of the peer activities of latency such as sports, crafts, reading,
and the like, thus contributing to problems in self-esteem regulation.

Language. The emergence of language, and later reading
and its comprehension, is central to countless aspects of differentiation and growth of the ego and object relations. As noted above,
within the sphere of budding object relations, its precursor, vocali-
zation, affords a channel for reciprocal exchange with mother
and/or maintenance of contact in the absence of visual or tactile
availability. As the child is increasingly able to comprehend and
communicate words meaningfully, the distinction between "me"
and "not me" is strengthened. In the context of brief separations,
mother is now able to provide reassurance that she will return.

In a similar vein, with increasing linguistic and cognitive
development the child is gradually able to tolerate greater periods
of delay and dosages of frustration, in part related to mother's
explanation first that there *is* a "later," and ultimately her identification of time sequences in the past and future: "before," "yesterday,"
"after," "tomorrow." Verbalization of the baby's experience and
feelings contributes to drive and affect modulation (Katan, 1961)
and the curbing of their discharge through motor channels. Weil
(1971) comments on the miscarriage of this process in the form of
exacerbation of motor activity in the constitutionally hyperactive
child who additionally suffers from a language disorder: "Dysfunctions in the areas of language and speech will further spur such
trends toward hyperactiveness. Dysnomias and language difficul-

ties foster discharge in action (at an age when verbalization would usually take over) and this tendency toward action then interacts unfavorably with the child's general basic hyperkinetic drivenness" (p. 85). This failure or delay is also characteristic of the dysnomic child without neuropsychologically based hyperactivity.

Simultaneously, mother expands the baby's knowledge of the world as she supplies information, points out interesting events, and answers questions. The child's reality testing is fostered as he can express his observations and feelings and, therefore, make them available for mother to correct and elaborate (Katan, 1961). Language development coincides with the discovery of sexual differences to which there is an unavoidably disturbing reaction due to the conclusion that to not have externally visible genitalia is equivalent to castration. Through language mother can correct this theory by providing information that the child is like his (her) mother or father, thus fostering pride in likenesses to loved and admired parents. Other magical and omnipotent beliefs and fears about the child's and parents' powers can similarly be corrected as language permits distancing from the immediacy of the situation.

Not only does mother expand the child's horizon and better adjust his beliefs to the bounds of reality, but she utilizes language to organize and integrate his experience into meaningful segments. In the absence of language, much as in the presence of hyperactivity, the child's taking in of his surroundings is more fragmented and diffuse. Verbalization of time sequences, spatial relationships, and causal relationships contributes to the stabilization of experience and the establishment of secondary process thinking. Furthermore, concept formation and symbolic thinking is stimulated by mother's identification of connections between like objects, events, and people in the environment.

All of the above ego functions so heavily reliant upon language—self-object differentiation, reality testing, frustration tolerance, secondary process thinking, concept formation, modulation of drives, and the development of sublimations—are essential for the tasks of learning expected from latency onward, which in turn further contribute to ego development. A specific example is the contribution of reading to reality mastery. Learning to read—in the sense of decoding unfamiliar words—assumes a complex array of functions, as detailed above. These range from those highly specific to reading and, therefore, less likely to affect early psychic

development in general (e.g., the blending together of discrete
sounds) to those with more general import for development (e.g.,
conditional thinking which, in the case of reading, relates to mastery of varying phonic associates dependent upon contextual
placement of a letter). Grasp of conditional concepts, taken more
broadly, is one of the many higher level organizing principles which
may be recognized as deficient in some neuropsychologically
impaired children somewhat later in their lives. The genesis of a
dysfunction in conditional concepts can itself have multiple roots;
for example, it may reflect disorders of syntax, sequencing, phonic
associates, and/or visual discrimination. Conversely, it may be one
of what Weil (1978) refers to as the "organizing faculties" that are
required, beginning in the second half of elementary school, when
learning is no longer predominantly rote, but instead requires
conceptualization, reasoning, and organization of various sorts.
If neuropsychologically based—and these are the most difficult
interferences in learning to diagnose in the sense of untangling their
neuropsychological from their neurotic roots—this disorder stands
as an exception to the general rule that the later emerging deficits
have less profound impact. It remains true, however, that the
impact of this limitation will vary greatly depending upon the
degree of parental investment in intellectual pursuits.

   Motor coordination.   Just as a spatial disorientation renders
the developing child more dependent upon mother, so will a prolonged delay or deficit in gross motor coordination. Difficulties of
fine motor coordination will hinder self–object differentiation
given the import of exploration of the self and other through the
tactile mode for this developmental trend. As Weil (1978) has
stated, "It is obvious that the infant who is able to grasp at an early
age likewise touches his mother, himself, and objects at an early
age. This in turn has a bearing on separation–individuation and
reality testing. Likewise the earlier the infant crawls the earlier he
will engage in exploration and reality testing" (p. 463).
   Pronounced clumsiness, particularly when it persists for an
extensive period of time, interferes with multiple acquisitions in ego
functioning and object relations. The child's proneness to injuring
himself or the inanimate environment is likely to elicit special
protection and/or prohibitions from mother which may in turn

exacerbate the toddler's typical tendency to negativism. Further-more, since touching, handling, and visually exploring are impor-tant intellectual modes for the baby, severe curbing on mother's part in the interest of caution may have the effect of teaching the baby not to be inquiring, to avoid prohibited objects, and, there-fore, to inhibit curiosity—all with important effects on intellectual development. Coping efforts, for example, in the differentiating toddler's following after mother or approaching a substitute at a moment when an imminent separation portends excessive discom-fort, are made more difficult in the absence of age-appropriate motility.

Incapacities in the fine or gross motor realm pose a major challenge to the toddler's—and later the oedipal and latency child's—emerging sense of effectiveness and control over the environment, as noted earlier. Mocking and rejection by peers due to incoordination in sports or manifest peculiarities of gait and the like may leave prominent stamps on the child's self-image and sense of worth.

Memory functions. Memory functions are so finely inter-laced with all of the above neuropsychological features—and espe-cially those which involve processing stimuli since this is an essential precursor to their recording in memory—that they have in many respects already been considered. Nevertheless they are consi-dered separately to highlight several issues. These functions are discussed in their plural form since they encompass multiple modes (auditory, visual, tactile, and the like) and types in each of these modalities (immediate, short term, and long term). A deficit in one type or modality has no necessary bearing upon another. This needs to be added to Weil's (1978) observation of change of function of memory in the course of development which she discusses as if it were a unitary phenomenon: "Memory, also an autonomous appa-ratus, functions differently at different stages and in different spheres. It participates in the smile as much as in the discovery of the permanence of the object, in remembering the physiognomy of a face or the acoustical sequence of a phrase as much as in remem-bering the physiognomy of a printed word" (p. 464). In actuality it is necessary to assess the psychological implications of an individu-al's particular memory disorder. The more severe and pervasive is the involvement of an array of memory functions, the greater the likelihood that the earliest features of ego development and object relations will be compromised. Disorders of more delimited scope and lesser severity are more prone to affect specific school acquisitions but not major psychological sectors of the personality in that the existence of other intact channels facilitates spontaneous compensations.

Chapter 2

The Complexities of
Definition and Diagnosis

DEFINITIONS

Since language not only conveys but structures meanings (Whorf, 1956), careful and thoughtful usage of terms is necessary to facilitate communication; furthermore, it is reflective of the state of clarity of a field. Viewed from this perspective, the field of learning disorders is frequently muddied by imprecise, overlapping, or contradictory terminology. To some degree this is symptomatic of the universal problem in achieving objective examination. In all fields, the data observed are to some degree colored and shaped by the theoretical perspectives which individual investigators bring to them.

The great currency of the term "learning disability," for example, exemplifies this inevitable fact of human inquiry. It is used variously in the literature in a descriptive and etiological sense. It sometimes indicates that a child is functioning at a grade level two years below that expected, without regard for the cause of that delay. When the term is used to convey etiology, one clinician may be considering a neuropsychological dysfunction, while another views the problem in learning as a symptom of psychological conflict. To further confuse matters, it may refer to a deficit in many aspects of learning or to one which is highly delimited. The countless books and papers on this subject sometimes suffer from a failure to identify the boundaries of the views to which their authors subscribe and the definition of their terms. For example, an author may be talking about a specific subgroup of children with learning difficulties without making this explicit.

In the interests both of maintaining clarity and forwarding an integrative approach to problems in learning, we will define the major terms to be employed in this book and identify their relationship to some of the voluminous vocabulary which appears in the existing literature (for more complete surveys and discussions of terminology see Johnson and Myklebust, 1967; Sapir and Nitzburg, 1973; Black, 1974; L. B. Silver, 1975; and Kinsbourne and Caplan, 1979). The terms in the literature which follow will only be referenced if they are original to a particular author.

"Learning disorder" is here employed as a generic term for any impairment in learning of serious proportions in a child who has been given adequate educational opportunities; this is regardless of whether the impairment is comprehensive (e.g., total school failure) or delimited (e.g., deficits in arithmetic computation or reading). This term is descriptive and does not specify etiology. Other nonspecific synonyms are "learning problems," "learning difficulties," "learning disturbances," and "school failure." Under this broad umbrella definition, three major subcategories may be delineated: (1) those which represent a *primary* psychogenic etiology; (2) those which convey a *primary* neuropsychological etiology; and (3) those which are based on conditions such as mental retardation or sensory impairment, for example, blindness and deafness. While these three categories may be found in "pure" form, and have been delineated as such for heuristic purposes, it is important to recognize that they do not exhaust the possible clinical manifestations of learning disorders. That is, they may be found in an array of combinations with one another, as will be elaborated in the diagnostic classificatory scheme which follows.

Those disorders in learning of primary psychogenic origin, some other frequently used terms for which are "learning inhibition," "psychogenic disorders," or "pervasive pseudoimbecility," may encompass any or all academic subjects. Their varied clinical manifestations will be described in detail in the review of the psychoanalytic literature which follows in chapter 3.

Learning disabilities are those learning disorders in children of normal intelligence, normal educational background, and age-appropriate grade placement for chronological age which are primarily based on unspecified but assumed neurocortical abnormalities or developmental lags.[1] While children with such disorders need not be free of emotional problems or sensory deficits, these must not be the *primary* cause of the disorder in learning. We intentionally avoid using this term in a generic sense because of its multiple, irreconcilable, and therefore confusing usages by an array of clinicians. Instead we believe the term learning disability is best reserved to convey a learning disorder in which neuropsychological factors are primary. Several synonyms found in the literature are "cognitive power disorders" (Kinsbourne and Caplan, 1979), "neuropsychological learning disability," "neurologically based learning disability," "specific learning disability" (Adamson and Adamson, 1979), and "neurogenic learning disorder." Belonging here also is Myklebust's (1964) term "psychoneurological learning disorder," the sequencing of which is meant to emphasize that "the primary manifestations [of dysfunction in the brain in these learning disorders] usually are behavioral, not neurological; the more obvious involvements are psychological in nature" (p. 260).

A cluster of terms found in the literature which we would classify under the rubric of "learning disabilities" describes the functions and/or academic subjects affected. For example, several pertaining to reading are "strephosymbolia" (Orton, 1937), "dyslexia," "specific dyslexia," "specific reading disability," "congenital word blindness," and "developmental alexia" (see Boder [1971b] for a more extensive review of these terms). Some relevant to disabilities in expressive and receptive language are "dysgraphia," "agraphia," "language disorder," "aphasia," "anomia," and "expressive-receptive language disorder." Disabilities in arithmetic are referred to as "dyscalculia," "acalculia," and the like. There is, in addition, a cluster of terms which signify neuropsychological disorders which

---

[1]We do not concur with the common practice of specifying a degree of performance deficit (Cantwell and Forness, 1982). The standard operational definition of performance two years below expected grade level may be necessary for group research and public policy which requires inclusionary–exclusionary criteria. However, such criteria become complicated and/or inapplicable in the clinical situation. For example, the child with an IQ of 140 who performs at grade level may nevertheless have a learning disability.

may, but do not inevitably, eventuate in a problem in learning. When they do, they belong among the learning disabilities. Some are general terms of which learning disabilities may be one manifestation: "minimal brain dysfunction," "minimal brain damage," "minimal brain disorder," "minimal cerebral dysfunction," "neuropsychological dysfunction," "neuropsychological disorder," "developmental disability," "developmental lag," "maturational lag," "neurological immaturity," "soft signs." There is another set of terms which more specifically describe the functions disordered. These too may have no implications for learning if they are either of minor degree or naturally find compensation. Some examples are "perceptual disorder, disturbance, or deficit," "visual–motor integration disorders," "hyperactivity" or "hyperkinesis," "distractibility," "attention deficit disorder," "short-term auditory memory disorder," "short-term visual memory disorder," "association disorder," "graphesthesia," "finger agnosia," "ataxia," "dyskinesia," "apraxia," and the like.

To reiterate, the third discrete subgroup of learning disorders are those due to more global deficits, for example, mental retardation or sensory impairments such as deafness and blindness.

CLASSIFICATION OF LEARNING DISORDERS: THE DIAGNOSTIC SPECTRUM

The frameworks and principles delineated in chapter 1 suggest the need for a classification system that covers the spectrum of learning disorders and recognizes and permits integration of the array of possible contributory factors. Distinctions between categories would be in some instances categorical and in others only a matter of emphasis. In the literature numerous efforts at classification may be found with different degrees of scope. For the most part they focus upon the nuances and subdivisions within several of the points on the spectrum to be proposed, without mention of the others.[2]

We would like to propose a classification scheme in the spirit of a network of beacons to guide further diagnostic and treatment efforts. Work with learning disordered patients is by no means

---

[2]Of those contributions reviewed after this classification was developed, the schemata of Heinicke (1972) and Pine (1980) most closely approximate the one presented here.

static. It is best characterized as a continuous process of exploration and refinement, even after the formal diagnostic period is completed. Therefore, flexibility in revision of original impressions is demanded.

Four broad landmark categories exist: (1) learning disorders of primary psychogenic etiology; (2) learning disorders of primary neuropsychological etiology; (3) admixtures of psychogenic and neuropsychological etiology; and (4) learning disorders attributable to intellectual limitations. The extremes of this spectrum are easiest to define, yet least reflective of the clinical realities of complexity and overdetermination. We shall, therefore, focus equally upon the in-between points.

Primary Psychogenic Learning Disorders

Neurotic Level Symptoms of Intrapsychic Conflict. This appears in the child whose impulse–defense constellation and its symptomatic manifestations center upon the arena of learning. Learning in general or specific aspects of learning (e.g., arithmetic or reading) may be affected. Other features of the child's development—his object relationships and ego functioning—are relatively unimpaired. The learning process as a whole or delimited aspects of learning have been imbued with unconscious symbolic meaning which eventuates in inhibitions. Only the gradual uncovering of these unconscious conflicts will release the child's inherent, unimpaired ability to learn. A careful formal assessment is essential to accurate diagnosis of this type of learning disorder. Such assessment is especially crucial when only highly specific aspects of learning are involved since, as Weil (1977) noted: "Neurosis does not create a dyslexia. Neurotic development may lead to diminished learning capacity and inhibition of curiosity, but I have not seen it specifically and solely affect reading. Neurosis does not create reversal of letters and words. However, if a child has such a maturational weakness, tending to reversals and poor reading, neurotic conflicts may bring it out much more" (p. 58). This latter clinical situation is subsumed by the third type of mixed etiological disorder described below.

Case 1, Noah, the boy with the eye tic and "yucky eyeballs," to whom we return in chapters 5 and 7, illustrates the unfolding of a global learning disorder as a symptom of neurotic conflict. This category of learning disorders has received extensive consideration by psychoanalysts and psychoanalytically oriented clinicians, as will be elaborated in chapter 3.

Disturbances in Cognitive Style. This type of disorder in learning emphasizes difficulties in stylistic features of approaching the learning situation. In the absence of a neuropsychological substrate, such children evidence problems in focusing upon, conceptualizing, and taking in knowledge which, in some instances, result from neurotic conflict. Thus this category may overlap with the previous one in some cases. However, a differential diagnosis helps to determine whether the learning problem can be ameliorated by attention to these aspects of style alone or whether intensive psychodynamic psychotherapeutic work (as in the above category) is essential to uncovering impulse–defense configurations underlying the learning problem. In addition the degree to which these features of cognitive style are confined to the learning situation, as opposed to being central features of personality functioning in general, may aid in deciding between this category and the previous one.

The work of Santostefano (1978, 1980), which adds a developmental perspective to Klein's (1951, 1954, 1970) earlier studies of cognitive controls, addresses the dimension of human functioning intended here: "that individuals consistently use particular cognitive ego strategies or attitudes to approach, avoid, select, register, pace, compare and cluster information, and that individuals differ in the use they make of one or another strategy" (1980, p. 48). He reports several normal developmental shifts between early and late latency from (1) global registration of body percepts and lack of differentiation between slow and fast tempos of motility to more differentiated percepts and tempo regulation; (2) slow, passive and narrow approaches to scanning information to a more active and broad focus; (3) failure to distinguish between relevant and irrelevant stimuli to an ability to do so; (4) global memory images to more focused, detailed and subtle memories; and (5) more narrow and concrete concepts in organizing information to more broad and abstract categories. Psychopathological populations and those under stress do not evidence these trends and thus he concludes "the efforts of these persons to adapt to and assimilate information usually are limited, whether the tasks involve learning in school, learning in a hospital milieu program, or learning in psychotherapy sessions" (1980, p. 54).

Looked at from another perspective, children whose cognitive controls are immature probably are those who receive diagnoses in the personality, and especially conduct disorder, range since they are likely to act impulsively and without sufficient forethought. Difficulties in learning stand, therefore, among others of a broader scope. The other end of the differential diagnosis relevant to this category of learning disorders requires a careful exclusion of the presence of neuropsychologically based distractibility, hyperactivity, concreteness, and the like, since such characteristics may similarly intrude upon learning. These obstacles to learning constitute another category to be delineated below. A related problem characterizes Kinsbourne and Caplan's (1979) diagnostic category "cognitive style disorder." Because it encompasses problems in attention due both to primarily emotional and primarily "brain based" or "physiological predispositions" (the latter included under the lower category "neuropsychological disorders of dysinhibition" in the current classification), it is potentially confusing in its heterogeneity and, therefore, has not been adopted as such.

Learning Disorder as a Function of More Severe Psychological Disturbance in the Absence of Neuropsychological Dysfunction. Children in this category evidence deviations in the development of ego functioning and object relations of sufficient severity to warrant diagnoses of borderline personality or psychosis. Their learning difficulties are secondary to these more pervasive disturbances which result in an inability to invest in learning. This type of learning disorder is especially well delineated by Pine (1980) who outlined three developmental lines necessary for learning, on at least two of which these children manifest disorder: (1) a basic biological and psychological intactness; (2) an ability to control and adaptively channel affects and impulses; and (3) a good measure of autonomy of the learning process which is for the most part invulnerable to disruption by impulse and fantasy. The knotty diagnostic issue—and one in relation to which many contributions to this field are unconvincing or at least inconclusive due to inadequately comprehensive assessment—is establishment of the intactness of biological apparatuses. Some of the "pervasive developmental disorders" of *The Diagnostic and Statistical Manual* (DSM-III) may fall in this category, while others belong in our category "severe developmental disorders," which are admixtures of psychogenic and neuropsychological contributions. DSM-III fails to consider this distinction based on etiology, that is, whether or not neuropsychological dysfunction is contributory.

Environmental Interferences in Learning. This type of learning disordered child lives in an environment which does not provide the necessary stability, encouragement, and calm that are essential nutriments for learning. Not infrequently such familial deprivation also eventuates in the broader developmental disturbances encompassed by the previous diagnostic category. It is when these interferences are primarily confined to the learning process that consideration of this type of disorder is warranted. Also relevant to this distinction is the timing—onset and chronicity—of these interferences. If the environment has been deleterious to the development of essential structural capacities for learning from early on, it is unlikely that ego deviations will be limited to learning. The degree to which learning difficulties are reactive to ongoing stress versus a manifestation of internalized, structuralized deviations is the major issue at stake. Weil (1977) offered a succinct and vivid picture of one deleterious environment which might result in a learning disorder of the type intended:

> Unfortunately, for some deprived children, this is a pattern in their environment; not only are they not given the words for expressing their feelings, but they see the adults in their lives act emotions rather than verbalize them. Exposure to sexual and aggressive scenes is not rare. Constant excitement thus often leads to sexualization and aggressivization of their own functioning and hinders learning. Moreover, the prevalence of irritation and hostile aggression in their environment necessitates that a good deal of their energy goes into vigilance, alertness, avoidance of unpleasantness, searching for little advantages, instead of into productiveness and learning [p. 57].

Learning Problems of Primary Neuropsychological Etiology: Learning Disabilities

Focalized Findings. This type of learning disorder stems from constitutionally based deviations in neuropsychological organization which affect specifiable cognitive functions, such as the ones necessary for academic skills as outlined in chapter 1. Typically these do not result in a pervasive disorder in learning to which the child would be likely to evidence a psychological reaction (see categories below). We do not distinguish between deficits of this sort due to "maturational lag," minimal brain dysfunction, and "constitutionally determined patterns of disturbed neurological organization" (p. 663) as does Heinicke (1972), since these conditions do not have different implications for either the patient's self-experience or treatment. Furthermore, in selected ways the terms "maturational lag" and "MBD" are ill-advised. It is not possible, except retrospectively, to determine whether a child's disorder reflects a lag or an enduring dysfunction. Therefore, we do not concur with Weil's (1961) statement that "in general, children with developmental lags show a good prognosis, with gradual improvement" (p. 84). Children frequently fail to "grow out of" so-called "lags" or, even if they do, they have, due to the "lag," already missed basic academic acquisitions upon which later learning depends. The term "minimal brain dysfunction" refers to such a vastly varying array of minimal (and maximal) difficulties that its use, which is suggestive of a specifiable syndrome, is frequently misleading. Instead it is more accurate to designate whether or not the learning problem has a neuropsychological basis which may be due to slower than usual *or* deviant development.

Within this category are multiple discrete, as well as clustered deficits which have been carefully delineated by many renowned neuropsychologists. A description of some of the more common syndromes will be found in chapter 6 and a critique of contributions to this subject in chapter 3. Also pertinent to this category are the "specific developmental disorders" of DSM-III. However, the subtypes specified in DSM-III are insufficiently inclusive: "developmental reading disorder," "developmental language disorder," "developmental articulation disorder," "mixed specific developmental disorder" (some combination of the above at approximately the same level of difficulty), and "atypical specific developmental disorder" (a disorder not included among the above). There are additional disorders, however, which are not at all atypical—in spelling, sequencing, spatial organization, blending, and the like—which are not encompassed by the DSM-III framework.

Neuropsychological Disorders of Dysinhibition. Children who suffer from neuropsychologically based hyperactivity and/or distractibility (the "attention deficit disorders" of DSM-III) in the absence of focal findings or syndromes are nevertheless highly prone to difficulties in learning. Their quick pace, diffuseness, and/or lack of distinction between relevant and irrelevant stimuli, among other characteristics, interfere with the way in which information is perceived and processed (as described in the section of chapter 1 on the interplay between neuropsychological disorder and the development of ego functions). If not severe—and if properly diagnosed and controlled early enough by medication and/or environmental modifications—such children often need not develop reactive and intermeshing psychopathology of a serious magnitude. Those who are not so fortunate are included in the below category of "developmental disorders."

Focalized Neuropsychological Findings Accompanied by Disorders of Dysinhibition. The above two categories were separated to highlight the fact that neuropsychological impairments with consequences for learning are not necessarily associated with hyperactivity or distractibility as all too many studies assume. Those children who do manifest such disorders may be prone to earlier identification by parents and teachers because of the disruption they cause. More subtle focalized deficits, some of which will not be diagnosed until the middle school years, are more easily misinterpreted in psychodynamic terms. This category accounts for the child who manifests a combination of focal deficits *and* disorders of dysinhibition, who is early and correctly diagnosed; thus the deficits do not take on symbolic meanings and are not recruited for the expression of psychodynamic conflict.

Admixtures of Psychogenic and Neuropsychological Contributions

Psychological Disorders Reactive to Neuropsychologically Based

Difficulties.   These are disorders of acute onset in the early school years as neuropsychologically based deficits come to light in the context of the new cognitive demands made of the child when he enters school. While the child or his parents may to some degree have perceived difficulty in functions such as auditory sequential memory (e.g., following several step instructions) or right–left orientation (as in turning the wrong way to his room), they reassured themselves that "he would grow out of it." School creates an arena in which comparison with peers brings the deficit(s) into the foreground. The reassurance that he has a "lag" no longer suffices to relieve the child's and/or parents' humiliation. Proper diagnosis and treatment of the deficit, accompanied by clarification of its extent and implications, will frequently resolve the acute reaction. In other cases, particularly when the resulting sense of deficit builds upon an earlier developed negative self-representation, psychotherapy is essential for its resolution. Case 3, Matthew, illustrates such a disorder. He was previewed in the Introduction (and will be further elaborated in chapters 5 and 7) as "a blank wall" in that he was a puzzling combination of boisterous hyperactivity, leading others "in the wrong direction," and charm with a capacity to calmly involve himself in work. A failure to consider the possibility of neuropsychological contributions to learning problems, and thus a prolonged period of psychodynamic interpretation of such problems, is likely to result in the more chronic enmeshment of these deficits with trends in character development which are subsumed by the next category.

Severe Developmental Disorder with Neuropsychological Substrate.
This is a disorder in which neither neuropsychological dysfunction nor neurotic conflict formation may be designated as primary since they are so inextricably interwoven. In the context of these children's chronic difficulties, learning disorders typically emerge with the new academic and behavioral demands imposed by school. This type of child is similar to the one described above (learning disorders as a function of more severe psychological disturbance) except that neuropsychological dysfunction has been one of the major interferences in the development of ego functions and object relations. While there may be focal, remediable deficits which interfere with basic academic acquisitions, remediation alone would not address the more pervasive and chronic developmental failures. Case 8, Brad, discussed in chapter 7, illustrates the complex

interplay of factors and the exquisite diagnostic and treatment methods essential to their amelioration. The disorganization many of these children manifest sometimes makes it mandatory that psychotherapeutic work precede remedial efforts, as was the case with Brad.

Developmental Disorder in the Character Pathology or Neurotic Range with Neuropsychological Substrate. This is the child whose undiagnosed neuropsychological dysfunction has seriously compromised some aspects of learning over at least a period of years. In so doing, problems of self-esteem have arisen, as have maladaptive defenses. Several of those most commonly seen will be described, both in their surface manifestations and the underlying feelings they express or protect against.

There is the child who feels "better bad than dumb," or the acting out child. A child with a propensity for impulsivity may use this tendency to avoid exposure of incompetence; for example, when called on to read, he pushes the person next to him. Thus his aggressiveness rather than his academic incompetence appears paramount. Another type of child protests, "I'm bored" or "I just don't want to do it; I could if I wanted to." Both of these are forms of denial that the incapacity exists. The child who proclaims, "I just can't do it" exhibits a form of exaggerated helplessness, dependency, and passivity. "Let those goody-goodies do it, I have better things to do with my time. I'm really better than they are, they just don't know it." Along with excessive daydreaming and involvement with superheroes, this grandiose stance is an effort to defend against and repair feelings of defect. The child who complains, "My teacher is awful. Why does she do this to me?" manifests a form of externalization of blame for the difficulties experienced. The cry "I don't want to go to school" accompanied by vomiting, headaches, and the like is a phobic defense. A tendency to perfectionism, seen in reworking of assignments, procrastination in undertaking them, excessive sensitivity to the discovery of an error—as if the error destroys the entire effort—is an obsessive–compulsive style of avoiding whatever the next task might be for fear that it cannot be managed. Some of the "conduct disorders" and "anxiety disorders" of DSM-III may be included among these developmental disorders, although their neuropsychological substrate is not acknowledged in DSM-III.

In some of these children, the deficits which exist have already developed, or proceed to develop, specific symbolic meaning such that there is a convergence of channels of expression for neurotic conflicts and neuropsychological dysfunction. Case 4, Joseph, discussed in chapter 5, illustrates a remarkable coincidence of deficits and a genetic history which rendered them particularly fertile for psychodynamic elaboration. In other cases in which family pathology demands that some members be identified as deficient or different, the neuropsychologically impaired child's constitutional limitations readily offer themselves for selection. Case 5, Rachel, in chapter 5 exemplifies such a clinical situation.

Intellectual Limitations

All too often in this age of alertness to "minimal brain dysfunction," parents and professionals alike overlook two other possible routes to a learning disorder:

Mental Retardation.   There is the bona fide retarded child whose clinical presentation, due to physical beauty or personal charm, masks an underlying low intellectual capability.

Average Intelligence.   Although not retarded, the child of average intelligence in a highly successful, ambitious family and cultural setting is retarded relative to the goals and aspirations of his parents. Typically, by the time such a child is brought for psychological evaluation, a vast array of explanations for his poor school performance have been propounded and internalized by the child. They may include variants of poor motivation, laziness, or neuropsychological dysfunction. Unraveling the by then well-entrenched self-esteem problems and family conflicts from the realities of the child's original potential is frequently a delicate and difficult task. Case 7, Eloise, discussed in chapter 5, illustrates the erroneous conclusions to which parents and professionals may adhere in work with such children.

It should be noted that neither of these last categories precludes the possibility of neuropsychological dysfunction. However, its presence would require a diagnosis of mixed etiology.

Chapter 3

A Critique of the Literature

Given the vast body of literature that now exists on this subject, and therefore the impossibility of an exhaustive study, contributions were selected with the aim of examining three major controversies and evaluating representative contributions to each side. Two controversies are primarily within the diagnostic realm: disputes over whether learning disorders reflect (1) neuropsychological versus psychodynamic and ego psychological etiologies, or (2) developmental lags versus structural anomalies. The other controversy is in the remedial field and concerns the issue of whether it is preferable to strengthen the disordered function or to construct alternative pathways to achievement of a particular skill.

In light of the book's major goal—the development of an integrative perspective on learning disorders—an attempt will be made to determine the extent to which these controversies represent truly irreconcilable differences of opinion or straw men based on polemical divisiveness. Toward that end, several interrelated questions will be asked of the contributions reviewed: (1) Are the evaluations that have been performed adequate to support the diagnostic conclusions reached? If not, the contribution may well suffer from polemical leanings. (2) Is the reported scope of the formulations valid, or is it too broad or narrow? Keeping in mind the spectrum of diagnostic categories and the importance of precise terminology discussed in the previous chapter, are the author's conclusions applicable to all learning disordered patients or only to one or several categories of the spectrum of such disorders? If there is limited applicability, but this fact is not explicitly indicated, an apparent controversy may be mounted on a shaky scaffolding: a failure to identify the appropriate scope of the patients to whom a particular viewpoint is relevant. Formulations so derived are also likely to suffer from a lack of parsimony or, alternatively, excessively simplistic thinking which does not allow for overdetermination. (3) Related to the second question is that of whether the scope of the proposed treatment methods is accurately identified. Are the claims regarding their efficacy too few or too many?

THE PSYCHOANALYTIC VERSUS NEUROPSYCHOLOGICAL CONTROVERSY

Assignment of contributions to the body of psychoanalytic literature, as opposed to the body of neuropsychological and/or educational literature, is in some instances debatable. Forcing a decision in such instances might in that sense be criticized as itself polemical, the very kind of thinking this book aims at discouraging. What governed assignment in these cases was the type of journal, edited compendium, or book in which the contribution appeared, rather than the author's stated purpose. This decision was reached for two reasons. First, the author's statement of his or her purpose did not always seem to be actualized; alternatively, since terms are used so variously (as discussed in chapter 2) an author's explicit declaration of intent might misrepresent what he actually proceeded to communicate to the reader. Second, what seemed salient was which kind of professional a particular contribution might reach and, therefore, how it would expand or complement the understanding that the reader already had of the subject. By the same reasoning, two contributions by the same author may be classified differently.

Contributions considered psychoanalytic, or more broadly psychodynamic, are those appearing in psychoanalytic and psychotherapeutic journals and books likely to be read by clinicians who treat patients in one or another psychoanalytically oriented psychotherapy. Those classified as neuropsychological and/or educational are likely to appear in journals and books tending to reach professionals in educational and cognitive psychology, special education, learning disabilities, neuropsychology, pediatric neurology, language pathology, and the like. Each of these two groups of contributions will be examined in light of the major facets of learning disorders they consider and their fulfillment of the above-mentioned criteria for integrative thinking.

Psychoanalytic and Other Psychodynamic Contributions

Although the field of learning disorders has burgeoned into public awareness in the last two decades, it is noteworthy that psychoanalytic contributions appeared as early as the 1920s and 1930s by such prominent authors as Abraham (1924), Glover (1925), Bornstein (1930), Strachey (1930), M. Klein (1931), and Fenichel (1937). Early interest may have reflected the excitement of the 1920s and 1930s sparked by Freud's (1923) introduction of the structural hypothesis and subsequent advances in ego psychology. This fueled exploration of the impact of the drives and the superego on various functions of the ego. Attention continued at full strength into the 1940s, 1950s, and mid-1960s until it all but ceased in the late 1960s, some notable exceptions being Weil, 1970, 1971, 1977, 1978; Millman and Canter, 1972; Newman, Dember, and Krug, 1973; Berger and Kennedy, 1975; and De Hirsch, 1975. This was precisely at a time when papers on "learning disabilities" and "minimal brain dysfunction" proliferated (Black, 1974) with the result that these became household phrases and heated controversy about etiology and treatment was brought to public attention.

At least one of the effects of declining psychoanalytic interest in childhood learning disorders is clear. Psychoanalytic perspectives on etiology and treatment are not expressed in the form of an enriching and vital dialogue with proponents of nondynamic approaches to such clinical phenomena. What obtains is the situation illustrated by De Hirsch (1975); reports submitted by individual professionals (teacher, neurologist, psychiatrist) about the same child can readily be mistaken for reports written about different children, rather than facets of a single child which interact and are capable of integration.

However, the problem is not simply one of "lack of press." There are limitations from which many of these papers suffer which compromise their value. These can be summarized as follows: (1) they do not perform evaluations sufficient to rule out neuropsychological contributions but nevertheless claim an exclusively psychogenic etiology; (2) they frequently address themselves to a limited spectrum of learning disordered patients without explicitly so stating; and (3) when a neuropsychological etiology is evident, they may relegate such patients to a group with which they do not deal therapeutically. Valuable applications of psychoanalytic concepts are therefore lost. Such problems are then seized upon by nonpsychoanalysts to repudiate the usefulness of psychoanalytic contributions, in toto. An example is the following introduction to a book on learning disorders in which the authors report their exclusively psychopharmacological treatment of 1,000 minimal brain dysfunction (MBD) cases, despite their disclaimer about ignoring psychodynamic factors:

> Until the early 1960s, the term "Minimal Brain Dysfunction" was hardly known to professionals. . . . Now it has acquired a wide currency. . . . Yet, one cannot believe that this condition arose de novo in one decade. The reason for this sudden appearance of a new syndrome can be understood by a brief excursion into the state of child psychiatry in the first half of this century. Psychoanalysis had created a true revolution in thought about child development, a field of study which prior to 1900 hardly existed at all in any form. So much new was learned about children through reconstruction of adults' memories of their own childhood as brought out in psychoanalytic therapy, and later through direct observation of children, that in a few decades the fields of child psychiatry and child psychology came to be dominated by psychoanalytic thinking, at least in the English-speaking world.
>
> Like everything new, what was once revolutionary became, after a time, ultraconservative. A hard and fast doctrine soon permeated the thinking of clinicians. . . . The success of this procedure in many cases led to the belief that *all* psychological problems of children—problems of behavior, neuroses, psychoses, learning disorders, speech disorders— had essentially the same etiology in disturbed family relationships and required the same treatment [Gross and Wilson, 1974, pp. 1–2].

Psychoanalytic contributors to the field of learning disorders focus predominantly on describing the varied clinical manifestations of psychologically based learning disorders and their etiologies from the psychodynamic and genetic viewpoints. Little attention has been given to the subject of diagnosis and not much more to the question of treatment.

Diagnosis.   In general these authors give inadequate consideration to the possibility of neuropsychological contributions to learning disorders and, therefore, to the necessity of carefully assessing their existence in each individual case. Three excellent exceptions are papers by Heinicke (1972), M. A. Silverman (1976), and Pine (1980), in which the multiple etiologies of these disorders and their varied clinical manifestations are carefully delineated. Pearson (1952) long ago cautioned against the disregard characteristic of so many contributions reviewed:

> [E]very child who shows any form of steeple-like or valley-like learning patterns requires an evaluation by a psychoanalyst. It is important that those psychoanalysts who specialize in the psychoanalysis of children have a broad knowledge of the factors which may produce such problems and of how they may be cured . . . [p. 322]. Most of this data [neuropsychological bases for learning problems] is well known to physicians and educators but I have felt it necessary to re-emphasize it because at the present time when there is so much emphasis on the importance of intrapsychic processes in all phases of medicine and education, psychiatrists tend to become overenthusiastic about dynamic intrapsychic processes to the complete neglect of physiological and organic processes, for which they seem to have a psychic blind spot [p. 328].

Blanchard (1946) and Liss (1955) also emphasized the need for more wide-ranging assessments (e.g., physical, hearing, and vision examinations) in the language and techniques of their day and, most recently, Weil (1961, 1971) has mentioned the availability of more specific and modern techniques. However, she is not sufficiently insistent upon their use. Her discussion and clinical examples emphasize one type of learning disordered child, the neuropsychologically impaired child who presents with hyperactivity and attention deficits, for whom these behavioral indicators coupled with an

IQ test may be sufficiently diagnostic. However, even with such children an IQ assessment alone would be inadequate for remedial purposes, as will be demonstrated in chapters 4, 5, and 7.

The contributions of these authors notwithstanding, there are countless cases reported, not only in the 1950s and 1960s (Plank and Plank, 1954; Jarvis, 1958; Vereecken, 1965) but more recently (Newman et al., 1973; Berger and Kennedy, 1975) which do not reflect the greater sophistication and comprehensiveness with which such diagnostic studies can be performed. Moreover, there is a frequent misconception in the literature about what constitutes an adequate assessment of the intactness of ego equipment [Hartocollis (1968) has commented upon this situation in the evaluation of adults]. Many papers reviewed reveal an erroneous assumption that an average or superior IQ score precludes the possibility of neuro-psychological factors and is, therefore, a sufficient measure. A technical examination of the problems which characterize these contributions will be reserved for the section of chapter 5 entitled "Pitfalls of a Partial Evaluation," once the nature of a reliable examination has been delineated in chapter 4.

Etiology. With rare exceptions, the psychoanalytic literature primarily attributes learning disorders to psychodynamic factors. Even in as sophisticated a journal as *The Psychoanalytic Study of the Child* which so sensitively renders the overdetermination of symptoms and psychopathology in general, other factors are given short shrift. All contributions, many of which are found in this publication, are elaborations of the fountainhead, "Inhibitions, Symptoms and Anxiety" (Freud, 1926):

> [T]he ego function of an organ is impaired if its eroto-genicity—its sexual significance—is increased. . . . The ego renounces these functions, which are within its sphere, in order not to have to undertake fresh measures of repression—in order to avoid a conflict with the id.
>
> There are clearly also inhibitions which serve the purpose of self-punishment. . . . The ego is not allowed to carry on those activities, because they would bring success and gain, and these are things which the severe super-ego has forbidden. . . .
>
> The more generalized inhibitions of the ego obey a different mechanism of a simple kind. When the ego is involved

in a particularly difficult psychical task . . . when a continual flood of sexual phantasies has to be kept down, it loses so much of the energy at its disposal that it has to cut down the expenditure of it at many points at once [pp. 89–90].

Since that time authors have concerned themselves with an array of disorders: pervasive pseudoimbecility; school failure despite obvious intelligence or specific difficulties, for example, hypertrophied verbal as compared with visual–motor functions; deficient or exceptional arithmetic abilities; reading disorders in the context of other intact functions; and limited conceptual abilities side by side with factual knowledge which proceeds normally. Differential emphasis has been laid upon one or more of the following factors: dynamic, genetic, structural, representational, and environmental.

In these contributions authors have varied widely in appreciating and clearly reporting the appropriate scope of the conclusions they reached. Some (Blanchard, 1946; Newman et al., 1973; and Berger and Kennedy, 1975) thoughtfully identify the subgroup with which they are concerned. For example, in her contribution to reading disorders, Blanchard notes that her psychogenic explanations pertain only to, "the smaller group of reading disabilities . . . the probably 20 percent . . . in which the trouble in learning to read is an outgrowth of personality maladjustments and is one of the child's neurotic symptoms" (p. 164). Unfortunately, more typical are publications (e.g., those of Plank and Plank, 1954; J. S. Silverman, Fite, and Mosher, 1959; Buxbaum, 1964; Bettelheim and Zelan, 1981; and Kaye, 1982) which, by failing to identify the patients studied, implicitly and incorrectly claim the universal relevance of their findings:

Reading disabilities occurring in children in the critical period from eight to ten years are so widespread and disabling that parents and school authorities are greatly concerned. Moreover, work with these children has shown repeatedly that the reading disability is only one aspect or symptom of a more basic disturbance in the child's emotional life. . . . Reading disability was surveyed as it is found in fourth-grade children of about nine years, of average intelligence, and with reading retardation of at least one and a half to two years. The premise urged here is that reading disability in such children is a specific case of intellectual inhibition . . . of learning disorder... [resulting from] a constellation of factors, conscious and unconscious, particularly conflicts around curiosity and aggression involving oral and anal ambivalence [J. S. Silverman et al., pp. 298–299].

Buxbaum (1964) propounds a theory of *all* learning disturbances with distinctions based on patterning:

> All-pervasive learning disorders are different from circumscribed, symptomatic disorders. All-pervasive learning disorders, like primary behavior disorders, are the result of a continuing conflict with the mother. Symptomatic learning disorders are to some degree the result of internalized conflicts, although here, as in other neuroses of childhood, the battle with the environment continues and shapes the child's behavior [p. 425].

Plank and Plank (1954) offer a single explanation for intraindividual differences in reading versus arithmetic abilities:

> This disparity is the starting point of the present paper. We shall try to show how different constellations in the preoedipal period and differences in the effort to resolve the oedipal conflict influence the ability for and interest in arithmetical learning... [p. 274]. The overprotected children being poor in arithmetic while relatively good in reading... [p. 284] learning of mathematics becomes blocked where the first and strongest object relationship cannot replace objects . . . [p. 291].

Even very recently, highly polemical dismissals of neuropsychological contributions appear. Bettelheim and Zelan (1981) state that children do not evidence problems in reading due to dyslexia or hyperkinesis or any of the other so-called neurological disorders, but rather due to the fantasy that words are magic and by manipulating them one can manipulate whatever they symbolize. Kaye (1982) refutes the "neurological position" and offers instead a purely psychoanalytic construction of the learning disordered child's disturbance in his "system of learning." A recent example of a more subtle biased approach is Heinicke's (1980) study of the "origins of the child's learning difficulties" in poor "task orientation" which he in turn associates with less than optimally empathic and efficient responsiveness to, and communication and mutual gazing with, the infant. Despite his disclaimer that he does not view this as a sole factor, his failure to neuropsychologically assess the children studied lends a polemical tone to this effort.

Bearing in mind these reservations about the psychoanalytic literature, it does offer a rich explication of psychodynamic aspects of problems in learning, a summary of which now follows. Conflicts—whether predominantly oral, anal, or oedipal—have been shown to result in a great variety of manifestations: general disruption of the learning activity itself, specific kinds of errors (e.g., misinterpretation of words based on drive-determined distortions), or particular conditions under which the activity finds interference (e.g., in the presence of special dynamically laden contents). Other authors consider the relative involvement of the three psychic structures, ego, id, and superego, in a particular learning pattern (Pearson, 1952). This approach highlights the fact that the psychodynamic meanings of learning may fuel a disruptive breakthrough of impulses or, conversely, a special investment and high level of proficiency (Plank and Plank, 1954). Disorders may arise where there is (1) failure to achieve sublimation in a child who has not experienced optimal frustration or gratification (E. Klein, 1949; Plank and Plank, 1954; Rubenstein, Falick, Levitt, and Eckstein, 1959; Vereecken, 1965); or (2) deneutralization of drives (E. Klein, 1949; Plank and Plank, 1954; Newman et al., 1973). The latter may be due to the ego's impoverishment with respect to energy available for learning by virtue of its absorption in other tasks, a punitive superego's demands for failure or libidinization or aggressivization of an activity.

Psychodynamic formulations of both extensive and delimited learning disorders differ in their relative emphasis upon preoedipal and oedipal factors. Theories of unconscious oral conflicts find especially great currency in the literature on reading problems, although they are also called upon to explain general problems in learning. Reading is viewed as a derivative and symbolic expression of the following oral activities: when done in bed, a nightcap or goodnight kiss (Glover, 1925), "eating" another's words (Strachey, 1930), or incorporation by way of the eye (Fenichel, 1937). Oral conflicts and consequent reading disorders may include fear of

destroying the object through incorporation (Pearson, 1952), reluctance to relinquish oral passivity as seen in difficulties in shifting
from the passivity of being read to, to the activity and initial
frustration of being the reader (E. Klein, 1949). Plank and Plank
(1954) offered a similar formulation for arithmetic disabilities. The
persons whose autobiographical statements they reviewed could
not give up the desire for maternal oral gratification necessary to
move into a world of symbols. Conversely, those who excelled in
arithmetic evidenced special maternal deprivation.

Learning impairment in general may reflect an equation with
having food shoved down the throat (Pearson, 1952), given the
association between imbibing knowledge and eating (Abraham,
1924; E. Klein, 1949), or a disorder of frustration tolerance (Pearson,
1952). Narcissistic issues are also thought to contribute to stunted
learning, as when the child cannot bear to suffer comparison and
possible competitive loss. He attempts to maintain a superior stance
by virtue of apparently not needing to study, holding those who do
in contempt (E. Klein, 1949; Newman et al., 1973). A somewhat
different emphasis is given by Kaye (1982) who views the learning
problem as a manifestation of the maintenance of "innocence in
relation to the self-system" (p. 92).

Anal issues and conflicts which are said to contribute to or
interfere with learning include the special appeal of particular
subjects (e.g., arithmetic) because of their demands for precision,
the possible use of knowledge to express anal sadistic and exhibitionistic impulses (Pearson, 1952), and the negativity or hostility
manifested in a specific symptom, for example, writing words
backwards or not learning at all (Blanchard, 1946).

Oedipal determinants of learning disorders have been much
discussed. Intellectual inhibition as a whole or in a particular subject with sexual associations (e.g., biology), may be a symbolic
derivative of the suppression of sexual curiosity (Mahler, 1942;
Blanchard, 1946; E. Klein, 1949; Pearson, 1952; Jarvis, 1958;
Vereecken, 1965). Pseudoimbecility, for example, permits the
child to do, see, and say things otherwise not permissible. Inhibition
may also reflect associations between learning and femininity,
creating a conflict for boys, or masculine strivings with resulting
conflicts for girls (E. Klein, 1949; Pearson, 1952; Plank and Plank,
1954; Jarvis, 1958). Castration anxiety elicited by the prospect of
excelling over parents or older siblings is another commonly noted

contributor to learning problems (E. Klein, 1949; Pearson, 1952; Jarvis, 1958; Vereecken, 1965) and other kinds of success neuroses (Buxbaum, 1964).

Arithmetic disorders are attributed to aggressivization of the processes of manipulating numbers: breaking them up, taking parts away, and the like. Such concerns over aggression and integrity of the object may be orally colored as well. Jarvis (1958) discusses reading disorders which force a situation of being read to, rather than reading oneself, as a regressive solution to oedipal dangers. This general idea is further elaborated by some to explain fear of use, but not acquisition, of knowledge which is equated with use of the penis, often beginning in early adolescence (Pearson, 1952). The sense of having a damaged head is construed as an upward displacement of castration anxiety. Fears of humiliation in examination of one's learning are symbolically related to the boy's humiliation in the course of having his genitals compared with those of his father.

Several authors (Hellman, 1954; Rubenstein et al., 1959; Buxbaum, 1964; Newman et al., 1973; Berger and Kennedy, 1975) emphasize the impact of environmental rather than intrapsychic factors, although their clinical illustrations suggest that, when prolonged, environmental stress will result in internalized conflicts and maladaptive identifications. Various constellations of parental psychopathology are posited to shape the child's development at particular stages. In some cases, the mother's unconscious need to externalize her own sense of inadequacy, which finds embodiment in her child, is highlighted (Blanchard, 1946; Buxbaum, 1964; Berger and Kennedy, 1975). In their patients, Berger and Kennedy note the mother's early expectation of defectiveness and consequent failure to nurture development. Faulty maternal resolution of separation–individuation processes is emphasized in others. The child's ability to learn threatens an especially intimate tie between mother and child. Preoedipal encouragement of oral fixation was suggested by histories of excessive stimulation or inconsistent patterns of excessive indulgence and frustration. In these cases, general stupidity or a particular disorder represented an unconscious collusion with mother in order to preserve her love by remaining in a partially symbiotic relationship. This precluded independent functioning or recognition of ability. This might later be oedipally elaborated as an impairment of ego function and inhibition of curiosity and scoptophilia as a defense against knowing forbidden family secrets, especially when they were sexual (Mahler, 1942; Staver, 1953; Hellman, 1954; Buxbaum, 1964; Sprince, 1967). Pseudoimbecility permits looking without being thought to be able to see. Hellman (1954) describes a special situation in which mothers' distortion of reality made it impossible for their children to see realistically without compromising closeness.

A predominantly preoedipal constellation which incorporates some of the above elements is elaborated by Newman et al. (1973) to account for poor academic performance in boys with exceptionally high IQs. Uneven development, a strong command of language, accompanied by poor conceptualization, attention, and motor functions, is attributed to the mother's excessive valuation of verbal production without concomitant encouragement of motor activity, since the latter signals the child's ability to separate. This early imbalance interferes with the normal intertwining of such functions necessary for the formation of sensorimotor schemata, lending a shallowness to later language and other higher cortical functions. Maternal attitudes are noted to reflect their depression and devaluation of spouses in the child's early years, rendering them excessively needy of the child for companionship. The child's precocious speech leads mother to believe he *is* a genius, without need for ongoing stimulation. Lack of activity and autonomy, not regarded as problem areas by mother, are identified as such only at school age. This preoedipal substratum sets the stage for a difficult oedipal phase. Having earlier gained a sense of omnipotence associated with talking, the child has exaggerated expectations that talking alone will help him negotiate. In school, where this is not the case, he experiences intense narcissistic injury at the prospect of having to struggle and not know immediately. This leads him to avoid less developed areas, resulting in a further disequilibrium of functions. Conflicts with father are significant as well. In some respects the child has already won an oedipal victory, which makes the ultimate oedipal defeat more humiliating, and simultaneously fuels fears of retaliation by the father he defeated. The learning disorder is conceptualized as an expression of ambivalence toward mother—verbal facility expresses love, and failure in performance expresses hostility—as well as a means of maintaining closeness with mother through verbalization, and both provocatively defying father by physical inadequacy and school failure and placating him by not being more successful academically.

Other environmental contributions to learning disorders of a current, rather than chronic nature are noted by Pearson (1952): unpleasant conflictual experiences with teachers, ongoing family traumata (e.g., parental fighting) which absorb ego energies, and pressure from or identification with peers who discourage learning.

Treatment. In contrast to the tendency of many psychoanalytic authors to claim that their formulations apply to a broader range of patients than is accurate, statements regarding the applicability of their clinical methods are typically too narrow. With several exceptions (Sarvis, 1960; Rappaport, 1961; Hartocollis, 1968; Weil, 1971, 1977; De Hirsch, 1975; M. A. Silverman, 1976; Pine, 1980; and Kafka, 1984), the contributions reviewed do not sufficiently appreciate the value of psychoanalytic concepts and techniques in treatment planning for children with neuropsychological dysfunction. The growth of techniques for diagnosing neuropsychological dysfunction in children did not contribute to a "widening scope" (Stone, 1954) of patients considered treatable by psychoanalysis. Children without intact "equipment" were frequently dismissed as unsuitable. This was particularly true when the aspects of functioning involved were of central importance to psychoanalytic work, for example, expressive language and conceptualization (Waldhorn, 1960). Several other considerations may have fostered either/or thinking. As analytic concepts and techniques were increasingly applied to children, the intensiveness of this approach left little room, practically speaking, for adjunct treatments. There may also have been concerns about their effect upon the transference and analytic process.

This either/or thinking is exemplified by Pearson (1952) who, despite his caution that assessment must be broad enough to encompass the complexities of diagnosis, is overly schematic in his treatment recommendations. He does not fully develop the interplay of the "basic core" and "experiential factors" (Weil, 1970) for later ego development, character, and psychopathology. Pearson regards diagnostic evaluation as a prelude to prescription of the relative contribution(s) of psychoanalyst, physician, psychologist, and psychoanalytically trained educator in diagnosis and treatment. In his view, the diagnosis and treatment of a child who evidences neuropsychological pathology is said to be "largely the function of the psychoanalytic trained educator assisted by the psychologist and the physician. Here the psychoanalyst can contribute nothing to therapy but occasionally be of help in making a diagnosis" (p. 328).

The cases of Daniel (case 2) and Brad (case 8), discussed in chapter 7, illustrate that psychoanalytic concepts are relevant and frequently essential in working with neuropsychologically impaired children who should not be dismissed as unsuitable for psychoanalytic treatment or modified approaches informed by these concepts.

In contrast to Pearson, in a recent case study, Kafka (1984) reports his process of discovery of the neuropsychological dysfunction of his adult analytic patient and discusses its possible implication for analytic technique and character development. Had he referred his patient for a neuropsychological diagnostic assessment, these issues might have been elaborated upon even more informatively. Erring in a direction opposite to that of Pearson is Heinicke (1972) who concludes that "only the extensive procedure of child psychoanalysis goes some way in ensuring continued progressive development at the period of treatment" (p. 690). This is despite his stated intention "to summarize what is known about these [i.e., learning] disturbances and to integrate this knowledge in a way that will enhance progress in diagnostic classification, in the understanding of their etiology, and in their treatment" (p. 662).

The one psychoanalytic contribution to treatment of cognitive problems—but not learning disorders per se—which promotes a possible combination of psychoanalysis with another treatment modality is that of Santostefano (1978, 1980). However, since he assumes neuropsychological factors are not at play in the cognitive lags he considers himself to treat, yet does not specify whether they have initially been ruled out in a formal assessment, his position suffers in that sense from polemicism. He proposes methods which specifically address the patient's cognitive difficulties either as an alternative to psychotherapy, a preparation for it, or as an adjunct approach:

> Because cognitive controls serve in the structuring and maintenance of defenses, I am working with the hypothesis that the analysis of cognitive controls should precede the analysis of defenses. As a cognitive control is reformed . . . the

restructuring of defenses . . . can then take place more effectively with the assistance of the cognitive scaffold constructed.
Analytic work could move from cognitive controls to defenses
to controls and back to defenses and so on in point-counter-
point fashion. At each step throughout this process the gradual
reformation and growth of cognitive controls is seen as serving
the reformation of defenses [p. 65].

Neuropsychological and Educational Contributions

Another substantial body of contributions predominantly concerns
the child's neuropsychological functions and corresponding educational requirements, both behavioral and cognitive. Authors in this
field focus upon one or more of the following facets of the neuropsychology of learning problems: diagnosis, the phenomenology
and/or localization of an array of disabilities, correlations between
these symptoms and other aspects of functioning, learning disability syndromes, etiology, and approach to and outcome of treatment.

In addition to being wide ranging in the aspects of this vast
topic they consider, these authors vary greatly with regard to the
adequacy of their recognition of the possibility of other than neuropsychological factors and, consequently, the degree to which
they would be likely to promote a dialogue with professionals of a
primarily psychodynamic orientation. Three broad groups of
authors can be identified: (1) those who are integrative in their
conceptualization of the multiple routes to disorders in learning,
some of whom nevertheless elect to focus primarily on neuropsychological features of learning "disabilities"; (2) those who are
neither integrative in their consideration of the etiology and treatment of problems in learning nor polemical; they identify their
limited purpose of discussing subgroups of learning disabled
patients whose characteristics are not purported to be universal;
and (3) those who do not successfully approach the integration of
multiple causes of learning problems either in failing to acknowl-
edge the possibility of psychodynamic contributions, referring to
them in the service of dismissing their value, or alternatively, in
ostensibly acknowledging their existence but subtly proceeding to
devalue their usefulness. In so doing the latter authors do not
document their points of view.

Since an exhaustive survey of this vast literature is neither possible nor appropriate to our purposes (see, for example, Strother, 1972; Gross and Wilson, 1974; and L. B. Silver, 1979 for historical discussions of the subject), some of the major contributions to each facet of the neuropsychological and educational management of learning disabilities will be reviewed, and examples of characteristic polemical and integrative approaches selected for discussion.

Diagnosis. Perspectives on the diagnosis of learning disordered children are implicit in all contributions to the subject, but we will review only some of these which have as a major aim delineation of the diagnostic process. With a few exceptions (John, Kamel, Corning, Easton, Brown, Ahn, John, Harmony, Prichep, Toro, Gerson, Bartlett, Thatcher, Kaye, Valdes, and Schwartz, 1977; and Elliott, Halliday, and Calloway, 1978 to be discussed below) the procedures recommended are not themselves novel. Rather, authors generally differ in the scope they view as essential and the approaches they take to data analysis.

One group of authors conveys an extremely broad and integrative view of the array of possible contributing factors. Some undertake to describe the very comprehensive assessment required to survey all such factors. Another subgroup acknowledges the multiple routes to disorders in learning but elects to focus on assessment of one or more specific factors. Whether evaluating the child's reading (Rabinovitch, 1972) or learning as a whole (Clements, 1966a; Rubin, 1971; Meier, 1976; Hagin and Silver, 1977; Kinsbourne and Caplan, 1979; Forness, 1982; Rothstein, 1982), authors in the first subgroup recommend that the following be included: a history of the child's development, as reported by his parents and/or other sources; a school report; clinical interviews with the child; diagnostic testing (encompassing examination of the child's IQ, academic functioning, more specialized aspects of neuropsychological organization and personality, all of which are then interpreted from the standpoint of part-functions, i.e., task analytically), and a neurological evaluation. Within this general consensus, there are minor differences as to whether additional procedures need be routine, for example, general physical, audiological, and opthalmological examinations, electroencephalographs (EEGs), and observation of the child in the classroom.

Most of those authors included in the second subgroup of integrative contributors elaborate upon the diagnostic testing process. Myklebust (1964), a foremost contributor, emphasizes the extensive battery of psychological and educational tests necessary "to appraise each psychoneurosensory system as it functions semi-autonomously, in coordination with other systems and as all of the systems function simultaneously" (p. 262). He further (1968) details the insufficiency of discussing learning disabilities in terms of the number of years below grade level, since verbal and nonverbal (i.e., right and left hemisphere) functions need be treated separately in relation to the child's mental age and chronological age; he terms such ratios "learning quotients." A very subtle polemical tone might be conveyed by this work if read alone, although a complete reading of the works Myklebust has edited and his other contributions (1964, 1968, 1971, 1975a, 1975b, 1978a, 1978b, 1983) would correct this impression. His 1964 paper on assessment begins with the statement that psychological factors are too often exclusively considered. He proceeds to delineate the need for test, behavioral, neurological, and EEG data without mention of psychological assessment, in the sense of features of ego functions and psychodynamics. Although it is true that he is writing about learning disabilities, that is, those disorders with a neuropsychological basis, one cannot know this to be the case prior to the conclusion of the period of assessment. Similarly, Myklebust, Frostig (1968), and Frostig and Orpet (1972) especially emphasize the necessity of a task analytic examination of all sensorimotor, perceptual, and language data derived from specialized as well as more conventional tests.

Jansky (1980)who makes another such contribution within the context of an integrative perspective concludes, however, with a polemical tone. The psychiatric and neurological components of the assessments she recommends are said to be merely "adjunctive" to remedial work with children who have specific learning disabilities. Gardner (1979, 1980), who believes that minimal brain dysfunction (MBD)[1] has become overdiagnosed, delineates what he regards as a more precise diagnostic process with specified norms for many aspects of functioning, for example, hyperactivity, visual processing, motor coordination, persistence, and overflow. As with Myklebust, if read out of the context of his total work, Gardner's

---

[1]Despite our belief that MBD is a poor term, it will appear frequently in this chapter since it would be cumbersome to discuss many contributions without employing the term they themselves employ. We would prefer terms such as neuropsychological impairment or learning disability when learning is affected, since MBD implies a degree of clinical specificity which does not actually exist.

paper could be misconstrued as polemical since he omits specific mention of the need for evaluation of psychological factors. Kinsbourne (1973b), like Gardner, attempts to reduce confusion by underlining the importance of including IQ as well as achievement tests. He notes how frequently learning disabilities are erroneously diagnosed on the basis of a presumed discrepancy between achievement level and IQ when in fact a child's mild retardation is not detected by clinical impression. Somewhat different contributions in this cluster are those by Ong (1968) and Voeller (1981) who, while maintaining an integrative perspective, describe the specific diagnostic functions and procedures of the pediatrician and pediatric neurologists respectively.

A second cluster of contributions can be characterized as neither integrative nor polemical. Particular aspects of the diagnosis of children already determined to be learning disabled are highlighted. Boder (1971b) notes the importance of obtaining direct evidence of dyslexia to prevent the insufficient conclusion that a "nonspecific disability" exists. Ozer and Richardson (1974) underline that the evaluation of learning disabled children must involve a "process approach"; that is, a task which poses difficulty must be broken down into its parts, akin to the task analytic principles espoused in chapter 1. Rourke (1978) emphasizes that a developmental approach should be taken with regard to the various "brain-related abilities" and difficulties of learning disabled children 5–15 years of age. In so doing data need simultaneously to be analyzed from the standpoint of pathognomonic signs, contrasts between scores and between the two sides of the body, and expectations of the normal rate of development of abilities.

A third cluster of contributions is polemical in that the scope of the evaluation recommended is too narrow and/or there is overt devaluation of selected procedures without adequate evidence to substantiate this position. The classic book by Wender (1971), *Minimal Brain Dysfunction*, suffers seriously from such thinking. Having arrived at the diagnosis of MBD even prior to evaluation, Wender proceeds to recommend only those assessment techniques which are needed to substantiate this diagnosis. In his words:

> I draw two pragmatic conclusions from the prevalence data [i.e., the statistics regarding the prevalence of MBD]: (1) the MBD syndrome should be a major target for "secondary

prevention" (i.e., treatment) in the school-age population, as it apparently constitutes the major fraction of psychiatrically disturbed children. (2) With no further knowledge, any preadolescent child admitted to a child guidance clinic [later on p. 59, he says "appearance at a child guidance clinic with a learning problem"] is most probably in the category unless proven otherwise. If, in addition, one knows that a child is not bizarre or retarded and has not been recently disturbed by a presumably noxious environment, one can make the diagnosis with some certainty. This diagnostic technique lacks subtle nicety but is quite effective [p. 61].

According to Wender the most salient datum is the child's response to amphetamine treatment. Interviews with parents are not considered valuable since Wender assumes parents are poor informants in contrast to whom teachers give more valid reports; nor is a psychiatric interview with the child necessarily useful. Neurological examination and EEGs are "irrelevant" since neurological abnormalities presumably bear no relation to MBD. Psychological test evaluations are not useful unless required for educational placement. The only exception is the Rorschach which may reveal borderline pathology; the import of this is that such patients are prone to differential responses to pharmacotherapy. Other projective data are unnecessary since "knowledge of children's dynamics may be epiphenomenal" (p. 71). Testing is discouraged as a whole, despite the admission that it is not clear whether amphetamines affect specific learning disabilities (p. 93). Thus, Wender gives no credence to educational or psychological implications of presumed MBD, much less the possibility that the surface manifestations of pathology (frequently including a disorder in learning) which brought the child to professional attention might have other roots. Wender's own statement, "If a disorder is common, one will make the diagnosis readily; similarly if a disorder is rare, one will hesitate to make the diagnosis even if an individual has pathognomic symptoms . . ." (p. 59), should be regarded as an unfortunate possibility which one attempts to guard against and to transcend rather than as an acceptable reality.

Gross and Wilson's (1974) study is similar in viewpoint. Upon becoming disillusioned with the low success rate with children with MBD seen in a conventional mental health center—notwithstanding the enormous amount of time spent in their evaluation—they felt it preferable to institute their own abbreviated diagnostic process. What they failed to observe is that despite the prevalence of learning disorders in the children seen in such a mental health center, neuropsychological testing was not performed, and thus the evaluation was not as complete as they perceived it to be. Their shortened diagnostic evaluation included an EEG, neuropsychiatric examination of the child, and a history taken from at least one parent. Psychological testing—typically meaning merely the Bender-Gestalt and Wechsler Intelligence Scale for Children (WISC)—was administered in only half of the cases: when school problems were minimal or "no other strong indications" existed (the meaning of this was not spelled out). Thus, even in children who presumably had some form of brain abnormality, the authors saw fit to decide, on the basis of surface symptomatology, against exploring all possible contributions to their patients' pathology in the interests of time. A further problem is that when they did recommend a testing evaluation, it was an inadequate one, therefore promoting the possibility of false negatives.

John et al. (1977) present one of the few truly original diagnostic techniques in recent times. Using neurometric computer analyses of EEG and evoked potential data, they claim the ability to estimate the presence and extent of maturational lags or deviant development of each brain region, and possibly to identify learning disabled children before their symptoms appear clinically. They proceed in a polemical fashion to offer these techniques not as complements to already existing methods but as superior, particularly to diagnostic testing. The arguments proposed, however, are not always founded. Neurometric evaluation is said to be preferable to testing because tests only measure products, not processes; however, this is true only when they are poorly interpreted or reported. Second, tests have "developmental, linguistic and cultural limitations" (p. 1397) from which neurometric techniques do not suffer. While it is necessary to take such limitations into account in interpreting these tests, it is not valid to dismiss them on this basis. Third, neurometric measures are cited as better discriminators between normal and learning disabled children than were "psychometric measures." However, the psychometric battery used in this study is not adequately sensitive to learning disabilities; thus, it is not surprising that cases would be missed. Interestingly, in the brochure which advertises the neurometric diagnostic service (*The Neurometric Evaluation Service*) run by John and his co-workers, less sweeping claims are made: "neurometrics *assists* the clinician in distinguishing between problems of primarily neurological versus psychological origins and *supplements* conventional neurological, neuropsychological and psychometric examinations" (undated, emphasis added).

A more balanced exposition of the contribution of evoked potential data to assessment of learning disorders is that by Elliott et al. (1978). They emphasize the sensitivity of such data in supplying convergent information and note that the relationship between evoked potential data and behavioral data remains to be elaborated. Thus, assertion of its clinical utility still requires great caution.

Symptom Description and/or Localization. The contributions of this type (as well as those in the next two categories) are so numerous (Black, 1974) that only a small portion can be considered. Many authors have delineated the phenomenology of a particular type of learning disability, such as Myklebust's (1978b) work on dyslexia in contrast to other types of reading disabilities, and Slade and Russell's (1971) work on developmental acalculia, while others have focused on a combination of disabilities in writing, reading, spelling, and arithmetic (Orton, 1937; De Hirsch, 1952; A. A. Silver and Hagin, 1960). Another perspective is the elaboration of various manifestations of the disorder of a particular sensory function or set of functions, such as Wepman's (1972) emphasis on auditory imperception and Myklebust's (1975a) exposition on "nonverbal learning disabilities." Several typical contributions to localization of function are Basso, Taborelli, and Vignolo's (1978) paper on the dissociation between oral and written language in left brain-damaged patients, and Heilman's (1978) work on localization of language functions.

Syndromes. Contributions to this subject include delineation of typical clusters of neuropsychological symptoms, amongst which are learning disabilities, as well as clusters of deficient functions postulated to constitute subtypes of specific learning disabilities (reading, language). Finally, the co-occurrence of particular types of learning disabilities and deficits in part-functions is described. Our perspectives on common neuropsychological syndromes will be reviewed in chapter 6.

Of those neuropsychological syndromes, MBD is far and away the most commonly cited. Nonetheless, although given validation and specification in 1966 in a federally sponsored monograph (Clements, 1966a), it has by no means gained universal acceptance. Clements reviewed the by then numerous publications on the subject and formulated an exhaustive list of the symptoms and terms cited to describe children of approximately average intelligence whose mild to severe behavioral and/or learning disabilities were associated with deviations of central nervous system dysfunction and not primarily attributable to psychogenic factors. Of these the 10 most common symptoms of the MBD syndrome were described: hyperactivity, perceptual-motor impairments, emotional lability, general deficits, disorders of attention, impulsivity, disorders of memory and thinking, specific learning disabilities involving reading, arithmetic, writing, and/or spelling, disorders of speech and hearing, equivocal neurological signs and EEG irregularities. Noting that each child presents his own individual cluster of these and other symptoms, such clusters were conceptualized as a variety of subsyndromes within the primary diagnosis of MBD, for example, the hyperactive syndrome, primary reading disability, aphasia, and the like.

Stevens, Boydstun, Dykman, Peters, and Sinton (1967) corroborated the existence of the MBD syndrome in an experimental study of the incidence of "organic-like" symptoms in children with MBD as compared with normal controls. They found that the MBD group indeed differed, exhibiting slower responses, less ability to follow verbal instructions, to discriminate tones, and to tap in rhythm, and inferior scores on the WISC Information, Arithmetic, Digit Span, and Coding subtests. Although a creatively designed study in terms of the tasks used to measure some of these functions, it could be criticized for its insufficient examination of the subjects' psychological status, making some assignments to the MBD group open to question. Wender (1971) also fervently upheld the existence of this syndrome, emphasizing the decreased experience of pleasure and pain, the high and poorly controlled activation level, and the extroversion of these children. Disorders in learning were considered one of their most common symptoms.

As Dykman, Ackerman, Clements, and Peters (1971) note, a host of professionals (Birch, 1964; Johnson and Myklebust, 1967; Werry, 1968, 1972; Benton, 1973; Kinsbourne, 1973a) argue against the idea that a syndrome truly exists, given the diversity of clinical manifestations of the symptoms involved. More specifically Benton comments on the lack of evidence that the varying abnormalities warrant the designation "syndrome," either in that separate elements reliably occur together or in the sense that they arise from a shared underlying abnormality. He grants that more limited syndromes (e.g., Clements' subsyndromes) may have useful treatment implications. Werry (1972) points to the future for the establishment of valid criteria for formulating syndromes and notes the importance of beginning efforts at symptom grouping on the basis of localization of brain function, empirically derived symptom clusters, psychophysiological response patterns, presence of neuropsychological anomalies or, finally, response to medication. A number of contributors focus on one or more aspects of the MBD syndrome and postulate the existence of another different but related syndrome. Dykman et al.'s (1971) response to this dissension from the concept of MBD is to argue, through research, that there *is* an attentional deficit syndrome involving alertness, stimulus selection, focusing, and vigilance. Rappaport (1964) presents the "brain damage syndrome" encompassing a combination of response patterns reflecting ego dysfunctions of impulse control, integration, a defective self-concept, and narcissistic sensitivity. L. B. Silver (1971) describes the "neurological learning disability syndrome" characterized by: hyperactivity, distractibility, short-attention span, occasional perseveration, specific learning disabilities of many possible kinds (e.g., in the interpretation, sequencing, abstracting, or storing of stimuli), and emotional problems secondary to frustration related to the above and manifested in lability, low frustration tolerance, and poor impulse control. In a similar vein, Jansky (1980) elaborates on specific learning disabilities which show characteristic but not invariant clusters of symptoms, for example, problems in language, coordination, and graphomotor competence, handedness and directionality, academic performance, and developmental and emotional maturity.

Another syndrome in which a learning disability is considered to be a major symptom is the Gerstmann syndrome initially described by Gerstmann (1940) and placed in a developmental context by Kinsbourne and Warrington (1963) and Kinsbourne (1968). They postulate a developmental lag in the ability to recognize, recall, and utilize information regarding relative spatial or temporal positions, which is manifested variously in finger agnosia, agraphia, acalculia, and right–left orientation.

Another large group of contributions describes syndromes of specific learning disabilities, for example, in language (Bender, 1958; Heilman, 1978) or in reading, an area of widespread interest. Formulations of subtypes of reading disabilities are offered by many clinicians (Kinsbourne and Warrington, 1963; McGrady, 1968; Rabinovitch, 1968; Mattis, French, and Rapin, 1975), and a review by Boder (1971b). In addition, Rabinovitch (1972) presents a classification of three disorders in reading in which one subtype is of psychogenic origin. Rourke (1978) delineates neuropsychologically a series of subtypes of general learning disabilities (i.e., including reading, spelling, and arithmetic) which have common underlying deficits.

A third type of contribution of this sort describes correlations between specific learning disabilities and other aspects of neuropsychological dysfunction, sometimes with the implication that one may account for the other. Explicit etiological statements will be examined in a section below. For example, Jansky (1980) writes of the relationship between dysfunction in one or more aspects of language functioning and disabilities in reading, writing, and spelling. In this regard reading is most frequently studied. De Hirsch (1963) believes reading disabilities to be only one of several difficulties with integration and differentiation of visual patterns including dyspraxia, spatial organization—sequences, reversals, left–right discrimination—and poor motor–speech patterns. This is related to Kinsbourne and Warrington's (1963) clinical correlation of dyslexia and the Gerstmann syndrome and A. A. Silver and Hagin's (1960, 1964) findings of a 92 percent evidence of problems in perceptual skills relating to spatial and temporal organization among children with specific reading disabilities. The other 8 percent are postulated to be the "emotional" group of poor readers, despite the absence of psychiatric assessment of all these children.

Denckla, Rudel, and Broman (1981) find certain language deficits to be more common among dyslexic than other learning disabled boys; they are less accurate on sentence completion tests, slower in naming, and make more dysphasic errors. In contrast McGrady (1968) views the so-called syndrome of dyslexia as a variable syndrome. He reviews the work of authors who differ in noting relationships between dyslexia and one or more of the following: disturbances of orientation, topographic representation, time, written language, spelling, numerical functions, memory, auditorization or visualization, motor skills, and neurological deficits. Although not commenting upon the validity of attempting to universally account for reading problems on the basis of specific dysfunctions, Heinicke (1972) also reviews correlational studies between dyslexia and various aspects of cognitive functioning (e.g., auditory–visual integration and auditory perception, mixed dominance, IQ, right–left discrimination).

Correlational Studies of Learning Disorder and Other Forms of Pathology. A common type of study examines the statistical or clinical relationship between learning disorders—in general or of a particular kind—and a host of other forms of pathology. Bateman (1972) and Sapir and Wilson (1978) argue the lack of any predictable relationship between MBD and learning disabilities. In contrast, Denhoff (1973), in a study of "the natural life history" of children with MBD, reports a highly significant correlation between what he terms signs of hyperreactivity and hyporeactivity at 1 year of age and inefficient learning and poor school performance at 7 years of age. Connolly (1971) notes that although many authors believe there is a positive relationship between learning disorders and emotional problems (Bender, 1956; Harris, 1966; Giffin, 1968; L. B. Silver, 1974a, 1974b, 1979), few have attempted to validate this belief. Citing Orton's (1937) view that "no generalization is possible concerning the appearance of emotional disturbance" (p. 132), Connolly similarly argues against the existence of such a generalization. He cautions that such factors as severity and chronicity of the learning problem and subcultural group, socioeconomic level, and intelligence of the child must be kept in mind. However, he arrives at a no more validated opinion than the authors he criticizes. Several related contributions address the association of soft signs of MBD and psychiatric disorder. Shaffer (1978), who examines the correlation between soft signs (e.g., dysgraphesthesia and dysdiadocho-kinesis) in early life and later disturbance, reports that such children may develop specific psychiatric syndromes. Yet it is not clear, he argues, whether this is due to a persisting central nervous system (CNS) abnormality or a less direct association. In a lengthy review article, Werry (1972) comments that those who take brain damage as an independent variable find there is an increased risk of psychopathology. However, the risk is small, difficult to detect, and of a nonspecific type, making it inaccurate to conclude that one is a necessary or even frequent correlate of the other. He suggests that if brain damage is not taken as a homogeneous grouping, a more compelling relationship may be demonstrable. When psychiatric disorder is examined as the independent variable, it is seen that as a group emotionally disturbed children have an increased frequency of EEG abnormalities, soft signs, and mixed physical anomalies. Boshes and Myklebust (1964) who examine the relationship between learning disorder and neurological status, find that neurological integrity is more closely related to behavior and social maturity. They qualify the report of their findings with the statement that sometimes differences are qualitative and are not evident quantitatively.

With regard to specific learning disabilities in the language sphere, Bender (1958) describes a clinical relationship between "developmental language lags" (in reading, writing, and spelling) and disturbances in body image concept. Cantwell and Baker (1980) report that children who present for speech and language evaluations are likely to have academic problems and to be at risk for psychiatric disorders, most frequently conduct and attention deficit disorders. Correlational studies of reading disabilities and psychiatric disorder, or particular personality characteristics, do not arrive at a consensus. Gottesman, Belmont, and Kaminer (1976) and Eisenberg (1975) find them to be unrelated and Connolly (1971) concludes there is no evidence for a "dyslexic personality," although such children tend to be immature and impulsive. In contrast Berger, Yules, and Rutter (1975) report that psychiatric problems are three times more common in children with "specific reading retardation" (p. 510).

Etiology.   Contributors to the question of the etiology of learning disorders are diverse both in their conclusions and in the polemicism or integration which characterizes the route by which they arrive at these conclusions. One cluster of authors identifies one or another type of neuropsychological basis: a maturational lag, a constitutional neurological deficit, and/or MBD. A second cluster emphasizes maladaptive aspects of cognitive style (e.g., passivity or distractibility), often with the implicit or explicit notion that these are in and of themselves of neuropsychological origin. In this sense they may also be considered a subset of the first cluster mentioned. A third cluster addresses the array of possible etiological factors, either as their major purpose or as a background for more specific consideration of one or more selected factors.

Of the first cluster of authors, Orton (1937), Bender (1958), and Kinsbourne (1973a, 1973b) are some of the foremost proponents of the idea that learning disabilities—not learning disorders as a whole—are a function of slowness to mature of at least some aspects of the CNS. The controversy over the validity of soft signs (or a maturational lag) versus the need to document hard neurological signs will be taken up in some detail in the next section of this chapter. Here suffice it to say that the above authors, following a careful diagnostic assessment, clearly define the limits of applicability of their conclusions, that is, the particular group of learning disordered children to which they pertain. This is in contrast to Ames' (1968) presentation of her view of maturational lags. She asserts that 50 percent of learning disorders could be reduced by not teaching children material beyond their developmental capacities. This is despite the fact that she does not base her views on a proper neuropsychological and psychological evaluation.

Other contributors postulate deficits: L. B. Silver (1971) identifies one group of learning disordered children, those who have the "neurological learning disability syndrome" mentioned above, whose problems he bases in a "neurohumoral deficiency which results in physiological dysfunction of the ascending reticular activating system and secondly of the limbic system" (p. 126). Myklebust (1968), with a broad appreciation of five sources of learning impairment—peripheral nervous system involvement, mental retardation, emotional disturbance, cultural disadvantage, and neurological involvement—selectively devotes his efforts to investigation of minor disturbances of brain function and their psychological concomitants. The work of Wender (1971), which seems on the surface to reflect an integrative appreciation of etiology (in this case MBD, of which problems in learning are a cardinal symptom) when read more carefully is disappointingly polemical. He initially proposes the possibility of several distinct etiologies which, he notes, may interact with one another: brain damage and genetic transmission under which he includes "polygenetic abnormality, extreme placement on the normal distribution curve, intrauterine random variation in biological development, fetal maldevelopment and psychogenetic determinants, i.e., deviant psychological experience" (p. 37). However, these postulations notwithstanding, Wender states that MBD can be assigned to "a possible neuroanatomical and/or biochemical locus for this physiological defect" (p. 2). In regard to learning problems in particular, Wender notes their non-specific etiology; neurotics, dysphasics, and retarded children all manifest them. Yet without adequate documentation he claims, "probably the single most common subgroup, however, consists of children with the MBD syndrome" (p. 16). He proceeds to use the diagnosis "neurotic" (the quotes are his), emphasizing the importance of sorting out causes and effects. He presents a classification scheme with MBD as the main diagnosis under which five subtypes exist, one of which is the neurotic type. Thus, he relegates neurosis to a reaction to a specific constitutional abnormality rather than possibly an equal or singular contributory factor in some cases. This is in contrast to Clements (1966a) who regards MBD as an important root of learning disabilities, while at the same time giving full weight to the possibility of psychological determinants of other kinds of learning problems.

A second cluster of contributions posits particular dysfunctions of style, individual sensory modalities, or their interaction—all on a neuropsychological basis. Most of these authors are neither integrative nor polemical in claiming exclusively neuropsychological etiologies when psychogenic factors should be considered. They address a delimited subgroup of learning disabled children—often dyslexics—to which their statements of etiology apply. However, in another sense their work sometimes suffers from a tendency to promote unifactorial cognitive explanations, when multiple cognitive explanations on a neuropsychological basis might be more accurate. For example, De Hirsch (1965) attributes reading disabilities to difficulty in perceiving or responding to complex gestalten which integrate short units into larger ones. These are some of many possible difficulties with integration and differentiation of visual patterns. McGrady (1968) identifies two types of reading disabilities, one due to trouble perceiving visual stimuli and another to difficulty with auditory stimuli. He notes there may also be concurrent difficulty with both senses or in their association. Birch and Lefford (1964) study defects of cross-modal integration in obviously brain-injured subjects. Blank and Bridger (1966) reevaluate and revise their findings, arriving at the conclusion that reading disabilities reflect deficits in conceptualization insofar as the child is required to apply verbal labels to visual stimuli. Schilder (1944) thought the basic problem in alexia to be a gnostic disorder in integration and differentiation of the sounds of the spoken word and its parts in connection with the formation of the written word and its parts. In contrast, Vellutino (1977) offered a more general verbal deficit hypothesis of reading.

Two examples of the "style" hypothesis are the work of Rudel (1980) who states that failure of the generalization of "response strategies for encoding incoming information . . . may be key to understanding the discrepancies that define learning disabilities" (p. 566), and Ross (1976) who focuses on problems in selective attention in learning disabled children, but with a somewhat different emphasis. Torgesen (1975) underlines the passive learning strategies of these children; this paper is the only one in the group which does not make clear whether such strategies are or are not attributed to neuropsychological dysfunction.

An extensive review of the literature on etiology of reading disabilities—although her titles suggest she is addressing learning disabilities in general—is offered by Wong (1979a, 1979b). Her major critique concerns the unidimensionality of the explanations offered, despite the documented heterogeneity of the population. She further notes that regardless of how many studies refute the idea of causal relationships between MBD or other perspectives on neuropsychological dysfunction, others will confirm the link. Closure is not reached because definitions are not clarified and measures are inadequate.

In contrast, a group of excellent contributions is devoted to a truly integrative consideration of the multiple etiological explanations and their possible combinations. They make clear the insufficiency of forced dichotomous classifications of neuropsychological versus psychogenic disorders in learning, and the need for an etiological model which is based on a notion of cumulative vulnerabilities and a "complemental series" (Freud, 1916–1917); the greater the vulnerability of a child to one factor, the more likely another vulnerability—even of minor magnitude—is to have an impact on that child (Giffin, 1968; Werry, 1968, 1972; Rubin, 1971; Mattick and Murphy, 1971; Meier, 1976; Arnold, 1976; Kinsbourne and Caplan, 1979 on learning disorders in general; Critchley, 1968 and Rabinovitch, 1972 on reading disabilities; and De Hirsch, 1965 on language disabilities). The work of A. A. Silver and Hagin (A. A. Silver and Hagin, 1960, 1964, 1980; A. A. Silver, Hagin, and Hersch, 1967; Hagin, 1973; Hagin, Silver, and Kreeger, 1976; A. A. Silver, Hagin, De Vito, Kreeger, and Scully, 1976; Hagin and Silver, 1977) is also in this spirit, although until the paper by Hagin and Silver in 1977 there was a tendency to forced choices; they did not deal with admixtures of neuropsychological dysfunction and psychological conflicts. Several other contributions deserve mention for their integrative perspective on etiology, although they focus on a particular subgroup: the neuropsychologically impaired, learning disabled child (Eisenberg, 1964; Kinsbourne, 1973a, 1973b). For example, Eisenberg emphasizes the almost inevitable contribution to the child's psychology of such disabilities.

Treatment.   Not surprisingly the authors just discussed who offer an integrative conceptualization of the etiology of learning disorders are equally appreciative of the possible complexities of therapeutic needs. These are most often addressed in remediation, psychotherapy, pharmacotherapy, or some combination thereof. Several other contributions in this spirit were found to be specifically concerned with the subject of treatment. Frostig (1968) writes of the need for remediation and psychiatric or neurological help, depending upon the individual case, as does Thompson (1974), who only deals with reading disorders. Clements (1966b) gives special emphasis to the importance of interpretation of findings and the offer of counseling to parents, including help with home management and educational planning. At the same time he is subtly negative about the MBD child's need for psychotherapy, probably because the thrust of his effort is to establish the existence in children of a type of learning disorder which does not have a primarily psychogenic basis. However, such distinctions for definitional purposes do not justify overshadowing the complexity of clinical realities.

Another basically integrative effort with, however, some polemical leanings, is that of Gardner (1968, 1973). Accompanying a valuable exposition of typical character defenses of the MBD child, he states that such children require medication, education, parental guidance, and psychotherapy—in that order. Psychotherapy is indicated only if a combination of medication, education, and parental guidance is not effective. While it would certainly be clinically imprudent to recommend psychotherapy without a great deal of forethought, it seems equally imprudent to foreclose the possibility as a general rule unless other treatment modalities fail. The other limitation of Gardner's work is that he writes as if there is *an* MBD child. This is the basis for an assumption that MBD children cannot engage in analytic work because of impairments in conceptualizing and abstracting but can profit from noninsight forms of treatment with the goal of achieving a better appreciation of reality. Since the postulation of this syndrome is a practical convention to refer to symptoms that are likely, but not inevitably, clustered such assumptions seem hazardous.

One other generally integrative contribution to the subject of treatment worthy of note is that by Doris and Solnit (1963) who demonstrate the efficacy of psychotherapy in "brain-damaged" children, particularly when it is offered in combination with special education and consultation to parents and teachers. In comparing psychotherapy with these children with that of neurotic children, their paper suffers, but to a lesser degree, from the same faulty assumption made by Gardner that all such children present with deficits which interfere with insight. The authors state that while principles of verbalization, clarification, and interpretation are the same, they play a less dominant role than in the treatment of children with more intact language and thought processes. Furthermore, the development of insight and resolution of internalized conflicts are sometimes replaced by other purposes.

Several contributions reviewed are neither specifically integrative nor polemical. Having carefully delineated the learning disabled subgroup about which they write, they recommend remediation as the treatment of choice (Bender, 1958; Birch and Lefford, 1964; Myklebust, 1964; L. B. Silver, 1975).

Another group of contributions does manifest polemicism in the form of predominantly recommending only one treatment modality in all cases and dismissing out of hand other modalities without a sound explanation. Denhoff (1973), Gross and Wilson (1974), and Wender (1971) fervently advocate the sole use of medication in the treatment of children with MBD, as if there were only one possible clinical manifestation of this syndrome. Wender's work will be examined in some detail because of the problems it so vividly illustrates. At a superficial glance, Wender would appear to be quite even-handed in his recommendations, but upon closer examination it becomes evident that he dismisses the efficacy of psychotherapy and remediation on the basis of flimsy evidence— even by his own admission. For example, in the service of discouraging the implementation of remediation, Wender (1971) writes: "Remedial education for children with 'special learning disorders' is currently a subject of considerable dispute. If one can generalize from experience in medicine, the presence of considerable dispute probably documents the lack of clear-cut advantages for any of the proposed treatment programs" (p. 125).

Of course such an argument could be equally applied to the use of medication, which is by no means immune from controversy. Furthermore, it has been reported in some studies that while amphetamines are effective in diminishing the child's hyperactivity and/or distractibility, they do not treat the learning disability for which remediation is the treatment of choice (Gittelman, 1980). Another specious argument is used by Wender to discourage the recommendation of psychotherapy:

> Since the decision not to medicate is usually a decision to substitute another form of treatment, namely psychotherapy, one must also weigh the relative merits and demerits of such treatment. In addition to the possible advantages and disadvantages of psychotherapy that have been discussed previously, there is another psychonoxious effect that should be mentioned. Since psychotherapy is quite clearly ineffective in the vast majority of MBD children, it frequently serves to worsen the rapport between the parents and the therapist [p. 129].

Neither assertion—that a decision for psychotherapy precludes a decision for medication, nor that psychotherapy is ineffective with the vast majority of these children—is documented. Wender repeatedly states that parents have been oversold on psychotherapy, to which they are far less resistant than the use of medication. This is a blatantly invalid clinical generalization; many parents are relieved to think their child's problem is biochemical in origin. Furthermore, despite a theoretical section on extensive secondary psychological reactions to MBD—including marital stress, superego pathology, low self-esteem, cross-sexual identification, guilt and anxiety, narcissism, and the like (pp. 143ff.)—Wender only regards the following as meaningful interventions: explanation to the child of his problem and the need for medication, psychotherapy "narrowly construed," by which he means structuring of the environment to have consistent and predictable contingencies and educational intervention when medication does not suffice.

Jansky (1980) and Connolly (1971) are subtly polemical in their views that while learning disabled children may have psychiatric problems, the most effective treatment is remediation, in Jansky's opinion, and counseling offered by teachers or parents, in Connolly's view.

Finally there are a few contributions on treatment outcome, a relatively unchartered area, as Black (1974) notes. To cite a few, Gittelman (1980) concluded it was unjustified to assert that the use of methylphenidate is effective in the treatment of children with pure learning disabilities (i.e., without a psychiatric diagnosis) or subgroups of these children. Gottesman et al. (1976) found that intervention for reading disabilities over a 3- to 5-year period yielded poor results, in contrast to Hagin and Silver's (1977) reports of the efficacy of these interventions. These conclusions may be reconcilable in that Gottesman et al. did not perform an adequate evaluation to determine the type of reading disability, and thus intervention may not have been appropriate in all cases. Furthermore, adequate psychiatric evaluations were not done, so that additional and/or supplementary intervention may have been necessary to successful treatment.

As late as 1975 Torgesen pointed out that despite a great number of attempts to indicate one or another form of brain dysfunction in the etiology of learning disorders, there is a relative absence of practical information relevant to educational and remedial procedures. Studies conflicted because subject selection was not standardized or properly described. Some populations were clinical ones and others were not; some were controlled for IQ and age, while others were not. Werry (1972), who reviewed the literature on treatment of hyperactive children, found that unlike neurotic children they were refractory to brief psychotherapy and responded better to stimulant drugs, but were equally responsive to principles of behavior therapy.

THE DEVELOPMENTAL LAG VERSUS STRUCTURAL ANOMALY CONTROVERSY

A debate exists in the literature about what constitutes sufficient grounds for attribution of the learning disability of a child without sensory handicap, retardation, or significant psychological conflict to neuropsychological dysfunction. Some authors insist that such a conclusion is valid only in the face of decisive neuropsychological evidence of structural anomaly, while others maintain that a developmental lag, not damage, both constitutes adequate grounds for and a more accurate perspective on childhood learning disorders.

This seemingly straightforward surface description of the controversy belies, however, a more complicated and sometimes confusing series of branching questions and occasional polemical debates. They may be summarized as follows: (1) Is presumptive diagnosis of brain damage or dysfunction legitimate; that is, how "hard" or "soft" must the evidence be? (2) How valid is the diagnostic category of MBD? (3) Are authors who employ terms such as hard and soft signs, defining them in the same manner? (4) Which techniques and types of data constitute sufficient grounds for the conclusion of brain dysfunction? The most reasonable and clinically useful response to these questions is one which allows for multiple relationships between brain dysfunction and learning disability. These relationships will vary in the degree to which they are presumptive, and the techniques and combinations thereof required for their diagnosis. This point of view will be further elaborated following the review of associated controversies.

The first question is to what degree it is legitimate to presume a disorder in brain functioning (i.e., is presumptive diagnosis acceptable?). One group of contributors insists that the diagnostic process and the conclusions deriving from this process be maintained within highly restrictive limits. Although it is often stated that neurologists are the major proponents of this position, they neither appear to have a monopoly on it, nor are they in agreement; many neurologists were found to take issue with one or another facet of the following ideas. The reasoning is as follows: if one is to accurately reach the diagnosis of brain damage, there must by definition be positive proof of damage. They maintain that so-called "soft" signs are insufficient confirmation because they are prone to imprecision, error, and lack of objectification either in administration or interpretation (Cohn, 1964; Ingram, 1973; Schain, 1977). Furthermore, empirical studies have not shown them to distinguish between normal and brain damaged populations (Boshes and Myklebust, 1964; Critchley, 1970; Ingram, 1973; Adams, Kocsis, and Estes, 1974). This latter argument is not accepted by other investigators (Kennard, 1960; Stevens et al., 1967; Peters, Roming, and Dykman, 1975; Shaffer, 1978). Shaffer, for example, found that not all, but rather specifiable neurologic signs—involuntary choreic or athetoid movements, synkinesis, dysdiachokinesis, general clumsiness, and sensory abnormalities such as dysgraphesthesia—differentiated normal from brain damaged children. Even Boshes and Myklebust (1964) who found that quantitative scores did not separate these two types of children, nevertheless argued that there may be important qualitative distinctions in processes of task solution not reflected by quantitative scores. Voeller (1981), who did an extensive review of the literature on the incidence of "soft signs" in brain damaged as compared with normal children, concluded there was no consensus about their ability to distinguish between these groups.

In the absence of definitive neurological findings, some of those who argue against presumptive diagnosis of brain damage assume a "maturational" or "developmental lag." One such contributor is Ross (1976) who states this position succinctly: "In the absence of clear-cut signs of neurological damage . . . the learning-disabled child is principally an immature child, a child whose central nervous system (or a crucial part thereof) has lagged in the development of functions that are essential for learning under the conditions and expectations encountered in the ordinary environment" (pp. 70–71). This is in harmony with the thinking of Bender (1956, 1958) and De Hirsch (1963) who, while they do not recommend immediate dismissal of the import of "soft" signs, maintain that it is preferable to use descriptive terms about observable clinical phenomena which do not require inference when referring to children others might consider "organic" or "brain injured." In a related vein, Kinsbourne (1973b) feels promotion of "soft" signs to the status of a diagnosis is confusing since it implies a "coherence and finality," a relationship of selective damage to a neurological location or system which such signs do not have; some are of consequence and others are not.

Another group of contributors supports the practice of presumptive diagnosis of brain damage when a convincing constellation of symptoms exists (Kennard, 1960; Eisenberg, 1964; Myklebust, 1964; Clements, 1966a; Benton, 1973). They maintain this position in recognition of the current inconclusive state of the art of assessment and the absence of one-to-one correspondences between even documented lesions and behavioral symptoms. They point out that most medical diagnostic efforts rely upon inference, a statement especially true of pediatric neurology (Eisenberg, 1964; Vuckovich, 1968; Voeller, 1981) except in the rare instances when autopsy findings are available. If one confined oneself solely to neurological examination and EEG data to establish the existence of pathology, it might be possible to eliminate false positives, but only at the expense of an excess of false negatives (Eisenberg, 1964; Voeller, 1981). This possibility is beautifully illustrated by M. A. Silverman's (1976) case report of the emerging learning disability of a child who at preschool age evidenced no neuropsychological dysfunction upon neurological (or psychological testing)[2] evaluation. Towbin (1971) has elaborated the significant incidence of undetected neonatal damage, that is, false negatives, which may be linked to the later appearance of MBD. As Werry (1972) notes, "Because of the delicacy, inaccessibility, and complexity of the brain, most of the diagnostic techniques aimed at evaluating its status in vivo are necessarily indirect and inferential" (p. 93).

To make matters more complex, even a documented structural defect may be linked to behavior problems considered to be manifestations of brain damage only by presumption. Such relationships vary from case to case; there are brain damaged children without such behavioral manifestations, as well as an array of possible consequences for behavior in the event of a demonstrable lesion, making prediction of outcome or postulation of cause and effect very imperfect indeed (Eisenberg, 1964; Denckla, 1977).

Although the above-delineated differences of opinion about the legitimacy of presumptive diagnosis are rather distinct and irreconcilable, for some contributors a resolution may hinge upon whether one concludes brain damage, as opposed to brain dysfunction, in the absence of clear-cut evidence of neurological deficit; the latter is acceptable and the former unacceptable (Strother, 1972). This is closely associated with the question of the validity of the diagnosis of MBD, about which there is no consen-

---

[2] We have some question about the adequacy of the initial testing evaluation of the child described since a second evaluation "employing specialized tests in addition to the routine ones" (p. 296) when the child was 5 years old, did detect evidence of neuropsychological dysfunction. While we agree with the author that such diagnosis is difficult in the preschool years, it might be that with attention to the need for comprehensive testing, as delineated in chapter 4, such dysfunction could have been diagnosed.

sus, nearly 20 years after its adoption. Even interpretation of the words represented by this abbreviation is variable; some use the term minimal brain damage and others minimal brain dysfunction or dysfunctions (Rie and Rie, 1980). There is a group of authors, Denckla (1977) being one of them, who regard the designation MBD as a reasonable and useful initial step in diagnosis:

> [A] broad category to indicate that attention should be paid not only to undeniably important social-emotional factors of "nurture" but also quite centrally to brain factors, whether they were called "organic" or "constitutional" or "innate" of "nature." . . . a miscellany of permutations and combinations of brain dysfunctions, whether neurological impairment (genetic or acquired) or neurological immaturity ("maturational lag," "late bloomers") [p. 244].

However, having done so, further diagnostic work remains; it is confusing and may be erroneous to assume that MBD implies acquired brain damage in the absence of additional evidence.

Even among those like Denckla, who find some utility in the concept MBD, there is dissatisfaction with its terminology. The word "minimal" is thought to be a misplaced modifier; that is, it properly applies to the extent of the consequences of brain dysfunction or damage, not to the extent of the area of the brain which is involved. It is noted that damage or dysfunction in a small portion of the brain may have major impact upon behavior while involvement of a large portion of the brain may have a minor effect (Cohn, 1964; Myklebust, 1964; Benton, 1973; Denckla, 1977).

Another set of contributors recommends that the term be discontinued for a variety of reasons. It is confusing by virtue of its inclusion of an excessively heterogeneous group of patients (Gomez, 1967). It is invalid and does not qualify as a syndrome in the medical sense of a consistent combination of symptoms (Rourke, 1975; Ross, 1976). Harmful consequences may arise from its unjustified implication of brain damage in the minds of the lay public, most particularly in patients and their families (Abrams, 1968; Thompson, 1974; Rourke, 1975; Schmitt, 1975). One additional argument against the use of the term MBD is that it reflects fallacious logic; it is circular reasoning to conclude that all symptoms of children documented to be brain injured, when seen in children not documented to be brain injured, signal brain injury. Minimal brain dysfunction is based on a series of behavioral symptoms which may have multiple etiologies. To assume one etiology over others with insufficient proof is invalid. Strother (1972) who makes this point quotes an instance of just such fallacious reasoning in 1948 by seminal contributors to this field, Strauss and Kephart (1955), who note but nevertheless accept its circularity:

> [We] select a group of individuals who behave in a certain fashion. The vast majority of these individuals display definite signs of brain injury. About the few remaining, we do not know one way or the other. It would seem that we are justified in assuming that the factor which is causative in the vast majority is causative in the few remaining, especially in view of the fact that the common neurological examination is known not to be infallible. Such a line of reasoning may be open to the criticism that it is circular in nature. . . . If this reasoning is circular it may yet lead us to the goal without undue error [quoted by Strother (1972) on pp. 177–178].

Ingram (1973) is a very harsh critic of this line of reasoning, feeling that such "soft signs" of MBD do not constitute a diagnosis but rather a symptom in need of a diagnosis. Reasoning such as that of Strauss and Werner represents "soft" thinking.

To some degree the above differences of opinion are rendered less capable of resolution or even of discussion by problems of definition. Terms are used variously by different contributors, at times making communication and comparison of positions difficult, and in some instances, exaggerating differences, thus contributing to polemicism. Two examples are "maturational (or developmental) lag" and "soft signs." The former seems to have originated with Bender (1958) who defined it as follows:

> It [the maturational or developmental lag] is based on a concept of functional areas of the brain and of personality which maturate according to a recognized pattern longitudinally. A maturational lag signifies a slow differentiation in this pattern. It does not indicate a structural defect, deficiency, or loss. There is not necessarily a limitation in the potentialities and at variable levels maturation may tend to accelerate, but

often unevenly. Again one has to use the concept of plasticity in the way the embryologists use the term, being as yet unformed, but capable of being formed, being impressionable and responsive to patterning, and carrying within itself the potentialities of patterns which have not yet become fixed. ... It is this particular characteristic of developmental lags that effects such a variety of symptoms that they defy classification and make it possible for each investigator to emphasize those factors that best fit his experience and theories [p. 533].

Thus Bender, like Weil (1961), De Hirsch (1965), Satz, Taylor, Friel, and Fletcher (1978), and Kinsbourne and Caplan (1979), quite explicitly use this term in the sense of CNS abnormality in rate of development, but not structural damage. Ames (1968), for example, employs the term to indicate a lack of readiness for academic demands of unspecified etiology, which is expected to correct itself spontaneously over time. No implications of CNS abnormality are intended. Some authors use "maturational lag" as a wastebasket category without regard for the future consequences of the so-called lag, that is, whether it will or will not be spontaneously outgrown, while others employ the term "lag" synonymously with "soft" signs which are themselves variously defined.

Two or three usages of "soft" signs are discussed by Rutter, Graham, and Yule (1970), Werry (1972), Ingram (1973), Shaffer (1978), and Gardner (1980). Actually four were noted in the current review of relevant literature, some contributors employing several and others only one or two. To make matters more complicated, it was only in the minority of cases that a contributor explicitly identified the sense(s) in which he intended the term. One meaning, that of delay (Kinsbourne, 1973b; Kinsbourne and Caplan, 1979), is itself divided into two subcategories by Ingram (1973): a failure to develop normal milestones at the usual time and a persistence of immature reflex patterns of neurological behavior. A second meaning is borderline or slight forms of traditional neurological abnormalities (Denckla, 1977), while a third involves signs which are inconsistently present and not clearly associated with neuroanatomical lesions (Wender, 1971; Adams et al., 1974). A fourth meaning signifies minor discrepancies upon neurological examination of a child with educational handicaps (Ingram, 1973). Schain (1977) deplores the confusion of two of these usages—

borderline neurological findings and delays—since he feels they have significantly different implications.

Assessment of a particular author's acceptance or dismissal of "soft" signs as meaningful diagnostic data will necessarily depend upon the way in which he uses this term. Some authors regard "soft" signs as one manifestation of maturational lag or as one of its criteria (Kinsbourne, 1973b; Thompson, 1974; Kinsbourne and Caplan, 1979) thus viewing such signs as due not to damage but to individual variations in genetic programming. Yet others use "soft" signs as the basis for conclusion of brain damage or dysfunction. Were the variety of definitions to be differentiated and given distinct designations, certain apparent differences of opinion about the usefulness and/or the implications of "soft" signs might be resolved.

Furthermore, how these are defined has significant bearing on the question of what constitutes sufficient data for the diagnosis of neuropsychological dysfunction: which individual diagnostic technique or combination thereof—neurological examination, history, neuropsychological testing, EEG, and the like—and the elicitation of so-called "soft" versus "hard" signs.

In general those who regard "soft" signs as meaningful—either in the sense of a maturational lag or a borderline neurological finding suggestive of brain damage or dysfunction—consider a wide-ranging assessment of the learning disordered child to be essential to the establishment or dismissal of a neuropsychological diagnosis. While striving to achieve maximum diagnostic precision, they have no philosophical opposition to a presumptive conclusion of brain dysfunction when "hard" neurological findings do not emerge, if convincing and objective clusters of "soft" signs are present (Gardner, 1979, 1980). In short, they do not regard so-called "soft" signs as any softer in their meaning than so-called "hard" signs. In contrast, those contributors who believe "soft" signs to be meaningless recommend a more circumscribed diagnostic procedure consisting of a neurological examination and sometimes an EEG. These tend to be the authors who define "soft" signs as those which are inconsistently present and not clearly associated with neuroanatomical lesions or as minor discrepancies between various neuropsychological functions upon neurological examination. Thus, they are regarded as incapable of objectification (Ingram, 1973; Schmitt, 1975) and/or a function of anxiety, distractibility, or hyperactivity (Schmitt, 1975; Schain, 1977).

Perspectives on several other issues contribute to opinions about the necessity of obtaining "hard" findings and thus the type of data which must be elicited. The first is the adequacy of the standard neurological examination to tap subtle higher CNS dysfunction. Schain (1977), a major spokesman for its efficacy, maintains that most neurologists feel that if performed carefully, this examination will elicit bona fide "hard" findings in the event of brain damage; they are thus dubious about the value of borderline neurological findings or results of other data. Another proponent of this position, Schmitt (1975), explicitly dismisses the usefulness of diagnostic test findings for establishing a conclusion of neuropsychological dysfunction; in his view only statements about strengths and weaknesses can be made. Furthermore, both Schain and Schmitt argue that the notion that a standard examination fails to detect subtle dysfunctions is not adequate grounds for failing to provide solid documentation of neurological abnormality.

Schain's statement notwithstanding, many neurologists, child psychiatrists, and neuropsychologists could be found to question the infallibility of the standard neurological examination for assessment of higher cortical functions. Voeller (1981), a neurologist, offers a very informative discussion of its shortcomings, and proposes a far more comprehensive examination which encompasses much of the wide-ranging neuropsychological testing evaluation to be delineated in chapter 4. Thus, she supports the position that the most efficacious diagnostic procedure is one which casts the broadest net. She questions why the conventional neurological examination has failed to distinguish between learning disabled and normal populations, offering several explanations. This examination results in many false negatives since the abnormalities it detects—difficulties in gross, fine, and graphomotor coordination—are secondary to cortical spinal tract abnormalities and thus irrelevant to many disorders in learning, for example, a child's inability to read. Therefore, an adequate examination must deal with a full range of cognitive processes, not simply sensorimotor functions. Furthermore, it is constructed to localize lesions, but those of the learning disabled child are typically subtle and different from circumscribed lesions of the mature brain. Furthermore, even when "hard" and "soft" signs are detected, they must be evaluated in light of the child's age since both types of signs are more frequent in young children. Finally, Voeller notes the importance of examining not only quantitative findings but coping strategies to ascertain the nature of the child's deficits and his abilities to transcend and correct for them.

Similar reservations about the singular accuracy and comprehensiveness of the neurological examination are echoed by Kennard (1960), Vuckovich (1968), Werry (1972), Kinsbourne (1973b), Peters, Roming, and Dykman (1975), Rabinovitch, Drew, De Jong, Russell, Ingram, and Withey (1954), Werry and Aman (1976), and Denckla (1977). While all authors, therefore, suggest an expansion of the conventional examination to enhance its contribution, they note that evidence of abnormality on the neurological examination is not essential to diagnosis of a constitutionally determined disturbance in neurological organization and/or a specific learning disability.

Some authors provide a slightly different emphasis, stating that the best diagnostic process involves the interrelating of multiple types of data. For example, Denckla (1977) who distinguishes between types of "soft" signs—"developmental soft signs" which involve delays and "pastel soft signs" which are reminiscences of "hard" neurological findings—feels that the former are neither necessary nor sufficient for implication of permanent brain damage, as compared with the latter which are necessary but not sufficient evidence of damage. Therefore, in conjunction with these data one must examine historical data, school records, and neuropsychological test results, taking into account the multiple etiologies of brain dysfunction in any one individual (see also Myklebust, 1964). Vuckovich (1968) feels that it is rarely possible to establish a clear-cut pathological diagnosis on the basis of the neurological exam alone; its interpretation is most meaningful in conjunction with a detailed history. Birch and Lefford (1964) note that even in clearly brain damaged children, for example, those with cerebral palsy, one may need tests of higher cortical functions to diagnose deficits in intersensory integration, while difficulties in simple perceptual discrimination may be discerned on neurological examination alone. Kinsbourne (1973b) and Kinsbourne and Caplan (1979) comment that children with documented neurological abnormality may evidence no disorder in learning and, conversely, those without neurological abnormality on examination may have reading disabilities which are developmentally or neuropsychologically based.

In review of the controversy as to whether learning disabilities are due to developmental lags or structural anomalies—as well as the additional issues embedded in this controversy—it seems most accurate and efficacious to assume an approach to diagnosis which encompasses multiple models of brain involvement. Correspondingly, the casting of a broad net in data collection and interpretation in which "soft signs" (a poor term) are considered neither more nor less conclusive than so-called "hard signs" is a most relevant approach. Thus, a model or a diagnostic technique which is especially germane to one child may be unsuitable or uninformative in the case of another.

An interesting conception of multiple models of brain involvement in cognitive functioning is presented by Kinsbourne and Caplan (1979) (see also Hynd and Obrzut, 1981). The three models they delineate are: (1) the "deficit" model which attributes a child's lack of school-related abilities to demonstrable structural damage, one indicator of which would be "hard" signs; (2) the "delay" model which involves selective lags in neurological development, not necessarily from structural damage; thus "hard" evidence of gross damage is less likely than "soft" signs; and (3) the "difference" model which does not assume structural or even "molecular" deviation, but rather variations in the pattern and emergence of cognitive skills which are only problematic insofar as society demands adequate functioning; "soft" signs may themselves be manifestations of difference. Kinsbourne and Caplan designate these models in the service of pointing out the polemical thinking and self-fulfilling use of data in which proponents of each model engage to validate their own positions:

> Each of the three models can fit many situations; more important, it is rarely possible to prove that one model is more applicable to an individual case than the other two. Whereas the presence of hard signs might arguably support the deficit model, a proponent might see their absence as merely suggesting that the structural damage was too localized to generate hard signs, even though such signs could be detected by other methods. The presence of soft signs is easily attributable to structural damage, since the typical effect of early structural damage is to retard the onset of development of those functions which are normally the responsibility of the damaged brain section. The delay model views hard signs as coincidental and the absence of neurological soft signs as indicating a narrowly focused delay with regard to cognition only. The

difference model would regard the presence of hard signs, neurological soft signs, or both as coincidental and unillumi- nating.

The effect of these considerations is to highlight the use- lessness, with respect to school failure, of the much-discussed MBD phenomena. Inferences made from the presence or absence of signs of one or another kind are at best problematic in nature. Worse still, the probabilities attached to each finding are quite unknown. This type of information is not useful in the individual case. Only when the finding relates directly to the school failure is it of interest. Thus, when clumsiness is one cause of a child's difficulty in the classroom, then soft signs of motor immaturity are relevant to the complaint. The same applies to selective cognitive deficits and to cognitive style abnormalities, but these are better regarded as primary com- plaints than as associated findings [pp. 102-103].

However, informative empirical research by Rourke (Rourke, 1978; Rourke, Bakker, Fisk, and Strang, 1983) suggests the efficacy of using varying models, depending upon the clinical presentation of the individual case, for example, the employment of both a developmental lag and a deficit model for children with reading disabilities. As Rourke reported the findings of his longitudinal study of reading disabilities:

The results of this study offered some support for the developmental lag view of Satz and his colleagues (e.g., Satz et al., 1978) in that "younger" (ages 7–8) retarded readers exhibited particularly poor performance as compared to age- matched normal readers on tasks that seem to require primar- ily visual-perceptual and visual-motor abilities (e.g., the Underlining Test). However, it should be noted that, at the time of study 1, the normal and retarded reading groups did not differ significantly on the WISC Performance IQ measure (which is composed primarily of tests heavily weighted in terms of visual-spatial and visual-motor components). In addition, as was pointed out above, it may be the case that verbal labeling of the complex visual forms of the Underlining Test was one of the crucial elements responsible for success on them.

Finally, the fact that the accurate predictive antecedents at ages 7 to 8 of reading and spelling levels at ages 11 to 12 for the retarded readers differed markedly from those for the normal readers could be construed as evidence in support of either the developmental-lag or the deficit position. However, it should be emphasized that only 5 of the 19 subjects originally classified as "retarded readers" made fairly substantial (and, on the basis of the results of this study, predictable) gains in reading achievement (i.e., more than 20 centile points on the MAT Reading subtest), whereas approximately three-quarters of this group made little, if any, progress. This being the case, it may be that a developmental lag model would be appropriate for those few who made significant advances, whereas a deficit interpretation would be appropriate for those who did not [Rourke, 1978, pp. 109–110].

Thus, consideration of all available data and models (Bender, 1956, 1958; De Hirsch, 1963; Ames, 1968; L. B. Silver, 1971; Ross, 1976; Satz et al., 1978) is preferable to single model frameworks which tend to rely upon specific data and to dismiss others (Thompson, 1974; L. B. Silver, 1979).

CONTROVERSIES WITHIN THE REMEDIAL FIELD

Two major controversies may be identified among the myriad techniques and philosophical approaches to remediation which appear in the literature. The first concerns the advisability of strengthening disordered functions or revisiting deviant phases of early development assumed to be the basis for a problem in learning; the purpose of such intervention is to render them normal, in contrast to constructing alternative pathways to learning by circumventing the deficits. A second debate—one often inseparable from the first—surrounds the validity of assuming that the restoration of a skill, neuropsychological function, or deviant stage of development to its normal mode of operation will necessarily have implications for the normality of other aspects of cognitive functioning. These two controversies are interrelated in that those who advocate the strengthening of a particular function frequently assume success in this effort will result in cure of the learning disability.

In general there has been remarkably little empirical study of either controversy. Instead, fervent beliefs reign, with the rationale for these beliefs better delineated in some instances than others.

However, one may find many critical commentaries concerning both controversies, which trench upon the indications of polemicism we have been stressing: (1) Too often either the appropriate scope of the recommended methods remains unspecified or it is exaggerated. The method is claimed to be of universal value. And frequently related to this, (2) insufficient attention is given to assessment of individual differences among learning disabled children; thus such differences cannot be taken into account in remedial approaches.

While there are countless minor variations in approach to the remediation of learning disabilities, the array of methods and their philosophical underpinnings can be clustered into four broad perspectives. One calls for a "repatterning" of the learning process. It assumes that learning problems are residua of early deviations in the child's sensorimotor development. A second argues that learning disabilities are due to one or more specific cognitive deficits. Retraining in these deficit areas permits a restoration of normality, thus allowing learning to proceed in the conventional manner. A third, comparable to the second in that specific deficits are also recognized, calls for the discovery of alternate means of teaching which involve the construction of detours around the deficit area. Rather than strengthening the deficit area, already existing smoothly functioning capacities are utilized. A subtype of this perspective may be called "multisensory" in that the child is taught with a variety of simultaneously presented stimuli: auditory, visual, kinesthetic, and tactile. Proponents of the fourth perspective, which is eclectic in nature, urge the employment of any effective remedial–educative method, regardless of its theoretical rationale. They request that in the absence of clear-cut documentation of the success of any one position, it is preferable to focus on the functions or skills which have not been acquired rather than upon why these acquisitions have not taken place.

A brief overview of each of these perspectives—the nature of the approach, its stance on the two major controversies, and the degree of its polemicism—will be presented. The remediation of reading disorders will be emphasized since these are the problems most commonly addressed in the literature. However, the issues raised in this discussion are equally applicable to remediation of other disorders.

Repatterning

The major proponent of this method, Delacato (1963), believes that the child with learning disabilities has suffered a serious alteration in an essentially immutable series of steps in sensorimotor development. By virtue of not having gone through the requisite steps, the child has lost something in cognitive development. Delacato maintains that the only form of restoration, or "repatterning," involves a return to very early stages of development.

This method is polemical in several respects. There is no convincing empirical support for its efficacy in general or for its claim that sensorimotor retraining will transfer to and thus enhance learning. Reviews of this approach have been almost uniformly negative in their conclusions. L. B. Silver (1975) notes that since little description of actual interventions and results has been provided, replication studies are impossible. This has led the American Academy of Pediatrics, the American Academy of Cerebral Palsy, and the United Cerebral Palsy Association of Texas to issue statements questioning the effectiveness of the approach. Heinicke (1972) finds no evidence to support the notion that the retraining of basic motor activities results in increased reading achievement. Kinsbourne and Caplan (1979) believe patterning to be irrational in its goal of "helping learning disabled children's brains to develop by training them in abilities that have no self-evident relationship to reading, writing or arithmetic readiness, but which are alleged to be prerequisites for readiness to acquire these skills" (p. 196).

Other critics challenge Delacato's belief that one can concretely return to an earlier phase of development, as if it were identical in the older child. Sapir and Wilson (1978) state that: "When an older child has a deficit at a lower order of thinking or perceiving, it is not possible to retrace one's steps and simply retrain . . ." (p. 133). Wong (1979a, 1979b) cogently comments that the motor and perceptual systems become less autonomous and increasingly dominated by cognition; there is nothing in developmental theory to argue for the need to strengthen either motor or perceptual activities to aid cognition.

It seems clear that there is no reason to date to consider patterning a viable method of remediation for the learning disabled child. It suffers from the basic flaw that it does not teach the child to read; he may crawl better, but whether he will read better is left to chance.

Retraining of Specific Deficits

Proponents of the retraining approach may be compared to Delacato with regard to their positions on the two major remedial controversies. They subscribe to the view that remediation should attempt to strengthen the identified disordered function or developmental stage. Furthermore, they typically believe that such work will generalize to academic functioning, even if the disorder in academic functioning is not itself directly treated. At the same time significant differences between their perspectives deserve to be highlighted. Repatterning, as conceived by Delacato, is far more reductionistic in its theory of the etiology of learning disorders. Thus it more markedly overestimates its range of applicability and gives no attention to individual differences in the children for whom it is prescribed. Although contributions to retraining may be subject to the same criticisms, these problems are not of the same magnitude, as will be further explicated below.

The notion that a specific diagnosable deficit must be retrained and, therefore, removed so that the child's learning may progress, has been most forcefully promulgated by Frostig (1968) and Kephart (1960, 1968). Frostig emphasizes the visual perceptual system while Kephart focuses on problems in the motor system. Kephart's system is reminiscent of the patterning approach in that motor activity is emphasized, but different in that it does not call for the child to return to much earlier modes of activity. Instead it centers on activities that are common for the child at his age. Since children with learning problems evidence a disproportionate number of problems with such functions as balance and bodily orientation, it is argued that a variety of activities should be introduced to strengthen them. For instance, children walk on balance beams and jump on trampolines. There is no direct teaching of reading or other basic skills.

Frostig's program aims to retrain a postulated defect in the child's perceptual system since its functions are considered essential building blocks for the aspects of reading mastered from ages 3 to 7 1/2 (Frostig, 1964, 1968; Frostig and Horne, 1965). For example, children who had trouble learning to read were noted to have difficulty copying geometric forms. Thus, a series of exercises including matching and discrimination of forms and shapes was developed. Another body of work (A. A. Silver, Hagin, and Hersh, 1967; Hagin and Silver, 1977; Hagin, Silver, and Breecher, 1978) maintains that while deficient perceptual functions must be retrained, this will not suffice; instead it must occur concomitant with the continued teaching of reading.

Several other contributors have targeted for retraining alternate singular perceptual deficits or combinations thereof. Chalfant and Flathouse (1971) note that many children are referred for help with reading because they do not have good visual and auditory discrimination skills. They suggest the need for identifying which children have which deficiencies; following this appropriate training is instituted. Children with auditory discrimination problems are taught to distinguish various dimensions of sound, one speech sound from another, and meaningful from nonsense words. They are also helped to identify the location of a sound source. They suggest training in visual perception to be purely perceptual in contrast to Frostig or Kephart's methods in which the training is visual–motor. The bases of hue, brightness, form, and vertical versus horizontal movements are taught. Yet another emphasis is provided by Klueur (1971) who believes that poor readers are deficient in memory and thus require training in this function.

Two broad problems characterize all of these approaches to retraining and partially reflect a polemical spirit in which contributors forward their own approach as universally preferable. First, there are questions about the validity of assuming that once the child has mastered the function that was retrained, this will necessarily generalize to all skills or academic functions in which the particular function comes into play. Second, many approaches neither recognize nor leave room for individual differences; children are assigned to programs with little understanding of why they cannot read. Related to this, the complexities of and multiple routes to disabilities in learning frequently remain unappreciated. The reasons for recommending a particular approach have not been explained theoretically; nor have their claims been documented empirically.

The assumption of generalizability has been contradicted by the findings of many studies. Heinicke (1972) reports that neither the Frostig program nor auditory training results in reading improvement. Sapir (1973) found that children who had received training in a variety of tasks generally thought to be prerequisites of reading—lateral awareness, spatial orientation, and the like—did no better on follow-up studies of academic achievement than those children who had not received the training. Those children with the training did do better on a variety of measures of these specific functions, however. Rourke et al. (1983) note that the use of the Frostig program seems to teach the child to do well on the Frostig test but does little to improve reading. They do, however, go on to say that some skill training is necessary, although skills such as those taught by the Frostig program have a limited impact on the higher order visual perceptual processes crucial to academic functioning.

The expectation that training in one area will automatically transfer to another may be particularly ill-founded in the case of learning disabled children who typically evidence problems with generalizing (Johnson and Myklebust, 1967; Luria, 1973). In this vein Guthrie and Seifert (1978) argue for the necessity of identifying and teaching in a painstaking manner all of the underlying cognitive processes involved in reading. Particularly important are decoding accuracy, decoding speed, and perception of orthographic regularity (i.e., the ability to recognize the similarity of elements when embedded in different contexts, e.g., "who" is always "who" no matter what precedes or follows it). They feel that normal readers typically discover the various aspects of reading on their own, but that many children do not possess this ability to "invent" reading.

The other difficulty with retraining concerns the accuracy of its authors' theories of learning and how these theories dovetail with individual children's needs. As Zigmund (1977) indicates, the evidence supporting Kephart and Frostig is equivocal and unconvincing. One "must question the assumption that perceptual-motor inadequacy causes reading problems" (p. 439) since correlational studies cannot be used to impute causality. Clearly, many children with learning problems have motor or visual–motor integration problems, but this does not mean a coexisting reading problem is caused by the difficulty. Wong's (1979a, 1979b) criticism of the patterning approach, noted earlier, is also pertinent here. There is no reason to argue that, because one stage precedes another and there are problems in that later stage, retraining of the skills thought to be acquired in the earlier stage is essential to adequate performance in the later stage.

Some contributors thus conclude that retraining methods are generally inefficacious; others feel that these methods may be useful for some children but not for others, careful diagnostic study being the only way of making such distinctions. Pihl (1975), Benton (1977), Guthrie (1977), and Kinsbourne and Caplan (1979) regard perceptual–motor, fine and gross motor activities as among those methods without promise for learning disabled children. There is no evidence that supplying a child with a superabundance of normal experience will accelerate brain development (Kinsbourne and Caplan, 1979). An especially adamant critic is Farnham-Diggory (1980) who believes:

> If a diagnostician claims to know that something is wrong with a child's "visual perception," "auditory memory," or the like, and claims to have remedial tutoring programs for their "weaknesses," they are themselves poorly informed. It is important that parents and professionals alike understand that the scientific evidence on this point is conclusive: no matter what one may wish to believe, remedial teaching procedures of the foregoing type are useless. . . [p. 577].

Some authors emphasize not only the lack of empirical findings, but the fallacious reasoning which they believe to underly such approaches. Guthrie and Seifert (1978) comment that the visual processes involved in geometric form discrimination are distinct from those involved in the perception of words. They note the flaw in thinking which maintains that because perception is involved in both, the type of perception used is identical. Myklebust (1975a) believes that in children with perceptual problems it is not perception itself which is disturbed but the child's ability to gain significance or meaning beyond perception; the implication is that some important language aspect is missing.

One of the commonest criticisms of perceptual–motor retraining programs is that they do not sufficiently take into account the variety of clinical situations for which they may be recommended and thus the possible limits of their application. They do not recognize the differences among various disabled children and/or that not all problems with reading stem from disturbed perceptual–motor processes. For these reasons no one program, process, or procedure is universally applicable (Johnson and Myklebust, 1967; Sapir and Wilson, 1978). Rourke et al. (1983) point out that even two children who have a similar pattern of neuropsychological strengths and weaknesses may respond differently to the same therapeutic techniques. Addressing this subject from another perspective, Luria and Tzvetkova (1968) say, "it is senseless for a patient whose writing trouble derives from damage of the auditory analytic and synthesizing process to be exercised at copying tasks" (p. 143). They discuss the importance of developing specific techniques that meet the needs of each individual patient. For instance, if there are problems with the comprehension of logical–grammatical structures such as "up," "down," "under," then tasks must be devised which use these structures specifically.

Teaching via Alternate Pathways

The third perspective on remediation, like the fourth—the eclectic approach—tends to be less polemical than repatterning or retraining. Both perspectives convey a recognition that each child is unique and that the learning process in general, and reading in particular, is highly complex. Thus, effective diagnosis of disorders in reading requires differentiation into its various components, and remedial techniques useful for one child may not be useful for another. In this way both the alternate pathway and eclectic perspectives do not routinely exaggerate the scope of their applicability.

However, a more careful analysis of individual contributions reveals the existence of variations in this regard. Within the broad perspective of teaching via alternate pathways, a subdivision may be identified. One trend argues for the use of multisensory stimulation; another dichotomizes visual and auditory learning styles, arguing that teaching should occur within the stronger modality. All of these approaches maintain that deficits in neuropsychological function should be circumvented and that generalization from one area to another should not be assumed. The area or areas of learning difficulty are directly addressed; for example, the child is taught to read by using reading and language materials, not by walking on balance beams, making angels in the snow, or copying geometric forms.

As a whole, contributions to the multisensory trend are rather weak in their theoretical rationale. For example, why instructing a child to look at a letter while tracing it in sandpaper and saying its sound should result in a greater likelihood of committing the sound to memory is not grounded in a neuropsychological explanation. Contributors vary both in the combination of modalities they suggest and the degree of certainty with which suggestions are made. For example, Johnson and Myklebust (1967) suggest a combination of auditory, visual, tactile, and kinesthetic stimulation may be useful in remediation of reading disorders. However, they offer the cautionary note that some learning disabled children, because of their difficulty in dealing with large amounts of stimulation, may actually suffer from this approach; the multiple stimuli may be overwhelming (Johnson and Myklebust, 1967; Myklebust, Bannochie, and Kellen, 1971). Meier (1976) suggests that multisensory techniques such as the use of color to aid in discriminating phonics may be useful but that evidence on this point is by no means clear or consistent. Fernald (1943), takes the view that more is better, and relies heavily upon multisensory stimulation. Orton (1937), Anderson (1966), Thompson (1974), and Golden (1978) argue for the introduction of tactile and/or kinesthetic stimuli to strengthen the verbal–auditory associations necessary for reading, while L. B. Silver (1975) adds to this the utilization of visual stimuli in the form of wooden blocks covered with sandpaper.

Those who promote the diagnosis of deficit in the visual or auditory sphere, with the recommendation that remedial efforts employ the functions of the remaining sphere of strength, do not sufficiently recognize two clinical realities. One is that it is not possible to neatly separate the visual from the auditory. Reading is a complex task that intimately commingles visual and auditory processes. Nor is it simply audition or vision that is involved in reading, but an array of cognitive processes that employ various types and levels of skill within each of these areas. By using a task analytic method the various skills can be identified, the deficit areas delineated, and remedial techniques derived to teach that aspect of the function. The idea is neither to ignore the deficit nor really to circumvent it, but simply to teach what needs to be learned by a particular child using any means necessary.

The other reality is that for any individual, deficits may exist in one, both, or neither spheres; thus the existence of deficits in the visual sphere does not preclude those in the auditory sphere, and vice versa. Zentall (1981), one representative of the authors who dichotomize auditory and visual functions, describes a variety of auditory problems and suggests that if they are of significant magnitude, the child should be taught via the visual mode. Hynd and Obrzut's (1981) "key" approach attempts to provide a systematic means of diagnosis based more on cognitive functions than on underlying brain structures. Although diagnosis is meant to indicate the teaching approaches to be used, little discussion of remedial approaches is actually presented. It is only stated that diagnostic differences suggest some children learn better through a phonetic and others a visual approach. Myklebust (1964) feels that if there is a disturbance of the auditory process, learning should be approached through visual processes. Similarly, L. B. Silver (1975) claims that "knowing a child has auditory perceptual difficulties the educator would not use a phonics method to teach reading" (p. 408).

The Eclectic Approach

Voluminous contributors emphasize the importance of pragmatism by stressing the disadvantages of slavish commitment to a particular theoretical perspective on remediation. Some more extreme in their thinking than others, seem to need to shock the field back to the hard realities that many children have languished in programs inappropriate to their needs. All seem to believe that theories have gone too far afield of the data and thus do not adequately serve the children for whom these theories were initially conceived. They assume a commonsense approach, therefore, maintaining that one needs specifically to address the disordered area of learning; if one method does not result in progress, it should be discarded and another attempted. Thus, they do not take a stance on the controversy concerning strengthening of disordered functions versus creation of alternate pathways. However, in the case of the second remedial controversy, they oppose the assumption of generalizability from intervention in one area of cognitive function to another.

Some authors support an eclectic perspective on remediation in general, while others focus upon remediation of reading. Among the former are Rourke et al. (1983) who echo the belief of many others (Orton, 1937; Strauss and Lehtinen, 1947; Nelville, 1966; Bateman, 1972; Opperman, 1978; Sapir and Wilson, 1978; Kinsbourne and Caplan, 1979; Rourke et al., 1983) that because each child is different, to have one system of remediation ignores the complexity of the problem. The approach suggested is one of practicality, teaching what needs to be learned, which sometimes involves teaching "to strengths" and sometimes strengthening areas of weakness. Contributors of this persuasion emphasize the need to carefully define educational objectives prior to embarking upon a remedial program. Equally essential is constant monitoring of the child's rate of progress, accompanied by a willingness to discard unsuccessful interventions.

Several characteristic contributions of this perspective to the remediation of reading disorders are those of Pihl (1975), Zigmund (1977), and Guthrie (Guthrie, 1977; Guthrie and Seifert, 1978). Guthrie, in a simplified but important approach, argues for close definition of the reading process so that it may be taught without reference to any one specific remedial theory. Pihl reports that no one approach leads to a demonstrable long-term impact on reading level, and, in his review of remedial approaches, finds none that is always efficacious. He suggests abandoning adherence to any one method and the employment of more direct teaching. Zigmund, in a radical statement, contends that so-called dyslexics are not truly dyslexic but rather children who are "hard to teach." He argues that perhaps "true dyslexics" should not have to rely upon reading or writing procedures and presents a notion of "bookless learning."

In summary, while various controversies about remedial approaches continue to rage, it seems clear that not all approaches are effective; even those that are successful are not of universal benefit. Dismissal of the Delacato approach seems justified since evidence for perceptual–motor training approaches is at best scanty and that against it rather damning. Those who support the necessity of determining whether a child is primarily visual or auditory, and then teaching within the area of strength, have not adequately delineated the reasons why this should be done. Furthermore, this perspective makes little sense since it is erroneous exclusively to attribute reading or learning in general to visual or auditory functions; nor has the rationale behind multisensory approaches been explained in a convincing manner. What seems most reasonable to us is an approach which encompasses elements of the alternate pathway and eclectic perspectives. A clear description of the child's strengths and weaknesses is essential to the development of a remedial program that capitalizes upon the individual's strengths. At the same time, such a program is viewed pragmatically in that it is constantly under review and, when needed, revision. In chapter 7 there is further delineation of these views on remediation and the technical approaches deriving from them.

Chapter 4

Diagnostic Principles and Process

Rather than a radical revision of the traditional clinical evaluation, what is urged in this chapter is an augmented conceptual scope in diagnostic work with learning disordered patients. In some instances this involves deriving additional data of special relevance to learning, for example, in the course of assessing the patient's mental status or developing a history. In other instances it is a question of considering conventionally derived data from supplementary perspectives. Diagnosis is here separated from treatment for purposes of exposition. However, they are frequently overlapping and continuous processes characterized by reassessment and/or deepening of the formulations initially gained. A study that attempts to achieve the greatest precision possible, must not contribute to forced primary diagnoses.

The first section of this chapter concerns the development of a history—with the patient's parents, the patient, and school personnel—of the nature of the child's disorder and previous efforts at intervention. Salient features of this phase of the diagnostic process, and the types of data specific to each of these sources, will be noted and special problems in history development will be highlighted. The phrase "developing a history *with*" rather than "taking a history *from*" is employed to convey the activity and shared participation of interviewer and one or more interviewees in this process. The clinician aims to elicit the interviewees' valuable observations. In part this involves educating them about the potential importance of data previously regarded as insignificant. In the course of the interview, descriptions and beliefs may consequently be amended, expanded, or deepened.

Following this, screening procedures are presented for incorporation in the clinician's early contacts with the patient, whether they be in the form of semistructured mental status examinations or unstructured initial clinical interviews. Even if not carried out as such, awareness of these procedures may shed additional perspectives on the interview situation.

Special emphasis is placed upon the composition and rationale of an adequate diagnostic testing evaluation. Although some readers who are not psychologists may be tempted to skip over this section, it is hoped they will at least skim it sufficiently to ascertain whether the evaluations they typically receive and/or request encompass the guidelines and principles recommended here. If not, they are urged to proceed to cases illustrative of the miscarriage of diagnostic efforts in the absence of such evaluation. These will be found in the last section of chapter 5, "Pitfalls of a Partial Evaluation." A perusal of the section on diagnostic testing in the current chapter may also be valuable in that it further elucidates task analytic principles detailed in chapter 1. These are applicable to the interpretation of historical and clinical interview data as well.

After brief discussion of indications for referral for neurological evaluation, consideration will be given to selected aspects of the reporting of findings to the patient, his parents, and school personnel which are especially pertinent to patients with learning disorders. The inclusion of this stage of clinical work in a chapter on diagnosis reflects a belief that the manner in which patients and their parents receive diagnostic conclusions significantly influences their ability to embark on the treatment recommended. In this sense it is part of the diagnostic process. In some instances assessment of such reactions may lead to a revision of recommendations or an extension of the diagnostic period in an effort to more effectively prepare those persons involved for treatment.

In illustration of these principles of diagnosis, the process of assessment of the three major cases previously introduced will be presented in chapter 5. These will be contrasted with other cases in which the diagnostic process floundered for a variety of reasons.

DEVELOPMENT OF THE HISTORY

With the Patient's Parents

While there is nothing categorically unique about developing a history[1] in the course of evaluating a learning disordered child, there are differences of emphasis which stem from the multiple perspectives which must be firmly kept in mind to effectively diagnose such conditions. This goal is most successfully achieved when the clinician is able to hold aside his preferred theoretical framework. Although all clinicians inevitably favor some orientations over others, when such preferences serve to distort or color data—or even worse preclude their consideration—major inaccuracies may result.

At the same time, the history ought to clearly delineate the parents' implicit theory (or theories, since those of mother and father may radically differ) about the origin and nature of their child's disorder in learning. Should there be a previously undiagnosed neuropsychological substrate, an understanding of parental theories will be an important key to its psychodynamic elaboration. It may also lend clarification to parents' failure to have observed or registered cues that should have raised this possibility, or to their dismissal of the opinions of professionals previously encountered. Equally significant is their view of the child's experience of the

---

[1]The reader is referred to several excellent discussions of conventional approaches to history taking by Chess (1969), Goodman and Sours (1967), Sours (1978), and Cohen (1979a, 1979b). Exception is taken, however, to Sours' view of the potentially disruptive or competitive effect of diagnostic testing on the consultation process (pp. 600, 602), assuming of course that the psychologist is a carefully chosen collaborator. It is agreed that parents who have made contact with an evaluating clinician should be discouraged from arranging for testing prior to consultation with the evaluating clinician, but for different reasons. To assure that they seek an adequate evaluation it may be necessary to provide education about what is involved or to suggest referral to specific psychologists. Additionally, it is preferable that the clinician fully explore with parents the observations which may very legitimately have raised their concern about the possibility of neuropsychological dysfunction. In our experience testing is rarely as anxiety provoking as Sours indicates, unless it is perceived as threatening by the evaluator. Finally, we distinctly disagree with the practice of postponing testing until after the completion of the consultation (p. 602). It is best viewed as an integral part of the consultation for reasons which will be explicated in the later sections on psychological testing and in our clinical illustrations of effective and problematic consultations.

problems for which they seek consultation. Most basic is their assessment of whether he is aware of and/or troubled by the difficulties they identify. Alternatively, the child may be troubled, but by different issues (nightmares, parental marital discord, an inability to accomplish homework quickly enough to play with friends) or by a different sense of the locus of the difficulty (his rotten teachers or nagging parents rather than his incapacity). This background will also undoubtedly facilitate effective communication of the findings of the current evaluation insofar as parental responses can be anticipated.

In the service of understanding parents' expectations and theories, the initial interview is best begun in an open-ended manner. This will permit the emergence of observations and ideas as parents spontaneously organize and connect them. Implicit assumptions and conflicting opinions should subsequently be highlighted by the clinician and raised for parents' consideration. The impetus for the present evaluation is especially important to clarify. Very different clinical situations obtain when parents wish to open-mindedly explore the etiology of their child's learning disorder (as in cases 2 and 3, Daniel and Matthew) from those instances in which they have a distinct investment in seeing the problem as a manifestation of an underlying neuropsychological condition (as in case 1, Noah) or, conversely, dread such a diagnostic impression and favor a psychodynamic formulation (e.g., the fathers in cases 5 and 7, Rachel and Eloise). Different again is the clinical situation in which parents bring their child as a result of pressure from the school whose concern they do not share (as in case 4, Joseph). (All cases mentioned are elaborated in chapter 5.)

Parental investment in a particular perspective may reflect an expectation that one or the other causation is more amenable to effective intervention and/or more directly related to parental failings. A review of the existence and nature of previous evaluations will often reveal parental theories and hopes. Dissatisfactions may reflect valid complaints about the quality of such evaluations or the clarity with which findings were conveyed or, alternatively, a wish to disconfirm these findings because they run counter to wished-for conclusions or too directly threaten characteristic defenses and fantasies. In some instances, for example, case 4, Joseph, the child is relied upon to be a perfect repository of one or both parents' unfulfilled expectations.

In other families, the presenting child is associated by one parent with the hated spouse and is, therefore, regarded as equally "dumb" or "sick." The problem in learning is recruited to this set of beliefs (see case 5, Rachel). In contrast, a parent may himself have a deeply felt identification with the learning disordered child. Diagnosis of a neuropsychological or psychological basis to this symptom highlights differences between parent and child and thus fractures this identification. Another common clinical situation is that in which a highly successful parent has had the same specific difficulty as his school-age child. Having transcended the deficit in any one of a number of ways, the parent has typically repressed the pain and humiliation it caused him at his child's age. Furthermore, since he has personally either been able to compensate or to choose a field of work which does not require proficiency in the disordered function(s), he feels it is of no consequence or, alternatively, does not regard it as a disorder.

Below is a series of investigative areas which may not be routinely included in conventional clinical evaluations. Their statement in everyday, commonsense terms will yield the richest data since parents' memories will be jogged by questions meaningful to their day-to-day lives. Direct and specific questions, rather than global or open-ended and broad ones, will also be more effective at this point since parents may have made observations of which they are unaware, and which, therefore, they are unlikely to report spontaneously. Alternatively, painful or guilt-ridden events and experiences (e.g., accidents, birth or perinatal trauma, early separations, and the like) may be momentarily repressed or sometimes withheld in the clinician's office.

In addition to standard questions concerning the length and normalcy of pregnancy and delivery, parents should be asked about the existence in their child's past and present of seizures, convulsions, staring spells, high fevers, and periods of unconsciousness. The occurrence of a number of physical conditions with high risk for neuropsychological dysfunction, masked by other more apparent conditions, should be ruled out. One of these is childhood diseases accompanied by high fevers and encephalitis which present as a personality change. Another is abdominal epilepsy appearing as sporadic stomachaches which, upon evaluation, have been found to be "nothing." They have, therefore, been regarded as a psychosomatic symptom. These are distinct from those stomach-

aches which occur Monday through Friday mornings in anticipation of school. Another form of epilepsy presents as a mood
alteration with diurnal variations associated with an array of epilep-
tic phenomena (see Carter and Gold, 1973 for a discussion of other
somatic complaints of possible neuropsychological etiology).

Beyond the normally requested developmental milestones, a
series of questions about motor, language, spatial, and memory
functions should be posed. Depending upon the child's age, it is
important to know about capacities related to eating, for example,
whether he can cut his meat and pour from a bottle. Sometimes the
clumsiness of neuropsychologically impaired children emerges in
this way. Eye–hand dyscoordination will be reported by parents in
terms of inordinate sloppiness or clumsiness, as in knocking over a
glass of milk, not knowing when to stop pouring, missing the glass in
so doing, tearing the meat, and the like. One should also inquire as
to whether there was a significant delay in mastery of riding a
tricycle and a bicycle. Parental attitudes toward the child's maturation (e.g., in not letting the child cut his own meat) and/or aggression (not letting the child use sharp utensils or other instruments at
an age when this would normally be considered permissible) will
emerge in this way as well.

In parallel fashion, the child's ability to handle age-appropriate
skills in dressing should be assessed. Inabilities and aberrations
should be ascertained with direct questions, for example, about
whether there is any history of reversing shoes (right to left and vice
versa) or clothing (inside to outside, front to back). These actions
often foreshadow left–right disorientation in reading, writing, and
letter reversals in later life. In addition to these spatial elements of
dressing, any unusual or deficient motor elements should be
explored, especially fine motor dexterity, such as in zipping, but-
toning, and tying shoelaces.

A related issue is the performance of other daily tasks with
significant spatial elements. For example, do parents report that
regardless of repeated instruction, the child inevitably confuses
positions of fork and knife in setting the table? Does the same child
run or throw to the wrong base on the baseball field? Does he
confuse the direction in which one must move when playing a
board game? Alternatively, are actions taken in the right direction
but out of sequence? Can the child learn new games easily or are
directions readily forgotten?

Exploration of parents' comfort with allowing the child to travel alone in familiar places without fear that he will get lost, may yield data suggestive of their unconscious perception of spatial orientation problems. The way in which they describe their doubts will aid in distinguishing between a reasonable concern and a need to infantilize the child for a panoply of dynamic reasons. Does the child tend to know the way home in the car, does he get lost in a familiar store or on the beach? Possibly related to this is an assessment of parents' comfort with relying upon their child to take on at least minor responsibilities. One should be alert to complaints about the child's "unwillingness" or "irresponsibility" which may mask immediate auditory memory or auditory sequential problems.

A host of questions surround language development and current capacities. Is the child's use of language—both its meaning and the way in which it is articulated—generally understandable to his parents and to strangers? In the realm of language, one should inquire about whether the child knows the name of colors (especially the primary ones), the child's ability to remember what ought to be familiar phone numbers, the misnaming of what ought to be familiar people, the misuse of common words (e.g., "fork" for "spoon," "up" for "down," "before" for "after"), or the use of simpler words where more complex ones would be more appropriate. Another important observation is whether the child can convey in a sensible and sequential manner an experience at school or with a friend.

The child's ability to tell time and to use time as an organizational framework is another important area of investigation. Related to this, does he grasp time sequences as regular, predictable events? Is he generally on time or late? If the latter, is this associated with rebelliousness, obliviousness to time, or confusion about its organization? Inquiry should reflect the significant distinction between the decoding of a clock and the comprehension of time relationships conveyed in language (e.g., "before–after," "yesterday–tomorrow"). A disturbance in one has no necessary bearing upon the other.

In the absence of a spontaneously emerging and detailed picture of the child's and his parents' responses to school, several features should be specifically elicited. The child's attitude toward going to school and undertaking homework is important to discern. Is work begun without prodding, or only with parental structuring or help? Can the child concentrate and, if not, is this a global difficulty or one limited to particular types of work? Do parents have any special observations of the child's approach to task solution, for example, confusion in directionality on the page, a discrepancy between highly complex ideas and elementary efforts at writing, or the forgetting of orally delivered instructions and explanations?

In this context, it is extremely valuable to inquire into each parent's school history with regard to areas of proficiency and difficulty, aspirations and the degree to which they have been reached and, finally, symbolic meanings which education may have acquired. Revelation of unconscious family dynamics centered around learning—as well as inherited deficits in specific areas—may come about in this way. Not infrequently, a previously unrecognized association between the child's and parent's conflicts over and problems in learning will come to awareness as a parent reviews his own history and that of important others, such as siblings and parents.

A central framework to be kept in mind as one listens to parents' organized and random observations about their child and their opinions of him and his problems is the task analytic approach described in chapter 1. As the interviewer sorts through the vast array of data provided by parents, he should begin to formulate hypotheses and to identify contradictions and confirmations implicit in them. Further questions should occur to him to clarify contradictions and to expand his understanding of apparent difficulties.

An example is in order: if parents complain that their son "does not listen" at home or at school, several considerations may more finely delineate the nature of this problem and contribute to the discovery of its roots. Initially, the clinician must gain a more detailed picture of the behaviors characterized as "not listening" by parents. There are innumerable possibilities, several of which are suggestive of a differential diagnosis of neuropsychological versus psychogenic etiology. For example, the child listens to sounds out on the street when his mother gives him an order; this requires a differential diagnosis of avoidance and oppositionalism versus distractibility. When given directions, the child carries them out in the wrong order. Does this reflect oppositionalism or an auditory sequencing disorder? The child carries out only part of the parent's orders. Is this an instance of oppositionalism or an immediate auditory memory disorder? Another possibility is the parent who has repeatedly and unsuccessfully tried to teach his child a skill heavily laden with spatial and memory demands, for example, multiple-column division or chess. He concludes that the child "does not listen." Finer scrutiny of whether "not listening" set in at predictable stages (e.g., when left–right choices had to be made), may shed a new perspective on its causation. In this vein, it is important to determine the extent to which the complaint is general or specific and, if specific, the nature of the circumstances under which it occurs.

This example regarding the child who "does not listen" is one in which the clinician arouses curiosity and uncertainty in parents'[2] minds. They learn that what they considered an explanation is merely a surface description. A relevant phenomenon is the effect of "cognitive dissonance" (Festinger, 1957). Due to the natural inclination to resolve apparently conflicting observations of the child, premature and incorrect conclusions about etiology may be formed. In such cases the interviewer serves an educational function by reopening a matter that has reached premature closure. He communicates that questions of etiology remain to be answered after a careful examination has been made of the range of underlying routes to this surface. Conversely, the clinician may dispel and resolve what from parents' perspectives are contradictions by promoting a more differentiated view of the child's functioning.

In order to convey these latter functions of the interview, we will review an array of clinical presentations which are experienced by parents as puzzling and, therefore, contradictory. Ways of reconciling these only apparently mutually exclusive possibilities will be suggested, employing the task analytic perspective.

Disparities between performance in what are considered equivalent facets of the same ability, for example, memory or motor functions, pose especially thorny obstacles to parents' efforts at understanding. It may be recalled from the Introduction that it was difficult for Matthew's parents and teachers to understand several apparent inconsistencies in his memory. Matthew (case 3) was the boy who boisterously "led others in the wrong direction" yet was sometimes able to calmly involve himself in work. It was

---

[2]Although we generally refer to parents, the same problems and confusion may be experienced by teachers, mental health professionals, or the patient himself.

found confusing that he could not retain a few sight words or
phonic associates when he had a fine memory for day-to-day
events: actions he had taken, promises made to him, and places he
had visited. Another ostensible contradiction is experienced by
parents whose child has a superb memory for details and events of
long ago but who cannot recall the correct words with which to
describe them. These confusions derive from the misconception
that memory is a unitary function without an appreciation of its
manifold variations. Among others, these include the time span
involved (immediate, short term, or long term), the sensory modality utilized (auditory, visual, or kinesthetic), and the presence or
absence of sequential and/or spatial demands. Viewing memory as
a complex set of functions in this way, the child who cannot
remember a word after reading only three lines, but has a phenom-
enal memory for family outings might have an immediate visual
memory disorder in the context of intact, even exceptional long-
term memory. Similarly, motor functions must be differentiated
with regard to gross or fine motor coordination, the part(s) of the
body required for the task at hand, and the presence or absence of
prominent demands for spatial organization and orientation. Thus,
it is possible to unscramble the confusion precipitated in Matthew's
parents (because he was an outstanding athlete and had fine constructional abilities but exceptionally poor handwriting) as follows:
the latter is a language-dominated motor task as contrasted with the
former which are not language related. A high level of functioning
in one has no necessary implications for functioning in the other.

Another common class of apparent contradictions might be
entitled "the child who is bright but does not learn." The classification of learning disorders proposed in chapter 2 was in one sense an
attempt to identify the multiple varieties and etiologies subsumed
by this global surface description. One set of parents may apply this
phrase to their child who is truly bright but does not learn for
psychodynamic reasons, as in the case of Noah (case 1), the boy
with the eye tic and "yucky eyeballs." Another set of parents may
characterize in this way their impressions of a child who appears
intelligent up to a certain point in school, during which he can
master the initial acquisition of reading and spelling at a level
concomitant with his peers. However, mathematics suffers all
along, as do all aspects of learning upon entry into the latter half of
elementary school since he is unable to manage the conceptual

demands implicit in these areas. The same description may be applied to the child who evidences a rapid drop in aspects of academic functioning in the second or third grade after a promising beginning. This might be due to psychogenic factors or, alternatively, the acute emergence of areas of neuropsychological dysfunction not clinically apparent until task demands were increased. The retarded child who has social charm and poise that mask the retardation until school entry may also be viewed in this way. A variation on this theme is the child who is thought to be retarded in school but not at home, where his development seemed to be fine until the onset of school. Evaluation may reveal that such a child is not truly retarded but has massive disabilities in the functions required for attainment of the most basic academic acquisitions.

A third class of learning phenomena puzzling to many parents includes discrepancies in learning among academic subjects. Knowledge of localization of function and the task analytic concept of multiple determinants of adequate functioning in complex skills becomes essential to unscrambling these puzzles. It is particularly crucial to grasping the idea that excellence in one area has no necessary implications for another, if they are unrelated neuropsychologically. The student who excels in science and history but cannot read is one such example. A combination of intense motivation, outstanding intelligence, and excellent memory may enable such a dyslexic child to learn through listening and discussion. Incredulity in relation to the child who reads and speaks beautifully but cannot spell—the latter being viewed as a sign of "laziness"— suggests a lack of awareness of the independence of these functions. In fact, however, outstanding conceptual and expressive abilities may exist in the dysgraphic child. Again in the case of Matthew (case 3), his parent and teachers tended to discount a nagging suspicion that his letter reversals might be one manifestation of a learning disability because he had highly tuned fine and gross motor capacities. They had read in magazines and other popular literature that children with such disabilities had poor coordination. The notion that he could have a disorder in perceptual discrimination (e.g., not perceiving "d" and "b" as meaningfully different) in the presence of excellent motor skills was not grasped. Matthew's parents and teachers were similarly confused by his difficulty in remembering sight words and phonic associates in contrast to the ease with which he retained arithmetic facts and operations. Thus, he could easily attach meaning to the symbols "+" and "−" but was unable to remember that the configuration "boy" had a specific significance. This is another illustration of the importance of bearing in mind that memory is not a unitary function.

Yet another type of confusion expressed by parents and teachers concerns the apparent ability of the child to learn a particular subject in one setting but not in another. An illustration is the child who performs complex arithmetic operations in a one-to-one setting but is unable to do the same in a group situation. Thus, his teacher concludes that he requires individual instruction for motivational problems. In fact what may have happened is that the teacher has unconsciously provided cues to this child who has an undiagnosed right–left disorientation. In the absence of these cues in the group setting, his "ability" will not be carried over. A similar situation may obtain when parents report their child can read at home but not in school, with the implication that the school must be doing something wrong. In reality the child may have a blending disorder with an intact knowledge of phonic associates. He sounds out individual letters and his parents reward this by "helping him along" with the blending process, thus averting the very area of dysfunction.

A final group of "contradictions" surrounds another type of disparity between behaviors in one setting as compared with another. The child who is "lazy" about schoolwork, but highly motivated with regard to activities outside of school, provides a typically perplexing perception of the learning disabled child's avoidant adaptation to sensed areas of incompetence. A similar explanation can be posited for the child who fights and/or daydreams at school but is obedient at home and at camp. The contrast between a child's hyperactivity and distractibility in class, as compared with his far greater capacity for attention and concentration in a one-to-one setting, is frequently cited to discount the possibility of a neuropsychologically based condition. While hyperactivity and distractibility may exist on the basis of anxiety or depression, such automatic dismissal of a neuropsychological basis overlooks the toned down stimulation level and the organizing influence of individual attention. Yet another type of differential behavior pattern is illustrated by Daniel (case 2), the boy who was pleasurably at ease in social contacts with adults but paralyzed and ineffective with peers. While there are multiple possible explanations for such a disparity in object relations, one often overlooked is the added cues adults may unknowingly provide for the child with deficient temporal, spatial, and language concepts. Given this additional organization, the child is capable of more relaxed and pleasurable relatedness. In their typically more egocentric fashion, peers are unlikely to offer comparable structure.

With the Patient

While it may not be common practice to develop a history with the child patient himself, there are at least three important reasons for doing so. Such a clinical approach contributes to the child's active sense of participation in the investigative process and implicitly conveys the belief that his difficulties can be objectively addressed and understood. Second, the patient may have valuable observations to impart about his own style of learning and areas of dysfunction of which his parents and other adults are unaware. This might be a function of his lack of comfort in discussing such observations with them due to their real or imagined responses. Alternatively, the clinician's manner of framing questions or inquiry into global or vague statements made by the child, may spur ideas not previously available to him. Third, the process of history development with the patient may serve as an additional barometer of his accessibility to exploration and treatment of his disorder in learning and the nature of the defenses he has utilized in this regard in the past. Such data will subsequently aid in most effectively framing the explanation of findings and in eliciting his cooperation in treatment efforts.

As in developing a history with parents, it is typically most efficacious initially to permit the child to express his perceptions, theories, and feelings about his problem in learning in a maximally unstructured atmosphere. Subsequently, more specific questions and follow-up inquiry about earlier communications may be effectively introduced.

Since the initial contact with the child typically follows that with his parents, it is useful, as in any evaluation, to determine how he perceived his parents to have explained the purpose of the interview. Was he given any explanation and, if so, was it truthful and/or accurate? Did it suggest an open sense of interest in clarifying the nature of the problem or was there a tone of blame and/or disapproval? It must be kept in mind that while what the child conveys may be realistic, it should not automatically be taken at face value. The child's experience of his parents' attitude toward his learning disorder, and the consultation related to it, may or may not accurately reflect their actual feelings. For example, the child may project his intense humiliation at failure onto his parents and appear consciously unconcerned. Or he may complain that one or both parents are not sufficiently concerned about his learning problem, that they wish him to fail in school. This could represent a projection of intense oedipal rivalrous wishes. Despite the possible existence of unconscious defensive distortion of parental responses, one can gain an impression of the degree to which the child experiences his parents as resources in his effort to cope with the panoply of feelings about his disorder in learning.

If, in explaining what his parents have told him, the child conveys a significantly distorted picture of the nature of the evaluation, it will be important to provide some clarification of its goals. It might be conceptualized as follows: some person or persons have thought that he has a problem in school related to learning and/or behavior. There are multiple possible reasons for such problems. The evaluation is intended to determine, first, if he actually has difficulties in school and, if so, what they are and to which factor or factors they may be attributed.

The above comments trench upon the issue of the defensive modes utilized by the child. To what degree does the child accept or deny the suspicion or conclusion that he has a disorder in learning? If this possibility is accepted, what is the child's attitude toward it? Does he evidence relatively open curiosity and a sense of relief that he may find help? Is much of his energy channeled instead into protecting himself against feelings of intense humiliation? Is this problem the source of deeper and more pervasive self-esteem problems or one manifestation of such underlying issues?

Another value of collaborating with the child in developing a history of his suspected learning disorder is the opportunity it allows to assess his theory or theories of the etiology of this disorder. Is it viewed as internally or externally generated? If the former, is it thought to be a static defect or something amenable to modification? There are, of course, possibilities between these two extremes. For example, the child may have an unconscious fantasy that the learning disorder is a punishment for murderous wishes toward a sibling or for oedipal strivings. Thus the locus of responsibility would be experienced both as inside and outside; something outside originally caused the damage which is now inside.

The task analytic perspective is again important in guiding efforts to elicit the child's own observations of his difficulties in learning or other aspects of functioning which may be associated with learning, although not necessarily in the child's mind. Success in eliciting the child's collaboration in delineating the nature of his learning disorder will naturally vary with his attitude, defensive constellation, and/or degree of talent in verbal expressiveness. Some children may spontaneously and insightfully describe their experience of differential capacities in one school subject as opposed to another, one setting as compared with another, or one function vis-à-vis others (e.g., memory or writing). Even in these cases inquiry deriving from a task analytic approach may lead to further elucidation of the child's self-observations. For example, did the child who regards himself as "bad" in arithmetic in third grade similarly regard himself the previous year? The demands of third grade typically involve a grasp of right–left orientation and other spatial concepts which are not required for more elementary arithmetic calculation. Thus it is possible that the sudden onset of difficulty reflects a dysfunction in right–left discrimination.

A similar approach is useful in exploring vaguer or more global reports from the less articulate or less self-observant child. For example, when a child asserts that he "hates school," it is important to further delineate the nature and origins of this "hatred." Does he dislike all academic subjects and all teachers, or are there distinctions he can be helped to make? Are there particular demands an individual teacher makes on the child which encroach upon undiagnosed areas of dysfunction? The following are a few of the numerous possibilities to be considered. Does the teacher tend to teach or give homework assignments in an oral manner without the aid of written cues? The child with immediate auditory memory problems will no doubt find this an extremely frustrating situation which may subsequently be translated into "hating" the teacher or school in general. Does the teacher give particular types of tests which hinge on other disordered capacities? Several examples are essay tests on which the child is penalized for his spelling disorder, those which involve interpretation or execution of diagrams on which the child fails because of his spatial disorder, those which require processing of sequential information which is difficult or impossible for the child with a sequencing disorder or those which are timed and thus penalize the child with graphomotor problems. Is the "hated" teacher one who assigns the child the responsibility of delivering materials or information to another classroom? Does this become a dreaded experience because the child has right–left or other forms of spatial disorientation and gets lost, or suffers auditory sequential memory problems and forgets or confuses one or more parts of the message to be delivered? Does the teacher in other ways require that the child perform in public—such as doing work on the blackboard or reading aloud—in ways which expose his incapacities?

An analogous set of considerations needs to be brought to bear upon any of the child's complaints, whether these considerations are raised only in the clinician's mind or explicitly discussed with the patient. Many common complaints and the issues and questions pertinent to them were elaborated in the section on developing a history with parents. Therefore, only one additional illustration of the importance of integrating the task analytic perspective with psychodynamic considerations will be given. The child reports he does not like his parents to go out on weekends and adds that he does not object when they go out during the week. It emerges that a different baby-sitter is present on weekends and further that the weekend baby-sitter is likely to engage the child in playing board games. Is it possible that the child suffers from an undiagnosed problem in sequencing or spatial organization, both functions essential to most board games?

With School Personnel

Multiple perspectives are as essential in tracing a child's school history as in developing a history with parents and with the patient himself. The perspectives in this case include attention to teachers' theories regarding a child's learning difficulties, the historical course of these difficulties, and the application of a task analytic approach in understanding them. This frame of reference can be applied in varying degrees to all of the data collected, including standardized test scores, grades, narrative descriptions, and interview reports.

It is crucial that the clinician's theoretical leanings not render him unable to listen openly to the observations of educators. When this does happen valuable data may be lost either because school data may be interpreted in a distorted manner to fit the clinician's theory or dismissed entirely if they are felt to be conflicting. Like clinicians and parents, educators develop explicit or implicit theories about the origin and nature of a particular child's learning difficulties. It is important to delineate what these theories are and to determine whether the child is perceived similarly by a number of school personnel (both at the time of evaluation and throughout his school years) or, alternatively, whether there is considerable disagreement.

There may also be an erratic school history about which there is consensus. Since trends in the history of the child's school functioning may be informative, each type of data, be it a formal test score, a description, or a grade, needs to be followed over time. Chronic school difficulties, sudden marked changes in academic functioning, or onset of difficulties in fourth, fifth, or sixth grade would each lead to the development of different hypotheses regarding the origin and nature of learning problems. For example, chronic school problems might be suggestive of long-standing learning disabilities which have been interfering with the acquisition of basic academic skills. Sudden marked changes would raise the possibility of the onset of neurological disease (e.g., a tumor or other neurological disorder). Emergence of learning problems in the fourth, fifth, or sixth grade might be indicative of mild learning disabilities which were compensated for in the early elementary school years but have become more evident with the increasing complexity of academic demands in the upper grades.

While development of a history with parents takes place in a face-to-face interview, tracing a child's school history often involves a number of data gathering procedures, including a careful interview of the child's teacher(s) and guidance counselor. Frequently, the process begins with a review of standardized test scores, grades, and narrative data sent by the school in written form. Test scores are generally normative and, therefore, give a picture of a particular child's standing relative to children of his age and grade placement. Several types of information may be included. One is the standard score which expresses the individual's distance from the mean in terms of the standard deviation of the distribution. It shows where a person falls in a given distribution and thus permits comparison with himself on other tests as well as with others on the same test. A second type of information derives from the percentile which indicates the individual's relative position in the standardization sample. It is expressed in terms of the percentage of persons in the standardization sample who fall below a given raw score; the 50th percentile corresponds to the median, with percentiles above 50 representing above average performance and those below 50 signifying inferior performance. A third type is the stanine, a single-digit system of scores with a mean of 5 and a standard deviation of approximately 2, with scores running from 1–9. Frequently, two sets of norms are presented, national and local, between which there can be a substantial discrepancy. When a child's local scores are considerably lower than his national scores, it is important to consider the possibility that the child's learning problems are in some measure determined by his particular school community (e.g., the child of normal intelligence who attends a school with a population in the superior intellectual range).

In addition to quantitative information gleaned from standardized test scores, the clinician can derive other kinds of information if he is familiar with the structure, format, content, and nature of the demands placed on a student by various tests. For example, there are significant differences between the demands placed on the student, as well as the cues provided, on individual-, as compared with group-administered tests. Individual tests offer more opportunities to ask clarifying questions, to elaborate upon answers, and to note whether the child is satisfied with a response offered. Structured multiple-choice tests that involve selecting the correct answer from among four choices require different kinds of task solutions than do tests in which one is asked to supply the answer. The former is more reliant upon discriminatory memory and the latter upon recall. Tests with separate computer answer sheets which require that one line up question and answer booklets and fill in a blank space may, for children with difficulties in spatial organization, evaluate their ability to do this, rather than their knowledge of the test's content. An understanding of the demands of a particular test is also important as one compares test scores with daily academic functioning. Such a comparison may lead to the finding that while a child scores adequately on structured tests, he does poorly in the classroom on open-ended assignments requiring internal organizational abilities.

Narrative material in school files needs to be carefully examined in order to distinguish between direct observations and interpretations reflective of the educator's theory about the child. Such words as "unmotivated," "daydreaming," "aggressive," "provocative," "lazy," "bored," and "inappropriate," for example, require further inquiry if they are to be meaningfully understood. Often, this can be done only in face-to-face or phone interviews with teachers. As with parents, it is important to start in an open-ended manner and to work toward further delineating the meaning of any noteworthy features of academic, interpersonal, and group behavior. Especially salient are apparent contradictions within a particular academic area, between academic areas, and/or in response to different teachers or modes of instruction.

Standard inquiries regarding academic functioning (e.g., reading and arithmetic grade levels), should be augmented by the task analytic approach. For example, teachers should be asked whether a particular child's difficulty involves decoding or comprehension? Or is memory a mitigating factor, as in the case of a child who is able to handle higher order concepts when new material is presented in the classroom but cannot answer conceptually based questions about a chapter he read the night before? Are sequential abilities impaired as evidenced in the child who understands what he reads but cannot express his thoughts in a meaningful sequential order? Is there a discrepancy between a child's silent and oral reading?

Similarly, an investigation of writing skills should include consideration of possible differences between the child's writing skills on a spelling test as compared with spontaneous writing tasks. One should note, too, whether there is a discrepancy between the level and complexity of the child's oral and written language. Thus, for example, if a child's oral language is rich and his written narratives are sparse, there is reason to hypothesize that this child may have learned to limit his written expression to coincide with his spelling or other writing capabilities. Attempts should also be made to differentiate among difficulties with spatial organization, fine motor dexterity, and sequencing. Different hypotheses may be generated depending upon whether the child transposes letters and numbers (suggestive of sequencing problems); evidences spatial discontinuities, for example, "thel ight" (suggestive of spatial organization and orientation problems); writes in a very difficult to decipher scrawl (suggestive of motor control or praxic difficulties), or in an unusually small, very compressed manner (suggestive of efforts to compensate for poor control in earlier years). Such differentiations can only be made if the clinician asks specific rather than global questions in tracing the child's school history. A general comment such as "a child's writing skills are poor" yields little useful information.

A related issue is the child's style of learning, coping, and socializing. For example, does the teacher report that assignments requiring organization, planning, and some independent effort are overwhelming for a particular child? This might suggest the possibility of frontal disorder. Does the child seem to require endless repetition of directions? This raises the possibility of an auditory memory problem.

Does the child have difficulty differentiating left from right and keeping complex sequences of material in order, which might reflect temporal–parietal dysfunction? On a more descriptive level, when given the choice, does the child frequently choose to attend to visually presented versus auditorally presented material (e.g., pictures or graphs instead of verbal descriptions)? This would be suggestive of auditory processing problems. Visual spatial functioning should also be investigated as it is a significant component in the successful handling of numerous academic tasks. With this in mind, questions regarding the child's ability to copy off the blackboard, to keep his place on a page while reading, to find his way around the school building, and to follow directions with spatial referents will yield meaningful information.

In addition to these specific features of functioning, it is important to determine the consistency of a child's performance. Does he inevitably do poorly or is there considerable variability in his functioning in a particular area? How assiduously is he struggling to keep up with his classmates? How tired is he?

A host of questions needs to be entertained about other kinds of classroom behaviors which may not be routinely included in the development of a school history. They may be subsumed under two broad investigative areas: attention and activity level. With regard to attention one needs to ask, is the child able to concentrate for the period of time expected of someone of his age? Is he able to focus on a particular task? Does he seem to move in and out of a discussion, as if he were not sustaining his attention for the duration? Is he highly distractible and unable to filter out surrounding noises (e.g., pencil sharpening, paper shuffling, voices in the hall)? Does he appear to stare blankly into space for relatively long periods of time? The area of activity level needs to be carefully evaluated since important mitigating factors may be involved: the age of the child and expectations of teachers, as well as the possibility that a high activity level may be a defensive mode in coping with difficulties in academic functioning. The child may feel that his only choice is to flee, either via activity or fantasy, leading the clinician to an incorrect diagnosis of hyperactivity or attention deficit. Finally, one should explore the possibility that some body movements (e.g., constant doodling), are attempts on the part of the child to control much greater movement. For example, one boy, when asked why he was constantly drawing circles, said, "If I didn't draw them over and over again, I'd be running around in circles." Is the child in question one who moves in his seat even when sitting or one who frequently falls off the chair?

Finally, while the whole area of social–interpersonal functioning is obviously very important in tracing a child's school history, certain aspects are particularly relevant to learning problems. One would wish to ask about the child's level of frustration tolerance, the intensity of his need to control, and the degree of maturity he evidences in interpersonal functioning. Does he cry easily or give up quickly? Does he fly into a rage with no obvious cause? Is he fearful of trying new games or activities? Does he lie or cheat in games? Is he frequently unable to tolerate losing? Is he overly controlling in other ways? Does he exclusively seek the company of younger children? Does he find it difficult to sustain friendships? Is he unable to handle the give and take of interpersonal relationships leading him to prefer solitary activities? While each of these behaviors may be symptomatic of a variety of underlying factors, the possibility that they are manifestations of a disability in learning should be considered until it is adequately ruled out.

Even if specific answers to each of these questions cannot be found at this stage of the evaluation, the posing of such questions may catalyze a systematic and collaborative process of thinking in the clinician and educators. One often finds that sensitization to such differential observations endures beyond the time of the interview as school personnel continue to work with the child.

ADDITIONAL PERSPECTIVES ON THE
CLINICAL INTERVIEW

Clinicians vary greatly in their approach to initial contacts with children and adolescents. Some create an entirely open-ended atmosphere (Goodman and Sours, 1967; Sours, 1978) while others conduct a far more structured interview (Hodges, McKnew, Cytryn, Stern, and Kline, 1982) in some respects equivalent to an adult mental status examination. Of course there are many variations between these two extremes (Chess, 1969; Cohen, 1979c, 1979d). Although general considerations in child consultation will not be taken up here, a few words are necessary to set the stage for the perspectives and procedures to be introduced.

Of the above spectrum of possibilities, the relatively unstructured interview reveals most about the patient's style of perceiving and organizing the world and the expectations, attitudes, and representations he brings to new object relationships. While not behaviorally active, the interviewer who uses such a clinical approach is required to call forth active and incisive observational and organizational capacities which are reflective of a conceptual framework. As Sours (1978) writes of this clinical style:

During consultation hours the therapist thinks about the child in categories referred to in the mental status examination. His approach is not methodological and procedural. It is a way of seeing and thinking about the child and his behavior. He carefully follows the child's motor behavior, play, and affects. Questions are asked only to clarify what the child is doing. They are kept at a minimum. . . . The child is not encouraged to do any specific thing in the session . . . [p. 605].

The entire mental status can be done by observation, a kind of free-floating attention, following the child's affect and only asking questions which resonate with the child's affects. This is the activity involved in the assessment of the child: general appearance, motility, coordination, speech, intelligence, thinking and perception, emotional reaction, manner of relating, fantasies, dreams, and character of play (Goodman and Sours, 1967). The assessment presupposes the knowledge of childhood psychopathology and its common ground with adult psychopathology (Freeman, 1974; Flappan and Neubauer, 1975) [p. 606].

We might add that the assessment should also presuppose a grasp of neuropsychological dysfunction, including a developmental perspective on its ramifications for the development of ego functions and object relations. This is especially mandatory when the clinical picture includes a learning disorder (L. B. Silver, 1976).

This leaning toward less structured interviews may be partially modified when the evaluating clinician knows from the outset that he is merely a consultant and thus whatever the recommendation, ongoing work will be initiated with another professional. In such instances it is not uncommon, and typically not contraindicated, for the consultant to be more active in an effort to learn as much as possible about the patient. In contrast to the above approach, clinicians in this role, or those who routinely structure their initial contacts, may pursue the procedures described below in a more formal manner.

Nevertheless there is often a "hands off" response to the idea of direct assessment of academic areas or functions related to them, even in children and adolescents whose major presenting problems involve behavior or learning disorders in school. Undoubtedly there are multiple reasons for this, two of which have arisen with particular frequency in our experience. Clinicians of all disciplines who have been trained in a psychodynamic tradition have concerns about introducing an evaluative component into their relationship with the patient. Allied to this is a feeling that the three Rs is the stuff of schoolteachers, not psychotherapists. The second reason is derived from an assumption that the learning disordered child will recoil from such activities. In the service of establishing rapport, direct assessment, and sometimes even mention of academic functions, is avoided. Such an outlook may also contribute to the unnecessary postponement of referral for formal psychological testing in some cases.

Contrary to this expectation, it is often seen in the course of testing that the child who suffers from a learning disorder is not only unstressed, but even expectant of and relieved by the opportunity to reveal and discuss the very difficulties which have brought him for consultation. Typically the same response is noted when a potential psychotherapist addresses the patient's problems in learning in either a formal or informal sense. The problem of creating an atmosphere in which the therapist is a judge or teacher is greatly diminished or even bypassed when this is done in the spirit of "let's see what we can understand about the sources of your problem," as would be the approach to any other symptom or complaint. Indeed the child's motivation may be increased if he feels the consultation has the potential to provide solutions for long-sensed problems.

The following is a series of categories of neuropsychological part functions—the building blocks for higher cortical functions such as those required for academic acquisitions—and some possible informal procedures to screen for their intactness. Even if carried out in its totality, this list of tasks can in no way substitute for the rigor, scope, and breadth of the formal testing evaluation to be described.[3] However, it can impart important insights into the child's abilities, his processes of task solution, and his psychological contributions and reactions to confrontation with areas of challenge and dysfunction. For the clinician who wishes to preserve an open-ended field the inclusion of a few narrative and arithmetic books, along with other standard playroom equipment such as paper and crayons, may elicit some of the same data if the child chooses to examine them. Furthermore, the child's spontaneous drawings and approach to games and other materials may all be simultaneously and interdependently considered from the standpoints of what they reveal psychodynamically and neuropsychologically, the latter guided by the categories below.

Approximate age norms for their acquisition are noted in parentheses. Further commentary on interpretation of these tasks will be found in the next section of this chapter, "Formal Testing Evaluation." Parentheses enclosing procedures indicate that they have already been described or will subsequently be described.

---

[3]A more extreme position is taken by Gardner (1979, 1980) who insists upon the *Objective Diagnosis of Minimal Brain Dysfunction,* for which he has developed extensive formal procedures and norms. He would probably argue against the value of the informal assessment of neuropsychological dysfunction proposed here because he would believe it left too much room for impressionistic error. While we heartily concur with the necessity of subsequent formal verification, we feel that important hunches (but by no means conclusions) may be raised with the use of these procedures and/or the concepts they reflect. The reader is referred to Gardner's work for norms more detailed than those reported here.

They have been cross-referenced because they are functions which can be examined from more than one neuropsychological perspective, for example, language and sequencing.

Time Orientation

(By 8 or 9 years)
1. Ask the patient to write numbers on a circle as if it were a clock.

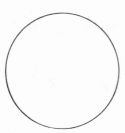

2. Ask the patient to indicate an array of times, for example:
   25 minutes before 3:00
   10 minutes after 7:00
   5:30
   If any errors are committed, ask the patient to explain how he arrived at his answer.

3. Ask the patient to show the "before" and "after" sides of the clock.

4. After placing the numbers and hands on a second clock, ask the
   patient to read an array of times such as the following:
       15 minutes after 4:00
       10 minutes before 11:00
       1:20

If any errors are committed, ask the patient to explain how he
arrived at his answer.

5. Ask the patient to name the days of the week in order.

(By 10 or 11 years)

6. Ask the patient to name the months of the year in order.
   In case of errors, note whether the sequence and/or verbal labels
   are the source of difficulty.

Sequencing

(By 8 or 9 years)

1. Temporal and Numerical

   a. (Names of days of the week in proper sequence)

   b. Ask the patient to name the days of the week beginning with
      Wednesday to see if the sequential concept holds up when
      embedded in a more difficult and less automatic context.

   c. (Names of months of the year in proper sequence)

d. Ask the patient to name the following days:
   Today:
   Yesterday:
   Tomorrow:
   Day before yesterday:
   Day after tomorrow:

e. Choose a hypothetical day and ask the patient to name the following:
   If today is (name of hypothetical day), what is:
   Yesterday:
   Tomorrow:
   Day before yesterday:
   Day after tomorrow:

f. Ask the patient which number (or day) is "before" (b), "after" (a), or "between" (bet) the following:

	(By 6 or 7 years)		
(b)	6	(b)	30
(a)	9	(a)	59
(b)	16	(a)	70
(a)	11	(b)	20
(bet)	4 and 6	(bet)	17 and 19

	(By 8 or 9 years)
(a)	Wed
(b)	Sun
(a)	Fri
(b)	Thurs
(bet)	Sun and Tues

2. Spatial

   a. Ask the patient to name the shapes below first, to rule out an anomia. If none, proceed to ask which shape is "before" (b) or "after" (a) another, as indicated below. If there is difficulty with naming, point and say, "which one is before (or after) this one?" and ask the patient to answer by pointing.

(b) triangle   (b) diamond
(a) square   (a) rectangle
(b) rectangle   (b) square
(a) triangle   (a) circle

b. (Note whether "before" and "after" concepts were understood on the clock.)

Laterality and Dominance

*(Sometimes established by 3 or 4 years,
sometimes never established and not
necessarily pathologic)*

Ask the patient to do—or pretend to do—the following and note
whether right or left is used:

1. Writing

2. Throwing and catching

3. Eating

4. Kicking and hopping

5. Eyedness
   Place a hole in the middle of a sheet of paper and ask the patient
   to wrap it around his face like a mask and look through it.

(Established by 9 years)
6. Awareness of right (R) and left (L) on self and other

After checking whether youngster knows body part labels ask him to point to:

His	L elbow	R elbow
	R knee	L knee
	R shoulder	L shoulder
	L ankle	R ankle
	R shin	
Your	L elbow	R elbow
	R knee	L knee
	R shoulder	L shoulder
	L ankle	R ankle
	R shin	

Ask the patient, "How did you figure it out?"

7. Left to right orientation
   a. Ask the patient to count aloud the dots below. Note whether the direction taken is left to right or right to left.

   . . . .

   b. (Check problems involving borrowing and carrying)

   c. (Check whether dictated numbers are lined up on the right or left and whether they are written left to right)

Motor Functions

Note how well these tasks are executed (apraxias) and the presence or absence of overflow (synkinesia).

Demonstrate and then ask the patient to do the following:

*(Can be performed by 3 years.
No overflow by 8 or 9 years.)*

1. Wiggle thumb, independent of hand or arm, eyes opened. Note chin rotations, wrist arm movement.
   Left
   Right

Wiggle thumb, eyes closed
   Left
   Right

(3 1/2–4 years. 7–8 years without overflow)
2. Sequencing fingers
Demonstrate for the patient opposing the thumb to each
finger in sequence and ask the patient to do the same.
Eyes opened. Do each hand at least 3 times.
   Left
   Right
Eyes closed. Do each hand at least 3 times.
   Left
   Right

3. Rapid alternating movements.
Demonstrate for the patient opening and closing the fist in
alternation, palm down on a tabletop.
   Left
   Right
   Together: Both open and closed at same time
   One open and the other closed at same time

4. Throwing and kicking

5. Eye tracking
Following examiner's fingers with eyes. Note eye jumping,
eyelid drooping, head movements with each of the following
directions:
   Left
   Right
   Circular motion
   In toward nose
   All the way from left to right and back

6. "Touching" the chin with the tongue
"Touching" the nose with the tongue
Demonstrate putting the tongue in the left and right cheeks
alternately and ask the child to imitate.

7. Pushing out the cheeks as if blowing

8. Winking one eye independent of the other
   Left
   Right

9. Whistling

10. Articulation
    Ask the patient to say each of the following:
    Episcopal
    Connecticut
    Massachusetts
    Put-a-kuh—(several times
    rapidly in succession)
    The sick animal went to the hospital
    Spaghetti and meatballs

11. Graphomotor coordination
    Note the quality of the patient's spontaneous drawings.
    Ask the patient to write a paragraph on any topic and note the
    quality of the effort.

Sensory Processing

1. Tactile
   (90% of children by 8 or 9 years)
   a. Graphesthesia
      Trace each of the following numbers on the patient's palm
      out of view.
      Left: 7 3 8 2 1 5 9 4 10 6
      Right: 8 5 7 10 6 2 9 1 3 4

   (90% of children by 7 years)
   b. Finger agnosia[4]
      Out of view in a series such as the one below, touch one or

---

[4] Kinsbourne and Warrington's (1966) technique.

two fingers of patient's hand which is palm down on a table. When you touch one finger, touch both the proximal and distal joints; when you touch two, touch one proximal and one distal joint of two adjacent fingers.

   i. Differentiation between 1 or 2 fingers

      Left: 2 2 1 2 1 1 2 1

      Right: 1 1 2 1 2 2 1 2

  ii. How many fingers are between those being touched? Out of view touch two fingers of the patient's hand which is palm down on a table, varying the number of fingers between the two touched as follows:

      Left: 1 0 2 1 2 0 1 1

      Right: 0 1 0 2 1 0 2 1

(7 or 8 years)

2. Visual

(Mistakes on letter naming, e.g., "p" for "q" or "d" for "b")

(early)

3. Auditory discrimination

Say each set of sounds with the examiner's mouth out of the patient's view and ask whether they are the "same or not the same." If the patient does not grasp this concept, ask him to repeat what is said.

pat-put	may-may	p-z	t-t
red-rod	can-con	g-b	b-p
chin-shin	end-and	d-p	g-g
let-let	sit-sit	b-v	z-c
ten-tin	last-lost	e-c	d-z

Memory

1. Visual

  a. Immediate

    Put three or four objects on a table and cover them, immediately asking the patient what has been concealed.

  b. Short-term

    Put several objects on a table and cover them, telling the patient you will ask him what they are in 15 minutes.

c. Long-term
Put several objects on a table and cover them, telling the patient you will ask him what they are when you see him next week.

2. Auditory

a. Immediate
Say a sentence or number series including five units and ask the patient to repeat it immediately afterwards.

b. Short-term
Say a sentence of five words and tell the patient you will ask him to repeat it in 15 minutes.

c. Long-term
Say a sentence of five words and tell the patient you will ask him to repeat it when you see him next week.

Language

1. Expressive

a. Autotopagnosia
Have child name parts of the body you point to, e.g., ear, shoulder, chin, knee, nose, eye, wrist, knuckle, elbows.

b. Have the child name colors drawn with five or six different crayons.

c. Have the child name objects around the room: paper clip, key, pencil, ashtray, curtain, doorknob, and the like.

2. Receptive

a. Ask the patient questions, e.g.,
"On what do you sleep?"
"What do you wear on your feet?"
"What do you buy in a bakery?"

b. Ask the patient to "Show me the table, chair, floor, ceiling, red object" and the like.

Lexic and Arithmetic Functions

(End of 1st grade)

1. Spelling and Reading

a. Ask the patient to write the alphabet

b. Ask the patient to name the following letters:
   p f s t e j n q a l m x h d v i b c g z k o r u w y

c. Ask the patient to produce the sounds associated with the following letters. Then produce the sounds and ask the patient to point to, write, or say the associated letter.

t	b	r
d	i	u
a	o	k
s	f	z
l	e	n

   (No specific age norms, but by age 6 years and above child should identify some nonsense words)

d. Auditory blending.
   Tell the patient, "I am going to say some sounds and I want you to put them all together and tell me me what you get." Enunciate each sound separately.

a	p	
o	t	
a	z	
c	a	t
r	e	d
s	i	p
t	o	p
g	u	m
t	i	z
k	a	l

```
r   u   p
s   o   f
l   e   k
```

e. Ask the child to write a paragraph about a selected topic. Look for spelling, organizational, capitalization, punctuation, and/or language errors.

(End of 2nd grade)

2. Arithmetic

   a. Dictate a column of numbers and ask the patient to, "Line them up as if you're going to add them." Include an array of numbers of varying digits, e.g., 16, 8, 102, 145, 19, 1031, with special attention to "teen" numbers and their obverse (for example, 14 and 41).

   b. Arithmetic operations
      Ask the child to calculate and then explain how he performed the calculations.

$$
\begin{array}{rrrr}
6 & 47 & 85 & 193 \\
+4 & +25 & -14 & -29 \\
\hline
\end{array}
$$

$$
\begin{array}{rr}
21 & 235 \\
\times 2 & \times 12 \\
\hline
\end{array}
$$

$$2\,\overline{)\,64} \qquad 31\,\overline{)\,428}$$

FORMAL TESTING EVALUATION

The concept of a formal testing evaluation to be presented derives from the same task analytic principles which have already been applied to historical and clinical interview data. The underlying hypothesis of an extensive, unbiased, and integrative evaluation is that something may be awry in the intellectual–cognitive, neuro-psychological, or emotional aspects of a child's functioning, or in their interaction. The goal of the evaluation is, therefore, to arrive at a picture of the whole child, whose particular learning problems may be understood to stem from difficulties in one of these areas or, when the data argue for it, from an interaction of any of these.

The comprehensive assessment thus involves a systematic and critical method of thinking with the ultimate aim of delineating a child's strengths and weaknesses in the intellectual–cognitive, neuropsychological, and emotional spheres of functioning. It is not simply a matter of administering a series of tests and reporting their associated scores, but rather a creative clinical investigative process which is applied to a variety of standardized psychological tests as well as informal measures. A series of hypotheses are formed which are ruled in or out based on the data rather than the evaluator's theoretical orientation. The focus of observation is as much on the manner in which a child processes information and negotiates tasks as it is on the content of his productions (see also Dennis, 1979). Therefore, inquiry is frequently needed to ascertain, "How do you know that, do that or solve that?" Furthermore, there is interest not only in the pattern of strengths and weaknesses but in making clinical sense of the particular kinds of errors which a child commits in each area investigated. Given the fact that most tasks or tests tend to be "confounded," that is, they tap more than one underlying function, it is essential to establish which aspect(s) of the task pose the stumbling block for a particular child. The mode of solution may vary greatly in two individuals who achieve similar scores on aparticular test or subtest.

A related issue is that of compensation, which in this context means the use of an alternate pathway for task solution when a deficit exists in a circumscribed area of cognitive functioning. Thus, for example, the child who relies upon verbalization to solve the Block Design subtest of the Wechsler Intelligence Scale for Children-Revised (WISC-R), rather than the more typical method of visual–spatial processing, may be attempting to compensate for difficulties. Evaluation of compensatory mechanisms encompasses their identification as well as assessment of their effectiveness. For example, does the amount of energy expended at compensation outweigh its usefulness? In those instances in which a deficit exists alongside a strength, diagnostic teaching within the evaluation, or a minilesson, may be employed to assess the usefulness of introducing the child to a particular method of compensation based on his strengths. On the other hand, some children who already use successful compensatory techniques on circumscribed tasks, without realizing that they are doing so, may be encouraged to generalize these techniques to a wider array of tasks. Diagnostic teaching as part of a total evaluation is also valuable in establishing whether certain academic problems reflect simply a gap in instruction or, alternatively, an area unresponsive to conventional modes of instruction. The latter would be due to a deficit in one or several underlying functions, or building blocks, necessary for effective learning in this area.

In keeping with the overall concept of an adequate evaluation, several additional considerations may be useful in arriving at effective interpretations. No single test should be analyzed in isolation from other diagnostic data. Such phenomena as motivation, examinee–examiner rapport, and problems in attending must be carefully weighed in evaluating the reliability of findings. Finally, while specific subtests are purported to measure a particular function, in reality they usually measure several, making it necessary, as noted above, to carefully observe that aspect (or those aspects) which is (are) problematic in the performance of a particular child. For these reasons it is distinctly disadvantageous to subdivide the testing evaluation into multiple separate assessments of narrower scope, for example, those of the clinical psychologist, neuropsychologist, and educator, a practice recommended by many authors (some recent examples being Dennis, 1979; Harway, 1979; and Magnussen, 1979).

Examination of Overall Intelligence

Examination of overall intelligence in school-age children typically involves administration of the Wechsler Intelligence Scale for Children-Revised (Wechsler, 1974), the WISC-R, an individually administered intelligence test for ages 6 years 0 months to 16 years 11 months. It should be noted, however, that manifestations of level and quality of intelligence may be observed throughout the clinical evaluation, including the interview and all other portions of the test battery. Such components of intelligence as language, conceptual abilities, and creativity are in fact sometimes better observed in nonstandardized aspects of the assessment. Although there are other intelligence tests (e.g., the Stanford-Binet), the WISC-R is most frequently used because it best lends itself to a task analytic approach. Furthermore, the WISC-R offers for examination a wide array of skills, both verbal and nonverbal.

This test is divided into two sections, Verbal and Performance, and yields three major IQ scores: Full Scale, Verbal, and Performance. In general the Verbal subtests call upon the child's ability to use language for cognition, while the Performance subtests rely upon manipulation of materials with a focus on visual–spatial processing and visual–motor abilities. Five subtests comprise the Verbal and/or Performance portions, respectively, and an additional optional subtest is included in each.[5] In reality each subtest measures the interaction of several functions in such a way that any failure requires more refined diagnosis of its origins.

To make matters more complex, an important consideration in analyzing WISC-R results is the factor of age.[6] In general, it can be said that at the younger ages the WISC-R measures more varied abilities whereas at 12 years and beyond the overriding factor examined is conceptualization. Items for children below age 12, therefore, tend to require a more personal and concrete level of thinking even though the subtest purports to measure abstract thinking. Thus, for example, the early items of the Similarities subtest really assess categorizing ability, for example, "How are a wheel and a ball the same?" Later items touch upon higher order conceptual ability and facility with language with such questions as, "How are anger and joy the same?" If one looks back to an evaluation conducted when a child, now 12, was 6 years old, it may be found that the earlier IQ score reflects an accumulation of correct but concrete responses, whereas more correct and higher level conceptual responses will be needed to achieve the same IQ at the age of 12.

Another factor lending complexity to interpretation of the WISC-R is that most Performance subtests are timed while most Verbal subtests are not. It is possible for a child to achieve a significantly lower Performance IQ score, not because of visual–spatial processing difficulties, but rather due to a problem in handling tasks with time constraints. Therefore, it is important to allow the child to finish an item, even after the allotted time has expired, in order to determine whether operating within a time frame is the major source of difficulty.

---

[5] The Verbal subtest traditionally thought of as optional, Digit Span, we believe to assess an important component of intellectual functioning, particularly in an evaluation of learning disorders. In that sense we do not consider it optional. Its significance will be discussed below.

[6] It should be noted that the subtest scores are compared to those of peers and, therefore, an older child is expected to correctly answer more items in order to achieve the same score as a younger child.

Each subtest will now be briefly described in terms of what it is purported to measure as well as some additional considerations and nuances relevant to task analytic interpretation. Excellent and detailed explications of the traditional perspective on abilities measured by individual subtests may be found in Glasser and Zimmerman (1967) and Kaufman (1979); however, these contributions do not adequately consider the neuropsychological components of WISC-R subtests. The present discussion is not intended to be exhaustive but instead complementary to such contributions, highlighting some of the less obvious elements which may come into play. Subsequently, various ways of comparing and contrasting subtest findings will be delineated.

Verbal Subtests. The Information subtest is intended to evaluate the child's basic fund of factual information. In addition, however, long-term memory and general experience within the culture are also assessed. Furthermore, certain items on this subtest may reveal possible sequential organization or time orientation difficulties to be corroborated or ruled out by other data in the evaluation. Thus, if a child misses or has difficulty answering, "How many pennies make a nickel?," "How many days make a week?," "Name the month that comes next after March," and "What are the four seasons of the year?," a hypothesized deficit in sequential organization or time orientation needs to be considered.

Traditionally, the Similarities subtest is considered to evaluate the child's ability to form abstract verbal concepts. However, some further distinctions are necessary in describing what it actually measures. The early items of this subtest assess categorizing ability (e.g., "How are a wheel and a ball the same?"), while the later items evaluate higher order conceptual ability (e.g., "In what way are liberty and justice alike?"). Furthermore, on most items, responses which refer to concrete or action properties receive a lower level score of 1 point, while those which reflect concepts receive a higher level score of 2 points. The meaning of a child's total score on this subtest thus needs further refinement. The overall score may not in and of itself adequately capture qualitative features of his abilities in this area; it may represent in one case numerous 1-point answers which would be indicative of concrete thinking, while in another it involves an accumulation of fewer 2-point answers indicative of more abstract abilities. While this subtest taps language facility to some degree, it does not address elaborative linguistic capacities such as one might see on the Vocabulary or Comprehension subtest; rather, it reflects the ability to reduce a concept to a one- or two-word response.

The Arithmetic subtest requires a child to mentally compute arithmetic problems presented orally. It is typically thought to measure the capacity to attend and concentrate, but also involves auditory memory. For the child who asks that questions be repeated and who cannot seem to hold them in memory long enough to negotiate the arithmetic operations, this test in effect becomes a measure of auditory memory. It is important, therefore, to compare the score and the quality of task solution on this subtest with written arithmetic tests in order to tease out what is actually problematic for the child. This is a timed test and it is useful to note whether the child's functioning improves dramatically when one eliminates time as a factor.

In the Vocabulary subtest the child is asked to define words, starting with those that are concrete such as "clock" and "hat" and progressing to more abstract words such as "rivalry" and "amendment." While this test is generally thought to measure knowledge of vocabulary, it also assesses expressive language. In addition, it may yield information regarding efficiency of language usage; the examiner may note whether definitions are succinct and to the point rather than full of hesitations and circumlocutions suggestive of word-finding problems.

The focus of the Comprehension subtest is the child's ability to understand and interpret the demands of social situations. While the beginning items are personal (e.g., "What is the thing to do if a boy [girl] much smaller than yourself starts to fight with you?"), the higher level items tap the child's understanding of the role of societal institutions and procedures and as such are far more conceptual. In addition this subtest assesses higher level receptive and expressive language abilities, along with the capacity to retain complex oral language in memory.

The Digit Span subtest is particularly reliant upon intact attention and short-term memory. The child is asked to repeat, both forward and backward, a series of numbers in correct order. Generally this subtest is purported to measure auditory sequential memory, as it is administered orally. The ability to repeat digits backward, however, may in some instances be reflective of visual sequential memory since this task may be executed by visualizing the auditorally presented numbers and then reading them off in the mind's eye, as it were.

Performance Subtests. In the Picture Completion subtest the child is presented with a series of individual pictures and asked to identify the important missing element. The subtest is conventionally thought to assess attention to visual detail, as well as the grasp of part–whole relationships. It should be noted, however, that this subtest is also highly sensitive to word-finding difficulties. Thus, while credit is given so long as a child points correctly, excessive pointing and circumlocutions (e.g., "the thing the buttons go in" instead of "buttonholes") may be indicative of a dysnomia. This subtest also taps long-term visual memory as it requires the child to recall what a particular item actually looks like in the service of determining what is missing from the picture presented.

The Picture Arrangement subtest is conventionally thought to assess the child's ability to arrange a series of pictures in the correct order so that they tell a sensible story. Included is a variety of abilities such as visual sequencing, planning, appreciation of relationships between events and people, and overall social awareness. For some children it can also become a measure of their ability to use language in order to organize the perceptual world. While it is common practice to ask children who miss a particular item to tell the story they have created, it can be very useful to ask that stories be given for each of the items. In so doing, one can note whether use of the storytelling technique allows the child to self-correct. Often one may also find that the child has arranged the pictures correctly, but has nevertheless missed a subtle nuance in the story which may suggest that his social awareness is limited and that the task was handled largely via visual cues. This is a timed subtest, interpretation of which requires alertness to the above-mentioned features.

The Block Design subtest requires the child to copy designs using blocks with sides of different color. It is typically regarded as a measure of visual–spatial awareness and visual–motor integration in the presence of a model, as well as nonverbal conceptualization in that it requires both analysis and synthesis of spatial part–whole relationships. For some children, however, it becomes in part a verbal task as they use words to break down the visual stimulus. This too is a timed test.

The Object Assembly subtest demands that the child assemble four puzzles: a child, a horse, a car, and a human face. While it, like Block Design, purportedly measures visual–motor integration, there are the additional components of visual memory and revisualization because no model is provided to guide the child. Instead he is required to revisualize the object and to construct it from memory. Occasionally a child may be observed to attempt a solution of the human face item, for example, by touching his own face or carefully observing the examiner's face; this is suggestive of an inability to envision interrelationships of the parts of the face. For some children this subtest can also become a measure of visual sequential memory in that the ability to judge which piece comes next is an important component. Both the Object Assembly and Block Design subtests require construction skills at acceptable rates of speed which make them good measures of constructional apraxia.

The Coding subtest requires the child to draw symbols which correspond to a particular number by writing the symbol below the number. The associated symbol is indicated by a key. This test is traditionally thought of as a measure of the ability to engage in new rote learning, visual–motor coordination, fine-motor efficiency, and short-term visual memory, since the task can be performed more efficiently when the symbols are memorized. In addition, it can measure a child's ability to focus, attend, and follow through independently. It also encompasses a spatial sequential element, as the task is handled with greater efficiency if the child moves fluidly along the sequence.

Mazes is an optional subtest which requires the child to find his way out of a maze using paper and pencil and without going into any blind alleys. While in younger children primarily visual–motor skills and visualization are assessed, this subtest is conventionally considered to measure planning and anticipation.

Analysis of Inter- and Intratest Scatter. An understanding of those functions purportedly assessed by each of the WISC-R subtests, augmented by attention to those additional aspects which present the stumbling block for an individual child, is essential to interpretation of both inter- and intratest scatter. Intertest scatter is the configuration formed by the distribution of scaled subtest scores. Since the same IQ can be the product of very different patterns of intellectual functioning—given the fact that the Full Scale IQ is merely a statistical averaging of scaled scores—what is of interest is the individual's pattern of relative strengths and weaknesses. In general, the practice of using discrepancies of 3 points or more from the child's own mean to determine relative strengths or weaknesses prevents overinterpretation of chance variations. Intratest scatter refers to an uneven pattern of successes and failures within any one subtest of the WISC-R such that a child passes more difficult items and fails easier ones.

The terms "inter-" and "intratest" scatter refer specifically to the WISC-R. However, the principles of analyzing discrepancies in performance are equally applicable, and indeed must be extended to the test findings at large. It is hoped the reader will refer back to these principles as he proceeds with the presentation of other tests later in this section. In keeping with the task analytic perspective, examination of both forms of scatter emphasizes the individual's performance on various functions underlying these tests. Thus subtest scores may be grouped and regrouped according to an array of organizing principles in order to make sense of an individual's pattern.

The first and simplest pattern would be that of greater strength or weakness in either verbal processing or visual–spatial functioning. This would be suggested by a marked discrepancy between the Verbal and Performance IQ scores. If, however, findings are less clear-cut, for example, in the event that several of the verbal subtest scores (e.g., Information, Comprehension, Similarities, and Vocabulary) are low while others (e.g., Arithmetic and Digit Span) are high, one might still hypothesize a linguistic processing problem which has not affected number skills. Similarly, low scores on Picture Completion, Block Design, and Object Assembly in the context of high Picture Arrangement and Coding does not necessarily rule out a visual perceptual deficit. It may simply indicate a relative strength in linguistic compensation as the latter subtests are most likely to profit from such intervention.

Another approach might be to group those subtests tapping memory or acquired knowledge as contrasted with those calling upon reasoning. Low scores on Arithmetic, Coding, Information, and Digit Span—the ACID-Pattern (Rourke, 1981)—therefore, may be reflective of a deficit in either information storage or retrieval. Filskov and Boll (1981) report that, "There are at least two definable subgroups of reading disabled children who exhibit this pattern: one with particularly poor immediate memory for short bursts of nonredundant auditory-verbal information and another with particularly poor visual imaging" (p. 460).

When, however, only Arithmetic, Digit Span, and Coding are relatively low one might entertain the hypothesis that the common underlying impaired function is the ability to attend. When results of other tests, particularly projective test data, are integrated with these findings, it is possible to determine whether the ability to attend is compromised by anxiety or by an attention deficit disorder.

It is also possible, however, to cluster low scores in Arithmetic, Coding, Digit Span, and Picture Arrangement on the basis of an underlying deficit in sequencing. When Object Assembly is the only other low Performance score, and when it appears in conjunction with the above-noted depressed scores, it can be hypothesized that the deficit in sequencing affects the handling of visual–spatial material as well. Such a hypothesis would then have to be borne out by other test data, particularly indications of weakness in telling time and knowing the sequential order of days, months, and numbers. However, it might also be that the underlying issue is a processing deficiency rooted in the interaction of poor memory and a deficit in sequential processing reported by Bannantyne (1971) in dyslexic readers.

It should be noted that placement of a particular subtest in one or another cluster of functions is at times dependent on the way in which the task has been negotiated. This can be ascertained either by examining the incorrect responses or by asking the individual how he arrived at them. Thus, for example, arithmetic may be viewed either as a task tapping reasoning or recall, among many other functions. If errors are due to the fact that the child has not been able to memorize the basic number facts, then a memory deficit may be suspected. If, however, an examination of errors reveals that the child does not know whether to add or subtract in a particular example, then inadequate numerical reasoning may be considered.

Within the Performance area, clustering of relatively low scores on Picture Completion, Picture Arrangement, Block Design, and Object Assembly is typically reflective of visual processing difficulties. Visual–spatial and/or visual–motor constructional functioning may also be considered impaired when the Block Design and Object Assembly subtests are particularly low. A depressed score on Picture Arrangement within the context of adequate functioning on Picture Completion, Block Design, and Object Assembly, however, may be reflective of linguistic processing difficulties as this Performance subtest is most amenable to a linguistic cognitive approach. Alternatively, it may be indicative of interpersonal difficulties as it requires the ability to understand the nuances inherent in interpersonal relationships. A choice of this point of view or hypothesis would have to be corroborated by other data such as responses to the Comprehension subtest.

Another approach entirely might be to understand clustering in terms of the way in which subtests are presented, that is, the nature of the input and output required of the child. Thus, for example, one might consider the length of the presentation of instructions as the important variable. Subtests with relatively long instructions include Arithmetic, Comprehension, Picture Arrangement, and Coding, when compared with the brief instructions for Similarities, Vocabulary, and Digit Span. Thus one might keep in mind that a child with an auditory receptive processing deficiency, which results in difficulty in deriving meaning from spoken language, may experience more problems in handling successively lengthy questions or verbal instructions. Similarly, one might consider as the significant underlying variable the amount and complexity of verbal expression required for successful performance on a particular test. Tests which require little elaboration include Information, Similarities, Arithmetic, and Digit Span, while those requiring more verbal expression include Vocabulary and Comprehension.

Thus, analysis of each child's pattern of processing requires a flexible approach which takes into account not only quantitative scores but also the manner in which they were achieved. The above-mentioned possibilities by no means constitute an exhaustive list but rather an attempt to highlight selected patterns reflective of differential strengths and weaknesses in neuropsychological processing as they impact upon cognitive functioning.

The focus of this discussion has been on the task analytic perspective on neuropsychological functioning which is crucial to the diagnostic process with learning disordered children. Effective evaluation must also encompass the aspects of ego functioning and

psychodynamic issues which may intrude upon intellectual functioning in equal or intertwining fashion. Therefore, one should
always be attuned to the possibility of disorders of thinking, bizarre
ideation, breaks in reality testing, regressive elaboration, or personalized responses evident in an individual's approach to the WISC-R,
in the same manner as one would be alert to these in any clinical
interaction or in the use of projective techniques. In addition, one
may also find evidence of emotional intrusion in a child's approach
to the array of subtests. For example, if one sees a slowing down of
responsiveness on the timed tasks of the protocol, one can consider
that this may be a manifestation of depression, anxiety, or oppositionalism. One can also inspect scatter from the vantage point of the
child's capacity for independent functioning. Certain tasks, by
definition, do not require the child to maintain investment independent of the examiner, for example, the Verbal subtests and
Picture Completion. In contrast most Performance tests demand
greater concentration and sustained autonomous output.

Traditionally, the existence of intratest variability has been
interpreted to indicate the presence of anxiety or the elicitation of
specific conflicts by the content of selected items. For example, the
Picture Completion subtest appears to be sensitive to projection of
psychodynamic issues. A recurrent pattern of considering the pictured object to need an accompanying element to complete it (in
contrast to the instruction to identify the missing portion of the item
already pictured) may suggest a sense of incompleteness reflective
of separation issues. This view is best exemplified by responses
such as food or chairs for the table rather than the correct response
of the missing table leg, a person for the coat rather than buttonholes, and wood for the screw rather than a groove. Failure of
certain Picture Arrangement items may be another example of
emotional intrusions within a cognitive task. For example, problems with authority figures may be reflected in distorted interpretations of the roles or motivations of the characters depicted and thus
in incorrect arrangements.

While such conclusions about intratest scatter may be appropriate in the analysis of selected protocols, other possibilities must
simultaneously be considered. Different items on the same subtest
may require varied types of processing. For instance, on the Information subtest such items as "How many days make a week?,"
"Name the month that comes next after March," "How many things
make a dozen?," and "How many pennies make a nickel?" involve
aspects of general information which demand sequential process-

ing. Failure on these items, if corroborated by other findings of sequential disorder, does not necessarily indicate anxiety. Likewise, on the Object Assembly subtest the girl, face, and automobile puzzles offer greater perceptual cues than does the horse puzzle. Therefore, the inability to complete the latter in children with some visual perceptual weakness does not necessarily imply the interference of phallic concerns.

Examination of Academic Achievement

A comprehensive evaluation of children must include tests of academic achievement to confirm or rule out the existence of neuropsychological contributions to a child's difficulties in learning and/or in school as a whole. Although these tests are omitted with remarkable frequency in practice, in principle they should inevitably be part of the battery used to evaluate any presenting problems, since neuropsychological difficulties may be masked in a panoply of ways. In keeping with the underlying philosophy of assessment, interest is not confined to scores. Rather, it extends to an analysis of the functions or building blocks which they comprise. Thus, in recognition of the possibility that a child may arrive at the correct response for the wrong reason, attention must be paid to the way in which he processes the task rather than simply to the answers he offers.

Achievement tests are either norm referenced or criterion referenced. Norm-referenced tests indicate a child's achievement level in comparison to other children of the same age, while criterion-referenced tests address the specific question of those skills which pose difficulty for a particular individual. However, it is possible to use norm-referenced achievement tests for both purposes. The first is the examination of how much the child has learned relative both to other children his age and to his own assessed level of intelligence.[7] Second, achievement tests may provide clues to those aspects of the academic tasks presented which are responsible for the difficulties a child has in acquiring

---

[7]It is important to keep in mind that the score indicated by an achievement test may be an overestimation. This is due to the fact that the focus of these tests is often on one isolated component of an academic task, for example, decoding individual words or solving written arithmetic operations, while the demands of school tests are frequently more complex. Therefore, the appropriate instructional level should frequently be one grade level below that attained in an achievement test and independent work should be assigned at still a lower level.

the skills of reading, writing, spelling, and calculating. Criterion-referenced tests, as well as more informal educational inventories, may be used to enlarge upon the investigation of specific underlying deficits by providing more material for examination.

In chapter 1 a full description was presented of the building blocks involved in reading, writing, and arithmetic calculation. To briefly review, reading requires the following: perceptual discrimination, particularly visual and auditory, short- and long-term memory, smooth vocal–motor production, sound blending, left to right orientation, transmodal associations, conditional learning, and attentional shifting between modalities. In addition to these functions, arithmetic demands counting with one-to-one correspondence; adequate visual–spatial organizational abilities in conjunction with coordinated hand movements; the knowledge that each number has a visual counterpart called a numeral, and that these numerals placed in different juxtapositions represent different numbers, for example, "13" and "31"; good finger discrimination and recognition; the ability to shift set from left to right to right to left in executing arithmetic operations with more than one digit; the ability to attend to the significance of operation signs; sufficiently intact language to understand such concepts as "bigger-smaller," "greater-less than," and the like. Writing and spelling encompass visual sequential memory, visual–motor memory, the ability to recall a visual gestalt, and to integrate language with its written expression.

This review is presented to point out the array of underlying functions which must be kept in mind when interpreting achievement tests in conjunction with other test data. While many achievement tests are available for measuring children's reading, spelling, and arithmetic abilities, a strong preference is for those which are administered individually because they allow for the observation of task solution. The following is not an exhaustive list of available tests but rather an effort to highlight the ways in which achievement tests can best serve the overall objectives of the comprehensive evaluation.

The Wide Range Achievement Test (WRAT) (Jastak and Jastak, 1978), serves as a good jumping-off point since it covers all three areas of achievement (reading, spelling, and arithmetic) and offers a graduated selection of items at two age levels. Level I is applicable to children aged 5 through 11 and Level II is directed at those from age 12 on. The reading portion of the test includes letter and word recognition and thus focuses on the decoding process involved in reading without addressing the issue of comprehension. Within the context of decoding one can observe a number of qualitative aspects of this process. Thus, for example, one can evaluate the degree of fluency or laboriousness of the individual's efforts at decoding. It is also possible to determine whether the child is largely a sight word reader who has essentially bypassed the decoding process. If he is unable to apply a decoding procedure to words somewhat above his achievement level, one can predict difficulty in the upper grades when sight reading is no longer efficient or effective. More specifically, such phenomena as difficulties in visual discrimination can be seen in "b" and "d" reversals, sequencing problems as in reading "bulk" as "bluk", left to right disorientation in reading "was" as "saw", sound blending problems in correctly sounding out the syllables of a word but being unable to put them together to read the whole word, and tracking problems in skipping lines or words and the like. One can also explore whether the child can use linguistic processing to correct for mispronunciations by noting whether he self-corrects such distortions as "thres-hold" for "threshold" or "partikipate" for "participate."

The spelling portion of the WRAT involves copying marks and writing one's name and single words from dictation, thus focusing on the encoding process. It is important to note, however, that performance on this test may not necessarily coincide with the child's performance in the spontaneously written narrative requested at another point in the test evaluation. Observations similar to those noted above for reading may be made in analyzing data from the spelling subtest. The arduousness of the task must be determined with an emphasis on differentiating motor difficulty in writing from problems in recall or in the use of phonics. For example, a purely phonetic approach may be indicative of difficulties holding a visual gestalt in memory. In contrast, a pattern of correctly spelled words of increasing difficulty that ends abruptly, at which point the child is unable to sound out more difficult words phonetically, may imply an excessive reliance on visual memory. Visual sequencing difficulties may be observed in such misspellings as "lihgt" for "light" or "etner" for "enter." Unstable sound–symbol associations may be seen in misspelled words such as "well" for "will" and "hem" as "him."

The arithmetic portion of the WRAT entails counting, reading number symbols, solving simple oral problems, and performing written computations. It is primarily a test of written computation on which the child must work independently for 10 minutes. Oral problems are presented only at the precomputation level. Observation of the process of solution of these items allows one to note whether there is one-to-one correspondence between the child's verbal counting and attention to the visual material to be counted and whether the child knows that the last number he has counted signifies how many there are in the total group. Sequencing difficulties can be observed in number reading as in confusion between "14" and "41." One can also assess automatic memory for addition, subtraction, and multiplication number facts by noting whether the child needs to count fingers or use other devices in the process of calculation. The need to compensate in some fashion is always an indication that the process is arduous. Inattention to operation signs may be observed in children who continue to add when subtraction is required, while visual–spatial difficulties emerge in the handling of fractions as well as in double-digit multiplication. An inability to handle conversions, such as hours to minutes, years to months, or yards to inches, may reflect sequential as well as linguistic difficulties. Far poorer performance on this test, as compared with the Arithmetic subtest of the WISC-R, might be attributable to the more pronounced effect of a child's anxiety or depression when he has to work independently as the WRAT requires.

A variety of other achievement tests exist, some of which are generalized (i.e., they assess a number of academic areas), while others involve only one (in addition to the tests mentioned here, see Sapir and Wilson, 1978 for others). Most general achievement tests are group-administered and are, therefore, not amenable to the kind of process analysis discussed above. A notable exception is the Peabody Individual Achievement Test (PIAT) (Dunn and Markwardt, 1970), an individually administered test assessing mathematics, word recognition, reading comprehension, spelling, and general information. The test requires no written responses; the child is instead given multiple-choice items which he answers by pointing.

An individually administered general achievement test can be augmented by a variety of specialized achievement tests in reading and arithmetic. Within the reading area it is important to measure comprehension as well as decoding. The Gilmore Oral Reading Test (Gilmore and Gilmore, 1968) is an individually administered test encompassing grades 1 through 8. The child is presented with a paragraph to be read orally after which the paragraph is removed and he is asked five comprehension questions. There are 10 successively difficult paragraphs representing an increment of about one grade level. The Gilmore actually investigates three aspects of reading, namely accuracy, comprehension, and rate of reading. Whenever comprehension difficulties emerge, it is important to ascertain whether they are due to problems in linguistic processing, reasoning, or memory. In order to do that it is useful at first to administer the Gilmore according to the standard test instructions. If comprehension problems are suspected, then several paragraphs of an alternate form should be administered with the proviso that the paragraphs not be removed when the child is answering the question. Success in handling comprehension questions when paragraphs are available for rereading, as contrasted with failure when they are removed, suggests that memory rather than language or reasoning is the decisive factor. In addition, it is possible to analyze the nature of errors to see whether they reflect omissions, insertions, hesitations, mispronunciations, and the like. Children who substitute same meaning words may be using their developed semantic ability to compensate for a deficit in actual decoding. This test also allows discovery of whether contextual cues are beneficial to a particular child. For example, if the Gilmore accuracy score is higher than the WRAT reading score, one may entertain the hypothesis that contextual cues are effectively used by this individual. If, however, the WRAT reading score is higher, it might suggest that this individual does best with very limited stimuli presented one at a time. Other individually administered reading tests include the Durrell Analysis of Reading Difficulty (Durrell, 1955), the Gates-McKillop-Horowitz Reading Diagnostic Test (Gates, McKillop, and Horowitz, 1981), the Gray Oral Reading Test (Gray, 1963), and the Woodcock Reading Mastery Test (Woodcock, 1973). Irrespective of the individual test used, what remains most important is observation of the process of solution.

Individual arithmetic tests such as the Key Math Diagnostic Arithmetic Test (Connolly, Nachtman, and Pritchett, 1976) are helpful in that they expand the number of areas and problems assessed, thus permitting more time and contexts in which to observe the process. This individually administered mathematics test relies primarily on oral responses but does include some paper and pencil items. It spans preschool through grade 6 and includes 14 subtests which supplement findings on the WRAT since they include word problems, measurement, and time.

Examination of Part-Functions

Due to the fact that traditional intelligence and achievement tests involve tasks which are complex, each subsuming a number of underlying neuropsychological functions, it is important to further investigate problems of cognition by assessing each of these functions in as unconfounded a fashion as possible.

One way in which this can be achieved is by conceptualizing those neuropsychological or "part-functions" which are most relevant to cognitive performance in general, and to reading, writing, spelling, and arithmetic in particular. Such a conceptualization contributes to the selection of an inventory of tests which taps these functions as directly as possible. The set of items for screening neuropsychological dysfunction delineated earlier in this chapter in the section entitled "Additional Perspectives on the Clinical Interview" is one example of such an inventory based on informal procedures alone. It is meant to provide information regarding learning problems and other kinds of neuropsychological dysfunction not included in and/or sufficiently isolated by standardized tests. Like all other types of data, the data derived are not complete in and of themselves but must be used in conjunction with the broader formal test battery.

The following discussion is meant to highlight the underlying neuropsychological functions which this screening inventory investigates rather than commenting upon specific items. It is only in the context of an underlying neuropsychological perspective that these procedures have meaning. Approximate developmental expectations for these procedures are indicated next to each one in the inventory presented earlier. Age norms for the standardized tests mentioned are included in their accompanying manuals.

Perception. One part-function which enters into performance on many WISC-R and WRAT, or PIAT subtests is that of perception, by which is meant the integration of sensory impressions into psychologically meaningful data. Perception itself requires further analysis in that it is not a unitary phenomenon, but rather involves a number of functions: awareness, recognition, discrimination, patterning, and orientation. Perception is largely viewed as receptive in its visual, auditory, and tactile aspects.

The Raven Coloured Progressive Matrices (Raven, 1965), a test of visual perceptual functioning uncontaminated by motor requirements, is an important addition to the Performance subtests of the WISC-R in the assessment of visual processing. Although its norms range between 5 1/2 and 11 years of age, the simplest form of the Raven, Sets A, Ab, B, is used irrespective of the age of the individual being evaluated[8] because it is least confounded by additional task demands (e.g., that the individual solve visual analogies, as required by the adult form of the Raven). The simpler form includes three sets of 12 problems arranged in order of graduated difficulty. Generally, functioning on this test correlates well with that on the Block Design subtest of the WISC-R. When the Raven score is considerably higher, one may hypothesize that visual processing per se is adequate. However, such a discrepancy may reflect a breakdown in visual–motor integration suggestive of an expressive disorder such as a constructional apraxia. On this test, too, it is important to ask the individual how he arrived at his answers in order to assess the role of language in the processing procedure.

The ability to discriminate sounds may be assessed informally with a brief informal screening of auditory discrimination or with a more formal test such as the Wepman Auditory Discrimination Test (Wepman, 1973). In either case children are asked to indicate whether word pairs are the same or different. It is advisable to determine that the individual being evaluated understands the concept of "same" and "different" so that one does not mistake confusion of such concepts for auditory discrimination problems. In addition, it is important that the examiner screen his mouth when administering this test so that visual cues are not used, thereby contaminating the findings. If the child has difficulty discriminating word pairs one may temporarily modify the task, asking him to repeat each of the words in the pair in order to see whether his oral

---

[8]In the case of patients over 11 years of age, it is expected that most items will be solved correctly.

imitative abilities are intact. Some children are able to identify same and different word pairs after they have gone through this imitative procedure, suggesting that they need kinesthetic feedback to effectively discriminate auditorally.

Tactile discrimination may be assessed with a test of graphesthesia which involves the ability to detect numbers traced on the palms, both left and right, as well as two tests of finger agnosia (Kinsbourne, 1968). One requires that the individual differentiate whether one or two fingers are being touched and the other that he determine how many fingers there are between the two being touched. All of these tasks are executed with a shield so that the child must make such discriminations purely on the basis of tactile data and/or visual imaging. Tests of finger agnosia also assess the child's ability to differentiate certain sequences, in this instance the relative positions of the fingers on the hand. Immaturities in the development of this ability are often seen in conjunction with spelling and calculation disorders (Gerstmann, 1940). The constant need to monitor finger activity visually may have a negative effect on rate of written and other fine motor output. A further differentiation in interpretation of these tests, ostensibly of tactile discrimination, may be required in some cases. The child who demonstrates facility when asked to identify how many fingers are touched, but has marked difficulty when asked how many fingers are in between two that are touched and which number is being traced on his palm, may suffer from problems in visualization. The first of these tests does not rely on this function in conjunction with tactile discrimination, while solution of the second and third requires a visual spatial image in addition to intact tactile discrimination. This hypothesis would, of course, need to be corroborated by other positive findings, for example, on the Object Assembly Subtest of the WISC-R.

Motor and Graphomotor Coordination. Both gross and fine motor control are reflective of the organization of the central nervous system (CNS) and depend upon somatosensory cues from the muscles and joints in maintaining posture and sustaining movement. A number of standard examinations are available for evaluating motor functions. One of the most widely used is the Oseretsky Test of Motor Proficiency (Bruininks, 1978), an individually administered test which measures both gross and fine motor proficiency; norms exist for ages 4 through 16. Although an association between gross motor deficits and learning disorders has been postulated by some, research has not substantiated this.

For the purpose of evaluating children with learning disorders there is special interest in fine motor output, particularly of the hands, fingers, eyes, and tongue. The relevant factors regarding fine motor functioning are quality of eye–hand coordination as well as rate and efficiency of motor output. One indication of fine motor inefficiency is the existence of associated movements during the execution of a fine motor task. Excessive mouthing, whole body movement, or mirror movement—overflow or synkinesia—during fine motor activities may be suggestive of relative immaturity in this area. Among the hand and finger activities included in the informal neuropsychological screening are thumb wiggling, finger sequencing, and rapid alternating movements. The tester may also wish to use the Purdue Pegboard (Tiffin, 1948), a test of finger dexterity. Eye and tongue movements, puffing out cheeks, winking, and whistling are other examples of fine motor activities. Eye movements, otherwise known as ocular pursuit, are important to assess as possible indicators of difficulty in visual tracking. Articulation difficulties are also assessed since they may shed light on the relative efficiency of the oral apparatus for smooth vocal production.

Graphomotor functioning is such an important component of fine motor output that special attention must be given to its assessment. It can be observed throughout the evaluation whenever the child is engaged in any paper and pencil task. In all instances careful attention should be paid to the child's ability to control the pencil's movement and to the strength and effectiveness of pencil grasp. As noted in an earlier discussion, it is important to assess the degree of laboriousness with which a task is executed. Children who find writing tasks markedly awkward or arduous may inhibit their writing and thus become nonproductive with regard to written expression. Academic productivity, particularly in the upper grades, is highly dependent on speed of writing. It is often helpful to compare the child's written production of one word at a time with that in a spontaneous written sample. Thus, while one-word writing may be quite legible, a written narrative, which requires integration of language with spelling and motor output, may evidence disintegration of motor control. Furthermore, it is useful to compare oral and written expression. Often children with motor difficulties learn to tailor their written expression—its volume and complexity—to their motor rather than their cognitive capacity. In assessing motor production one must differentiate impulsivity from fine motor difficulties by encouraging the impulsive child to slow down so that his optimal fine motor abilities may be observed. In addition to samples of writing throughout the evaluation, graphomotor production may be assessed more formally with such tests of visual–motor integration as the Bender-Gestalt (Bender, 1946) and the Benton Test of Visual Retention (Benton, 1963). Of particular interest is the formation of angles, intersections, and fluidity of curved lines. The Koppitz (1964) system for scoring the Bender-Gestalt lends a useful developmental frame of reference, as well as providing cogent indications of compromised brain functioning.

Time Orientation and Sequential Organization. Throughout early life children gain experience with time and sequence as they are expected to assimilate data whose meaning is conveyed solely through a particular order. Time orientation and sequential organization function as interrelated phenomena in following directions, telling time, counting, and using a calendar. Indeed, much of learning depends in some measure upon the ability to put things in correct order and to comprehend time. Thus a wide array of tasks is necessary to evaluate a child's ability in this area: the organization of the face of the clock; telling time; knowledge of the days of the week and months of the year in their sequential order; comprehension of temporal and sequential vocabulary such as "before" and "after" and "today" and "tomorrow," as well as sequential concepts in relation to numbers. In older children these skills may have been overlearned and, therefore, may represent rote sequences. It is thus important to introduce some novelty by asking, for example, that the individual count backwards by 7s or entertain a hypothetical construct, for example, "If today were Wednesday, what would the day after tomorrow be?"

Dominance and Laterality. Consistent lateral dominance had been thought to reflect the development of one hemisphere of the brain for a particular group of functions. Hand preference is usually established between the ages of 4 and 6 and eye preference even earlier. The significance of dominance, particularly of mixed dominance as in the tendency to be right-handed and left-footed, has been associated by some with a higher incidence of reading disabilities. However, this has remained a controversial subject. What is perhaps of greater significance is the occurrence of left-handedness along with right-footedness in a child from a family of right-handed people. This constellation may reflect some aberration of the left hemisphere which caused the right hemisphere to take over; the result is that writing is carried out with the left hand contralaterally. That aberration may also be associated with other compromised functions. It is, therefore, important to inquire about family history vis-à-vis dominance.

Also significant is left–right discrimination, the ability to distinguish left and right on oneself, as well as to respond to left–right commands and to reverse these relationships in space. The ability to do the latter involves a high level of linguistic competence and has been associated with left–right reversal of letters and juxtaposition of numbers (e.g., "14" for "41"). It is important to note that children may be successful in executing left-right commands when this is tested explicitly but may have difficulty when performing another task, one element of which is the grasp of left–right commands. This would suggest that left–right discrimination is not firmly grasped and still requires a great deal of attention. It is of course always useful to ask the individual how he knows left from right and also whether it was difficult for him to learn the distinction.

Memory. Learning is cumulative and, therefore, reliant upon the ability to store previously acquired skills, experiences, and information. Both retention and retrieval of all of the above are thus essential. Since memory is not a unitary phenomenon, its evaluation must distinguish between immediate, long-, and short-term memory and memory for sequentially organized material as opposed to that for disparate gestalts. With regard to academic functioning, there is particular interest in visual and auditory memory. Long-term memory may be difficult to assess directly during an evaluation since it typically encompasses a relatively short-term time period. One possibility is to engage in some kind of instruction or mini-lesson in one session and to determine whether it has been retained at successive meetings. In addition, the Information and Picture Completion subtests of the WISC-R are generally good indicators of long-term memory.

Recall of Bender-Gestalt forms and designs of the Benton Test of Visual Retention reflect immediate visual recall, the Benton being particularly sensitive to retention of the visual spatial configuration of several designs. Visual sequential memory may be evaluated by means of that subtest of the Illinois Test of Psycholinguistic

Abilities (ITPA) (Kirk, McCarthy, and Kirk, 1968), which involves showing the child a sequence of geometric figures in printed form for five seconds after which he is required to duplicate the sequence with plastic chips in the absence of the model.

Auditory sequential memory may be assessed via the subtest of the ITPA bearing this name and the Digit Span subtest of the WISC-R. The difference between these two tests, both of which involve the repetition of a sequence of numbers, is the rate of presentation. The WISC-R sequences are read one digit per second and those of the ITPA at the rate of two digits per second. Some children are more successful with the WISC-R subtest because it gives them the opportunity to engage in verbal rehearsal. Other tests of auditory memory include Sentence Repetition from the Neurosensory Center Comprehensive Examination for Aphasia (Spreen and Benton, 1969) and selected subtests of the Detroit Test of Learning Aptitude (Baker and Leland, 1967) (e.g., auditory attention span for unrelated words, oral commissions, and auditory attention span for related syllables).

Language. The close relationship between academic functioning and language skill has become of increasing interest to psychologists and learning disabilities specialists in recent years. While the area of language subsumes a wide variety of complex skills, one can categorize these into two broad clusters, namely receptive and expressive. The first includes the interpretation and processing of auditory stimuli and may involve such simple tasks as discriminating sounds or such complex tasks as deriving meaning from individual words, sentences, and paragraphs. The second involves the ability to retrieve words previously stored in memory, the arrangement of these into sentences that conform to syntactical rules, the elaboration of meaningful thoughts, and the execution of the complex motor act of speech. In addition, both receptive and expressive skills must be executed in a rapid and efficient manner so that the demands of both social and academic settings may be adequately met.

Language skills are assessed throughout the clinical evaluation with observation of differences between spontaneous speech and speech in response to structured questions as well as between oral and written language. Throughout the assessment of intellectual functioning (e.g., the WISC-R) language facility is noted, as is the broader area of auditory processing. Stories produced in the course of projective testing (see below) provide excellent examples of language functioning and offer the opportunity to observe expressive elaborative abilities as well as syntax and conformity to grammatical rules. Furthermore, such stories offer the possibility of examining the child's ability to be focused, to speak coherently and cogently, and to generally communicate thoughts effectively.

In addition to more global clinical impressions, specific aspects of linguistic functioning need to be addressed as part of a comprehensive evaluation. First, one must rule out the possibility of hearing impairment in any child who presents with possible language disability. Attention in developing the history with parents should be paid to such problems as chronic otitis media in early stages of development as this may be related to later language difficulties. Second, one must evaluate the possibility of auditory inattention which may be reflected either in difficulties in blocking out background sounds or in a discrepancy between the child's response to auditory versus visual instructions. It is important to note, however, that this need not be a causal relationship; problems in auditory focusing may either reflect an existing language disorder or be the cause of it. Another aspect of language functioning which must be evaluated is that of auditory discrimination, the assessment of which has already been discussed.

Beyond the execution of individual words and sounds, the fluency with which speech is produced is an important component of language functioning. Fluency may be assessed qualitatively by attending to the child's narrative speech or more formally by giving a word fluency test, such as the one included in the Neurosensory Center Comprehensive Examination for Aphasia (Spreen and Benton, 1969), a comprehensive group of tests including a wide variety of receptive and expressive language tasks. Of particular interest are the Token Test which requires the ability to follow oral instructions, the Sentence Repetition Test which measures the ability to hold in memory and repeat sentences of increasing syntactic complexity, and the Sentence Construction Test which involves the ability to construct sentences from words presented by the examiner. Sentences must be grammatically correct and linguistically meaningful to receive full credit. Points are added for speed; speed and efficiency of verbal processing and expression are often critical factors in handling both school and life tasks. The child who experiences a lag in processing may miss a great deal of information. This becomes a serious problem as the child approaches late elementary grades in which classroom presentations involve greater speed of oral delivery and increasing complexity and quantity of verbal material.

It is important to note that children with developmental language disabilities may develop secondary problems such as inattention, emotional difficulty, and social inadequacy because the ability to comprehend and to communicate is essential in developing control of impulses, modulating feelings, developing awareness of self and others, and extracting meaning in all interpersonal and social encounters.

Lexic and Arithmetic Functions. Many building blocks underlying academic skills have already been referred to in earlier portions of this chapter. Several remain which are so basic as frequently to be forgotten. Nevertheless they are crucial to the assessment process and can be examined informally in the following manner.

The child is asked to write the letters of the alphabet across an unlined sheet of paper. The object of this task is to evaluate his knowledge of the letters and his ability to reproduce them in sequence. Pencil control as well as more generalized graphomotor abilities can also be observed as one notes the child's ability to control letter size, formation, placement, and spacing. Letter reversal and compensation for uncertainty about the direction in which letters are oriented, such as the substitution of capital "B" or "D" when all other letters are written in lower case, can also be noted. Observation of the child's process of execution is as important on this task as it is throughout the evaluation. The arduousness of graphomotor efforts, hesitations, or pauses and subvocalizations are significant aspects to be considered. If one suspects that graphomotor difficulty compromises performance, the child should be asked to recite the alphabet so that differences between verbal and written functioning may be noted.

To assess the child's mastering of all letter names and his ability to distinguish between visually similar letters, he is presented with a series of lower case letters out of alphabetical order and is asked to name them. Confusion with directionality of letters may be noted. Should difficulty in forming visual–auditory associations be observed, the possibility of a kind of anomia must be considered.

The child's grasp of symbol–sound associations is measured by asking him to produce the sounds of all letters. It is particularly important to note whether he gives the sounds with schwa endings (for example, saying the sound for "p" is "puh") as this tendency can interfere with the process of blending them together. In addition, it is important to note whether the child knows both the long and short vowel sounds.

It is also important to assess the child's ability to put disparate sounds together smoothly independent of their visual configuration. The ability to blend sounds may be evaluated informally with the instructions, "I'm going to say some words that are apart and I want you to put the sounds together." When testing young children it is helpful initially to present compound words such as "rain-coat," followed by multisyllabic words such as "ham-bur-ger" and, finally, one-syllable words such as "c-a-t." Since blending of simple words like "r-e-d" may be an example of overlearned behavior with familiar words, nonsense syllables are included to be certain that the ability to blend has in fact been well established. A more formal assessment of sound blending may be accomplished with the Sound Blending subtest of the ITPA (Kirk et al., 1968).

To assess the child's ability to organize and express thoughts in written form, he is asked to write a paragraph about a selected topic or one story of the Thematic Apperception Test (TAT) series. This is particularly helpful as a means of comparing oral and written language. In assessing the writing sample, attention should be paid to spelling, punctuation, and organizational errors. Mild graphomotor difficulties which do not emerge in simpler one-word writing tasks may be evidenced in this more complex context. Various components of a dysgraphia such as omission of letters or words, incomprehensible letter and word formations, sentences and phrases lacking in meaning to others may be observed.

Several additional tasks are needed to assess arithmetic skills presented in written form. Written examples involving simple addition, subtraction, multiplication, and division are visually presented to the child. In the absence of a more formal assessment, this enables the examiner to note whether basic number facts and operations are known. In addition, the child may be asked to line up a set of dictated numbers for the purpose of adding them up to evaluate whether he understands place value and the concept of aligning them on the right side.

Application of developmental norms to the assessment of all the building blocks described above is essential since the meaning of a child's difficulty in handling any of these tasks changes relative to age. Approximate developmental expectations are noted on pages 119–129.

Examination of Personality

Assessment of personality functioning is an essential component of comprehensive evaluation of the learning disordered child, even when there is no previous evidence of psychopathology. While it is carried out through analysis of every aspect of the clinical and testing evaluation, central data for this assessment derive from "projective tests." Because these tests are unstructured they allow for a wide variety of individual responses that are interpreted according to the projective hypothesis: individuals tend to project their own experiences and unique world views onto amorphous and unstructured stimuli. From study of these responses a picture emerges of each person's spontaneous concerns along with his characteristic pattern of personality organization.

Much has been written about personality assessment of children in general as well as about the use of projective techniques in particular (Halpern, 1953; Bellak and Adelman, 1960; Hammer, 1960; Hertz, 1960; Kagan, 1960; Machover, 1960; Koppitz, 1968; Levitt and Truuma, 1972; Mundy, 1972; Ames, Metraux, Rodell, and Walker, 1974; Magnussen, 1979). The present discussion will emphasize utilization of these techniques within the context of an integrative clinical evaluation focusing upon the possible interaction of a number of contributing variables in children with learning disorders. Within this context personality assessment is important both for evaluating emotional functioning per se and determining the impact of a cognitive or neuropsychological deficit on emotional functioning, or vice versa. Because such differential diagnoses are complex, they may not accurately derive from projective tests alone. Differentiation of neuropsychologically based disorders from those of psychogenic origin or of combined psychogenic–neuropsychological etiology requires the utilization of projective data, in conjunction with tests of intellectual and neuropsychological functioning.

Many different tests may be considered projective in nature. Psychological batteries, however, tend traditionally to include the

TAT (Murray, 1943), Rorschach ink blot test (Rorschach, 1948), or the Children's Apperception Test (CAT) (Bellak and Adelman, 1960) depending upon the child's age, and figure drawings. These tests will be discussed with the assumption that the reader is either already familiar with the way in which they are conventionally used or will refer to other sources such as those cited above for this purpose. The Rorschach, TAT and CAT are based on visual–perceptual stimuli which require the child initially to organize his perceptions and then to provide a verbal response. Drawings, particularly figure drawings, require the individual to represent his internalized body schema in graphomotor form. Unlike the Rorschach, the TAT, and the CAT, these productions are not elicited by external stimuli but are rather projections of inner images and perceptions. It is well known that perception is largely idiosyncratic, that each person has his own reactions to a stimulus, to a lesser or greater degree. These highly individual associations, along with some conventional responses, lend themselves to development of a picture of each person's personality organization. When, however, there is a deficit in perceptual, spatial organizational, psychomotor, sequential, and/or oral expressive function(s), the interpretation of responses must take this into account and its implications for individual personality organization must be carefully considered.

There has been a paucity of work regarding the response tendencies of neuropsychologically impaired adults irrespective of the projective technique employed (Burgemeister, 1962; Lezak, 1976). In addition, in recent years research has not substantiated the emergence of an "organic" personality pattern (Filskov and Boll, 1981). Even less has been said regarding the use of these techniques with neuropsychologically impaired children and less yet with children who have learning disorders of unspecified etiology. However, Lezak's (1976) excellent review of response tendencies of adults with neuropsychological dysfunction may, by extrapolation, be useful in analyzing the protocols of children. She includes "constriction," a reduction in response size; "stimulus-boundedness," a response lacking in the flexibility to shift both from one response to another or from one part of the stimulus to another; "structure-seeking," a clinging to structure provided by the stimulus or the examiner; "response rigidity," an inability to adapt to changes in instructions or stimuli, one example of which is perseveration; "fragmentation," responses which are unintegrated;

"simplification," a lack of elaboration; "conceptual confusion and spatial disorganization," responses lacking in logic and reflective of spatial disorganization; "confabulation," a tendency to link unrelated percepts on the basis of spatial contiguity; and "hesitancy and doubt," a continued dissatisfaction with and uncertainty regarding percepts.

While a number of these also appear in the protocols of functionally impaired individuals, when several appear on one test or in one protocol, and are also supported by neuropsychological findings on other tests, the possibility of some neuropsychological involvement must be seriously considered. It should be noted, however, that in the assessment of children with learning disorders in whom neuropsychological involvement is often implied or inferentially derived, these response tendencies are far more subtle than in frankly impaired adults or in children with focal neurological findings. Thus, for example, one may see some evidence of perseveration, constriction, or rigidity on tasks tapping the modality of weakness (e.g., in drawings of children with graphomotor difficulties), while spontaneity may emerge on storytelling tasks on which cognitive compensation is possible. Conversely, the child with an oral–expressive problem may tell constricted stories but draw scenes full of detail and spontaneity. As a result the response tendencies noted by Lezak (1976) are best applied to learning disordered children in the spirit of guideposts rather than signs concretely translatable into their childhood counterparts.

As in other portions of the neuropsychodiagnostic assessment, it is critical to consider the demands posed by the Rorschach, TAT, or figure drawings and to note individual variations in the ability to carry these out due to constitutional or acquired deficit. In addition, a thoughtful evaluation of personality organization with a special emphasis upon coping styles, controls, and defenses adds immeasurably to the assessment of a learning disordered child. An understanding of these may shed light on the behavioral characteristics which are in some children a salient component of the condition.

Selected features of the use of each of the conventional projective techniques within the context of the integrative evaluation will now be discussed.

Rorschach. The Rorschach test developed by Hermann Rorschach in the 1920s consists of a series of 10 inkblots to which the
individual is asked to respond by telling what each one looks like or
reminds one of. A number of scoring systems (Klopfer, Ainsworth,
Klopfer, and Holt, 1954; Beck, Beck, Levitt, and Molish, 1961;
Klopfer and Davidson, 1962; Rapaport, Gill, and Schafer, 1968;
Exner and Weiner, 1982) have been developed in order to categorize and quantify responses both in terms of content and style.
Despite their many differences, each method includes scoring for
the following variables: the part of the inkblot involved in the
response, for example, the whole, a small, or large commonly
included portion or one which is unusual or obscure; form level,
that is, how well the response conforms to perceptual reality; the
determinants of the response, including movement, color, shading,
and/or form; the nature of the content; the number of responses;
the speed of response; and the degree to which the percepts offered
are conventional.

Interpretation of Rorschach responses considers the individual's presentation on these variables relative to expectations for age
and gender, as well as in terms of what it may reveal about the
personality organization of each individual. This test adds to a
comprehensive assessment such information as degree of reality
testing in the form of perceptual accuracy, the effectiveness of
defenses, the nature of the child's perception of others and his
self-perception, the degree of his depression, and the level of his
impulse control and ability to delay, all of which must be viewed
within the context of neuropsychological dysfunction should it be
suggested by other data.

Thus, for example, individuals who have an impaired ability to
organize visual material may have more difficulty responding to
particular cards—most often Cards VI and IX—because they are
least clearly delineated perceptually. Conversely, color cards offering clearer distinctions among different areas of the blot are often
easier for the neuropsychologically impaired child to organize.
Figure–ground reversals may appear such that responses which
might otherwise be interpreted as evidence of poor reality testing,
bizarre ideation, or oppositionalism are present on a neuropsychological basis.

In addition, children with dysfunction in integrating disparate visual percepts into a meaningful whole may either tend to give details without being able to formulate one commonly unified percept or so desperately try to force an integration of unrelated percepts that they produce confabulations. In the presence of such perceptual and spatial organizational problems, the use of solely psychodynamic hypotheses, such as of castration anxiety, to account for poor responses may be inaccurate or at least incomplete.

Manifestations of defense on the Rorschach may also need to be understood in light of cognitive dysfunction. Thus, attention to minute detail, one feature of the development of an obsessive picture, may be the child's way of "hanging on" while feeling overwhelmed by stimuli which he cannot organize. Another example of "hanging on" in an attempt to maintain a sense of order or to compensate for impaired memory is a tendency to seek an excessive amount of direction from the examiner. With the presentation of each new card such children may repeatedly say, "What am I supposed to do?" as if making little or no use of earlier directions or previous experience. Conversely, stemming from the same sense of vulnerability and disorganization, some children become overly controlling, demanding to hold all the cards, to dictate the order of presentation, to reject some cards and to make notations on the examiner's location chart.

Finally, there are children who hide their disability not only from others but also from themselves, resulting in an excessive use of denial beyond the age when it is commonly expected. While denial typically diminishes in school-age children, it may remain a significant aspect of personality organization in the learning disordered child who in this way defends against overwhelming feelings of failure in handling daily school tasks. In those children who do not deny their disability, the need to hide from others any manifestation of dysfunction may result in a massive cover-up scheme which can include hypersensitivity or hypervigilance to nuances and cues in the environment, which may be used by the child with a learning disorder to negotiate school tasks successfully. This may manifest itself on the Rorschach in inordinate sensitivity to the examiner's approval. For example, should he feel himself to have succeeded with a particular response, such a child may offer it many times, irrespective of the features of the particular stimulus, in an effort to repeat a successful experience. Therefore, manifestations of rationalization, oppositionalism, pretentiousness, and excessive intellectualization, needs for control and compliance—in fact the entire defensive structure—must be evaluated not only developmentally but also in relation to areas of deficit.

Feelings of self-doubt, which develop as a result of actual repeated experiences of failure in negotiating age-appropriate life tasks, abound in the protocols of these children. On the Rorschach these may emerge both in a general tone of indecisiveness or in percepts which are continually modified but nevertheless fail to yield a sense of satisfaction. Responses to inquiry on the Rorschach may be particularly susceptible to indecision in the event of a memory disorder; the child may be unable to recall the location or content of previously offered percepts.

Thematic Apperception Test.[9]   This test developed by Murray (1943) is one of the most widely used storytelling techniques. It consists of a series of pictures of people often engaged with each other in a manner sufficiently ambiguous to allow for a variety of themes. The individual is instructed to tell a story about the picture which includes what is happening, what happened before, and how it is resolved. The goal is to present the individual with a wide variety of situations in order to elicit from him themes that preoccupy both his conscious and unconscious life. Inquiry is used here, as on the Rorschach, to clarify percepts, motivational features, or sequences of thought. This technique is particularly useful in evaluating the flow of verbal productions, the ability to organize ideas, and the existence of idiosyncratic attitudes or preoccupations.

With respect to neuropsychodiagnosis, such issues as fluency, sequential organization of thoughts, fragmentation of stories, and conceptual and perceptual misinterpretation must be specifically addressed. In addition, the series of stories elicited provides an excellent sample of the child's oral language. Integrity of semantics and syntax may be assessed and compared with the child's written language productions. Problems with word retrieval and richness of language are also easily observed. Response categories noted in discussion of the Rorschach are relevant to the TAT as well. Con-

---

[9]The CAT will not be taken up separately. In general, comments about the TAT are also applicable to the CAT.

striction, color naming, perseveration, rigidity, and a lack of popular themes may be characteristic of these children's protocols.

Figure Drawings.   When a child evidences cognitive, motor, or perceptual deficits, clinical interpretation of figure drawings becomes complex. Variables such as size, angulation, and line quality cannot be subject to projective interpretation alone but must additionally be understood in light of the particular disability. Figure drawings require graphomotor representation of an internalized body image. Distortions such as problems in visualizing body parts, their placement in relation to each other, fragmentation, and graphomotor incoordination are abundant in protocols of children with some form of neuropsychological deficit. Excessive elaboration of the head, either in the form of embellishment of features or in exaggerated or diminished size, frequently reflects conscious or unconscious preoccupation with impairment of brain functioning. The child who gropes to determine whether his nose lies above or below his mouth when asked to draw a human figure may evidence castration anxiety or, alternatively, a disorder in the capacity to visualize. Similarly, openings in body boundaries may express a bizarre sense of fragmentation, an overall sense of damage, and/or more specifically indicate a parietal lobe disorder.

What is essential is that such findings on figure drawings be evaluated in conjunction with data from other tests. When the data substantiate the diagnosis of some form of neuropsychological dysfunction, even if minimal, feelings of body damage and vulnerability need also to be understood as reactions to such dysfunction rather than solely as aspects of neurotic or psychotic development. At the same time, the particular fantasies the child has elaborated to explain his experience of dysfunction are psychological creations, a grasp of which may be critical to future intervention.

In the interest of differentiating pathological self-representations deriving from neurotic or more severe psychological disorders from those of neuropsychological origin, it may be helpful to offer a child with graphomotor problems conditions which optimally permit compensation for this difficulty. One example is the use of a marker, thick crayon, or pencil grip for producing drawings, thus facilitating assessment of body image representation apart from graphomotor functioning.

As is evident, the role of the assessment of personality functioning within the overall comprehensive evaluation is a complementary one in two ways. First, it augments the cognitive picture of the child by revealing additional aspects of ego functioning. Second, particular kinds of responses on projective tests may be used to corroborate findings of neuropsychological involvement noted in other parts of the evaluation.

INDICATIONS FOR NEUROLOGICAL EVALUATION

There is no consensus about the question of whether all children with learning disabilities and other soft signs need be referred to a pediatric neurologist. We believe that neurological evaluation is unnecessary in all cases and should derive instead from specific types of clinical and test findings (Kinsbourne, 1979). The clinical assessment delineated above will suffice for the large group of developmental disorders involving learning and other related functions.

However, at least two types of clinical findings are significant indicators requiring neurological evaluation. The first is hyperactivity and/or distractibility which appear to be on a neuropsychological rather than psychogenic basis. Such children may profit from the use of amphetamines, a possibility which must be assessed and monitored neurologically. An exception would be the case in which there is already ongoing psychotherapeutic intervention where the therapist happens to be a psychiatrist; in this context the psychiatrist may provide psychopharmacological supervision. Hyperactivity or distractibility may be the target symptom treated, problems in learning being secondary. Alternatively, relief of this symptom may be necessary to effective remedial and/or psychotherapeutic intervention. Second, any clinical evidence of seizure phenomena (e.g., absences due to petit mal) requires neurological evaluation and possibly medication.

A second group of indications for neurological evaluation derives from the nature of test findings. While an exhaustive discussion of these findings is beyond the scope of this book, several findings which are most common and/or salient will be delineated. Two suggestions of the possibility of an acute change in the child's ongoing cognitive functioning serve as indications for neurological referral. One is the finding of significant deterioration from performance on a previous evaluation. Another is behavioral, with implications for acute neuropsychological distress, such as a catastrophic reaction to a particular test with the possibility of a recent loss of function. In such cases the existence of tumors and degenerative diseases needs to be ruled out. Test findings or clinical observation of gross motor abnormalities, for example, peculiar gait or other deviant modes of executing motor and motor-related goals, should be followed up neurologically as they may be harbingers of a degenerative disease, especially when seen in the older latency age child or adolescent.

Psychotic-looking figure drawings (i.e., those which are fragmented or in other ways bizarre), in the absence of other manifestations of psychosis and in the presence of other parietal lobe findings, constitute another finding which requires neurological evaluation. Other related findings might be peculiar Block Design or Object Assembly solutions. Also warranting neurological evaluation is the child who has, not specific testing findings but a remarkable number of positive neuropsychological signs or, alternatively, a single finding or a few findings which are remarkably depressed when compared with the overall cognitive picture. The child who presents with findings which are unilaterally clustered requires such evaluation to rule out the possibility of a unilateral lesion. Yet another clinical situation leading to neurological referral is that of the child who reports auditory or visual hallucinations of a benign nature in the absence of other clinical or test findings suggestive of severe psychopathology. Especially when there are temporal lobe findings on testing, but even in their absence, neurological evaluation is mandatory.

A third and quite different indication for referral to a neurologist is unabating parental anxiety about the possibility of neurological dysfunction, despite the clinician's careful efforts to clarify that the child's learning disability is a psychogenic disorder. Only with further evaluation by a neurologist is there a reasonable hope of sufficiently diminishing the parents' concerns to enable them to proceed with recommendations for educational or psychotherapeutic intervention. Alternatively, in cases in which parents have a strong investment in believing their child to have some form of neuropsychological dysfunction, but none has been found in the evaluation, neurological examination may be essential to their ultimate acceptance of the conclusion that no intervention is necessary.

COMMUNICATION OF FINDINGS

Since effective communication of findings derived in evaluating a child with problems in learning is not categorically different from the art of conveying conclusions in any other clinical consultation, an attempt will not be made here to cover this vast and complex subject in its entirety. Instead, features especially salient in work with learning disordered patients and their families will be highlighted. As will become apparent to the reader, comments will be slanted toward difficulties encountered at this stage of consultation. This is not to imply that such difficulties are universal, but only to call attention to some of their manifestations and possible solutions. There are many parents who do not pose such problems, but rather with relief and appreciation profit from the professional's findings (as in cases 2 and 3, Daniel and Matthew, described in chapter 5). Such parents embark upon treatment courses without delay or conflict or, alternatively, accept the diagnostic conclusion that no treatment is indicated.

For heuristic purposes the communication of findings to parents, the patient, and school staff will be taken up separately, although there is much overlap between the principles which should be kept in mind in each of these clinical situations.

Communicating Findings to Parents

Regardless of parents' educational level and professional expertise, the sometimes complex and interweaving relationships between neuropsychological functions and their contribution to the development of the ego and object relations are likely to be difficult for them to grasp. This inherent difficulty is only magnified when such relationships pertain to one's own child, with all the hopes and aspirations he embodies. Therefore, two aspects of conveying findings to parents will receive special attention: the management of parental distortions and misconceptions in receiving the professional's communications and the educational functions of feedback.

A paramount consideration in conveying clinical impressions at the completion of a consultation is the possible types and sources of distortion with which parents may receive them. Although some degree of distortion is probably inevitable, a series of technical suggestions will be made in an effort to minimize this process. In the context of discussion with parents it is essential to keep in mind their individual and joint hypotheses about the nature of their child's difficulties, as ascertained in earlier contacts. Some frequent variations have been delineated in the section above on developing a history. Whether the findings corroborate or contradict these expectations or, alternatively, offer possibilities not previously fantasized, will likely affect in major ways a parent's ability to "metabolize" the conclusions that are presented.

In this vein, it is essential to bear in mind that each parent may have very different pet theories to explain the child's disorder in learning. For this reason, the common practice of conveying findings to the child's mother with the assumption that she will effectively pass them on to father is highly vulnerable to failure, if the ultimate purpose is accurate communication. This is not to imply that distortions are intentional, but rather to recognize the clinical inevitability that a person with intense wishes and fantasies is prone to some degree of misperception of complicated information. In addition, given the complexity of the data to be conveyed, each parent is best served by an opportunity to raise his or her questions and sources of confusion. While it is conceivable that the other parent may sufficiently replace the professional in this function, it is in reality unlikely that even highly sophisticated professional parents will accomplish this successfully. Another potential pitfall of conveying findings to only one parent is that, not infrequently, the one more opposed to the recommendations that the professional is expected to make may be prone to be absent. Yet at the stage of implementing the referral, that parent may pose an active interference.

Prior to proceeding with some of the specific difficulties that may be encountered in undertaking to clearly convey the complex relationships between neuropsychological and psychodynamic considerations, several technical recommendations will be made. Permitting parents a vivid visual and sensorimotor experience of the materials used for testing and the way in which the testing data emerge, followed by the process of hypothesis formation and confirmation or disconfirmation, can effectively prevent several typical problems. This approach can convey to either the skeptical or overly deferential parent that conclusions are neither precipitous and unfounded nor magical. It is more difficult to discount findings which appear to result from a solid, careful, and systematic approach. Where test data resonate with parents' observations of the child's behavior at home or at school, the highest degree of conviction is achieved. Thus wherever possible, linkage with such observations as they were reported in earlier contacts is effective. Not infrequently, more open-minded parents will associate to everyday examples of the test conclusions reported in the context of the feedback session. Attention to and elaboration of such spontaneous reports will be extraordinarily helpful in grounding what can be elusive statements in commonplace realities, and thus aid the parent in retaining these ideas by making practical sense of them.

When psychological testing has been administered by one professional, and clinical interviewing and history development by another (a primary therapist), it is not uncommon for the psychologist to submit a report of findings to the primary therapist. He or she then conveys his integration of both sets of findings to the child's parents. For many of the aforementioned reasons, difficulties may result when this is the sole method of communicating findings. Although there may occasionally be some valid clinical rationale for having the nontesting therapist act as the sole conveyor of test findings, there are also considerable potential losses in this arrangement. This is especially true when findings are counter to what parents wish to hear and/or when the clinical picture is a complicated one. Even if the primary therapist has a sophisticated appreciation of neuropsychological functioning, the nuances of the processes of testing and inference formation cannot be conveyed adequately by someone other than the examiner. Moreover, parents who are given conclusions which are unacceptable or disappointing to them may readily make use of this divided investigative situation to discount the conclusions they do not wish to hear— whether they be the test findings or those of the general clinical evaluation—rather than receiving them as different facets of the same child. Without exposure to the primary data of observation, concepts tend to remain murky or abstract and are more easily repressed, distorted, or not taken in at all. In a clinic setting, it is sometimes possible to deal with such parental "splitting" by instituting a joint feedback session in which the psychologist and primary therapist meet jointly with the child's parents. In private practice this is not feasible and may be clinically contraindicated. This imposes on the two collaborating professionals a responsibility to maintain close communication during this phase of clinical work about the nature of parental responses to their findings and recommendations.[10]

In the process of conveying a detailed and thoughtful picture of the findings suggested by the total evaluation, the clinician bears in mind how they dovetail or conflict with parental expectations. Such understanding is expressed in phrases such as, "I know you expected . . ." or "I know you will be relieved (or disappointed, or frightened) by the idea I am suggesting." A third ear is alerted to what the child's parents are processing, apart from what is said to them. For example, is there a developing atmosphere of "mea culpa" or "it's your fault" on the part of one or both parents? Is there depression in relation to the statement that the child has delimited neuropsychological deficits or a level of intelligence which is lower than expected? Does this distort the extent or nature of the actual problems cited? Conversely, is there relief that the suspected deficits were not confirmed or that the child is brighter than was previously apparent? On the crest of this relief, is there a resulting tendency to inflation of the child's intellectual potential or denial of the remaining, but far less than expected, manifestations of neuropsychological dysfunction? Such a parent may conclude that with just a little tutoring the child will catch up, the notion of remediation—that the child needs to learn in a different way—being too threatening. Having received a "clean bill of health" neuropsychologically, does one or both parents fail to integrate the very serious psychogenic problems which the professional has communicated? Are the originally held theories of the etiology of the child's problems likely to reinstate themselves because the conclusions suggested by the consultation so threaten an important family dynamic, for example, an investment in the child being just like one or another parent or parental sibling? These are, of course, only some of the manifold sources of distortion on the parents' part in receiving the professional's conclusions and actualizing effective forms of intervention.

In an effort to diminish the defensive processes mobilized when undesired findings are reported, some clinicians routinely

---

[10]Ochroch's (1981) concept of the "case manager" is one effort to resolve the clinical problems which may arise when multiple professionals address various perspectives of the same patient, both during and following this phase of diagnostic work.

schedule a second feedback session some one or two weeks later. This allows them to monitor what was digested, as well as affording parents an opportunity to ask questions which they could not formulate or did not think of at the time of the original appointment. Others make a clinical judgment about the intensity and deleterious influence of parents' defenses in coping with disappointing or threatening news and arrange such appointments only in those cases in which difficulties are pronounced.

Especially in the case of parents resistant to the consultant's conclusions—but not exclusively in such cases—the communication of findings may serve educational functions. Despite the widespread dissemination of the concept of "learning disabilities" there are many misconceptions or gaps in knowledge, the clarification of which may aid parents in digesting and implementing the professional's conclusions. Only a handful of many such examples follows: the issue of brain localization and the implications of clusters of findings; the psychogenic roots of pseudostupidity; the possibility of neuropsychological dysfunction unaccompanied by hyperactivity or motor dyscoordination, or of a memory disorder of one type in the absence of a memory disorder of another type; the distinction between tutoring and remediation; the existence of neuropsychological deficits of no consequence for learning; the possibility of equivocal neuropsychological findings in the early school years without assurance that the child will "outgrow" them; the existence of neuropsychological dysfunction which is untreatable except in the sense of altering the environment. (These and other examples will be further elaborated in chapters 5, 6, and 7.)

Communicating Findings to the Patient

Although the issues which characterize communication of findings to the child or adolescent are not very distinct from those relevant to his parents, this brief section is included to call attention to the fact that all too often clinicians overlook this part of the consultative process. Sometimes it is assumed that the patient's parents may be held responsible for explaining the evaluation's findings and at other times it is believed that the conclusions will be either too complex or too narcissistically injuring for the child to grasp. Furthermore, it may be thought that since parents have the responsibility of deciding upon the treatment which will address the child's difficulties, he may not require the type of explanation of goals which they do in order to resolve to undertake a treatment course.

However, paradoxically, avoiding such discussion may render "bad news" worse or complicated material less comprehensible. Leaving such explanations exclusively to the child's parents, who do not have the clinician's depth of understanding of the information to be conveyed, and who, in addition, may be subject to the impact of their own disappointments and fears, is creating a situation in which the child's needs are prone to be inadequately met.

There are occasional instances in which such an approach becomes exceedingly difficult for pragmatic reasons. However, the existence of obstacles notwithstanding, it becomes essential for the clinician to speak directly with the child when the clinical picture is complicated, narcissistically valent, or challenging of firmly held beliefs. Most parents do speak with their children about the findings reported, whether this be done in an accurate or distorted fashion or by omission. Therefore, it is important that the clinician carefully explore what it is they expect to convey. Correspondingly, inquiry into what the child has been told and how he integrated these findings is a significant beginning point with any child.

The age of the patient will determine in which order and combinations parents and child should be seen. This will generally follow the same guidelines as for other clinical work in which the latency age and preadolescent child is typically seen either alone after an interview with his parents or with them in a second interview, and the adolescent is seen alone prior to combined contact with him and his parents or in an initial joint interview.

When the child's difficulties are in small or large part neuropsychologically based, a simple and forthright explanation of areas of strength and weakness and the nature of these weaknesses will typically suffice. Reference to the specifics of tests done together will result in the child's most firmly planted understanding. More often than not the clinician is met with the child's profound sense of relief that his difficulties are identifiable and understandable. In all likelihood he has long been aware of them, although not necessarily able to articulate and delineate them in the clinician's manner.

Directness and honesty about their prognosis for improvement is also deeply appreciated by the child whose grasp of the reality of the situation—and his self-esteem related to what he can and cannot expect to do—is greatly promoted in this fashion. Distinctions should be drawn between those deficits which will profit from repetition, those which require that the child learn with methods different from those of his peers (albeit with the same final result) and those which cannot be improved except insofar as important adults in the child's environment can be helped to understand his legitimate need for altered requirements. Depending upon the availability of the child, it may be possible to briefly explore the self-attitudes which have been elaborated on the foundation of these deficits, as well as ways in which difficulties in one area may have become overgeneralized in fantasy to other areas in which there is no actual incapacity.

It is beyond the scope of this book to discuss the nature of feedback to a child who evidences no neuropsychological dysfunction, except to point out that, should the child have a stake in viewing himself as incapacitated and damaged, it is often useful to review the specifics of his ideas and the detailed manner in which the test and other evaluation findings ruled this out.

Communicating Findings to the School

The function of feedback to the school is to make the complex findings of an integrative clinical evaluation comprehensible, meaningful, and relevant to the school community. Regardless of the mode of feedback (e.g., written or oral report), it is important to avoid exchanging labels such as educational or behavioral ones for those which are technical and possibly obscure. In the interest of effective communication, the array of clinical data needs to be translated into the simpler language of instruction, learning style, behavior, and impact of the learning disability, should one exist, on the whole child.

Effective communication of findings to teachers and other school personnel requires consideration of a number of factors. First, the educational staff often await the results of evaluation with the expectation of receiving solutions to problems which have rendered them helpless. This perspective results in a rather passive stance wherein the clinician is cast in the role of prescribing answers. Second, there can be the expectation that answers be conveyed in the form of scores or grade levels, as this is frequently the language school staff use in describing children. Along with these expectations rest the educators' personal theories about the origin and nature of a particular child's learning difficulties to which they may adhere tenaciously despite their request for solutions.

In view of these expectations and theories it is helpful to establish a climate which facilitates active involvement of school personnel in the clinician's process of thinking. Their previously expressed hypotheses should be reviewed and either confirmed or ruled out. Specific examples may be drawn directly from the clinical data and linked with behavior, areas of puzzlement, or difficulties highlighted by school staff in the process of initial referral. This sets the tone for a collaborative effort in which the educator can actively relate clinical findings to his own experience of the child in question. Furthermore, such an approach sets the stage for a discussion which, while including scores and content of productions, has as its central focus delineation of the child's approach to processing information and solving tasks as well as his overall cognitive style. Such a description allows the educator to integrate his own experiences in teaching a child a particular skill with several aspects of the clinical findings: an appreciation of the demands placed upon the child in learning this skill, knowledge of whether these demands tap areas of deficit, and exploration of areas of strength which may be used in compensation to learn the skill. In addition to offering scores and prescriptions, a collaborative approach to feedback can open avenues of thinking about a child's strengths and weaknesses which the astute teacher can subsequently probe, verify, or modify. Prescriptions alone cannot continue to guide the instructional process over an extended period of time as learning of some new skills will inevitably require their modification. In effect, good teaching is a process of hypothesis generation, confirmation, or rejection.

Having set a collaborative tone, the clinician can then address the specific questions originally raised both by parents and school personnel. This approach should include both a description of overall levels of functioning and illustrations of areas of deficit as they impinge upon successful task solution. Thus, for example, the clinician can illustrate how an underlying memory deficit interferes with answering questions about a chapter read earlier; how an anomia impoverishes oral expression which requires verbal elaboration; and how a sparse written language sample in the context of rich oral productions may be reflective of an attempt to hide a dysgraphia. Therefore, just as the clinician should be specific in his questions when developing a child's school history, so can he attempt to be precise in differentiating various underlying functions which mitigate against adequate task solution.

In addressing school personnel the clinician is often asked for guidance regarding the kind of intervention to institute on behalf of a child, for example, full-time private school, self-contained special education classes, resource room, tutoring, and the like. Decisions regarding these options are best guided by a clear understanding of the pervasiveness of the deficit, including how broad a spectrum of school and other functions it affects. Thus, for example, difficulties with sequential organization may in some cases affect only spelling or writing; however, in others they may impact upon such varied tasks as organizing one's desk or assignments, the ability to carry out long-term projects, or to find the appropriate classroom on time. Since some of these behaviors may have been misconstrued as oppositionalism, such an analysis offers a radically different perspective. Clinicians also communicate information important to program decisions by assessing and reporting to school staff the child's use of compensatory mechanisms, as well as their degree of efficiency and efficacy. The important question in this regard is whether the child makes use of alternative ways of processing information when conventional methods tap an area of deficit. A related issue is the "cost" of the mechanism used or, stated another way, how effortful is the process and how tiring for the child. If the child has long struggled with multiple areas of deficit, he may require a more protected environment such as a self-contained classroom rather than out-of-class, once weekly remediation.

Recommendations regarding placement are also enhanced by communicating achievement test data in terms of levels of functioning, rather than by means of grade levels alone. Often the achievement test scores indicate only instructional levels (i.e., the level at which instruction can take place). Qualitative analysis of test data can yield information regarding functional level (i.e., the level at which a child is really comfortable and can work on his own). Finally, the clinician can pinpoint the frustration level, that is, the level or type of work which would be overwhelming to a particular child and thus lead to frustration. Communication of findings regarding all three levels makes the clinical data more relevant to the actual classroom experience.

Specific recommendations regarding methods of instruction or use of remedial techniques are best made in light of the personality and dynamics of the child. The child's stage of cognitive and affective development, acceptance or rejection of his disability, his central conflicts and defenses, all need to be translated into a behavioral picture of the way in which the child interacts with the world as a whole, as well as with academic tasks. Thus, for example, if one works with an adolescent who is engaged in an intense struggle to separate from adults, a recommendation of individual remediation which places him in an exaggerated state of dependency may be contraindicated. Such a person might benefit more from a resource room in which he can determine his own degree of reliance upon the teacher and thus experience a sense of independence by means of working with materials organized to assist him. Alternatively, the overly dependent child with difficulties in the area of concentration and attention is not likely to make good use of a resource room in which he is left to work somewhat independently. Since such a child may need the adult's ego to maintain his concentration and involvement in a task, intensive one-to-one remediation might be indicated.

Guidelines regarding methods of instruction or remediation derive both from assessment of neuropsychological functions underlying academic tasks and familiarity with varied instructional models and remedial techniques. Choice of a particular model is best guided by an understanding of the functions it assumes to be intact, for example, linguistic methods are based on the supposition that young children have well-integrated oral language skills. Such a blending of data from the clinical evaluation with knowledge of the structure of instructional models offers school staff the best possibility of effectively matching a child and an instructional method.

Chapter 5

Clinical Illustrations of the Diagnostic Process

We will now explicate in detail the necessarily comprehensive and integrative process of clinical investigation of disorders in learning with the aid of our three major cases, first described in the Introduction: Noah, Daniel, and Matthew. The nature of the clinical contacts and procedures performed will be sequentially delineated with commentary interspersed to convey the flow of emerging data and the process of clinical inference formation. The course of their treatment and extended evaluation will be presented in chapter 7. Later in this chapter, in the section entitled "Pitfalls of a Partial Evaluation," we will turn to additional cases which illustrate the problems which are likely to arise when less comprehensive diagnostic study takes place.

MAJOR CASES

Case 1: Noah, a Learning Disorder of Primary Psychogenic Etiology

The reader may recall that Noah was an 8-year-old boy who presented with an eye tic and a marked preoccupation with his "yucky eyeballs." Noah's parents, a professional couple, were seen by Dr. Meyers, a clinical psychologist with expertise in neuropsychological dysfunction, in order to obtain a history prior to clinical and psychological testing assessment of their son. They initially consulted with Dr. Gerard, pediatric neurologist, for Noah's learning difficulty. Implicitly, both parents were concerned with Noah's high activity level and his short attention span. In an appointment the previous week, Dr. Gerard found him neither hyperactive nor distractible. The only difficulty observed was Noah's poor reproduction of Bender-Gestalt triangles, diamonds, and dots.

Despite the fact that he had functioned at an average level since first grade, each year teachers complained of his poor attention span and distractibility. However, he had never been a behavior problem. In school, Noah received a lot of one-to-one attention which ultimately resulted in good progress at the end of each year but no alteration of his capacity to sustain attention. In addition, his educational history was marked by several changes of school early in life due to moves made by his family. In nursery school and kindergarten no problems were noted by teachers, except that he was always active, "high strung," and inquisitive but not hyperactive. Despite a major move from a less demanding to a more high-powered neighborhood and school system between first and second grades, his first and second grade teachers had similar impressions of him, each commenting upon his poor attention span.

A major current problem was in printing, although Noah was having more success with cursive writing. In reading, he generally understood what he read but frequently lost his sense of direction or was unable to follow through with written directions. During his first year in a highly competitive upper-middle-class school, there was a big contrast between him and the other children at the outset. Because he was both a half-year behind academically and young for the group, the demands upon him for social adjustment were great. However, he reportedly caught up in six months, moving up one whole reading group. Although his performance both in math and reading continued to be at a level apace of his peers, his teacher noted his difficulty in paying attention and his tendency to forget things. Newly taught mathematical concepts were forgotten over the summer, although an interest in learning—as seen in Noah's voracious reading of books—was evident. Recently despite his parents' impression that he understood place value concepts with 100s and 1,000s, he continually made errors. Then all of a sudden he seemed to grasp them, only to lose the concept once a new form of it was introduced. Dr. Meyers's inquiry about difficulties in sensory processing revealed that his sight and hearing were thought to be intact.

His parents observed that Noah picked up nervous habits each year with the beginning of school. In the first grade he would spit and then wipe his mouth on his shoulder. In second grade he picked on the skin near his nails. His father had a cousin who had an eye tic, with which they associated the onset of Noah's tic-ing in the past year, at the beginning of third grade. Their implicit assumption was that the tic reflected tiredness, an idea communicated to Noah.

Noah was described as kindhearted and curious. To illustrate the latter quality, his parents cited his great passion for science books. They recalled that he was always noticed a lot, stating "we couldn't go to a restaurant when he was 3 or 4 because he couldn't sit, but he was always well behaved." In class he liked to be alone and to create things. He was more interested in this than in formal instruction, for example, that sentences begin with a capital and end with a period. Noah would claim that he already understood it all, even though this was frequently not the case.

Noah was not competitive for marks and grades according to his mother, who was trying to "instill in him" a sense of competition. He was reportedly "well adjusted" about it, as exemplified by his never having let his parents know, in recent times, that he was worried about competition. By contrast, the previous year he could not tolerate losing games. His parents felt they were always doing schoolwork with him, in part because he made frequent mistakes which they required him to correct. This resulted in very lengthy sessions of two hours. In contrast other children in the class handled the same amount of homework in a much shorter period of time.

Jokingly, Noah's father indicated he felt that "only beating him up would help." With this he suddenly became more active in the interview, noting how little he and his wife understood about what would help Noah academically. "Was asking him to do math in his head too much?" Noah's writing was not neat, and this, he felt, was affecting his sentence structure. Noah's father had been told that he was the same way as a boy. "Since things worked out well for me, is this really something to worry about?" He had to take IQ tests because he only did half of the work that was assigned, instead watching a squirrel outside of his classroom or daydreaming. He then added, "We don't know what's wrong or how it's affecting Noah's performance. He should be able to read paragraphs and follow instructions and he can't. He still reverses 'b' and 'd' in his writing, his left–right orientation is not good." It was surprising to father that Noah was left-handed like him and that they also shared a tendency to write in an inverted position.

Inquiry about Noah's early history revealed that his birth was 2 weeks early but otherwise uneventful. Birth weight was 6 pounds, 1 ounce. Since the bilirubin level rose after 2 or 3 days, Noah stayed in the hospital for 10 days during which a transfusion was considered but ultimately not performed. As a newborn Noah had not taken the bottle well and consequently dropped in weight. Despite competent handling by a sympathetic pediatrician, mother had become anxious and in turn angry at her son over the anxiety he had caused her. She claimed that this state lasted until the middle child, also a boy, was born two years and nine months later. Although there was never a cessation of Noah's fussiness in eating, she believed that when she paid less attention to what he ate he tended to be less particular and to eat more. He was reported to have walked at 10 months and to have "learned all his letters and numbers" by 10 to 12 months. At 2 he "forgot" them all because he lost interest and by kindergarten he did not have any of these skills. Noah had no difficulty with toilet training and separated easily at the time of entry to nursery school.

His health had generally been good, with the exception of one transient fainting spell in school the year before that the pediatrician attributed to a virus accompanied by high fever. Seizures or febrile convulsions were denied. Noah did have roseola at age 2 but without complications and a mild case of chicken pox at age 3 or 4 without personality changes. There had been no hospitalizations or accidents.

On direct questioning about whether Noah was able to pour from a bottle and cut his own meat, his parents reported that he had no trouble in either activity. Indeed his small motor coordination in arts and crafts projects was excellent—and even quite imaginative and creative—as was his drawing. He was reportedly slow in dressing himself and needed to be reminded lest he dawdle, becoming distracted or absorbed in daydreaming. In self-care, he had the capacity to bathe and wash himself independently, but since mother liked him very clean she would participate. When asked about Noah's sleep patterns, his parents replied that they were "fine." He was said to protest a bit before going to bed, but to fall asleep readily and sleep through the night once he did.

Of Noah's peer relationships his parents stated that even though he had been living in the present neighborhood for only 1 1/2 years, he was happy and comfortable, had friends in school and at home, and was sometimes even a leader. He did tend to be shy at the beginning with unfamiliar people, particularly other children, who sometimes made fun of his surname that lent itself to punning. The previous year at school his teacher felt his social problems such as shyness played a part in his academic difficulties. Now, however, he had several friends, one of whom was a best friend.

When asked about his relationships with his siblings, Noah's parents reported that he loved his little sister, but there was rivalry with his brother with whom he fought a great deal. Noah was the eldest of three, the next younger child being a boy, and the youngest a girl. Spontaneously and with pride, Noah's parents commented upon his tendency to be expressive of his anger. If frustrated, he would bang on the table and throw his books down. They held the theory that if one had negative feelings, it was good to somehow get them out.

Although Noah complained about the nature and amount of schoolwork he had, he claimed to love his teacher. In math, he would start correctly but begin to commit simple errors as he continued. He did not "like" borrowing or carrying. He still typically used fingers for adding in school as well as in totaling the sums of dice in the course of a game. He was facile, however, with other games such as checkers.

Exploration of Noah's language capacities did not yield remarkable findings. He firmly knew colors, appropriately used common words, and comprehended prepositional and directional concepts (e.g., up-down, before-after, and the like). The previous year the school was surprised because Noah did not know the word "season." Otherwise there were no instances of aphasic symptomatology or difficulties with articulation. Direct inquiry revealed that he knew how to tell time and to organize himself around a clock in everyday activities (e.g., television and going to school). At this point Noah's parents offered that he was now going to a reading clinic to address his difficulty in writing sentences, which included a tendency to capitalize in the middle and to greatly vary the size of his letters.

Noah's father spontaneously expressed his view of the diagnosis and etiology of his son's learning disorder. He thought it was "laziness" but still sensed that "something is wrong and the something probably has an organic etiology"; that was why he and his wife originally went to see a neurologist. His confusion now rested in these two contradictory notions: "If something more is wrong," they did not want to treat him as though he were "lazy." He would prefer to arrive at a diagnostic understanding such as the one suggested by Dr. Gerard's tentative hypothesis of a fine motor problem. Noah's mother added that her son had had the Iowa test at the beginning of the previous year, second grade, on which he performed miserably. By the end of the year, he obtained a composite score at the 2.6 grade level. The learning disabilities specialist saw him and felt that she could work with him. However, after some additional tests, school personnel concluded there was no disability but rather an attentional problem for which they needed to work with him more closely in a one-to-one setting. Under these conditions, he better approximated his potential. Thus Noah's parents approached the evaluation with an expectation and wish that Dr. Gerard's impression of a neuropsychological basis would be further substantiated. This theory coexisted with an attitudinal explanation: "laziness."

At this point there was a negative history for inherited or acquired neuropsychological dysfunction. There were questions of disorders in memory, directionality, and graphomotor functions, all of which would render Noah at risk not only for difficulties in learning but also for self-esteem problems, given the high demands for academic performance characteristic of his family environment. The unevenness in his functioning and his repeated ability to catch up from behind in academic tasks—coupled with manifestations of inner preoccupation—also suggested the need to rule out psychogenic explanations for his problems in learning.

The following is a report of psychological test findings at the time of initial consultation.

Tests Administered

Wechsler Intelligence Scale for Children—Revised (WISC-R)
Illinois Test of Psycholinguistic Abilities: Auditory & Visual
    Sequential Memory; Sound Blending (Only)
Wide Range Achievement Test (WRAT)
Benton Test of Visual Retention
Raven Progressive Matrices
Rorschach
Thematic Apperception Test (TAT)
Purdue Pegboard
Motor Tests (Rapid Alternating Movements, Thumb Wiggling,
    Apraxias)
Laterality Tests
Figure Drawings & Most Horrible & Most Pleasant Concepts
Time Orientation
Finger Agnosia & Graphesthesia
Beery-Buktenica Visual-Motor Integration Test

General Findings

Intelligence: On the WISC-R, Noah obtained a Verbal IQ of 119 (90th percentile), a Performance IQ of 104 (60th percentile), and a Full Scale IQ of 113 (81st percentile). Below are the scaled scores:

Information	12	Picture Completion	11
Similarities	11	Picture Arrangement	12
Arithmetic	13	Block Design	11
Vocabulary	15	Object Assembly	11
Comprehension	14	Coding	8
(Digit Span)	(8)	(Mazes)	(11)

No scores fall into the deficit range though sequential memory is below expectations and influences the reduced Coding score. Often Noah would "give up" on manipulations tests and had to be encouraged to keep trying. Also characteristic of many of the scales was the failing of easy items and passing much harder items, suggesting (a) if consolidation takes place the IQ will probably rise and (b) current interference in continuous adaptive functioning.

Achievement: On the WRAT, Noah obtained a Reading Grade Score of 4.8 (87th percentile), a Spelling Grade Score of 3.5 (58th percentile), and an Arithmetic Grade Score of 3.2 (47th percentile). Qualitatively reading was done easily and well. Phonics have not been learned for vowels nor for the digraphs CH and SH in isolation.

His writing reveals reversals of form of b and d: body = "doby," as well as simple spelling errors: and = "a." Arithmetic skills are consistent for age and grade placement.

Part Functions

Perception: On the Raven, a test of visual–perceptual development, Noah scored at the 70th percentile. Clinically, and from the sound blending test there is no evidence of auditory imperception. Somatosensory tests revealed no finger agnosia nor difficulty with graphesthesia tests.

Motor: Fine finger speed and dexterity and gross motor coordination are intact. Mild synkinesia was noted on sequencing fingers in opposition to thumb. Rapid alternating movements (fist–palm) were done within normal limits, though Noah is not especially well coordinated. There was no evidence of eye, tongue, verbal, or facial dyspraxia. The constructional problem, noted by Dr. Gerard, is documented in an age score of 6–10 on the Beery and a 9th percentile score on the Benton copy series.

Laterality: Noah has a dominant left hand, right eye, and right foot, and because of the inverted position of his writing, the data suggest left cerebral dominance. The terms "left" and "right" are consistently reversed on himself though he uses imagery to decide left and right on someone else. These data are all suggestive of mild left hemisphere involvement. A left to right orientation is present for lexic and nonlexic material except for the persistence of the b–d reversals.

Time Orientation: Noah draws a clock well but becomes confused about reading a clock before the hour. The days of the week are known, with Wednesday misplaced after Friday. The temporal concepts are understood. The months have not been learned yet. Also Noah did not know that his birthday is on the same date every year. He said he has to wait until his mother tells him each year.

Memory: On the short-term auditory memory portion of the Illinois Test of Psycholinguistic Abilities Noah scored at age 9–2 in contrast to the low average WISC-R digit span score. He scored in the deficit range on a test of short-term visual spatial memory and at age 5–7 on a test of short-term visual sequential recall.

Language: There is no evidence of dysphasic phenomena. The terms "before" and "after" were understood temporally and spatially. Noah reads, writes, and aligns numbers accurately. Spontaneous, responsive, and automatic speech are intact. Autotopagnosia tests were negative.

In summary, Noah is a bright boy with soft signs of minimal cerebral dysfunction: constructional dyspraxia, left–right disorientation, and extreme variability in short-term memory functions. None of the above seems to be having major effects on intelligence or academic performance, and I would not intervene remedially at this time.

Personality

There is no evidence of psychosis or basic disturbance in Noah's sense of reality. He is aroused and stimulated by emotionally charged situations but he actively tries not to experience his own emotions for fear of being overwhelmed. Thus a somewhat rigid character formation is beginning to take place with fantasy supplanting emotional arousal. On the Rorschach he saw no human beings but saw parts of people, especially eyes and eyeballs. On the TAT the significance of eyes became clearly related to conflicts with adult males. It was on the father–son card that Noah lost distance (the picture shows "you sitting in the chair, and this looks like me. The boy's looking at the daddy and the daddy is making yucky eyeballs like this.") And then began incessant and uncontrollable blinking. Later on in the story Noah picks out a tiny detail never responded to which he calls a gun, then a water pistol, but he cannot integrate it into his story.

A mother figure is described in the first card as a statue and to another picture Noah has a phobic reaction and cannot even tolerate looking at the card.

"Yucky eyeballs" are mentioned over and over and ascribed to both mother and father images. The fact that they recur in card after card is highly suggestive of preoccupation and easily accounts for Noah's so-called distractibility. Because he is as visibly upset as he seems to be and because of his somatic reactions, as well as the pressured severe conflict with handling aggression and identifying with adult males, I would suggest psychotherapy be considered for Noah.

Thus, in some respects the current evaluation confirmed Dr. Gerard's findings and labeled them a constructional dyspraxia. In addition there was evidence of some variability in short-term auditory and visual memory functions, none of which appeared to be having any major effects on Noah's academic performance or intelligence. More salient were personality conflicts predominantly organized at an oedipal level. The existence of a high level of anxiety was noted, and the way in which it can simulate a neuropsychological disorder—in the form of distractibility, hyperactivity, and tics—was explained.

The major clinical problem was to convey Noah's need for psychotherapy despite some confirmatory evidence of neuropsychological dysfunction to parents who preferred a neuropsychological etiology. The relevance of two often perplexing clinical possibilities—those of neuropsychological dysfunction of no consequence and the equivocal nature of some neuropsychological findings in the early school years—was explained. In the course of discussion with Noah's parents, they presented observations which appeared to corroborate their son's need for psychotherapy. Additional symptoms had developed in the short course of the consultation: a mild phobic disposition and frightening dreams. Unexpectedly, neither mother nor father appeared to be markedly resistant to seeking help for their son. When they left Dr. Meyers expected that they would promptly pursue a consultation with the psychiatrist he recommended, Dr. Farber.

However, approximately 1 1/2 years later, when Noah was 9 years, 5 months, his mother called Dr. Meyers to say that she and her husband would like Noah to be reevaluated. They were willing at this time to follow his recommendation for psychotherapy if the same picture emerged. They chose, following the previous evaluation, to "wait it out." Another move, this one from their former high-pressured community to a more rural environment, left Noah feeling far more at ease and in the presence of better teachers. In the previous community, everyone was highly competitive and sophisticated. Noah, being a sensitive boy, was never happy with the social situation there. Now he had two "lovely insightful and empathic teachers who were not competitive" like those in the previous environment. All three children were very happy and mother was impressed with what they were learning. Furthermore, her own attitude and that of her husband toward Noah had changed considerably after the previous meeting, leading them to reduce the school pressure. Since they no longer viewed him as lazy and disobedient, the spiraling cycle of punishment and increased negativism had been interrupted. Mother left Noah with the responsibility for his own schoolwork and both praised and encouraged the efforts he made. There were reportedly no problems or tension at home, except that Noah saw little of his father who was working very hard in the business he initiated.

In the year and a half between the two consultations, the presence of the tic was variable. When it did occur it was accompanied by a noisy clacking of the tongue, a loud exhalation, and a grunt. Noah showed a several-year history of a mild, nonspecific phobic disposition characterized by fearfulness of going to an unoccupied floor in the house. Neither parent was aware of any bona fide nightmares, but it was evident from other things they said that their son suffered from very vivid and terrifying dreams and hypnagogic phenomena.

Noah was tested for placement when he enrolled in the new school and found to be in the high average group. He had some trouble with math since he had forgotten over the summer much of the material learned the previous academic year. Therefore, he was put in the third grade math group although he was in fourth grade. The teacher and program, which were excellent, allowed him to do assignments at his own pace. He quickly relearned the forgotten material with the aid of a tutor. He also started Hebrew school once a week without major difficulties. In fact in that sphere he was highly motivated and spontaneously did all his homework. In his regular school, all the teachers continued to report that his attention span was short and that, in addition, he daydreamed a lot. Daydreaming, a new symptom for Noah, had been part of the father's symptomatology as a boy. His mother continued to "instill a competitive spirit in him." Despite all these efforts, there had been only a slight improvement. Noah's mind wandered a lot and he did not express concern about tests or studying, apparently satisfied with his grades, characteristics which were a source of considerable dissatisfaction to his mother. Both parents appeared to be exhausted.

When Noah was seen the second time his vibrancy had disappeared. Where before he was animated and anxious in talking about his eyes, experienced manifest conflict about his somatic symptoms, and demonstrated seriousness and motivation in doing work, this time he had a blasé attitude. The only exception was his relief in having the opportunity to see the psychologist again and his eagerness about the prospect of finding a therapist. He reported that his eye blinking had stopped because his father "fixed them with drops." He still became car sick, a symptom which had become even worse in terms of the speed of onset. Nausea and headaches required him to stick his head out of the car window.

The following is a report of the second psychological evaluation:

Tests Administered

Wechsler Intelligence Scale for Children—Revised
Illinois Test of Psycholinguistic Abilities: Auditory & Visual
	Sequential Memory; Sound Blending (Only)
Wide Range Achievement Test
Benton Test of Visual Retention
Raven Progressive Matrices
Rorschach
Thematic Apperception Test
Purdue Pegboard
Motor Tests (Rapid Alternating Movements, Thumb Wiggling,
	Apraxias)
Laterality Tests
Figure Drawings & Most Horrible & Most Pleasant Concepts
Time Orientation
Finger Agnosia & Graphesthesia

Noah readily adopts an attitude which can only be described as pseudoretarded. He will protest incompetence or ask what you mean by something even when he knows perfectly well what is meant. If I would say, for example, about a story he was to tell, "What happened next?" he would ask, "What do you mean by 'what happened next?'" Or depending on the question, "What do you mean by, 'led up to this?'," or "What happened before?," or "What did I see?" Naturally, if I did not answer him, he went ahead and answered the questions without further clarification. Though he was cooperative throughout testing, Noah did not seem particularly invested in the intellectual exercise of the tests, seemingly more concerned about the interpersonal aspects of the situation.

General Findings

Intelligence: On the WISC-R, Noah obtained a Verbal IQ of 108 (70th percentile), a Performance IQ of 96 (40th percentile), a Full Scale IQ of 102 (55th percentile). These represent drops from 119, 104, and 113, respectively. Below are the scaled scores:

	Initial Consult	Second Consult		Initial Consult	Second Consult
Information	12	15	Picture Completion	11	13
Similarities	12	9	Picture Arrangement	12	9
Arithmetic	13	9	Block Design	11	9
Vocabulary	15	12	Object Assembly	11	10
Comprehension	14	12	Coding	8	7
(Digit Span)	(8)	(9)	(Mazes)	(11)	10

The pattern is very similar though the whole curve is depressed. On some subtests Noah did worse this time than last time in terms of raw scores. On those that he did better on, he did not do significantly better. One can only conclude that Noah has had an arrest of general intellectual development.

Achievement: On the WRAT, Noah obtained a Reading Grade of 6.1 (84th percentile), a Spelling Grade of 5.0 (73rd percentile), and an Arithmetic Grade score of 3.9 (50th percentile). Compared to last time the reading and arithmetic have progressed as expected and spelling has improved more than expected (previous spelling percentile 58th). Qualitative analysis of reading and spelling and arithmetic errors reveals no dyslexia, dysgraphia, or dyscalculia. Furthermore, no deterioration is seen.

Part Functions

Perception: On the Raven, a test of visual–perceptual development, Noah scored at the 78th percentile, ruling out a disorder in this area. Clinically and from the Blending test, there is no evidence of auditory imperception. Somatosensory tests revealed no finger agnosia or difficulty with graphesthesia tests.

Motor: Fine finger speed and dexterity are excellent; gross motor coordination is intact. Rapid alternating movements were done well and mild synkinesia was noted on sequencing fingers. All tests for dyspraxia (eye, tongue, verbal, facial, and constructional) were negative. The constructional dyspraxia seen at the time of initial evaluation is no longer present.

Laterality: Noah has a dominant left hand, right eye, and foot. Lateral awareness is intact on self and in extracorporeal space. A left to right orientation is present for lexic and nonlexic material.

Time Orientation: Noah can read and construct a clock accurately. The days and months and associated concepts are known. October is omitted from the month series.

Memory: Short-term visual–spatial and auditory-sequential memory are now intact. Visual–sequential memory is at age 7–10. All of these results represent an improvement.

Language: There were no dysphasic phenomena noted throughout testing. The terms "before" and "after" are understood spatially and temporally. Automatic, responsive, and spontaneous speech are intact. Numbers are read, written, and aligned accurately. Autotopagnosia tests were negative.

To summarize the above, despite rather dramatic drops in general intellectual functioning, Noah's performance on all tests usually sensitive to neuropsychological impairment has improved.

Personality

Projective test responses portray a boy with profound neurotic conflicts probably referable to primal scene fantasies and experiences (Card IV of the Rorschach, e.g., "is a butterfly that turned into a bat—a butterfly under a bat and they're mushed together"). It is of interest that that response occurs on the "father card" and then on the TAT card depicting a father and son, Noah starts blinking again. Seventeen months ago the same card produced blinking.

Noah has increased and solidified the use of repression to the point that his active fantasy life is drastically reduced from 1½ years ago. There is no question that he is as invested in "not knowing" now as he was in "not seeing" earlier, and again I would suggest a course of psychotherapy, especially now that he has practically asked for it.

With this picture of further decline in performance—in the context of resolution of the maturational lags which could have provided neuropsychological explanations for this decline—the power of psychodynamic factors made Noah's parents' dismissal of the recommendation for psychotherapy more difficult to sustain. With no other recourse this time, they displayed a passive willingness to follow directions and contacted the psychiatrist recommended without delay.

Their conflict over integrating a psychogenic explanation of their son's learning disorder persisted, nevertheless, into the period of consultation with the psychiatrist, Dr. Farber. Several highly significant observations of Noah's current presentation— and historical features newly revealed or emphasized— suggested his parents' attempt to work over and come to terms with the diagnostic impression rendered. While they no longer punished Noah for his laziness and immaturity in not doing homework, they sometimes confronted him in nonpunitive ways about the importance of his schooling for later life. His response was typically a negativistic and depressive one: "I don't care if I shovel dogshit when I grow up." Although this could be accounted for, in part, on the basis of the previous parental management and Noah's oppositionalism, it was also one aspect of his defective self-image. For instance, if pushed to study beyond his subjective capacity, he cursed at his parents, teachers, and at himself, saying, "I am dumb, I am stupid!" He frequently asked in a plaintive but serious way if his parents thought that he could be retarded.

A history of sexual exposure and seductiveness emerged with remarkable ease in the first appointment with the psychiatrist, having either been withheld or transiently repressed during consultation with the referring psychologist, Dr. Meyers. It was conceivable that this revelation grew out of the parents' review of the past from a new perspective in an attempt to make sense of what they had been told by Dr. Meyers. At any rate their reports certainly supported Dr. Meyers' notion that there were profound neurotic conflicts related to primal scene fantasies. What was inferred at age 8 as Noah's wish not to see was clearly understood by age 9 1/2 as his wish not to know. Mother admitted that Noah asked her to go to bed with him twice in the previous week, to lie down with him, and hold him "the way you hold Daddy." He was seductive with her, accusing her of not loving him as much as father, of not "snuggling" enough with him. Although she felt uncomfortable with this, she also felt guilty about her anger over his poor academic performance such that she found it very difficult to refrain from at least partially complying with these wishes. This behavior was no doubt further motivated by conflicts that she had with her husband over his long working hours and the loneliness and lack of sexual gratification she experienced. Although neither parent at first admitted to being aware that Noah had seen them in sexual intercourse, they did on initial consultation admit to mother's having taken showers with him until one or two years prior to treatment. There had also been easy access to observation of both mother and father naked while changing clothes.

Another profound stress to Noah's successful resolution of oedipal conflict was his father's medical history. When Noah was 4, his father had a grand mal seizure due to a cerebral abscess for which he had successful neurosurgery. A second operation a year later was needed to implant a metal plate to correct the cranial deformity. Noah had observed his father with a shaven head and stitches and experienced his transient hemiparesis following the first operation, as well as the residual weakness that followed for a year. Nevertheless, his parents had largely denied that Noah knew about this or, at the very least, grasped its import.

In the course of corroborating Dr. Meyers' impression that psychotherapy was indicated, Dr. Farber made an attempt to convey the multiple determinants of Noah's disorder and especially the concept of the psychopathology of pseudostupidity. At the same time, he emphasized that Noah's negative self-image no doubt found contribution from the maturational lags which, although now resolved, had been subjectively experienced as deficits and thus colored his earliest school experiences. While the lags could not themselves be treated, their symbolic elaborations could.

There were of course multiple additional dynamic formulations that were not shared with Noah's parents at this time: the relationships between Noah's inhibition in competitive pursuit of academic success and his fear of punishment—in the form of something wrong with his eyes—for aggressive impulses toward and fantasied oedipal victory over a father suddenly rendered weak and damaged by cranial surgery; conflicts over identification with such a defective paternal figure in a boy who himself had the experience of something wrong with his head (i.e., his maturational lags); conflicts over seeing and knowing related both to the atmosphere of secrecy about matters that could not be kept secret (e.g., his father's surgery and the overstimulation of primal scene exposure and maternal seductiveness). Indeed Noah's personal and family history fulfilled many of the conditions for and exemplified some of the most classical psychoanalytic formulations of learning disorders reviewed in chapter 3.

At the conclusion of the evaluation when diagnostic considerations were discussed with Noah's parents, in spite of the foregoing history and their intellectual understanding of Dr. Meyers's findings, both mother and father began to vigorously externalize the responsibility for their son's difficulties. It was the frequent moves the family had made, constitutional factors, and, finally, an unspecified "trauma." At this point they also displayed an unusually exaggerated concern that information about the "true cause" of Noah's trouble would be withheld from them. They began to insist on being allowed to learn from Dr. Farber "exactly how it had come about." It seemed as if anything less than such a promise from Dr. Farber would not still their anxiety and guilt. Noah's father wished to know how much more was being withheld from them. Noah's mother felt that she caught Dr. Farber in an inconsistency regarding the suggested frequency of sessions. All of this appeared to be their way of dealing, by projection and externalization, with their feelings of guilt about having contributed to the development of a learning disorder in their son. However, it was clear that despite a lingering wish to "solve the whole thing with one good spanking," they could no longer support the notion that Noah was merely misbehaving or obstinate. His psychotherapy began shortly thereafter.

Case 2: Daniel, A Learning Disorder of Mixed Neuropsychological and Psychogenic Etiology

It will be remembered that Daniel was a 7-year-old child who demonstrated remarkable social aplomb with adults side by side with massive anxiety when interacting with peers and separating from his mother. He was referred to Dr. Loni for consideration for psychoanalysis by an analytic colleague, Dr. Marks, who had initially been asked to evaluate him by the child's parents at the suggestion of Daniel's private school principal. The three major presenting symptoms included impoverished, anxiety-laden peer relationships, inability to work effectively in school, and profound difficulty in separating from his mother both in school and in social situations outside of school. It was a reflection of his complex pattern of strengths and weaknesses that the school did not recognize until the late spring that, despite a superficially adapted facade, Daniel was indeed not learning, not really participating in activities, and not developing peer relationships and skills.

Somewhat stunned by the extent of their only child's troubles, Daniel's parents swiftly arranged for an evaluation by a psychoanalyst and psychological testing by a psychodynamic psychologist who was in general highly competent but not conversant with neuropsychological assessment. The psychologist's description of Daniel's test behavior, psychodynamic constellation, and uneven cognitive functioning paralleled the impressions derived during the psychiatric examination. Excerpts from this initial psychological evaluation follow.

Tests Administered

Wechsler Intelligence Scale for Children
    Verbal Scale IQ   117
    Performance Scale IQ   91
    Full Scale IQ   105

Subtest Scores

Information	11	Picture Completion	10
Similarities	15	Picture Arrangement	7
Arithmetic	10	Block Design	10
Vocabulary	14	Object Assembly	11
Comprehension	14	Coding	6
Digit Span	11		

Bender-Gestalt
Make a Picture Test
Rorschach
Projective Drawings

Daniel, a small, good-looking, well-groomed, 6–11, 11-month-old boy, displayed marked difficulty in separating from his mother. Although he did so, he was tearful and whining, insisting that the door separating the office and waiting room remain open, complaining "I'm afraid it will take too long," "How long?" "How much more?" and so on. After about an hour, he stated that he was enjoying the tests and after a luncheon break, he willingly separated from his mother. Upon completion of the evaluation, Daniel refused to permit his mother to speak to the examiner unless he remained, crying, kicking, and hitting out at the mother.

Daniel was somewhat restless and fidgety, and appeared reluctant to expend any real effort on difficult tasks. He was manipulative, trying to avoid tasks, and was highly suspicious, stating that the examiner was tricking him.

His verbalizations are a mixture of sophisticated words and primitive, immature statements, with blatantly inaccurate syntax, surprisingly discrepant with the apparent sociocultural level of the family. He is a capable youngster whose intellectual potential is within the Superior range, but who is unable to fully utilize his resources, as seen in a Full Scale IQ of 105 (Verbal Scale IQ 117; Performance Scale IQ 91). Variability within the individual subtests, with Daniel failing easy items, and subtest scores, attests to uneven cognitive functioning.

Anxiety is manifest, interfering with attention and concentration, and thereby disrupting cognitive efficiency. Daniel seems to need interpersonal guidelines and limits in order to sustain his efforts. When required to work on his own, as, for example, on the coding subtest (a rote associative learning task), Daniel dawdled, often lost his place, or stopped intermittently to stare out the window. Likewise, on the Picture Arrangement sequences, Daniel's initial sequencing was often inaccurate, and it was only when the examiner imposed additional structure, by asking him to relate the story depicted, that he would recognize the flawed arrangement as he told the story, and then correct the sequencing. Even with this additional aid, there were indications of distortions of interpersonal nuances, difficulty in sizing-up social situations, and misperception of motivations. For example, to a sequence of a wife telling a husband he's late for work, Daniel said, "He wakes up and turns off the alarm and his mother, no his wife is forcing him to go." This appears to represent a major locus of difficulty. Daniel appears to be immersed in a battle for control of the relationships within the family, a battle which he perceives as a "death battle." However, he sees himself caught in a double-bind situation where he cannot really win. If he loses, he fears retribution, and if he is victorious, in essence more powerful than parental figures, then he is left with no one to turn to for protection.

Daniel is enmeshed in a highly disturbed relationship with an apparently seductive mother who attempts to symbiotically bind Daniel to her. The sexualization of the usual nurturing-dependent mother–child relationship has precluded effective sublimation of libidinal impulses. The distortions in this relationship have generalized and contaminated all aspects of familial and interpersonal interactions. Daniel perceives himself as aligned with the mother, in a relationship that totally excludes the father. Significant are a series of Rorschach percepts to cards eliciting sexual and maternal imagery. On the former card, Daniel perceived "a baby butterfly and a mother butterfly . . . flying around" followed by "a drill and these are the sparks and fire coming out." To the latter, Daniel perceived "a letter U"; "an open zipper"; "fingers pointing"; and "Fonze's thumbs going up when he says 'Cool man.'" Symbolically, these percepts suggest the open availability of the sexualized, seductive relationship with the mother, the anal sadistic sexualized component, and the feeling of being accused by the pointing finger. Daniel perceives the father as angry, but as helpless. In essence, he perceives himself as omnipotently controlling parental figures. However, this provides little satisfaction for him, and in fact, is frightening to him.

The alignment with the maternal figure is neither gratifying nor ego-syntonic. While he feels tied to her, there is rage and hostility evident. Daniel perceives the maternal figure as nonnurturing, forcing him to do things, and in essence as aiding and abetting his acting out. Thus, in one Make a Picture Test story, usually perceived as a policeman returning a lost boy to his mother, Daniel told of a woman and boy stealing jewelry.

Disturbance in self-concept and sexual identification are blatant. There is a lack of sexual differentiation and unstable self-concept. Daniel apparently diffused the sexually charged familial atmosphere via masturbation, but the ensuing guilt and fear of damage are overwhelming. Perseveration of pointing fingers on the Rorschach reveal the superego projections with a paranoid tinge to his fantasies and feelings of being accused for his sins.

Inner rage and guilt abound and are massively projected so that Daniel is in constant terror of retribution. In one story he told of a mother who is angry at her children because they "accidentally kicked her. She punishes them. Sends them into the forest . . . they get lost and are strays for the rest of their lives." In another story, a boy who "ruined nature" is handcuffed by police and the police lose the handcuffs. Death wishes toward both parents surface and are projected in a convoluted manner, so that Daniel is frightened that they will come true and backfire. In this context is the following story: "I don't like this. (?) Maybe there is a fire and the mother and parents got killed. The mother lighted a match to go in the oven and she dropped the napkin and she was scared to pick it up and it spread. The parents got killed and he went to a neighbor's house and his grandmother picked him up and he lived with her for the rest of his life. He remained that way till they both died. (?) The boy was at school when it happened. The parents were really out some place. He thought they got killed and he went to his grandmother. His parents came home and thought he was dead, but they didn't find no bones. So, they thought he went to the grandmother and they find him there. He lives with his mother the rest of his life." In light of Daniel's fantasies of death and destruction and his fear that in some magical manner these wishes will be actualized, it is understandable that he is unable to separate from the maternal figure.

A potential for acting out is indicated, representing efforts at warding off feelings of helpless vulnerability. Daniel is like his Rorschach percept of "a rabbit helping two mountain lions to climb a mountain"; he is as the weak rabbit who must help the strong lions who will, when he has served their purpose, then eat him. Thus, he feels a need to attach himself and cling permanently in a passive, submissive stance to a maternal figure, but this too is threatening.

In summary, Daniel is a highly conflicted youngster, caught in a web of disturbed familial interactions, who feels abandoned, manipulated, and damaged. His self-concept and sexual identification are unstable and distorted. Judgment is poor, which together with lability and inner tension, heighten the potential for acting-out behavior.

Denial, intellectualization, projection, and undoing are extensively relied on in efforts at maintaining an adequate adaptation. Reality testing is marginally adequate, and there is no evidence of a thought disorder. However, the defensive adaptation is being stressed by disturbed familial interactions.

Psychotherapy would seem imperative. In addition, the parents need help in establishing more appropriate interactions, and more adequately defining parent–child roles.

The diagnostic impression is that of severe neurotic conflicts with a marked paranoid component in a youngster whose adaptation is being taxed by disturbed familial patterns of interaction.

Thus this psychologist felt that the main etiology was functional and concluded that anxiety was manifestly interfering with attention and concentration and thereby disrupting cognitive efficiency. The psychological findings were consistent with those of the initial consulting analyst, Dr. Marks. Psychoanalysis was thought to be the optimal treatment to deal with Daniel's extreme anxiety, impaired development of stable self-concept and sexual identity, defective object relationships, and marked inhibition of meaningful learning. Furthermore, his areas of ego strength—intelligence, thrust for mastery, interpersonal appeal, and relatedness—and his parents' motivation and capacity to tolerate the emotional and practical demands of a four times a week analytic therapy were considered favorable and essential to recommending this treatment. It was felt that the parental, and especially maternal, emotional difficulties were serious, warranting appreciable attention and concern by the analyst.

This was the clinical picture presented to Dr. Loni when Daniel and his parents were referred to her for consideration for psychoanalysis. The parents were seen together to review the current problems, to develop a history, to confirm that Dr. Marks' findings and reasons for recommending a consultation for psychoanalysis had been understood, and to be sure that Daniel's parents and Dr. Loni would be able to establish a comfortable and constructive relationship.

In the course of developing a history with Daniel's parents Dr. Loni discovered long-standing and complex roots of Daniel's presenting problems. At the same time there was a diffuse and spotty quality to parental reports. This was partly symptomatic of the mother's psychopathology, especially her excessive identification with and yearnings for merger with her son.[1]

Daniel's separation difficulties were dated to the age of 2 1/2 when he refused to remain with a baby-sitter in a motel at which he and his parents were staying. By 3 he was unable to leave his mother to participate in a summer day playgroup at a swimming pool to which they belonged. When beginning nursery school, kindergarten, and first grade, he initially permitted separation and then quickly manifested anxiety and reluctance to go. At the time of consultation there were only two families he would visit without his mother. On outings he insisted that one parent attend.

Daniel's separation anxiety was intimately tied up with his peer difficulties. There was an astounding lack of exposure to children for the first 2 1/2 years of his life, most contacts being with immediate family and a few adult friends of his parents. His mother attributed this to her sense of awkwardness as a parent, given her relatively advanced age as a mother. She literally rarely took Daniel out except for visits to a few close, childless family members. She stated, almost with pride, "He was 2 years old before people in the apartment building knew he belonged to me." When at age 2 1/2 or 3 he had his initial exposure to other children, he singled out one child to whom he grimly attached himself in what his mother described as a "death grip." At summer camp at age 3 he finally ended up going with his only friend, Jane, to whom he stayed glued in the girls' group. He never really participated in the activities but stayed by her side all day. This attachment persisted through two years of nursery school until Jane's mother changed her school because of this relationship, a decision in which Daniel's mother shared. Jane was chosen to shift schools because Daniel was felt to be the more brittle of the two children. In kindergarten he again had one close companion and interacted little with other children in

---

[1]On occasion, some seemingly undocumented etiological assumptions will be suggested due to the need to delete some of the relevant genetic and familial history in the service of preserving confidentiality.

the class. In contrast he was reported to relate well to adults to whom he gravitated at family parties.

Daniel's nonachievement record at school, leading to his repetition of first grade, reflected his difficulty in working in one-to-one situations, his fear of failure, and his anxiety in unknown environments. Twice there was a precipitous decline in anxiety in school and a willingness to reveal more about the school situation at home, for example, to bring home stories and work. This took place transiently in kindergarten when his mother was advised to seek treatment for herself and again after he began analysis. Prior to that Daniel said nothing about school at home.

At 3 Daniel manifested excessive castration anxiety in relation to minor injuries and impairments in his peer relations and in his capacity to separate. He began to evidence food peculiarities such as refusing to taste others' food saying, "It has your taste on it." He would not even let his mother fill his glass for a second time without washing it. Other difficulties included finger sucking, facial tics, and impulsive pushing and hitting of other children. At the time of consultation, Daniel had no difficulty falling asleep but did find waking up difficult. He asked his mother to give him extra time to "warm up" to ease the transition.

The early developmental history mother and father were able to report was scanty and to some degree unreliable, although several features were remarkable. Physically there were no difficulties in delivery or the neonatal period. However, Daniel's mother's first reaction to her son was one of disgust: "My God he's ugly." Both mother and father felt awkward as parents of a baby but the father was clearly warmer and more spontaneous. Pictures showed him tossing Daniel in a mutually joyous manner in contrast to the mother who held him stiffly as if he were a toy. No eating or sleeping problems were noted. Daniel had "exquisite hearing" and sensitivity to light, often hearing something before his parents did. At 2 months he cried in panic at the sound of the blender. His mother handled this by going with him into his room and drowning out the sound of the blender with the roar of the vacuum cleaner. This type of history of congenital hypersensitivity to stimuli, combined with insufficient parental protection, was noted by Bergman and Escalona

(1949) to contribute to the later development of severe psychopathology. This hypersensitivity is also commonly reported in learning disabled children.

According to Daniel's parents no stranger anxiety was observed. As an infant he frequently smiled, generally appeared happy, and was able to amuse himself. It was unclear whether this was also symptomatic of understimulation, as mother found herself quite worn out by the task of caring for an infant. Contributory to this experience were her heavy burden of chronic anxiety and persistent criticism from her own mother.

Daniel's motor milestones were slightly slow but nevertheless within the normal range. Daniel sat with support at 8 months and walked at 15 months. He spoke words at 10 months and sentences at 2 or 2 1/2, generally showing a flair for linguistic nuances. His mother said of Daniel's toilet training, "He trained himself, no problem."

Daniel's mother was an American-born Jewish woman in her mid-40s who spoke with a heavy accent of unknown origin. An only child herself, she had a long-standing clinging–dependent relationship with her own mother that was further intensified when her father died almost two decades earlier. The maternal grandmother clearly resented the intrusion of Daniel into her relationship with Daniel's mother, often stating, "Things have never been the same since he came." There were many parallels between their relationship and Daniel's relationship with his mother. For example, the maternal grandmother was troubled by separations. When leaving her daughter as a child, she would say, "I swallowed a black olive and have to see a doctor." Social isolation also characterized her relationship with her daughter.

Daniel's mother suffered from many painful symptoms such as compulsive cleanliness, phobias in specific public places, social isolation, and somatic preoccupations. While many of her troubles stressed Daniel—her seductiveness, projection of her anxiety and distrust of people, wishes for fusion, and overidentification with the boy—she also had strengths which were indispensable in facilitating the analysis. These included the capacity to laugh at herself and see herself in perspective, honesty in reporting to the analyst, and a basic concern for her son.

The father was an accountant in his late 40s. While he was more gregarious and socially graceful than his wife, he was nevertheless markedly inhibited and socially isolated. He had chronic, unrealistic anxiety about losing his job. He described himself as a hypochondriac and saw himself as "touchy," awkward with Daniel and uncomfortable with closeness. The accuracy of these reports was in question since pictures of Daniel's earlier years were suggestive of glowing mutual pleasure between father and son.

At the close of the consultation for analysis, the plentiful and compelling psychodynamic explanations for Daniel's psychopathology—coupled with the absence of neuropsychological findings reported by the psychologist two months earlier and the lack of suspicion of a learning disability by his teachers—led to an initial underestimation of neuropsychological contributions to the clinical picture. Although the psychological test report described uneven cognitive functioning, intrapsychic turmoil and a disturbed parent–child relationship were posited as explanations. Also contributory to this underestimation were several aspects of Daniel's clinical presentation: his massive anxiety, his excellent language skills in communicating feelings, and the absence of motor stigmata.

Thus the preliminary formulation of the case was as follows: Daniel's mother was a woman who was openly ambivalent about motherhood, as seen in her near repulsion toward her son as a newborn, her inability to touch him warmly, and her almost literally hiding him from others for two years. She had a symbiotic relationship with her own mother that was stressed by Daniel's arrival. Maternal neglect, awkwardness, and ambivalence were combined with persistent seductiveness. The latter included unconscious pleasure in Daniel's inability to separate, offering her breasts and pubic area for "casual contacts," and frequent discussions about his genitals. While father provided a source of genuine warmth, there was passive neglect and an almost conscious relinquishment of his son for maternal identification and overinvolvement. The father admitted guilt over rejecting and ignoring the boy as he felt his own father to have done with him.

Developmentally there was significant preoedipal pathology including strong interferences with separation–individuation and pathological anal fixation. In the early contacts this was seen in Daniel's preoccupation with fecal equivalents: he called many items "doodies," he was curious as to whether the analyst enjoyed eating them, and compulsively engaged in anal play with frequent culmination in a bowel movement. Problems in individuation contributed to Daniel's inability to sustain meaningful peer relationships in contrast to his tendency to seek relationships with adults, especially mother surrogates. When separated from mother, he experienced an intolerable level of anxiety, particularly around fears of abandonment, low self-esteem, and fantasies of being damaged. His profound learning difficulties in school could be explained on similar bases: his poor capacity to tolerate frustration, his intense anxiety around separation, and his fear of failure. Aspects of his functioning in relation to school might also be viewed as symbolic efforts to separate, for example, not telling his mother anything about school, his teachers, or classmates.

However, features of the history and psychological testing suggested the need for further psychological evaluation to rule out neuropsychological dysfunction: Daniel's early hyperacusis and rather pronounced scatter on the WISC-R. At the end of the consultation Dr. Loni met with Daniel's parents to recommend that Daniel be seen in psychoanalysis four times weekly, as well as to explain her clinical impression that additional assessment by a clinical psychologist with expertise in neuropsychology was indicated. Neither of Daniel's parents ostensibly held specific personal theories of the etiology of his problems. His mother constantly saw parallels between Daniel's patterns and her own. These may well have reflected her wishes that they be identical, that she profoundly influence and affect him, and her guilt that she had damaged him.

Despite their personal psychopathologies, Daniel's mother and father had a strong core of genuine concern for their son and, recognizing the severity of his difficulties, rather readily agreed to embark upon treatment for him. Although his father seemed somewhat less sure, in his characteristic manner he went along with the suggestion. Nor did either of Daniel's parents object to the notion of further evaluation for neuropsychological dysfunction or view such a possibility as competing with the psychological explanations already offered to substantiate the need for psychoanalysis.

In consultation with the second psychologist, Dr. Hirsch, some two months after the beginning of Daniel's analysis, additional features of the current and past clinical picture and his parents' interpretation of them emerged. They spontaneously reported that he was having difficulty in school which the mother felt was not due to low intelligence, but to emotional difficulties and "some form of dyslexia with inverted perception." He inverted numbers and letters and confused the days of the week. This was his second time in first grade and they wished clarification of whether he was mainly emotionally immature or had some sort of specific learning problem, or both. They also reported that outside of school, life was different. For example, in school he would not do any woodwork, but at home he walked around with a screwdriver and fixed things.

An array of academic difficulties was noted. Daniel started to read only in the six weeks prior to this consultation; "he just decided to read and he did." Nevertheless he got lost in the pages that he started to read, became intimidated, and then gave up. He tired easily after a burst of enthusiasm and would rapidly forget a word, for example, between only the first and fourth sentences. He was going to a special reading class with three or four other children, although his parents did not understand what he did there. Sometimes he tried to sound out words, other times he made wild guesses, and at still other times he tried a phonetic approach but did not connect the proper sounds. The previous year teachers complained about his attention span, but this year in the classroom his attention had improved. When Dr. Hirsch asked how arithmetic was proceeding, they reported that Daniel's progress was satisfactory. Mother elaborated that he did arithmetic well if she sat near him but that he did not know what he was doing in school. She felt his intelligence was not being "harnessed." His handwriting was immature and he had difficulty making letters.

After exploring the initial complaints and Daniel's parents' observations about and conceptions of them, Dr. Hirsch asked about Daniel's medical history. No problems were reported with the exception of stomachaches, which his parents attributed to tension, since they were the early morning Monday-to-Friday type. Daniel never had any seizures, accidents, or hospitalizations. His birth weight was 7 pounds, 4 ounces. He was currently thin—about 4 feet high and 45 pounds—but "looked great."

In this context they spontaneously added that their pediatrician, whose own son had emotional problems, advised that seeking the help of a psychiatrist was advantageous. Physically, Daniel was "okay," but he had definite emotional problems which they repeatedly mentioned. Dr. Hirsch asked what led them to seek psychiatric help for Daniel and they said that two years ago he began to look very tense, clung, and was afraid to do anything on his own. Daniel's father resisted the idea of seeing a psychiatrist because he felt it was a phase of childhood, but when the school difficulties surfaced he acquiesced.

Dr. Hirsch inquired about Daniel's sleep habits and was told that once he went to sleep, he slept through the night. He usually fell asleep with his parents while they were in bed watching television. Sometimes they insisted that he go to his own bed, which he did without difficulty. He occasionally talked in his sleep but there was no sleepwalking and nightmares were rare. He was chipper on weekends when awakening, but during the week he was slow to rise and complained of stomachaches. He also reported stomachaches in the summer when he was upset. Although change was generally hard for him, he liked their recent move from an apartment to a house which took place simultaneously with the beginning of analysis. However, he had not yet made any friends in the neighborhood. Daniel's eating habits were good. He was "catholic" in his choice and did not overeat. He reportedly cut his meat by the age of 3 and poured into a glass with ease. He was currently able to dress himself, albeit with pronounced slowness as he liked to lounge around and watch television. He had been able to tie his shoelaces since the age of 4 or 5, although he liked his parents to do it. Now and again he dressed in reverse, to which they responded by making a joke of it. Bathing was performed independently and well if some prodding was provided. Once in the bathtub, Daniel stayed there and enjoyed it. Father and son jogged together and showered together upon return. At other times father jogged, Daniel riding his bicycle alongside. He learned to ride a two-wheeler quickly and continued to be a good rider, although he was sometimes slightly overcautious.

In terms of friends, Daniel was not a "mixer." He had some old friends at nursery school with whom he was in contact from time to time. He would not go to a friend's house regularly; when he did, should he hurt himself he wished to come home immediately. On one rare occasion he arranged to sleep at a friend's house, only to call up requesting to come home. In contrast he was apparently a great host when other children visited his home. At 4 years of age he went to day camp. The mornings were difficult but he had a good driver who knew how to ease him into the camp situation. However, the director of the camp asked that Daniel leave. Daniel's mother did not process this as a manifestation of trouble, but rather took away the understanding that camp was too exhausting for him. In general, Daniel was not a fighter but a child who kept completely to himself so there was never a behavior problem; in contrast he liked to mix with adults.

Daniel was subsequently seen four times to complete an extensive psychological evaluation, the findings of which were as follows:

Tests Administered

Wechsler Intelligence Scale for Children—Revised
Illinois Test of Psycholinguistic Abilities: Auditory & Visual
    Sequential Memory; Sound Blending (Only)
Wide Range Achievement Test
Raven Progressive Matrices
Rorschach
Children's Apperception Test
Purdue Pegboard
Motor Tests (Rapid Alternating Movements, Thumb Wiggling,
    Apraxias)
Laterality Tests

Figure Drawings & Most Horrible & Most Pleasant Concepts
Time Orientation
Finger Agnosia & Graphesthesia
Beery-Buktenica Visual-Motor Integration Test

    Daniel presents as a friendly, verbal, and cooperative boy suf-
fering from profound separation anxiety. He walked in like an old
man, his head bowed, slowly, lethargically in each session and, for a
7½-year-old boy, seemed very depressed, with a seemingly adult
clinical depression. In the first two sessions hyperacusis was noted in
his attentiveness to his mother's cough in the waiting room, his startle
at unexpected sounds, and his general hypervigilance. In the third
session, during the Rorschach he slipped from his chair and began to
cry profusely, well after the effects of physical pain subsided. He
protested he could not go on to me and to his mother, who induced
him to continue by offering to sit in the examining room. Her
presence was needed all during the third and fourth sessions. This
behavior, reflecting separation anxiety, was well beyond reasonable
expectations for a 7½-year-old.
    Daniel enjoyed the structured tests much more than the projec-
tive tests, the content of his responses to the latter indicating why.

General Findings

    Intelligence: On the WISC-R, Daniel obtained a Verbal IQ of
113 (81st percentile), a Performance IQ of 98 (45th percentile), and a
Full Scale IQ of 106 (66th percentile). Below are the scaled scores:

Information	10	Picture Completion	10
Similarities	14	Picture Arrangement	11
Arithmetic	9	Block Design	13
Vocabulary	17	Object Assembly	10
Comprehension	11	Coding	5
(Digit Span)	9	(Mazes)	11

    The results seem to be in general conformity with those
reported by the previous psychologist. There was the familiar triad
(lowered Arithmetic, Digit Span, and Coding) often fitting the diagnosis of learning disability because of a problem with sequential
organization, common to all three tasks. It should be noted, though,
that only the Coding score falls into the deficit range.
    Achievement: On the WRAT, Daniel obtained a Reading
Grade of 1.9 (21st percentile), a Spelling Grade of 1.6 (16th percen-

tile), and an Arithmetic Grade of 2.4 (47th percentile). The percentiles are for his age, not his current grade placement. Qualitatively reading is done very slowly and haltingly. On direct testing vowel phonics other than /a/ are not known, leaving Daniel totally unable to sound out a new word past the second letter. He then guesses, the only recourse open to him. Finger = "farger," weather = "water," work = "week," book = "bok," block = "book," etc. The digraphs th, sh, and ch are not known directly. Confusion of g and p and b and d were seen: deep = "beep."

Spelling shows the same problems. Other than four "sight" words no others were known, and aphonetic guesses were made: dress = "das," must = "mist," watch = "won."

In arithmetic single digit adding and subtracting are the limits of his learning so far.

Part Functions

Perception: On the Raven, a test of visual–perceptual development, Daniel scored at the 95th percentile ruling out a disorder in this area. Clinically and from the blending test, there is no evidence of auditory imperception. Somatosensory tests revealed no finger agnosia or difficulties with graphesthesia tests.

Motor: Fine finger speed and dexterity are excellent. Gross motor coordination is intact. Rapid alternating movements were done well and no synkinesia was noted. All tests for dyspraxia (eye, tongue, verbal, facial, and constructional) were negative.

Laterality: Left cerebral dominance is established for hand and foot. Left eye is dominant. The terms "left" and "right" were confused on self. Imagery is used accurately for making extracorporeal judgments. A left to right orientation is present for lexic and nonlexic material.

Time Orientation: Daniel constructs a clock fairly accurately for a 7-year-old but cannot tell time yet. The days are known as well as the concepts yesterday and tomorrow. However, he cannot figure out "day after tomorrow" nor "day before yesterday" given a hypothetical target date. The months have not been learned yet.

Memory: Short-term auditory–sequential memory (ITPA) is at age 6-3 and short-term visual–sequential memory (ITPA) is at 6-10.

Blending: Auditory blending skills are intact.

Language: There were no dysphasic phenomena noted throughout testing. The terms "before" and "after" are understood spatially and temporally. Automatic, responsive, and spontaneous speech are

intact. Numbers are read, written, and aligned accurately. Autotopagnosia tests were negative. The extent of Daniel's neuropsychological impairment was displayed in his total inability to count
backwards from 20. Witness the following interchange:

Daniel:	I can't 20, 19, I can't, I can't remember.
Dr. H.:	20, 19 . . .
Daniel:	I don't know.
Dr. H.:	What comes next—20, 19, 18
Daniel:	17, 16, 15, 14, 13, 20, twentyteen, thirty-teen, 19, 18, 17, 16, 15, 14, 14, I don't know what else. That's all I know.

He can count backwards from 10, which in these days is really a
"forward" series.

Diagnostically, the impression is of minimal cerebral dysfunction, probably left-temporal involvement. Affected are short-term
sequential memory independent of sense modality, sequential
organization, time disorientation, reading, and spelling. Remedial
work should definitely be considered since he is at risk and will be
going into second grade in a school of equally bright but academically superior peers. The effects on self-esteem of nonlearning in this
little fellow will be profound.

Personality

I will not dwell on the personality issues, since what emerged in
projective testing is repetitive of the material already known from
the analysis. However, I am quite concerned about the profound
depression this boy is capable of, a depression which has a life of its
own. This potential, in interaction with continuing lowered self-
esteem from school and elsewhere, as well as the evidence of peculiar thinking and breaks in reality testing render Daniel at great
psychological risk. Under anxiety conditions, Daniel's thinking is
regressive, unresponsive to reality check, and he can easily withdraw
into fantasy.

Continuing treatment is absolutely critical so that he can begin
to develop defenses against inordinate anxiety inundation. In the
meantime he requires a protective and supportive environment at
home and at school.

In addition to the obvious implications for self-esteem, peer
standing, and frustration in learning which Daniel's deficits

embodied, their contribution to his separation difficulties was important. The child who cannot comprehend sequences or orient himself will, in time, have difficulty grasping and feeling reassured by promises of mother's return and the routes by which this reunion is accomplished. This may also render the child more dependent upon mother and other adults for negotiating spatial and specifically academic instructions. These findings thus lent an additional dimension to the psychodynamic formulations previously proposed.

Case 3: Matthew, a Depressive Reaction to an Undiagnosed Learning Disorder of Neuropsychological Etiology

It will be recalled that Matthew's parents sought consultation with Dr. Trilling, a clinical psychologist who specialized in the diagnosis of neuropsychological dysfunction, to explore the reasons for their 5 1/2-year-old son's failure to progress academically and his behavior problems at school. Although teachers' reports precipitated the referral, Matthew's parents observed parallel difficulties at home; struggles over eating, dressing, bathing, and the like were a daily fare. He was considered a "blank wall" by both his teachers and parents in that he was a puzzling combination of boisterous hyperactivity—"leading others in the wrong direction"—and charm, with a capacity to calmly involve himself in work.

Exploration of Matthew's history revealed that there was never a period entirely free of stress. His birth, which was at full term, was uneventful with no complications. His birthweight was 7 pounds, 5 ounces. Matthew was the product of his mother's second pregnancy; the first terminated in a miscarriage. His mother had to remain in bed for five weeks at the beginning of her pregnancy with him. As an infant he was colicky with frequent diarrhea. Feeding was always difficult and remained a problem as he was finicky and preferred junk food. He was, probably due at least partly to the colic, a difficult baby to soothe and comfort; he cried frequently and for long periods. He did not sleep through the night until 1 1/2 years of age. General developmental milestones were all within normal limits.

When Matthew was 3 years old his brother was born amidst

much turmoil. Mother almost died of a life-threatening complication during the delivery and subsequently spent one month in
the hospital. She remained ill for 1 1/2 years after the delivery
until she had a hysterectomy when Matthew was 4 1/2 years old.
Matthew's mother reported not being very available to him in the
1 1/2 years that she was ill, especially after it was found that
Steven, Matthew's brother, had a heart murmur that would
require surgery. Steven was generally sickly and sluggish. The
parents said of this period of family life, "It was a traumatic time
for everyone." They reported little of specific note about Matthew except that he had to be careful when he dealt with his
brother. Steven's energy level was low, and as he clearly adored
Matthew, he typically struggled to keep up with him. Matthew
occasionally became exasperated and failed to modify his pace,
but was generally quite careful in attending to his brother's
needs.

This followed shortly upon Matthew's own surgery. When
he was 4 years old it was decided that a tonsillectomy and
adenoidectomy should be performed; he had been having too
frequent sore throats. Since at birth there had been some redden-
ing and swelling of his foreskin, circumcision was postponed.
Now, along with his tonsillectomy and adenoidectomy, it was
decided that Matthew should be circumcised. He was told about
the surgery beforehand but upon awakening in the recovery
room and seeing his penis "red with ugly stitches and a large scab
on it"—his mother's words—he wanted the scab off and had to
be restrained from pulling it off himself.

When Matthew was 5, his best friend moved to Florida,
after which his behavior "became impossible." He refused to go
to a day camp that he had attended the year before and became
withdrawn and angry. A sensitive pediatrician suggested that
Matthew might be responding to the move of his friend as if he
had died. Also of note was the fact that Matthew's father was
frequently absent at this time, traveling in his job for two to three
weeks at a time. His mother dated the emergence of Matthew's
truly erratic behavior to this period.

It seemed that Matthew had previously been capable of
control and modulation. Inquiry that typically elicits information
concomitant with a learning disability—questions about bicycle
riding, self-feeding, left–right differentiation, shoelace tying,

and the like—yielded nothing remarkable. Indeed Matthew had been able to do all these things with no particular difficulty either within normal limits or before the expected age.

Both Matthew's parents were very concerned about him, not only because they desired some quiet in the house but also because they were able to empathize with him. They knew he was in pain which they wanted very much to alleviate. Both parents were also intelligent, college educated, and well read. Education and academic achievement were clearly stated as important goals for Matthew. The evaluation was requested by them early in Matthew's life not only because his behavior was becoming more problematic but also because they wanted to insure a smooth entry into first grade. They wished him to start his academic career in the best possible manner. The father, while clearly very caring about his son, seemed to be somewhat of a task master. He had some difficulty reconciling what he knew to be Matthew's genuine unhappiness with his own tendency to feel Matthew should merely "buckle down and straighten out."

Both parents struggled against fully recognizing and accepting that Matthew had a problem because they had been burdened by so many other tangible stresses within only a few years (e.g., mother's and Steven's illnesses). A sense that they were fed up was conveyed from time to time, and both parents also appeared dispirited and overwhelmed. Matthew's physical prowess, cuteness, and apparent strong relatedness all served to mute and dilute the critical attitude they had toward him. Because of his mother's own athletic involvement—she had been a professional athlete and now taught younger athletes— Matthew's athleticism went a long way in engaging his parents. However, at the same time that his physical prowess was truly cherished, it was a source of confusion to his parents and something to which they kept returning, usually to make a point about how inconsistent he was. "He can do this, but can't or won't do that" was a frequent refrain. In contrast they talked about his athletic feats with awe and admiration.

Matthew was seen for evaluation, including psychological testing, at the age of 5 years, 10 months. He was tested during the first contact after a history was developed with his parents. Matthew found the work, which spanned four appointments, quite trying. In particular, he was not at all familiar with the process of being tested, and in general, never liked the idea of relinquishing control over what was happening to him. The testing was soon accomplished by means of an amicable truce. Matthew could do what was asked of him as long as he had plenty of opportunity to choose an activity in alternating intervals. Under these conditions he never overstepped this privilege, always attentive to the fact that he had a "job" to do. For example, his grave voice piped up in the midst of putting out the fire from a car accident, "It's all right, buddy. I'll come back soon's the fire is out!" Once in the interest of time some "force" was exerted and Matthew put up a remarkably stubborn resistance. It was clear that he was essentially unable to abdicate control. When he was in control and knew both the parameters of the situation and what was expected of him, he was most sensitive to the requirements demanded of him and to the need to fulfill them. He was then calm but still full of charm, humor, and wit.

The report of test findings was as follows.

Tests Administered

Wechsler Preschool and Primary Scale of Intelligence (WPPSI)
Illinois Test of Psycholinguistic Abilities: Auditory & Visual
    Sequential Memory; Sound Blending (Only)
Wide Range Achievement Test
Raven Progressive Matrices
Rorschach
Children's Apperception Test—Human figures
Purdue Pegboard
Motor Tests (Rapid Alternating Movements, Thumb Wiggling,
    Apraxias)
Laterality Tests
Figure Drawings & Most Horrible & Most Pleasant Concepts
Time Orientation
Beery-Buktenica Visual-Motor Integration Test

General Findings

Intelligence: On the WPPSI, Matthew received a Verbal IQ of 107 (68th percentile), a Performance IQ of 108 (70th percentile), and a Full Scale IQ of 109 (73rd percentile), all in the upper end of the average range of intellectual functioning. All subtest scores are shown below:

Information	10	Animal House	13
Vocabulary	13	Picture Completion	11
Arithmetic	13	Mazes	11
Similarities	7	Geometric Design	10
Comprehension	13	Block Design	11
Sentences	13		

Subtest scores are relatively consistent except for the lower score on Similarities. Matthew's responses to this subtest are quite concrete; he was unable to come up with a response to how two things are the same. It sometimes seemed as if he were refusing to really work at and think about the task.

Generally, thinking is clear and unaffected by any intrusion of personalized material. There is no apparent difficulty with perceptual motor tasks; graphomotor skills are adequate.

Achievement: On the WRAT, Matthew received a Reading Grade score of Kg9 (73rd percentile), a Spelling Grade score of 1.2 (91st percentile), and an Arithmetic Grade score of 1.2 (86th percentile).

Matthew matches letters adequately (makes discriminations) but makes some letter identification errors (H, P, Z were misidentified). He was able to read one sight word—"cat."

Spelling performance is characterized by adequate motor control to form letters and correct spelling of his first name. Last name was spelled with the second and third to last letters in reverse order.

Matthew's number concepts are adequate. He can count aloud and in reference to objects. Numbers up through 19 are identified correctly. Simple oral problems, both addition and subtraction, are done correctly. Matthew makes frequent reversals writing both numbers and letters.

Spatial aspects of academic performance (before and after, conceptually and perceptually) are understood and responded to correctly.

Part Functions

Perception: On the Raven, a test of visual–perceptual abilities, Matthew received a score between the 50th and 75th percentiles for 6 year olds. There was no clinical evidence of auditory imperception. Somatosensory testing revealed a mild finger agnosia on the right hand (number of fingers touched). Matthew was unable to respond to the number of fingers between tests for graphesthesia.

Motor: Thumb wiggling was done adequately and overflow was seen from the left hand to the right hand. Finger sequencing was done with difficulty and slight overflow was seen in both directions. Rapid alternating movements were done adequately. Tests of fine praxes revealed no difficulty except for trouble winking. Fine finger speed and dexterity were adequate. Graphomotor skills (Beery-Buktenica) were within normal limits.

Memory: Tests of auditory and visual–sequential memory (ITPA) were at the 8–8 and 6–10 year level, respectively, both clearly adequate.

Laterality: Matthew is right dominant for hand and foot and, on informal testing, left dominant for eye. Right–left awareness is accurate on himself but Matthew does not make the appropriate spatial correction for the other. Left-to-right orientation is not automatic.

Time Orientation: Matthew does not know the days of the week or months of the year and cannot tell time; this is all within normal limits.

Sound Blending: Matthew has slight difficulty with blending sounds; however, he is able to blend sounds into both familiar and nonsense words.

Language: There was no clinical evidence of language disorder.

In summary, the cognitive picture is of an almost 6-year-old boy of solidly average intelligence who is performing at age expectation in reading, spelling, and arithmetic skills. Cognitive tasks, while not approached with any particular relish, are done with no intrusion of personalized material as long as he is given some freedom in saying when and what he will do. Various "immaturities"—difficulty in letter recognition, reversals in writing letters and numbers—would seem to be simply immaturities, difficulties that will pass with further development. However, progress should, of course, be monitored.

Personality

Matthew is very concerned about maintaining himself intact in the face of what he perceives to be a threatening, dangerous world. He often feels quite frightened. His many concerns and fantasies about monsters are a real indication of a basic preoccupation with his safety. These fears are probably related to the surgery and circumcision in his fourth year. There is tremendous concern about the extensions of various things: people, objects, monsters, and so on. One monster—Godzilla—is drawn with a huge projecting phallus which Matthew says they do not usually show because it is so "gross and bloody." He says, however, that he saw it "once all bloody" but he is not sure whether others have seen it. This would seem to be the conscious part of a repressed memory of the aftermath of the circumcision. Much of Matthew's current concern and worry seems organized around his preoccupation with his ability to withstand assault and his fears that he will be damaged or has been damaged.

Matthew tends to see himself as a passive recipient of his experience—of what goes on around him, of what is done to him, and also of what he feels inside. Feelings are seen as washing over him with his having little ability to control or modulate them. The feelings themselves are not particularly distressing to him but he is bothered by the sense of passivity which they sometimes engender in him. This passivity is a pervasive difficulty and may be at the root of the trouble people have in getting him to cooperate. He is so attuned to these issues that he constantly feels the need to experience himself as being in control; he may appear negativistic when in fact he is simply trying to make certain that nothing terrible will happen to him.

These difficulties would seem to be in the neurotic range, with a major conflict about control and maintenance of phallic integrity requiring working through in intensive psychotherapy.

Therefore, it was anticipated that Matthew's learning would take hold with time, particularly as some of the turmoil of his inner life was alleviated. The multiple surgical procedures, separations, and threatened losses all through his oedipal period—his mother's difficult delivery and prolonged recuperation, his own surgery, followed by his brother's and then his mother's surgery— must have greatly exacerbated his castration anxiety and interfered with his sense of having an effective impact on his environment. Furthermore, both parents were sufficiently stressed during this period of time by fears of his mother's and younger brother's deaths, as well as by having to cope with the realities of their illnesses, that they were not able to be optimally available to Matthew as he weathered these traumata. Thus anxiety about loss of phallic intactness was repeatedly intertwined with threat of loss of the object. The move of his best friend concurrent with his father's increased absence when he was 5, to which he responded with withdrawal, recalcitrance, and refusal to separate, suggest that this event was experienced as one more frightening loss, not within his control. Moore (1975) has noted that surgical procedures inevitably disrupt the male child's (and his male sibling's) development until the ego is able to reestablish a psychic equilibrium. In Matthew's case the repetitive and prolonged nature of the traumata posed an especially difficult developmental challenge. It is not surprising that such a premium came to be placed on activity and control.

None of the positive neuropsychological findings were of particular note since they were equivocal at Matthew's age. Instead they were regarded as "immaturities" which needed to be monitored. However, given Matthew's great sensitivity to threats to bodily intactness and loss of control, even "immaturities" might be expected to provoke intense anxiety. He would not be able to grasp such a time perspective: that something which is currently a weakness will find later compensation.

Given these conclusions, it was felt that Matthew should be seen in psychotherapy. Although Matthew's parents were generally receptive to the results reported by Dr. Trilling and to his recommendations, they tended to disbelieve his clinical impression that Matthew did not have a learning disability. In part, the idea of a learning disability served an important defensive function for Matthew's parents who, racked with guilt, would find solace in ascribing Matthew's problems to "physical" factors. This seemed particularly true of his father whose "task master" approach was reflected in his adopting an attitude during the feedback session and subsequent parent consultation of, "Well, now that *we* know what the problem is, what are *we* going to do to solve it?" While in one sense the "we" indicated the strength of the therapeutic alliance he felt, its demanding, defiant tone also implied his skepticism that his son would be helped and his own difficulty in tolerating not being in control. Mostly, however, Matthew's parents were relieved that nothing was seriously wrong with their son. They seemed willing and able to try anything, feeling that they and Matthew desperately needed relief.

With the beginning of treatment shortly after the consultation the battlefield atmosphere at home diminished and the complaints and concerns from school were somewhat tempered. Matthew's parents seemed to feel that something was going to be done, that they and Matthew had been understood, and that there was hope.

PITFALLS OF A PARTIAL EVALUATION

The value and necessity of the comprehensive evaluation delineated in chapter 4 is not universally appreciated. Instead, where the learning disordered child happens to present will all too often determine the diagnostic conclusions reached and the treatment recommendations made. For example, if one arrives at the office of a private practitioner in psychotherapy or a conventional psychiatric clinic where a strictly psychoanalytically derived perspective prevails, a psychodynamic etiology will often be the conclusion. The same child, having been seen by a neurologist or educational specialist, might be referred for quite different procedures, eventuating in conflicting diagnostic formulations.

In this section several cases will be presented to illustrate the oversights, imprecision, or erroneous conclusions which may ensue when subtle biases in favor of one or another perspective on learning problems in particular, and psychopathology in general, exist in the minds of highly competent clinicians. These biases will be expressed in the nature and comprehensiveness of their evaluations and/or their approach to interpretation of the data derived.

Cases presented in several of the psychoanalytic contributions reviewed in chapter 3 are viewed in greater detail for clarification of more and less subtle omissions in diagnostic assessment. The evaluative processes in four other cases presented here for the first time illustrate additional potential problems at this phase of clinical work. Each of the latter patients was seen by at least two (and in one case five) well-known psychologists whose conclusions were to a lesser or greater degree conflicting. Attempting to resolve such confusion and contradictions is a common clinical experience for the child psychiatrist or other mental health professional working with learning disordered children. A secondary purpose is to demonstrate that many of these apparently conflicting conclusions could be reconciled if one kept in mind the varied scope and depth of the examinations from which they derive.

The case of Joseph (case 4) illustrates the oversights which may result when a neuropsychological assessment is not incorporated in the evaluation of a child presenting with school problems. In addition it exemplifies the fallacy of ruling out neuropsychological dysfunction on the basis of an average IQ score and, finally, the intimate intertwining of psychodynamic and ego psychological with neuropsychological factors.

The case of Rachel (case 5) exemplifies the unnecessarily vague state in which findings may remain in the absence of a complete educational and neuropsychological evaluation. Despite the elegant psychodynamic formulations made when Rachel was 9, the partial cognitive assessment performed without the perspective of a task analytic approach to interpretation afforded only the nonspecific conclusion that "obscure perceptual problems" existed. Another assessment two years later resulted in a far richer and more finely delineated description of these problems which facilitated effective clinical planning.

The case of Sara (case 6) portrays the massive confusion which may result when comprehensive evaluations are not performed and when data are viewed from the perspective of clinical bias. In the five test evaluations which span the ninth to sixteenth years of her life, Sara was variously diagnosed as learning disabled with reactive depression and anxiety, prepsychotic without significant neuropsychological contribution, psychotic with coexisting neuropsychological dysfunction, and learning disabled with an integrative language disorder and character problems but no disturbance in reality testing. These evaluations were performed by psychologists, all of whom are prominent in their various subspecialties and who vary in their orientations from psychoanalytic to exclusively neuropsychological.

The case of Eloise (case 7) illustrates the distortions which may the patient's personality. A girl of average intelligence in a highly successful and well-endowed family was diagnosed as having a learning disability in her latency years. A more comprehensive assessment years later revealed this to be a more acceptable, but erroneous impression of the girl's failure to live up to her family's expectations.

Cases in the Psychoanalytic Literature

Plank and Plank's (1954) formulation of the arithmetic disability of John Trumbull, the American Revolutionary painter, is a most blatant example of the pitfalls of a purely psychodynamic approach when it involves "stretching" or discounting conflicting data. In line with their general thesis that arithmetic disorders reflect an inability to relinquish a desire for oral–maternal gratification, the following data are presented:

In infancy Trumbull suffered from convulsions, which were supposedly caused by a too early closure of the fontanellae. Hope was given up until a famous physician advised his mother that only she could save the boy from idiocy or death—by massaging his head to reopen the fontanellae. This she did faithfully through his third year. One may conjecture that the difficulty of assuming an active role after so long playing a passive one brought about his blocking in arithmetic [p. 285].

While it was, of course, impossible to assess the intactness of Trumbull's equipment, such a conclusion seems rash, particularly when the few data available (e.g., the existence of seizures) strongly suggest neuropsychological involvement.

In a paper written a few years later about psychogenic reading disorders in children presenting at a college educational clinic (Jarvis, 1958), a more comprehensive evaluation could certainly have been accomplished. This study illustrates the very common assumption that academic disorder in a child of normal or superior intelligence is necessarily of psychodynamic etiology: "It is this visual problem (one with unconscious rather than organic meaning) in the retarded reader of average or better-than-average intelligence and its ramifications as we pursue its relation to the oedipal conflict, the problems of aggression and identification, to the fantasy of the preoedipal mother, to scoptophilia and exhibitionism, and to the defense mechanisms it evokes that will be the subject of this paper" (p. 452). In support of this notion Jarvis presents briefly the case of A., a 12-year-old boy of above-average intelligence who had difficulties reading double or "twin" letters. An array of psychodynamic explanations is posited, the major one involving conflict over scoptophilic impulses, particularly related to fears of punitive masculine women. The double letters are symbolically related to eyes. However, since it is reported in passing that A.'s father was a poor reader, the author most certainly should have ruled out the possibility of a genetically determined dyslexia. A normal IQ level does not adequately serve this purpose.

Even in the 1970s, in a period of diagnostic sophistication, and among psychoanalysts who are alert to the possibility of neuropsychological factors, studies appear which do not reflect this alertness. Berger and Kennedy (1975) propose to describe a subgroup of learning disordered children who suffer from psychodynamic conflicts. However, one of their case reports, that of a 10-year-old boy, Clement, raises ample data at least suggestive of the need for neuropsychological inquiry. Despite investment in his work, Clement's scholastic results were poor. Indeed, Berger and Kennedy noted initially: "The diagnostic assessment raised the question whether he was organically damaged. In spite of his good intellectual potential, indicated by the result of the intelligence test, Clement presented a picture of slow and delayed development from earliest childhood" (pp. 299–300). However, ultimately his learning problems are attributed to his "devalued self-image and his inability to compete with his brother," concentration difficulties associated with sexual impulses, masturbation, and sadomasochistic fantasies.

Despite very interesting psychoanalytic data, neuropsychological dysfunction is not sufficiently ruled out. At the same time, other data remain unaccounted for. The above quote again conveys an assumption that a high IQ is inconsistent with neuropsychological disorder. Clement's IQ scores, however, are highly suggestive of such disorder in that his Verbal IQ was 131 and Performance IQ, 91. Such a remarkable 40-point disparity deserves clarification and is frequently found in children with such difficulties. Paralleling this disparity is the fact that Clement's motor milestones were delayed— he walked when 2, his speech was delayed, slurred, and always difficult to understand, and bowel and bladder training were slow—and his birth was premature and marked by preeclamptic toxemia. In the absence of a more detailed profile of functioning, Clement cannot legitimately be classified among those children Berger and Kennedy seek to describe: those with intact equipment whose disturbances are attributable *only* to secondary interference of internal conflict or environmental response.

Writing 11 years later, Vereecken (1965), a psychologist, does evaluate the acalculia of his 6 1/2-year-old patient with psychological testing. Nevertheless, there is insufficient confirmation of his ultimate psychoanalytic formulation. Eddy's disorder is viewed as a "massive and generalized inhibition of ego functions" (p. 542) rather than as a symptom precipitated by specific psychosexual conflicts. As described, it is actually far more pervasive than acalculia, including "rigidity" in verbal and spatial concept formation and "constriction" in broader scanning of stimuli in order to form concepts and perform operations. The underlying dynamic is hypothesized to be a sense that all movement is dangerous because of its

multiple associations: with fears of masturbation and sexual excitement, intense orally elaborated castration anxiety, and primal scene
fantasies having implications for blocking of curiosity and comprehension and a wish to keep things the same through immobility in a
child with poorly structured ego defenses.

While Vereecken may be correct, further assessment would
make his presentation more convincing. Eddy obtained an overall
IQ of 94. Although the IQ test used does not lend itself to analysis of
separate Verbal and Performance IQ scores or to individual subtest
scores—as does the WISC-R more commonly used in the United
States—several pertinent details are added. Eddy passed all tests at
the 6-year level, solved analogies at the 7-year level, and failed
repetition of sentences at the 4- and 5-year level. Vereecken attributes this to resistance, but it could also reflect immediate auditory
memory problems often associated with dyscalculia. He evidenced
some delay on tests of constructive–praxic activities and marked
lack of motor initiative, coordination, and spontaneity on the Oseretsky Test. This is attributed to inhibition but could also reflect true
motor and visual–motor coordination difficulties. Rorschach percepts were perseverative and global. Results in reading and writing
are said to be normal, although since the tests given are not cited it is
unclear which aspects of these complex processes were examined.
Eddy's arithmetic difficulties are carefully detailed to illustrate
Vereecken's assumption of a functional disorder.

However, other explanations are equally plausible. Eddy was
unable to quickly identify the number of dots on a die (having
instead to count them), to count orally without seeing objects, to
count backwards or to calculate oral, in contrast to written arithmetic problems. Vereecken feels these deficits all reflect a lack of
mobility and flexibility. However, in the absence of specific tests of
immediate auditory and visual memory and visualization—the ability to call up a visual image, implicit in which is a capacity to
analyze and synthesize part–whole relationships—this explanation
is premature. For example, the capacity to recite number series
backwards generally involves intact sequential organization of a
number line which is then recited backwards. Calculation of oral
arithmetic problems, unlike written ones, involves auditory memory and sometimes visual representation of the problem. It will be
remembered that Eddy's earliest failure on his IQ test was on a task
of auditory memory: repeating sentences. Such dysfunction could

account for the patterning of Eddy's skills as well as the psychodynamic hypothesis; or, both could be contributory factors.

Similar problems characterize Newman et al.'s (1973) study of 15 "underachievers"—boys with IQs 130 and above and grades of C and below—performed in an age of diagnostic sophistication. Uneven development was also manifested in a strong command of language accompanied by poor conceptualization, attention, and motor functions. As noted in chapter 3, this was attributed to the mother's excessive valuation of verbal production without concomitant encouragement of motor activity which signals the child's ability to separate. The early imbalance was hypothesized to interfere with the normal intertwining of such functions necessary to the formation of sensorimotor schemata, lending a shallowness to later language and other higher cortical functions.

In detailing the contrasts between hypertrophied verbal capacities and impaired motor functioning, Newman et al. note their patients' sloppiness, restlessness, sluggishness, and poor handwriting which they do not regard as evidence of motor incoordination: "on their psychological tests they did not show even slight signs of any actual motor incoordination, and their total test performance was in no way suggestive of the presence of minimal brain damage" (p. 92). However, just preceding this statement is another: "Their scores on the coding subtest of the WISC, the only subtest that requires use of pencil, were the only scores that were almost uniformly low" (p. 92). These two assertions are contradictory: if visual–motor coordination problems are present, this is precisely where they are likely to be in evidence. A footnote to the first quotation cited is intended to further discount the possibility of neuropsychological dysfunction by equating an average IQ with intact ego equipment: "While their Performance IQ's were typically somewhat lower than their Verbal IQ's they were nevertheless well above average, in the superior range" (p. 92). Since the WISC is the only tool used to assess cognitive functioning and since there is a single finding suggestive of dysfunction, it is not possible to rule out a neuropsychological contribution to the constellation described.

Case 4: Joseph

Joseph, an 11 1/2-year-old boy hospitalized for psychiatric evaluation, had been known to a series of mental health facilities since he was 7 years old. Joseph's care was given over to his paternal grandparents at infancy by mutual consent of both parents. His mother had a history of drug addiction, imprisonment, and psychiatric hospitalization. His father was reportedly an eminent Juilliard-trained jazz singer who became a heroin addict and eventually overdosed when Joseph was 5. The plaques, record album covers, and other mementoes which were liberally displayed throughout the family apartment commemorated the purported fame of this man and resurrected his presence. At the same time, the circumstances of his death, his reason for giving Joseph to his own parents, and his relationship to Joseph's mother were all shrouded in mystery for Joseph.

The paternal grandfather was overseas during the first two years of his own son's life and felt responsible for what he called the "lifelong void" between himself and his son, and eventually for his son's death. It also emerged that in their younger years the paternal grandparents loved to party. Therefore, they had delegated the care of their own son and daughter to neighbors and relatives. In fantasy Joseph offered them the opportunity of making good for past neglect of their children and for the tragedy of their son's death. Stringent rules were designed to make sure that Joseph never be hurt or indeed leave their sight. Thus his social relationships were stunted. Contact with his mother was prohibited as well, despite the fact that she lived nearby and was known to have had several children by another man.

At the time of initial psychiatric consultation at 7, Joseph's school insisted that he be evaluated. He did not follow instructions, had a poor attention span, and was disruptive; he did not fight but distracted the other children from paying attention. Despite their having found Joseph to be oppositional and to have had a major sleep disturbance for years, it was not until the school demanded consultation that Joseph's grandparents followed through. The consulting psychiatrist did not consider Joseph to be hyperactive and, therefore, concluded that there could not be a neuropsychological basis to his school problems. He was referred neither for psychological nor neurological evaluation. Joseph's reports of seeing shadows and monsters at bedtime were interpreted as hallucinations, resulting in a trial on chlorpromazine and a referral for long-term psychotherapy which commenced about a year later.

During the three years of psychotherapy prior to hospitalization, Joseph's psychiatrist gradually increased his level of chlorpromazine to 250 mg and ultimately diagnosed Joseph as schizophrenic on the basis of intermittent experiences of voices at bedtime. In school he was considered very immature and functioned at a kindergarten level in all subjects besides reading. His teachers still complained that he did not pay attention and demanded constant individual care. Psychological testing at this time revealed Joseph to have a Full Scale IQ of 92, a Verbal IQ of 95, and a Performance IQ of 95, all in the Average range as measured by the WISC. He was not thought to have any neuropsychological difficulties. However, a deficit in arithmetic skills and abstraction was noted. Digit Span was not administered, thereby contributing to the failure to discern immediate auditory memory problems which later emerged. Learning and other problems were attributed to his anger and confusion over his father's death, the nature of his living arrangements as opposed to those of his half-siblings, and the strictness of his grandfather. Joseph was noted to feel like a sad, abandoned child.

Six months prior to Joseph's psychiatric hospitalization, his diabetic grandfather became blind, which had multiple repercussions for the family and resulted in an exacerbation of Joseph's behavior problems. Grandfather then retired and spent all his time at home. Joseph's mobility was even further curtailed since grandfather had been responsible for transporting him and grandmother did not drive. Previous monthly visits to the grave of his father were terminated for the same reason. Joseph now experienced mood swings and temper tantrums in which he threw chairs and broke valuable objects.

Joseph's grandfather ultimately contacted his biological mother "out of desperation" for the first time in three years and, as a result, Joseph spent his first weekend with her since infancy. This no doubt stirred up his longings for reunion. As contrasted with the very restrictive nature of his grandparents' home, Joseph was thrilled when his mother and her children engaged in stealing. Not surprisingly, mother's availability to Joseph was not sustained. While she promised to invite him again, she relocated and never did so. Joseph's behavior soon worsened. At home his outbursts included kicking his grandfather's legs. He refused to attend school after being told he could not participate in a school musicale because he was unable to follow the conductor or to keep the rhythm; hospitalization ensued.

The impression on admission corresponded to that held throughout his course of psychotherapy. Joseph's condition was believed to be the result of exclusively psychodynamic factors. He was born into a family in which intense demands were placed upon him. He was to be the perfect son his grandparents never had and to offer them an opportunity to be the perfect parents they had never been, thereby repairing the injury of and guilt over their biological son's death. Joseph was not to leave them. They had intense symbiotic needs of him and expressed the feeling they could not survive without him; at the same time he was felt to be unable to function without them. Being angry at his grandparents or wanting to pursue developmentally appropriate relationships with other than parental objects were experienced as desertions and thus not tolerated. Also felt as abandonment was curiosity about family secrets, foremost among them his father and mother's reasons for giving him away and the nature of his father's death. Such a psychodynamic constellation closely parallels that of the learning disordered patients described by Mahler (1942), Hellman (1954), and Buxbaum (1964), among others reviewed in chapter 3.

Joseph's neurological examination and electroencephalogram (EEG) were negative. Nevertheless, there were aspects of the history which argued for a neuropsychological component to his difficulties: his mother and father's drug addiction at the time of his conception and the absence of prenatal care. Prior to formal testing, observations reported at interdisciplinary meetings began to suggest the possibility of immediate auditory and visual memory problems. Nurses commented, for example, that Joseph had difficulty remembering the score in a Ping-Pong game or new rules of a card game. If his teacher wrote an arithmetic problem on the board and he copied it down, he usually had little difficulty with its solution. However, when orally delivered, Joseph often computed with the wrong figures. He frequently boasted of competence at games which he was later observed to be unable to play in diagnostic interviews. His intense sensitivity to humiliation was repeatedly noted. Saying "I don't know" did not seem to be a viable possibility for him.

A full battery of psychological tests dramatically bore out

clinical suggestions of neuropsychological disorder, particularly
with regard to temporal lobe functions. Joseph emerged as a boy
of average intelligence with marked variability in different
aspects of functioning. He evidenced strengths on tasks which
primarily tapped rote learning and social judgment and relied
minimally upon reasoning and immediate memory. In contrast
he had particular difficulty in forming verbal abstractions (e.g.,
how two things are alike), and conceptualizing part–whole relationships to replicate abstract block designs, although he had no
difficulty assembling representational puzzles. His immediate
visual memory was in the defective range. When asked to immediately reproduce designs which had been exposed to him for 10
seconds, Joseph commented, "I have to do it fast or it goes
away," and was noted to trace figures in the air with his finger to
aid him in remembering. In contrast, when asked to draw the
designs with the stimulus in front of him, productions were age
adequate.

Joseph's memory and conceptual problems had clear
effects upon his school-related learning. On the WRAT, he
scored at the 88th percentile in Reading, the 58th percentile in
Spelling, and only the 4th percentile in Arithmetic. He similarly
achieved a deficit score on the oral arithmetic portion of the
WISC-R. This variability in functioning reflected the greater
memory requirements of spelling and oral arithmetic and the
greater conceptual requirements of arithmetic. While Joseph
was able to recognize familiar words or letters and blend their
sounds together to read, spelling and arithmetic, particularly oral
arithmetic, items required that he call up or remember visual and
auditory stimuli. Once remembered, he had to work with the
figures, performing operations upon them which required conceptual skills. For example, when Joseph was asked the question,
"One and a half hours equals how many minutes?" he knew the
rote facts that 1 hour was 60 minutes and half an hour, 30 minutes,
but he did not know which operation to perform, and answered
"630." He similarly did not fully grasp concepts of division and
multiplication. Even simple arithmetic facts, when asked orally,
were answered incorrectly, since Joseph forgot the numbers
involved.

These data also shed some light upon the episode which
resulted in Joseph's not returning to school. The conceptual and

memory demands of keeping the beat in an orchestra are considerable. While failure in musical performance was undoubtedly laden with meaning—eliciting, for example, Joseph's oedipal competitive strivings with a rival, his father, who died at the height of Joseph's oedipal stage and his conflicted identification with his father—in the absence of an adequate evaluation it would have been possible to erroneously entertain an exclusively psychodynamic formulation. In fact temporal lobe dysfunction was clearly contributory; keeping beat is specifically a function localized in that portion of the brain (Myklebust, 1968, p. 12). Joseph's tendency to disturb the concentration of other students was also viewed, in part, as an attempt to equalize his memory disorder.

Testing did not markedly enrich the psychodynamic understanding gained through clinical evaluation. However, it did cast doubt upon the diagnostic conclusions previously reached. Joseph's perceptions were found to be entirely conventional and his reality testing intact. He did evidence perseveration and concreteness, which were probably related to his neuropsychological deficits. On the basis of this evaluation Joseph was diagnosed as a personality disorder with a learning disability involving immediate auditory and visual memory and conceptualization. It was strongly recommended that he receive more intensive psychotherapy in conjunction with work with his family to help explore family secrets and to make known and facilitate integration of his limitations. In addition he was referred for remediation to construct alternative pathways to learning which circumvented deficient temporal lobe functions.

It is clear that many features of Joseph's life contributed to his emerging personality disorder in general, and his self-esteem problems in particular: his having had an addict mother and an idealized addict father, being abandoned by them to grandparents who narcissistically invested in him as a perfect reparative object who was not to separate, a situation most recently exacerbated by his grandfather's blindness. His previously undiagnosed learning disability added to his sense of defect—additionally based upon identifications with defective adults and the experience of abandonment by important adults—especially because they were not recognized as such by himself or important others. Redefining aspects of his difficulties as neuropsychologically determined and capable of remediation, rather than evidence of his laziness and oppositionalism, offered the possibility of rebuilding an important aspect of his self-image. This could be accomplished both in mastery of previously impossible tasks and in continuing psychotherapeutic work.

Case 5: Rachel

At age 9 years, 7 months Rachel, the youngest of three girls born to professional parents, was referred for clinical evaluation at the school's suggestion. Unlike her two older sisters who were highly successful students, Rachel had chronic academic difficulties from which she "suffered miserably." She was viewed as a bright child who did not appreciate or live up to her capacities. Her parents shared the school's concern, noting Rachel's tendency to feel she could not do the work expected of her, especially when it involved acquisition of new skills. Furthermore, she frequently failed to take in what she read.

Because dramatic events in Rachel's life were viewed as adequate explanations of her poor academic progress it was not until fourth grade that a consultation was considered. Rachel's earliest years, beginning with the perinatal period, were stressed by her mother's episodic absence during brief psychiatric hospitalizations. More recently, but prior to the cessation of this series of maternal hospitalizations, Rachel's parents were divorced after many years of marital discord and relative absence of father, who frequently pursued an artistic avocation until the wee hours of the morning after a full day of professional work.

Having attempted to help Rachel, and having waited unsuccessfully for her to adjust to this renewed stress, her parents decided that a careful evaluation was in order. Her teachers' expectation was that psychotherapy would be recommended. Rachel was then referred to a respected clinical psychologist who interviewed the child and her parents and administered a standard battery of psychological tests—the WISC-R, Bender-Gestalt, Rorschach, Michigan Pictures Test, Sentence Completion Test, and Figure Drawings—which did not include educational or neuropsychological measures. Therefore, the type of evaluation performed was likely to bear out the school's suspicion of emotional interferences with learning, in that it would be less than optimally sensitive to the possibility of neuropsychological factors.

In the course of developing a history, there was considerable conflict in many aspects of the perspectives Rachel's parents held on the nature and etiology of their daughter's difficulties. However, they concurred in the general view that psychological factors were primarily responsible. There was an implicit tone of indictment and defense in their representations of and theories about Rachel. Father tended to emphasize her pathology, both associating her with his ex-wife and regarding her as damaged by her mother's illness. Mother stressed Rachel's assets: her creativity and sensitivity. When father noted Rachel's destructiveness of objects, mother viewed this as a manifestation of her curiosity. Rachel was in many ways mother's favorite and father's least preferred child. These differences of opinion also derived from the fact that Rachel tended to behave more immaturely when with father and more responsibly when with mother. Beneath both mother's defensive stance vis-à-vis father's criticisms of Rachel and her true appreciation of her daughter, mother harbored a deep sense of guilt that her own illness had irreparably harmed Rachel. Her favoritism was in part a function of her belief that Rachel was highly vulnerable and deserved special attention.

Apart from the familial atmosphere and events described, Rachel's early history was generally unremarkable. All milestones were achieved before or within normal limits. The only exception was her excessive passivity in the first year of life which led father to question the existence of a hearing impairment. However, this was ruled out. A renewed concern about hearing difficulty arose when Rachel was 5 as she complained of not hearing things. Once again an audiological examination proved negative.

The evaluating psychologist diagnosed Rachel as a neurotic child with "some developmental difficulties which may be related to some obscure perceptual problem. . . . She is very caught in a neurotic bind about being considered fragile and yet getting many secondary gains from this role." The psychologist's report continued:

The sense one gets from a great deal of the material is of a child who feels herself to be very bad. She has quite a highly developed superego and in many ways feels compelled to violate its standards. This may be related to some extent to the fact that her father, whose approval she so desperately wants to win, is quite a disciplinarian and certainly has standards much harder to meet than those of the mother. (Whether consciously or unconsciously, [her father] seems to be trying very hard to train and discipline Rachel so that she will not be the kind of disorganized slob whom he sees his ex-wife as epitomizing.) Badness on Rachel's part may be a further conviction, as noted above, in that she equates badness and stupidity and certainly feels the latter all too keenly. Her sense of having had a role in causing her mother's mental illness, while not directly expressed in the tests, was certainly hinted at and may play quite a large aspect in the chronic sense of guilt. What one also gets is a tremendous doubt of what one can count on or know and a lack of trust of one's own perceptions of other people's feelings or one's own.

The ambivalence that Rachel has toward herself is also paralleled by a highly ambivalent or polarized view of adults. She vacillates between seeing adults as far too grown up and harsh judges of the misbehavior of the child, harsh, but so righteous and impeccable themselves that the child will have little chance to rebel or object. And then she will see the adults as not any more mature than the child himself and an accomplice to the child's crime. It is most probable, one would judge from the history as well as my contacts with the parents, that in many ways Rachel, along with her older sisters, has had to be the parent to her mother and may both resent the premature responsibilities this has entailed and yet be very tender and protective of her mother. But at the same time, there is bewilderment about how the same child–mother is in some ways perfectly adult. A more complex state of affairs seems to exist in regard to her father, for she may be in awe of his righteousness and compulsiveness and high demands made upon her and yet also senses what she cannot really pinpoint, his own degree of impulsivity and infantilization, and not know what to make of the inconsistencies.

Within the body of the report there was some further commentary on aspects of cognitive functioning which probably contributed to the final conclusion of an "obscure perceptual problem" but yet did not truly lead to clarification of what was meant by this statement. Rachel was noted to have difficulties in left–right orientation, as seen in reproduction of Bender-Gestalt figures, and in spelling. The latter was referred to as a "language handicap." Aside from these difficulties, Rachel was regarded as a girl of potentially superior intelligence whose variability "in the way she uses her skills"—her scores spanned the Average to Very Superior ranges—was primarily attributed to inhibition and self-esteem problems. She was said to have "more ability than she gives herself credit for."

Thus a dual recommendation was made: tutoring for her "special language handicap" (spelling) and psychotherapy to enhance her poor self-image. It was suggested to the school that: "a greater push for mastery of the written word will be of real use for bolstering her sense of confidence. Besides the special tutorial work to aid in spelling, it might be of value if this child learned typing in the near future so she could better examine and proof-read what she writes." Of the two recommendations—psychotherapy and tutoring—the former was considered more essential.

Without delay, Rachel's parents arranged for individual psychotherapy. Their expectation that their daughter's learning difficulties were of psychogenic origin was essentially confirmed. While the contribution of perceptual difficulties was alluded to, its nature and ramifications were vaguely stated and an appropriate intervention on their behalf remained nonspecific. This left Rachel's parents sufficiently confused in their expectations, and unconsciously gratified that their theories about the nature of her learning disorder were correct, as to eventuate in inaction on their part.

Rachel was only minimally cooperative in individual psychotherapy, ultimately leading her therapist to suggest a family approach. However, intense resistance to this experience arose on the part of various family members at various times. Psychotherapy was discontinued one and a half years later, after much Sturm und Drang and a deterioration in Rachel's clinical picture—including a sleep disturbance and nightmares especially when she was at father's home, screaming and crying fits, poor peer relations, petty stealing at home in the service of bribing friends to like her, and no academic improvement. Several events had taken place which might well have contributed to this decline. Joint custody was established, including revised visitation arrangements such that Rachel spent alternate weeks with her mother and father, with a corresponding inconsistency in what was demanded of her. Furthermore, father had remarried quite suddenly, to which mother had a depressive response. At the same time mother was more consistently stable and had not required further hospitalization.

In her own treatment mother complained that Rachel had become increasingly uncommunicative. After reviewing the previous evaluation report, mother's therapist suggested a reevaluation of Rachel by a clinical psychologist with expertise in neuropsychological dysfunction. At this time Rachel was 11 years, 11 months and about to begin the seventh grade.

An extensive clinical assessment was performed including the following tests.

Tests Administered

Wechsler Intelligence Scale for Children—Revised (WISC-R)
Token Test
Raven Progressive (Coloured) Matrices
Visual Memory Test
Spatial Orientation Memory Test
Benton Visual Retention Test
Bender-Gestalt Visual-Motor Integration Test
Illinois Test of Psycholinguistic Abilities: Auditory & Visual
    Sequential Memory; Sound Blending
Auditory Discrimination Test
Sentence Repetition Test
Auditory Memory Span Test
Fine Motor Exercises
Test of Finger Agnosia
Test of Physical Dexterity (System of Multicultural Pluralistic
    Assessment)
Right-Left Screening Tasks,
Delayed Memory Tasks
Wide Range Achievement Test (WRAT)
Woodcock Reading Mastery Tests
House-Tree-Person
Rorschach
Thematic Apperception Test (TAT)

General Findings

A 12-year-old, early adolescent girl with overall high average intellectual skills with neuropsychological impairment, primarily involving left hemisphere verbal-auditory and spatial-sequential skills, contributing to a short-term (intermediate) memory deficit and a disturbance of the tonal quality of both attention and mood control. As a consequence, Rachel's academic skills, especially those involving more than one set of information (e.g., reading comprehension or computational arithmetic) fall below grade and intellectual expectation. However, less complex academic skills (as in word recognition or word attack tasks) fall at or above grade expectation. Associated with the attentional problem is Rachel's tendency to become physically lethargic when pushed beyond her capacity to assimilate material. Emotionally, her early experience of loss has become associated to even minor deprivations and has led to a tendency toward unpredictable outbursts. Her tendency to experience herself and her world in extremes seems related to her mood disturbance and seems to delay or dilute her awareness of her emotional sensations until they are reinforced by behavioral feedback.

Recommendations for Rachel are as follows:

1. Modification of classroom demands in line with suggestions previously described.

2. Psychoremedial therapy in an attempt to ameliorate the short-term memory problem, while simultaneously helping Rachel to sense, anticipate, and ultimately master her explosive tendencies.

3. A neurological consultation to explore more specifically the nature and possible psychopharmacological controls of her attentional/mood disturbance.

4. As needed, parental counseling to provide the ongoing supports within a structure that Rachel will need.

Although the results of this evaluation challenged their original beliefs and the complicated investments they had in them, Rachel's parents responded with relief and a sense of hope that something could be done to specifically address the long-standing problems in learning. While the dynamic formulations of the initial evaluation were all reasonable and were indeed born out in the second evaluation, the either/or thinking fostered contributed to somewhat misdirected treatment efforts. Some prominent examples are the conclusions that psychotherapy was more important than tutoring, the imprecise and even incorrect delineation of the nature of Rachel's neuropsychological dysfunction in the absence of the task analytic approach (i.e., there was no perceptual problem but rather a sequential and memory disorder) and, finally, a less than full appreciation of the scope and limitations of tutoring, which will be a subject of chapter 7.

Case 6: Sara

Sara, the first of two adoptive children of professional parents, was observed by her third-grade teachers to have difficulty in acquisition of reading and arithmetic skills. When this impression was shared with her parents at the end of third grade, at which time Sara was nearly 9, they arranged to have her tested by a psychologist known to be a specialist in neuropsychology. Sara's parents had themselves noticed some trouble with semantic naming and sequential, but not articulatory, aspects of expressive language as well as in comprehension of sequential temporal concepts (e.g., before and after). However, since some improvement had been shown they did not seek consultation until school staff brought additional problems in learning to their attention. Nothing else of a remarkable nature was reported to the evaluating psychologist. Whether or not this reflected the range and scope of questions posed to Sara's parents, or their tendency to selective reporting, is unclear. In contrast, some years later, in the context of another evaluation—this time by a dynamically oriented psychiatrist—several somewhat alarming observations of this period were revealed.

In this first of many psychological and psychiatric evaluations, a fairly extensive battery of tests was administered. Since it included an IQ and achievement test, tests of neuropsychological function and standard projective tests, it would not in and of itself be suggestive of bias. The diagnostic impression was of a "specific difficulty in retrieval of names of common objects and verbal organization of temporal–spatial events" with reactive feelings of low self-esteem and anxiety.

The summary of findings was as follows:

Sara, 8–8 years old, was referred by her parents for evaluation of difficulty in acquisition of reading and arithmetic skill. She is of average intelligence obtaining a WISC Verbal IQ of 99, Performance IQ of 107, and Full Scale IQ of 103. Sara was found to have specific difficulty in retrieval of names of common objects and verbal organization of temporal–spatial events.

All receptive modalities, short-term retention, and executive motor processes are at age-appropriate levels of development.

On the Wide Range Achievement Test Sara obtained a Reading grade of 3.3 (standard score of 97), Spelling grade of 2.2 (standard score of 35), and Arithmetic grade of 2.4 (standard score of 87). She has amassed an extensive "look-say" vocabulary but does not utilize a phonetic attack. Unfamiliar words are therefore poorly analyzed, reflected in reading errors which demonstrate relative disregard of consonant–vowel configurations and guesses based on the perceptual similarity of the grapheme to words already within her repertoire. Similarly, spelling errors tend to contain several of the correct letters; however, the product does not necessarily phonetically approximate the given word.

Sara's verbal difficulty has hampered her ability to utilize over-learned arithmetic relationships and grasp the temporal–spatial sequences necessary to perform the more complex calculations involving "carrying over."

Projective material and interview indicate that ego-strength, reality testing, and level of psychosocial development are excellent. Sara manifests moderate anxiety and depression reactive to her failure experiences in school. In order to protect self-esteem and minimize anxiety Sara tends to avoid specific situations threatening a high probability of failure. However, she has not generalized to avoidance of or pervasive negative reaction to school, teachers, and learning.

Therefore, remediation was recommended with a focus upon spatial and temporal sequential features of arithmetic and a phonetic approach to spelling and reading. The prognosis for improvement in these academic acquisitions was expected to be good given Sara's multiple intact areas of functioning and her perseverance. Her parents were led to believe that with a resolution of these difficulties, her depression and anxiety would resolve themselves without psychotherapeutic intervention, since they were symptomatic of her problems in learning.

Special help was instituted the following school year within the public school Sara attended, but without the expected success. Not only did her academic achievement fail to progress with the rapidity predicted, but she began to evidence difficulties with peers for the first time. She was reluctant to be with

friends and refused to have a birthday party. Her willingness to
engage in aspects of academic work which were difficult for her
had declined and she was more prone to withdraw into daydreams. Her parents who regarded this as an exacerbation of the
trends described to them by the evaluating psychologist, decided that a special school for learning disabled children would
relieve Sara's distress.

About 1½ years later, when Sara was 10 and had been in this
school for several months, she was screened by another psychologist with expertise in neuropsychology as well as general clinical
training, under whose supervision she was to be seen in individual remediation outside of school. The withdrawal Sara manifested in public school had to some degree abated in this new
school environment. Nevertheless she was not making the anticipated strides in her academic work. Since the previous evaluation had been performed by a highly reputable clinician, Sara
was not retested but seen in a clinical interview to assess her
suitability. Unexpectedly and astonishingly, delusional ideation
readily emerged. In a fully syntonic fashion, she described her
teddy bear who had a radio in his head through which she could
communicate with him when they were separated. The cotton
inside him was his fat among which his bones could be felt. There
was a crack in his brain. While deeply attached to this bear, she
sometimes wished to "get rid of him," which could be accomplished by splitting his throat open. Reexamination of the projective test data obtained earlier suggested that more severe
psychopathology had existed at that time as well, in conjunction
with the diagnosed neuropsychological features.

Several months later, Sara's parents, who began to become
concerned about her behavior at home, consulted with a psychiatrist, Dr. Reingold. Sara, who had chronically expressed feelings of inadequacy and inferiority, now was withdrawn and
unreachable. On several occasions she had run away, although to
spots where she was easily found. New also were temper outbursts and verbal abuse, especially directed toward her brother
who was four years younger and exceptionally bright. Her parents continued to attribute her difficulties to a disturbance in
self-esteem and frustration related to neuropsychologically based
deficits. However, at this point they considered these reactions to
be difficulties in their own right of a magnitude warranting
psychological intervention. Sara was characterized as "a private

child" whose withdrawal was a form of "withholding." Having heard about Sara's teddy bear delusions, Dr. Reingold viewed the original testing evaluation as entirely diagnostically inaccurate; that is, he dismissed the neuropsychological findings since the psychologist failed to recognize her serious psychological disturbance. Dr. Reingold conceptualized Sara's behavioral and self-esteem problems instead as symptomatic expressions of a more severe level of disturbance on a psychodynamic basis: a borderline personality organization.

In contrast both parents held to the original diagnostic impression, although Sara's father considered that the psychologist might have "gone light on the disturbance." They added some significant features of Sara's history which had apparently not been shared or requested two years before. Sara suffered several simultaneous stresses and disappointments to which her current pathology was possibly attributable. The fact that when she was 2, she and her parents spent the year abroad was forwarded as an explanation of her speech problems. When she was almost 4, her mother returned to work only several months after adopting Sara's brother. The bear Sara had been given at age 2 gradually became a powerful focus of her thoughts and emotions over the next years. She gave great attention to the bear's dress and communicated with him in her mind. At age 6, Sara entered what her mother termed her "murderous period." Sara, who showed no overt jealousy toward her brother at the time of his arrival, became intensely rivalrous when he "became a man" at age 2. Her bear expressed these feelings, as well as a wished-for solution, in his rageful jealousy of other animals who had to vacate the room he occupied, should he feel unhappy. In a pleading and mournful tone, Sara conveyed her wish to be newly adopted. Mother characterized the bear's functions for Sara as those of a "superego or alter ego."

Following the consultation Sara began intensive psychotherapy with Dr. Reingold which continued for two years until it was disrupted by the family's year away from home for professional reasons. A referral for another psychological testing evaluation was made as treatment began to reevaluate the state of Sara's ego functioning at this time and to explore the contrast between her clinical presentation and the impression previously gained through testing. Unlike two years before, Sara refused to complete tests other than the intelligence test.

Several months later, when Sara was 11 years old, Dr. Reingold referred her for testing by a psychoanalytically oriented
psychologist who was not trained in neuropsychological assessment. The standard battery (WISC-R, Rorschach, TAT, Figure
Drawings, and Bender-Gestalt) without achievement or neuropsychological tests was administered. This kind of evaluation
readily lent itself to overturning the original diagnostic impression since the tests which were likely to tap neuropsychological
dysfunction were omitted. The overall impression was of "an
atypical development with borderline features and a visual perceptual weakness" in a girl whose "pseudostupidity [has] corro-
sive effects on the maturational functions, including learning."
Academic difficulties were understood as "inhibitions," rather
than deficits, related to "wishes not to know, not to understand,
that may relate, in part, to her adoptive status" and to efforts to
restrain aggressive impulses. Noting the great variability in
scores obtained on some subtests of the WISC at age 11, when
compared with those at 10 years, 6 months and 8 years, 8 months,
it was reasonably concluded that "this is an unpredictable girl
whose earlier deficiency in this area cannot be attributed solely
to a neurological deficit."

An extensive analysis of projective data was not paralleled
by an equally detailed task analysis of cognitive functions. While
there was an apparent acceptance of the existence of neuropsychological dysfunction, it was implicitly discounted. The areas in
which neuropsychological factors would not be contributory
were cited, but those which might be affected were not delineated and integrated with the richly elaborated dynamic material. In summary, this psychologist wrote:

These tests reveal an intriguing child whose pathological findings are matched by her inner strengths. Sara's *learning disturbance
relates to pseudostupidity, more so than her neurological deficit.* She
has a superior intellectual potential and creative gifts. Her energies
that might be more appropriately directed toward maturational
growth, are dissipated by excessive sadomasochistic fantasies, and
the maintenance of an infantile facade. She does not present an overt
thinking disorder, but she gives an impression of a deviation held in
abeyance, that may resurface during adolescence. A delusional seed,
fantasies of death and reunion, are contained within her oral and anal

regressive content. Her obsessive sexual preoccupation and doubts about her identity may be enhanced by seductive punitive pressures within her household and by her adoptive status. A longitudinal study of Sara's three testing experiences, reflects her unpredictable ebb and flow, her readiness for panic, and her willingness to share, her distrust and affect hunger, her private qualities, and her emotional accessibility. Her many positives dilute a prognostic outlook that might otherwise be considered guarded [emphasis added].

Dr. Reingold took this report as confirmation of the inaccuracy of the previous test evaluation and worked with Sara in a psychoanalytically oriented psychotherapy for two years, while at her parents' insistence she simultaneously attended a school for learning disabled youngsters. She did reasonably well during this period.

Not quite a year after this test evaluation, Sara had to be retested for purposes of recertification of her eligibility for state funding of private school tuition. This time she was seen by the psychologist—both a specialist in neuropsychology and a psychodynamically trained clinical psychologist—who interviewed her at age 10 when private remediation was being considered.

An evaluation of broad scope was undertaken. This included tests of intelligence, neuropsychological functioning, and personality: the WISC, ITPA auditory and visual sequential memory and sound blending subtests, WRAT, Benton Test of Visual Retention, Bender-Gestalt, Raven Progressive Matrices, Purdue Pegboard, motor tests, tests of laterality, time orientation, finger agnosia and graphesthesia, and the Rorschach and TAT (as well as the CAT administered when the TAT was refused).

Sara emerged as a girl of average intelligence with neuropsychological dysfunction including difficulties in immediate visual memory and in replicating graphomotor productions. Receptive and expressive language difficulties appeared to have been resolved. Continued special education was recommended to aid in consolidating gains already manifest. Sara was cooperative throughout all intelligence, achievement, and academic tests, so that no clinical manifestations of psychopathology were evident. However, the patterning of scores on several of these tests—as well as Sara's response to and productions on projective testing—suggested the existence of serious disturbance with

some noteworthy improvement since treatment had begun.
Some excerpts from the report follow:

Sara's lowest scores on the WISC on both the Verbal and
Performance scales were on subtests tapping social awareness
(Comprehension and Picture Arrangement), both scores falling into
the deficit range, whereas all other scores were in the average range.
Such a pattern usually reflects psychological maladjustment, a finding not readily apparent on the Rorschach but profoundly manifest
on Thematic tests.

I do not have the original Rorschach record (of the first psychologist who tested Sara) but I recall from our telephone conversation a high degree of sensitivity to "holes" (which I related to Sara's
manifest concern with "Beary's" holes, and latently her own) and
many "invisible" responses. The present Rorschach is devoid of such
preoccupations. Instead one sees many popular responses being
given and several human responses. If one did not know the previous
history, the Rorschach looks relatively benign except for one fabul-
ized combination (two people holding onto a bell) and one response
of concern because of content (two people burned at the stake, tied
to a stake). Perceptually all responses were accurately seen, and if I
had not administered thematic tests I might even be suggesting the
discontinuation of therapy.

On the TAT Sara told a meager story to Card 1 and then
completely blocked on a picture of a farm scene showing a man, a
girl holding books, and a pregnant woman. Even direct questioning
yielded nothing as Sara assumed an almost catatonic position, sitting
and staring and saying nothing unless asked. Given the next card (a
person on the floor leaning on a couch), the same immobilization
occurred. I gave her another card and asked her to write a story.
Again, complete blocking, immobilization. I tried to help by telling
her to start writing "once upon a time" and got no response. I asked
her if she would just write the phrase and nothing more and got no
response as she sat and looked at the picture. Asking if she felt scared
yielded no reaction. Asking if the pictures looked real also produced
no reaction. I then put the cards away and administered the CAT,
which contained animal pictures and after 10 cards, administered
one more TAT card. The reaction to the last TAT card was the same
as the previously described reactions. Since she had freely told
stories to the CAT cards I asked her why she found those easier. She
said, "You can say *anything* about them" but could not explain
further.

Obviously, fantasies became almost real for Sara and only when
they are projected onto animals can she compartmentalize and
regard them in the realm of fantasy.

Sara feels relatively passive via-à-vis others and her own aggression, and there is almost total repression of aggressive drives. Only larger organisms have power and the only way one gains power is to become large. The danger with becoming large is that one also begins to become older and therefore weaker, thus losing power. This power urge is fraught with anxiety and Sara can only relegate it to animal and cartoon characters.

The dynamic material expressed in the CAT (such as nighttime anxiety, etc.) is less significant than the structural implications of the different reactions to the TAT and CAT. It is clear that Sara can become almost totally immobilized in thought and action when some fantasy (probably the pregnant woman was significant in the first card but I am not certain) is stimulated. This immobilization is total and recovery was not possible despite help. This reflects a severe nuclear problem still unresolved; you might be able to explore with Sara her experience during the TAT to see whether a severe break in reality testing did, as I suspect, in fact occur.

After two years of psychotherapy with Dr. Reingold and special school placement, Sara and her family moved for one year to a state distant from their home, for professional reasons. Psychotherapy was therefore interrupted with the likelihood of continuation upon Sara's return. Sara, now an early adolescent, began a period of decline resulting in increasing regression and alarming, although sporadic, breakdown of ego controls. During the year out-of-state she made a suicidal gesture following the diagnosis of a serious but not fatal medical condition in her father.

Upon her return, she resumed psychotherapy with Dr. Reingold for close to a year, during which she became mildly school phobic and did not reestablish the reasonably good adjustment previously achieved. She was observed at times to take a blanket and sleep under the piano. Two events, one in which she brandished a knife at the door of the parental bedroom and a second in which she pierced her mother's side of the bed with a knife, finally precipitated hospitalization. Upon discharge, after a long period of hospitalization, there were multiple attempts at different interventions. There was further consultation with Dr. Reingold, several briefer hospitalizations for suicidal gestures, placement in a residential treatment center from which Sara ran away, and another consultation with Dr. Reingold after which Sara broke off contact. For our present purposes, we will not further elaborate on these aspects of Sara's course.

One final testing evaluation was performed in conjunction with one of her hospitalizations when Sara was just 16 years old. This brought the diagnostic picture full circle, again illustrating the problems inherent in partial assessments. This time Sara was seen by a well-known neuropsychologist without general clinical training in psychopathology who administered the WISC-R and an extensive series of neuropsychological tests—Raven Progressive Matrices, Gray Oral Reading Test, Benton Test of Visual Retention, and the Wechsler Memory Scale, among many others—in the absence of projective data.

The diagnostic impression was most reminiscent of that of the first evaluation in its emphasis upon a primarily neuropsychologically based disorder with secondary psychological reaction:

The sheer specificity of Sara's impairment (i.e., an integrative language disorder), in itself suggests a genetic–neurological deficit. There is considerable evidence for this: (1) her late language acquisition; (2) the syntactic-semantic difficulty noted early in her development; and (3) her contrasting intactness in processing nonverbal material. Further, there is still some evidence of neurological developmental lag in her performance of certain motor acts. Her pencil grasp is infantile, her left hand is much slower than her right on rapid successive (thumb-in-opposition) movements, and there is dysrhythmia in her rapid repetitive and alternating foot movements. Further, her type of language disability is known to occur as a result of brain damage in adults in, of course, much more severe form. Transcortical aphasia is characterized by good naming ability, repetition, and learning for short term, but by poor comprehension and long-term storage. It occurs as a consequence of a very specific lesion of the left hemisphere. . . .

There are secondary emotional problems primarily due to a lack of acceptance by the child (and perhaps her parents) of the learning disability (diagnosed at least seven years ago) and a tendency instead to focus on rather more amorphous issues. There are also the emotional consequences of trying to function and to develop some rational self-appraisal with two such different sets of capabilities.

Several aspects of this evaluation contribute to a revival of the polemic created by the first two assessments, at ages 9 and 11. Its consideration of previous assessment favors the one more remote in time and nearly ignores those more recently performed. In contrast to only a brief mention and near dismissal of the second and third assessments which contradict this most recent psychologist's diagnostic impression, there are extensive references to the first evaluation performed—also by a neuro-psychologist who gave little weight to dynamic factors. Indeed, there was a near indictment of the efforts made to help Sara since that assessment: "Sara is a grown-up learning disabled child still suffering from a language disorder diagnosed at least as long ago as seven years." In failing to attempt the reconciliation of current results with these other findings—and further, in not administering the personality tests which were noted in these assessments to be sensitive to her psychopathology—this evaluation fosters either/or thinking and makes some poorly investigated and documented statements. For example, despite a disclaimer, "it should be noted that emotional and personality factors were not tested by projective techniques or other specific tests but are inferred from an interview with Sara's parents, her behavior, our conversations, and from disparities between what she says and what she does," complex formulations were made which rule out a primary psychogenic etiology:

Sara's problem instead seems to be one of reconciling the false introjected image of herself as having superior intellectual capacities with the learning disabled child she has always been and still is. Her second, related problem is with integrating a sense of self out of her disparate capacities. It is a question to which we have no ready answer: how does anyone integrate "dull normal" and "bright normal" intellectual capacities to achieve a sense of identity? She is aware of the problem and told a rather touching story of a friend who said to her, sometime after getting to know her, that she was "not as dumb as you first appeared to be." Sara is aware that her use of language makes her appear "dumb," and says she would like to change that. There does not appear to be anything deficient in Sara's interpersonal relationships. In every report on her it has been noted that her affect is quite appropriate, she makes friends easily, and her "psychosocial" development is excellent. We noted, in addition, her sensitivity to tone of voice and emotional expression. One needs to utilize these very positive factors in some effort to help her integrate her own sense of self.

Furthermore, in the absence of a specific assessment of the intactness of Sara's thinking, alternative explanations may be proposed for some of the findings reported. For example, this psychologist concluded that Sara has difficulty with aspects of language which are "at a secondary, more complex level" in contrast to intact functioning in language tasks which are rote and factual. The data selected to substantiate this impression might also appear in the record of a patient with a significant degree of psychopathology. The process of reaching one conclusion rather than another is not documented. For example, the highly variable distribution of subtest scores with, however, a consensus average IQ over years, and even in one instance within months, could suggest the possibility of intrusions of anxiety and/or personal concerns of major proportions. Furthermore, Sara's low score on a test measuring the grasp of cause and effect relationships in common social situations and her confused recall of a story from memory could be viewed in this light. The psychologist noted: "Similarly, but on a different level, she could not organize a story read to her (on the Wechsler Memory Scale) sufficiently well to come up with a logical ending. Indeed she dramatically altered the ending, possibly reflecting her own fears, but was not a bit constrained from doing so by the lack of coherence she thereby created." On yet another test which has rather complex questions and requires some complex responses, there was apparently no difficulty with receptive or expressive language: "Whatever antisocial inclinations she may have, Sara is well in control of them and can handle them with humor. On several of the Comprehension questions (WISC-R) Sara provided both the correct response and a humorous antisocial one. So close to the surface, these inclinations do not appear to be a problem." However, there is no explanation in light of the diagnosis rendered, of how she had sufficient language resources to be playful on such a task.

Based on the diagnostic impression, a radical revision of the previous approach to intervention was recommended:

> In our opinion Sara does not belong in a school for emotionally disturbed children. We believe that such placement merely reinforces a false emphasis, an attempt to cope with Sara's rebelliousness or stubbornness (as she calls it) when they are only a very flimsy facade. There seems to have been a tendency to reinforce and perpetuate her own poor defense, "I won't" instead of "I can't." The search should begin for an occupational direction, for a goal in life, for something that Sara can do very well. We believe the direction may be training in design, graphics, drafting, or artwork. Poor as her

pencil grasp is, Sara's reproduced designs are quite good and her performance on "block design" and "object assembly" was very good. She is interested in music and her talents in that direction might also be explored. . . . Remedial efforts must take the form of helping her overcome some of the language deficit while finding a vocational goal for her within the broad areas of her considerable competence.

In a dramatic gesture, Sara made a final visit to her psychiatrist, Dr. Reingold, whom she had not seen for a protracted period of time. After this she definitively refused further treatment. In this hour she entered the consultation room, deposited a copy of the report of this latest evaluation, and walked out, leaving Dr. Reingold to guess the message she wished to convey. It probably went something like this:

> I am thoroughly confused. For as long as I can remember, my parents have taken me from one expert to another to figure out what is wrong with me. At times they have been on target and at others I have felt misunderstood. They haven't all agreed with each other. Sometimes they think there is something wrong with my brain which makes it harder for me to learn. Another doctor felt it was all psychological. I think you agreed with that one. In some ways things have gotten better for me and in others they are worse. Now I am beside myself. I feel no trust in what the doctors say. The one who tested me when I was 16 returned to the same conclusion I heard when I was 9 which was then contradicted when I was 11 and partly reconfirmed when I was 13. No one has explained why they feel a previous doctor has been wrong and on what basis they have come to differ. Does each one have their own pet theory? I am confused. I feel let down, discouraged, and angry, with no one in whom I can place my trust.

Case 7: Eloise

Eloise, a 16 1/2 year-old high school junior and the youngest of three children of professional parents, was referred to a clinical psychologist with neuropsychological expertise for general consultation. Unlike her older sister and brother who had stellar academic records, Eloise had always been a mediocre student. Her grades fluctuated between Bs and Cs in a family context in which straight As and highly successful careers were the norm.

Nor did she seem to enjoy intellectual pursuits. She never spontaneously read a book but preferred to watch television.

Receipt of what they considered "disastrous" Standard Achievement Test (SAT) scores—a harbinger of opportunities closed to Eloise which had been open to all other family members—catapulted her parents into arranging for an evaluation. For years they had exercised what they termed "benign neglect." In reality this was not an entirely accurate self-characterization. Under similar circumstances two years before, when Eloise was 14 1/2, alarmingly low Preliminary Standard Achievement Test scores led her parents to seek consultation with a well-known neuropsychologist.

Several features of the history obtained at the time of the second evaluation when Eloise was 16 1/2 were suggestive of the possibility of neuropsychologically based learning difficulties. In the midst of an induced labor, Eloise experienced some respiratory distress. In the first year of life she contracted a severe ear infection which precipitated a regression in motor skills of several months' duration. However, by 1 year all milestones were within normal limits. Yet Eloise never found learning easy or pleasurable, even in a less than high-powered, public school setting and with the help of private tutors. In contrast, her brother and sister had moved out of this environment to excellent private schools because they were not sufficiently challenged. It was not until the impact of these college-related scores which had direct implications for the future that Eloise's parents actively sought to explore the reasons for these differences.

A detailed neuropsychological testing evaluation without projective tests or general clinical evaluation was performed during the first consultation when Eloise was 14 1/2. The diagnostic impression was as follows: "In sum, intelligence testing tells us that Eloise is at the upper end of the "average" range, with a possibly greater potential, that she has trouble maintaining concentration on sequences, that she has a word retrieval problem, and suffers effects of an inadequate education." The nature of Eloise's academic difficulties was further detailed:

This is reflected in a poor fund of information and an inadequate vocabulary. She is slow on nonverbal tasks but has no perceptual problems. Some inattention to the world around her is suggested not only by her poor information score but in her slowness with arranging time, her willingness to discard responses and improve them. . . .

While Eloise's early difficulty with reading appears not to have had any antecedents in later language development, her current school problems are clearly related to a central language processing deficit. She has difficulty distinguishing certain speech sounds and cannot read or spell them. Her problems with arithmetic seem to stem from not having automatized certain basic arithmetic combinations. She performs too slowly in arithmetic, paralleling the slowness of her response on other nonverbal, configurational tasks. Her poor vocabulary and information scores reflect a long-term language processing deficit, but may also be due to her inadequate reading and education. The "short attention span" of her childhood is manifested now in a difficulty with maintaining concentration on sequences of letters and words. This does not mean a lack of attention to detail; in fact, she has a superior capacity to notice details, to distinguish essential from unessential detail.

On another level, however, she is peculiarly oblivious to events around her and shows some slowness in appreciating human interaction. . . .

She has a superior capacity to learn if the material to be learned does not depend upon previously learned information. With this fine capacity to learn she should have a better vocabulary and fund of information. The discrepancy may signal some problem with long-term storage of information and retention of what is learned or, as suggested previously, her inadequate reading or education.

Eloise is good at abstraction and spatial relations, both indicators that her intelligence is hampered by poor language processing and slowness. When allowed enough time she does improve her performance. She can rise to the challenge of a new kind of test, and there are indications that she is learning to think.

Her scholastic achievement is at least two years behind what it should be given even "average" intelligence. Rapid reading and responding, both of which are extremely difficult for her, are essential for college entrance examinations. Eloise is going to require better schooling and considerable extra help in the next few years.

A close examination of the report as well as some of the original data on which it is based raised many questions and sources of confusion at the time of the second consultation. The IQ scores obtained were in the average range, as were most scores on specialized tests of neuropsychological function. The major discrepancy was the presumed two-year lag in academic tests. Much effort went into proposing a neuropsychological explanation for this when in fact this "lag" derived from a misinterpretation of the scores, as will be seen in the report of the second test evaluation which follows. There were also elaborate attempts to attribute Eloise's average intelligence to neuropsychological and psychological factors, that is, to discount the possibility that a girl from such an intelligent family could be merely average. For example, multiple references were made to the fact that Eloise's scores improved when time limits were discounted, a finding equally typical of the child of average intelligence. If no deficit in basic skills exists, more time should lead to improved performance. Furthermore, test data which could be suggestive of limited intelligence—terse and not highly imaginative sentence completion responses—were attributed to defensiveness:

While she was described as open and frank, we found her withdrawn and rather guarded. She completed some sentences for us as follows:
> When I have to read, I (long pause) read it.
> To be grown up is mature, probably.
> School is educational.
> To me homework is time consuming.

She was as noncommittal as one could be; cooperative without being informative.

Two other problems exist in this report. First, there are some internal contradictions, for example, the relatively high score in a subtest of abstract concept formation does not support the hypothesis of a central language processing deficit. Nor does the fact that language-based learning readily took place in the course of testing. Second, there are multiple, unreconciled explanations for the same phenomena. This is not to suggest that multiple factors may not simultaneously contribute to the same area of difficulty; of course they may. But when they are listed without any commentary on their relative contribution or their interrelation, it is difficult to develop proper interventions. For example, it was stated that Eloise's impoverished fund of information was due variously to her central language processing disorder, poor education, and long-term storage deficit. Yet she could learn in the testing sessions, as noted above, and had no apparent difficulty comprehending test instructions, at least insofar as the report indicated.

Eloise and her parents were given an elaborate list of recommendations as a result of this evaluation. They are reported below in the form of a letter sent to Eloise:

Dear Eloise,

Your mother has asked that I send a report of our testing directly to you, and I have agreed to do so because I have confidence in your capacity to cope with the problems it raises and with its recommendations. I say this in spite of the fact that you were very "guarded" during our discussions, sort of afraid to have us probe. In fact, when you were completing a sentence that started "I am afraid of" you said "being interviewed, I don't like being asked all these questions." We were asking them in an effort to help you, and I hope we may be able to do so in spite of your lack of candor. . . .

In summary, Eloise, you have difficulty distinguishing certain speech sounds and cannot read or spell them. Your trouble with arithmetic seems to stem from your not having automatized certain basic combinations and you therefore perform them too slowly. Your poor vocabulary and information levels may be due to your inadequate language and possibly a poor education. You have trouble maintaining attention to sequences.

You have, however, a superior capacity to learn; you are excellent at abstract reasoning and spatial relations, all indications that your intelligence is hampered by poor language processing. Your scholastic achievement is two or more years behind your age and more than that behind your capacity to learn.

You must learn to read and compute more accurately and rapidly if you are ever going to prepare for college. You must devote two to three hours a day (every day) to remediation and here are some recommendations:

1. You need general language tutoring and should learn lists of words by vision and audition simultaneously.

2. Learn the regular rules of English spelling and the exceptions.

3. Learn script, printing is too slow.

4. Learn to type and copy manuscript (pages out of books). This will help you with writing reports and may help with vocabulary building and spelling.

5. Read books and write summaries of each chapter (or of each story if they are short stories) and have these corrected by whoever is tutoring you.

6. Read the newspaper every day (and watch the news on TV if you like) and discuss current events with someone.

7. You need more repetition of basic arithmetic combinations. This can be done with flash cards. If the person helping you uses a stopwatch, you can see if your responses get faster.

8. Take an SAT preparatory course.

9. Should your reading improve sufficiently (at least up to grade level) you might take a speed-reading course so you can learn to read rapidly just for meaning.

10. Get a good, simple dictionary and whenever you come across a word you do not know or are not sure of, look it up, say it to yourself, and write it out several times. You might begin with any words in this letter that are unknown to you.

During the two-year period between the first and second consultation, Eloise's parents enrolled her in a private school based on the first psychologist's findings. There the teachers were unanimous in their positive feelings toward Eloise and their belief in her excellent, but unrealized capacities. A period of calm prevailed until her low SAT scores were reported, precipitating another evaluation. Since both parents were attuned to psychodynamic thinking and had themselves been in psychoanalysis, they sought referral to a psychoanalytically trained psychologist with expertise in neuropsychology. They were not necessarily invested in a repeated testing assessment—indeed father was distinctly opposed to this—but wished a comprehensive consideration of all factors contributing to Eloise's poor academic functioning. For the reasons noted above, it was felt that retesting, including projective testing, was indicated.

In the initial interview it became clear that Eloise's father viewed his daughter's poor academic performance as a psychogenically determined symptom. He framed his questions in an ostensibly open-minded fashion—he wanted to know, "How much is dyslexia, how much is deficit, and how much is emotional?"—yet it was clear that he did not put much stock in the findings of the previous evaluation. Although Eloise was the poorest student of his three children, he did not doubt her intellectual capabilities and indeed viewed her as the most insightful.

She suffered from a kind of "psychic malingering"; "she has a lot of things on her mind," and "thinks there will be someone to take care of her" if she fails.

Mother, despite success in her chosen profession, remarked upon her identification with Eloise's situation. She grew up in a far less competitive environment than her husband and children. She felt she could not herself have coped with the level of competition which Eloise must endure. She seemed to sincerely wish clarification of whether Eloise was doing the best she could. With some guilt mother noted that she and her husband had been relatively more absent during Eloise's early years than during those of her siblings due to the demands of professional training. Mother's own mother had served as a maternal surrogate. Her favoritism toward the older sister was keenly felt by Eloise who bore the brunt of her grandmother's critical nature. Mother also remarked that when father was around, he was typically in an angry mood.

When seen in consultation, Eloise presented as a mature, well-related, but clearly depressed girl who was cooperative with and invested in efforts to better understand the nature of her learning problems. She repeatedly traveled considerable distances to appointments on her own and openly expressed her feelings. It was clear that she had internalized an admixture of accusations of laziness and only half-understood explanations of the deficits which resulted in her poor school performance. Not much was explicitly retained about the test evaluation two years before—either its content or effectiveness—except a general feeling of resentment. She readily burst into tears as she spoke of her terror at report card time, in particular, fear of her father's scornful rage and her hopelessness about the possibility of communicating with or being appreciated by him.

Results of the testing reevaluation at this time suggested an entirely different impression than the one arrived at two years before. They will be reported in detail in the service of conveying the process of arriving at this impression and especially the way in which similar data were reinterpreted.

Tests Administered

Wechsler Adult Intelligence Scale (WAIS)
Illinois Test of Psycholinguistic Abilities: Auditory & Visual

Sequential Memory; Sound Blending (Only)
Wide Range Achievement Test (WRAT)
Benton Test of Visual Retention
Raven Progressive Matrices
Rorschach
Thematic Apperception Test (TAT)
Purdue Pegboard
Motor Tests (Rapid Alternating Movements, Thumb Wiggling, Apraxias)
Laterality Tests
Figure Drawings & Most Horrible & Most Pleasant Concepts
Time Orientation
Finger Agnosia & Graphesthesia

General Findings

Intelligence: On the WAIS, Eloise obtained a Verbal IQ of 106 (66th percentile), a Performance IQ of 106 (66th percentile), and a Full Scale IQ of 106 (66th percentile).

All scores are in the average range and are consistent with WISC-R findings two years ago (108, 104, 106, respectively). Below are the scaled scores:

Information	8	Digit Symbol	10
Comprehension	11	Picture Completion	10
Arithmetic	9	Block Design	10
Similarities	12	Picture Arrangement	10
Digit Span	11	Object Assembly	13
Vocabulary	10		

All subtest scores are in the average range except for Object Assembly which peaks to slightly above average (8–12 is the average range). The pattern is that of a person of average endowment. What was referred to two years ago as a word-finding difficulty was noted here also except not interpreted as an anomia. Eloise has a tendency to flail her arms and hands around and say, "You know what I mean," when she does not know something. The operation of repression is fantastic with her. What she does not know seems incredible. She "figures out" the number of weeks in a year (48), cannot accurately define the words "conceal" (to disguise), "hasten" (to disappear quickly), "commence" (to end), "domestic" (typical) etc. The hand waving also occurred during the Comprehension test and when one simply waited it out for her best explanation, she simply came up short. Proverbs elude her. The behavior, however, is a smokescreen for, or part of, her anxiety which rises when she feels she does not know something. Usually when she *feels* she does not, she *actually* does not.

Achievement: On the WRAT, Eloise obtained a Reading Grade at the 86th percentile, a Spelling Grade at the 89th percentile, and an Arithmetic Grade at the 42nd percentile.

If time is discounted the last rises to the 73rd percentile. An examination of errors reveals no qualitative signs of dyslexia, dysgraphia, or dyscalculia. Eloise can read and decode anything and as with most people, understands things within her intellectual level. Because so much was made of it earlier, I converted the previous findings on the WRAT to percentiles using the norms which were used then. At that time they resolved to 39th, 39th, and 70th, all in the average range (standard score equivalents of 96, 96, and 108) and consistent with her IQ. This misuse of grade equivalents which is quite explicit in the test manual and on each form of the record sheets was perhaps less clear when the test was first given. But even then a cautionary note was given on page 15. "The grade ratings above age 14 are more arbitrary than those below 14. . . . They are statistical anchors of achievement rather than precise grade placement measures." In the current version one is warned to "base all interpretations on standard scores." In the early testing and now academic achievement levels are consistent with IQ findings. (If anything Eloise's calculation abilities have improved as has her reading.)

Part Functions

Perception: On the Raven, a test of visual–perceptual development, Eloise answered 34 of 36 items correctly, ruling out a disorder in this area. Clinically and from the Blending test, there is no evidence of auditory imperception. Somatosensory tests revealed neither finger agnosia nor difficulties with graphesthesia tests.

Motor: Fine finger speed and dexterity are excellent. Gross motor coordination is intact. Rapid alternating movements were done well and no synkinesia was noted. All tests for dyspraxia (eye, tongue, verbal, facial, and constructional) were negative.

Laterality: Left cerebral dominance is established for eye, hand, and foot. Lateral awareness is intact on self and in extracorporeal space. A left to right orientation is present for lexic and nonlexic material.

Time Orientation: Eloise can read and construct a clock accurately. The days and months and associated concepts are known.

Memory: Short-term memory is variable. On a test of visual spatial memory she scored in the deficit range. When it was repeated with the instruction to "try harder," she scored within normal limits. Auditory short-term memory was average on the WAIS and at age 10–3 on the ITPA. I regard these findings as consistent with manifest anxiety, since no other findings suggestive of temporal lobe disorder are present and since there is manifest anxiety. Short-term visual–sequential memory is intact.

Language: There were no dysphasic phenomena noted throughout testing. The terms before and after are understood spatially and temporally. Automatic, responsive, and spontaneous speech are intact. Numbers are read, written, and aligned accurately. Autotopagnosia tests were negative.

To summarize the above, Eloise is a girl of average intelligence whose achievement levels are consistent with this. Although repression as a major defense is operative I would regard her current levels of functioning as quite representative of ability. There are no indications of central nervous system impairment as it usually is presented on these tests.

Personality

The Rorschach is that of a young woman whose emotions can be overwhelming and disruptive of good cognitive controls. Especially when emotionally aroused, her thinking can vary from overly concrete ("doesn't remind me of anything but it's pretty") to overly abstract ("reminds me of all different types of things: in general looks like unity with one central force in the middle, joins them all"). In particular, sexual arousal is disruptive, Eloise needing to take distance, even extreme distance, when sexual feelings are experienced. She vacillates therefore in her sense of herself as a vibrant female. This was displayed on the Rorschach in her converting feminine forms into abstractions: two ladies become angels, a fetus is followed by "an abstract person with sunglasses." Most confusion in thinking set is in her response to the "father card." It took her 80 seconds to start, indicating severe blocking and then began with fragmented perceptions proceeding to a near contamination: a dragon dog. Later this was explained as "not really a dog but something scary came to mind."

Eloise has strong exhibitionistic wishes which can be both acted on or lead to severe inhibition and "shyness." Narcissism, common at her age, is present, as is a pathological turning toward the self in the form of possible body concerns (hypochondriasis) and withdrawal through the use of drugs.

Eloise feels she should achieve more than she has and is disappointed in her lack of success. Denial of depression is her major defense against dysphoria. But depressive affect emerges and surprises her in its appearance. "How come all of these look so sad," she says of the TAT cards.

Although familial relations are fraught with distress, Eloise is most upset by the unpredictability of all adult men. Blocking of thought, forgetting, fragmentation take place in reaction to males and to some extent she fears a partial identification with their unpredictability. Sex and aggression are intertwined, sets of feelings she has not come to terms with.

Eloise has a vivid and active fantasy life. This, combined with her emotional lability leaves precious little energy for learning. Diagnostically the impression is of a hysterical character who under stress might become symptomatic. She needs therapy and an accurate picture of her intellectual capacities.

Thus the initial consultant's overzealous investment in a neuropsychological perspective—both manifested in and compounded by the omission of an assessment of personality— led to misdiagnosis and to two years of misdirected efforts at intervention.

Chapter 6

Common Neuropsychological Disorders

Prior to an exploration of treatment possibilities in chapter 7 we would like briefly to present common types of neuropsychological disorder which are the target of one form of treatment: remediation. These properly belong among the learning disorders of primary neuropsychological etiology in the classification offered in chapter 2, that is, learning disabilities. However, they have been reserved for more detailed description until the reader was better acquainted with the process necessary for their diagnosis.

While each child's learning disability is unique, there are commonalities among children which permit some degree of classification. Several diagnostic entities—visual perceptual disorders, the Gerstmann syndrome, dyslexia, dysgraphia, and dyscalculia—will be considered. The thread of our thinking generally runs counter to the tendency of many to emphasize syndromal aspects of each of these diagnostic entities. If diagnosis is to be pragmatic, attention to individual differences is of utmost importance. For instance, a child is said to be "dyslexic" because he cannot read. The assumption is made that a variety of possible factors may account for this failure to learn; it is irrelevant to treatment planning for an individual child whether or not he conforms to a particular subtype of dyslexia, reflective of some of these factors to the exclusion of others.

VISUAL PERCEPTUAL DISORDERS

Although visual perceptual disorders may contribute to learning disabilities and other cognitive disturbances (Johnson and Myklebust, 1967; Luria, 1973; Benton, 1979b), they are rarely the major causal factor (McGrady, 1968; Denckla, 1979). They are included here primarily to dispel the commonly held notion that dyslexia, and by implication other learning disabilities, is the result of perceptual disturbances. For example, letter reversals seen in many younger learning disabled children and sequential, or strephosymbolic, errors seen in children of all ages are not usually attributable to visual perceptual disorders; they are instead typically part of a more general confusion with spatial or lateral organization or orientation.

A visual perceptual disorder may properly be said to involve some difficulty in one or more perceptual processes: recognition of objects, faces, or pictorially represented stimuli, discrimination of complex figures, or localization of objects in space. These all represent a disorder in the "knowing" aspect of perception (i.e., in attaching meaning to what is perceived). Thus, they represent a kind of visual agnosia. To correctly classify a particular difficulty as a visual perceptual disorder, it is necessary to parcel out all other contributory possibilities. Only in differentiating visual perceptual from linguistic and motor elements can useful remedial strategies be developed. Luria (1973, 1980) and Benton (1979b) point out the linguistic component of visuoconstructional tasks such as copying geometric designs, as when a person guides his graphomotor efforts with verbal statements of the name of a shape ("circle" or "square") or its parts ("intersection of lines," "angle"). The diagnostic analysis of these tasks is further complicated by the existence of a motor component. Since these are the kinds of tasks often used to conclude that visual perceptual disorders are contributory to a specific learning disability, it is clear that care must be taken in arriving at such a diagnosis.

Another common example of erroneous diagnostic thinking is the automatic conclusion that a child who incorrectly names colors necessarily suffers from a visual perceptual disorder. Such difficulty may indicate an impairment in the perceptual–integrative or the associative process in the context of adequate sensory capacity, in that the child cannot reach an adequate level of recognition despite an adequate level of sensory information. These kinds of difficulties may either be more purely visual perceptual, with little reliance on language (as in problems with the perception and discrimination of color, or color blindness), or more closely linked with language (as in difficulty attaching the correct verbal label to a color, a color anomia, with no other associated language impairment). It would be incorrect to say that a person who can discriminate colors but cannot name them and has other signs of language impairment suffers from a visual perceptual disorder.

At the same time, we do not wish to ignore our own clinical experiences and data presented by others (Boder, 1971a, 1973; Mattis, French and Rapin, 1975) which do substantiate the occasional involvement of visual–spatial deficits in dyslexia. Such children typically evidence difficulty with constructional tasks in the absence of language involvement. However, because reading is so heavily reliant upon language, when visual perceptual disorders are contributory it is unlikely that dyslexia would be their only manifestation. Such perceptual disorders tend to be more widespread, with broader effects upon the child's life. For instance, a child with visual agnosia may indeed have difficulty recognizing letters of the alphabet which thus interferes with reading, but he would then be likely to evidence other more general findings of visual agnosia, for example, the inability to recognize an object or a person in a picture when they are recognizable in real life or difficulties in negotiating the perceptual demands of the world at large.

THE DEVELOPMENTAL GERSTMANN SYNDROME

Despite the debate (Benton, 1977, 1979a) as to whether the so-called "Gerstmann syndrome" may properly be called a syndrome, we believe the description serves a heuristic purpose and is, therefore, worthy of consideration as such. As defined by Gerstmann (1940) this syndrome encompasses four symptoms: (1) right–left confusion with regard only to one's own body or the body of another, unaccompanied by confusion in relation to space or objects in space; (2) finger agnosia; (3) a disturbance in spontaneous writing or writing to dictation; and (4) dyscalculia characterized by a difficulty with assessing the significance of numbers within a complex figure, particularly disorientation regarding the sequence and decimal values of numbers. The importance of this syndrome derives from the finding that these symptoms are seen in conjunc-

tion with each other in children who are not dyslexic, thus highlighting the diagnostic possibility that a child may be learning disabled
but not dyslexic. For example, significant arithmetic and spelling
difficulties may exist on a neuropsychological basis in the absence
of all other findings. Gerstmann (1940) also claims that these symptoms exist independent of other disorders: aphasia, apraxia, agnosia, and other motor or sensory findings. In contrast there is a
common failure to diagnose such children as suffering from a
specific learning disability when, in fact, the problem should be
recognized as such.

The observations of Benson and Geschwind (1970) notwithstanding, in our experience and that of others (Kinsbourne and
Warrington, 1966; Benton, 1977) cases of pure Gerstmann syndrome are at best rare. It is possible to see children with only two or
three of the four characteristics, for example, difficulties with spelling and arithmetic calculation, in the absence of other findings
indicative of neuropsychological dysfunction or the usual correlates
of dyslexia, dysgraphia, dyscalculia, or language problems.

Gerstmann's major thrust in identifying this syndrome was to
establish its localizing value for the parieto-occipital region of the
brain. Issue has been taken with this view by prominent contributors to the field. Kinsbourne (Kinsbourne and Warrington, 1966;
Kinsbourne, 1968) argues against the localizing significance of this
syndrome while nevertheless emphasizing its usefulness in postulat-
ing that children with this cluster of findings may have a residual
difficulty with spelling and arithmetic attributable to sequential
errors. Thus he identifies a "developmental Gerstmann syndrome ... of cognitive deficits ... in which there is selective delay in
the ability to recognize, recall and utilize information as regards the
relative position of certain items in spatial or temporal sequence"
(1968, p. 777).

Benton (1977, 1979a) and Poeck and Orgass (1966) not only
disagree with the claim that these symptoms are localizable to the
parieto-occipital region; they do not believe such a syndrome exists
at all, either because other symptoms are frequently associated or
because the four symptoms of the Gerstmann syndrome are viewed
as manifestations of an underlying language disturbance.

We have no essential quarrel with statements that the symptoms in question do not achieve the status of a bona fide syndrome.
Consideration of the Gerstmann "syndrome" is simply a means of

directing our thinking to the sequential problems consistent with this diagnosis when assessing sources of error in the older child with spelling and arithmetic disorders. Emphasis upon the developmental nature of the "syndrome" is in the service of highlighting the fact that aspects such as finger agnosia and right–left confusion which may have appeared early in a child's life are frequently absent in the older child due to maturation.

DYSLEXIA

Dyslexia is, very broadly, a disorder of the reading process in a child who is emotionally, motorically, sensorially, and intellectually intact (Johnson and Myklebust, 1967). This condition is attributable to "a dysfunction in the brain . . . the problem is one of altered processes, not of a generalized incapacity to learn" (p. 8). The explicit association of dyslexia with central nervous system (CNS) disorder does not imply that dyslexia is synonymous with neuropsychological dysfunction, since neuropsychological dysfunction may exist in the absence of dyslexia (Boder, 1971a, 1971b; Meier, 1976; Denckla, 1979; Luria, 1980).

Dyslexia is a diagnosis which can be made only in those who have reached the age when reading is expected to have developed, given proper education. Reading is a complex task demanding the intactness of many functions: visual perception; sequencing; the ability to make associations between visual and auditory modalities (Rutter, 1979); visual and auditory memory; spatial and lateral organization; blending of sounds and conditional learning. A difficulty in any one or a combination of these can result in difficulty with reading.

It is not surprising then that studies of dyslexia have noted numerous correlations (McGrady, 1968; Boder, 1971a, 1971b; Schain, 1977). Some of those most commonly cited are right–left orientation, time orientation, written language in general and spelling in particular, numerical functions, memory, auditorization, fine and gross motor coordination, consistent dominance, speech and language development, constructional abilities and finger discrimination and sequencing. An important distinction to be kept in mind is that such correlates do not reflect causal relationships between disorders in the above functions and dyslexia; rather they are due to structural relationships of the brain. For example, a dysfunction may find manifestation in both right–left disorientation and a disorder in reading. It would be erroneous to conclude that the child is unable to read because of such disorientation.

The importance of identifying these correlates notwithstanding, "no simple clinical factor can be accepted as pathognomonic of dyslexia" (McGrady, 1968, p. 225). Instead, the diagnosis of dyslexia is made on the basis of the reading problem alone; the variety of other disorders which may accompany it are useful in understanding the area of the brain that may be suspect.

Because dyslexia is popularly conceived to result from a visual perceptual disorder involving letter reversals, it must be emphasized that "there is little or no evidence in favor of the notion that visual perceptual disability is a significant correlate, much less a cause, of a reading disability" (Roswell and Natchez, 1977, p. 38). In fact, letter reversals are typically seen in children with fully intact visual perceptual systems. Although visual perceptual problems may be seen in conjunction with dyslexia, this tends to be a rare occurrence. Far more typically dyslexia is the most obvious expression, or one aspect, of a more pervasive or subtle language disorder or a disorder of those areas of the CNS responsible for language (Johnson and Myklebust, 1967; McGrady, 1968; Critchley, 1970; Boder, 1971a, 1971b, 1973; Mattis, 1979). Denckla's (1979) statement that there is "a remarkable confluence of evidence to support the view that dyslexia is usually the index symptom of a developmental language disorder too subtle to lead to a referral of the child in preschool life" (p. 550) is consistent with this view.

Nevertheless some dyslexics do seem to have a visual–spatial disturbance which, while not purely perceptual in nature, exists independent of a language impairment. Two examples are Boder's "dyseidetic dyslexia" (1971a, 1971b, 1973) characterized by a poor memory for gestalts and the necessity for sounding out even familiar words, and Mattis et al.'s (1975) third and smallest dyslexic type with poor constructional ability and difficulty with visual–spatial perception.

Since the approach to diagnosis recommended here is pragmatically geared to the individual child's specific clinical picture, not much attention is devoted to the postulation or identification of dyslexic types. However, many investigators have attempted to delineate classifications of dyslexia based on etiology, the nature of errors committed, and/or one of two kinds of correlations with other disordered functions or other types of learning disabilities. Some salient classification schemes will be reviewed to give the reader a flavor of the vast amount of work existing in this area.

One major example of an attempt to make distinctions on the basis of etiology is Critchley's (1968) "primary" and "secondary" dyslexia. "Primary dyslexia" is defined as developmental and constitutionally determined, and "secondary dyslexia" as being a result of brain insult in the perinatal period with which more and clearer signs of neuropsychological dysfunction are associated.

Among those classifications based on correlation with particular disordered functions there is no unanimity of opinion about which ones are most differentiating. Some emphasize the contribution of visual versus auditory disorders and others the presence versus absence of a language disorder. Johnson and Myklebust (1967) delineate differences between "visual" and "auditory" dyslexia. Visual dyslexics are said to have: (1) difficulty with visual discrimination as seen in confusion of letters or words of similar stimulus configuration; (2) a slow rate of perception; (3) a tendency to reversals and, less commonly, inversions ("u" for "n"); (4) problems in maintaining a visual sequence ("pan" may be produced as "apn" or "nap"); (5) visual memory problems; (6) drawings that are poorly executed and lacking in detail; and (7) difficulty with visual analysis and synthesis. In contrast auditory dyslexics evidence difficulty with: (1) auditory discrimination; (2) auditory synthesis or analysis; (3) sounding out words even when their meanings are known; and (4) auditory sequencing ("enemy" may be read as "emeny"). In a related vein Bateman (1968) distinguishes between dyslexics with poor auditory memory and intact visual memory, dyslexics with poor visual memory and adequate auditory memory, and dyslexics who have difficulty with both. She suggests that children in the third category have the most severe and persistent problems with reading. We agree with Albert (1979) who contends that although such classification systems have some merit, they pose many problems because children often present with disorders in both areas or a problem in "transducing information between the senses" (p. 226).

Two classifications emphasizing language functions are those by Kinsbourne and Warrington (1966) and Denckla (1979). Denckla proposes six "pure dyslexic" types. The first group is characterized by global language disorder with all tests of language falling below age level, and those in the nonlanguage sphere being of at least average level. The second group is marked by an articulatory graphomotor disorder with problems in fine motor coordination and articulation in the context of normal language functioning. An anomic-repetition disorder denotes the third group, encompassing evidence of circumlocution and paraphasias on confrontation and language comprehension and significant scatter in the Verbal IQ scale. A fourth group has a dysphonetic sequencing disorder evidenced in failed Sentence Repetition and Digit Span tests, occasional naming errors, confusion when faced with complex syntactical construction in the context of normal articulation and an at least average Verbal IQ. A fifth group is characterized by a verbal learning deficiency and a sixth group by difficulty with sequential material. Kinsbourne and Warrington (1966) categorize dyslexics into two groups. One is the "language retardation group," consisting of those with low Verbal IQ as well as clinical evidence of language disorder. The other is the Gerstmann group, those having a lower Performance than Verbal IQ, specific difficulty with finger differentiation and order, constructional tasks, and mathematical operations. Their first group of dyslexics is noted to produce more extraneous letter errors, reflective of problems in the language sphere, and their second group is said to produce more letter order errors, reflective of sequencing problems.

A quite different classification of dyslexia based on correlation with other disordered functions is that of Mattis (Mattis, 1979; Mattis et al., 1975) who suggests three independent syndromes. The "language disorder syndrome" involves reading difficulty in the presence of intact visual and constructional skills, graphomotor coordination, and speech and sound blending. Children in this group are found to have a specific language disorder, often including a delay in sight vocabulary due to anomia. The "articulation and graphomotor dyscoordination syndrome" is marked by intact visuospatial perception, language, and constructional skills as well as poor speech and graphomotor dyscoordination. The third and least common syndrome encompasses poor constructional ability and significant difficulty with visuospatial perception in conjunction with intact language, graphomotor coordination, and speech blending. Mattis et al. (1975) feel that "perception, storage and/or retrieval of visual stimuli are so inefficiently preserved that letters and letter sequences cannot be reliably associated with their sounds or linguistic referents" (p. 160).

Those contributors who offer classifications based upon correlations of dyslexia with other learning disabilities vary in the disabilities they consider. Geschwind (1968) and Albert (1979) find most
useful a classification scheme which distinguishes between dyslexia
with dysgraphia (i.e., difficulty with spelling) and dyslexia without
dysgraphia, since they reflect different underlying neuropsychological problems. Ingram, Mason, and Blackburn (1970) suggest
two categories for classification: (1) "specific dyslexia" in which the
disability is limited to reading and spelling, and (2) "general
dyslexia" in which arithmetic is also below expectation. They suggest that when there is evidence of neuropsychological impairment
there is also a tendency to see arithmetic problems.

Classifications reflective of types of errors are diverse as well.
Boder (1971a, 1971b, 1973) identifies three groups with differing
prognosis. She contends that reading requires a smooth interplay
between two processes: the gestalt and the analytic. In the dyslexic
child the two are dissociated. Using this model, the first of the three
groups is "dysphonetic dyslexia," typically characterized by a
limited sight vocabulary and a global rather than analytic process of
reading; with few word analysis skills, reading is attempted from
context. Spelling is not approached phonetically so that even simple
phonetic words can be grossly misspelled. Extraneous letter errors
and omitted syllable errors are frequent. The second is "dyseidetic
dyslexia" characterized by slow and halting reading, as if each
word is seen anew. Such a child has a poor memory for gestalts,
resulting in difficulty learning to distinguish among letters. Reading
is done analytically; sounding out of familiar as well as unfamiliar
words is the usual approach. Words that cannot be read phonetically tend to be read incorrectly. Sight vocabulary is limited
although reading may be done at or near grade level. Spelling is
poor but phonetic; misspellings are not as gross as those in dysphonetic dyslexia. The third group is "mixed dysphonetic-dyseidetic
dyslexia" which involves the most serious handicap and the worst
prognosis. Misspellings may be even more bizarre than those in the
first group. Mirror reading and writing, as well as confusion of
reversible letters, is common. Boder notes that a serious visuospatial
difficulty in reading and writing produces such errors.

DYSGRAPHIA

Dysgraphia is a neuropsychologically based (Orton, 1937; Critchley and Critchley, 1978; Marcie and Hécaen, 1979) disorder in the production of written language. Two broad types are observable (Johnson and Myklebust, 1967; Ingram, et al., 1970; Boder, 1971a, 1973; Albert, 1979; Marcie and Hécaen, 1979). One may be conceptualized as an aspect or derivative of a language disorder (Orton, 1937; Johnson and Myklebust, 1967; Ingram et al., 1970; Boder, 1971a, 1973; Meier, 1976; Critchley and Critchley, 1978; Marcie and Hécaen, 1979) in which problems in spelling and syntax predominate; this may include difficulty in organization of thoughts and their subsequent translation into written form. The other is characterized by disorders in spatial planning and organization, punctuation and, occasionally, spatial drift. This is in contrast to a pure graphomotor disorder affecting the ability to produce legible strokes on a page (Orton, 1937).

Although dysgraphia is frequently seen in conjunction with dyslexia or as a sequel of an earlier dyslexia (Orton, 1937; Boder, 1973; Critchley and Critchley, 1978), it may also be seen in "pure" form (McGrady, 1968; Marcie and Hécaen, 1979). Critchley and Critchley (1978) take issue with this view of dysgraphia, arguing that it is a specialized form of dyslexia.

Several classifications have been offered to further delineate variations within the two broad types of dysgraphia. Marcie and Hécaen (1979) propose four: (1) dysgraphia associated with dyslexia; (2) "pure" dysgraphia seen without any other language impairment; (3) dyspraxic dysgraphia, characterized by a difficulty with the production of those movements necessary for written expression; and (4) dysgraphia due to disorders that affect the spatial aspects of writing. Dividing up the array of clinical manifestations of dysgraphia somewhat differently, Johnson and Myklebust (1967) suggest that it may be viewed as: (1) a disorder in visual–motor integration or a type of dyspraxia with accompanying difficulty copying; (2) a deficit in revisualization of the visual image from the spoken form; or (3) a deficiency which affects the ability to organize and express thoughts in writing at a level comparable to spoken language.

Different remedial procedures are suggested by Johnson and Myklebust (1967) for each of these types of difficulty. This contribution is an exception since the prognosis for effective treatment of dysgraphia is generally acknowledged to be poor. Boder (1971a, 1973) alludes to the difficulty in remediation when she describes her combination group. Similarly, Orton (1937) and Critchley and Critchley (1978) note that while remedial input is frequently effective with dyslexics, those who are also dysgraphic tend to be left with serious deficits in that area. The progress in written production lags far behind the progress in reading.

DYSCALCULIA

Dyscalculia is a disorder in any of the many elements involved in arithmetic calculation: remembering and employing number tables (Cohn, 1961, 1968; Benson and Weir, 1972; Luria, 1973, 1980); visual–spatial organization as seen in difficulty with alignment of digits or their linear separation; confusion in maintenance of decimal positions or other place holders; right–left disorientation manifested by number reversals or the tendency to approach a problem from the left rather than the right (Cohn, 1961, 1968; Johnson and Myklebust, 1967; Benson and Weir, 1972; Luria, 1973, 1980); failure to recognize the meaning of signs (Cohn, 1961, 1968); sign inattention (Luria, 1973, 1980); linguistic features (Benson and Weir, 1972); confusion in deciphering the order value of multiple-digit numbers (Cohn, 1961, 1968); loss of the meaning of such numbers as in reading "729" as "7-2-9" (Luria, 1973, 1980); visual–motor difficulties evidenced by malformed or excessively large numerical symbols (Cohn, 1961, 1968; Johnson and Myklebust, 1967); disorder in maintaining the sequence of multiple computational steps or the conceptual elements involved in knowing which operation or operations to perform on which numbers.

Like dyslexia and dysgraphia, dyscalculia is understood to be secondary to underlying neuropsychological dysfunction and may, therefore, have a variety of correlates; frequently there are body image problems or right–left disorientation. Dyscalculia is neither rare nor necessarily concomitant with dyslexia as Critchley and Critchley (1978) maintain (Johnson and Myklebust, 1967). Dyscalculia may be seen either in isolation or in conjunction with dyslexia, dysgraphia, or both (Albert, 1979; Marcie and Hécaen, 1979).

The thrust of our thinking about dyscalculia is toward delineating those aspects of the arithmetic process that are disordered so that remedial procedures can be instituted. Toward this pragmatic end three rough types of dyscalculia are useful to bear in mind. One type is characterized predominantly by the linguistic elements of arithmetic: problems with concepts such as "less than" and "more than" and/or with following a sequence of steps. The second is attributable to memory problems as seen in difficulty with the retention and retrieval of number tables. The third is more typically characterized by visual–spatial problems such as misalignment of numbers or confusion in carrying and borrowing, for example, taking the smaller number from the larger one, regardless of position, or beginning computation on the left rather than the right. Very similar classifications are offered by Benson and Weir (1972) and Levin (1979).

Given the frequency of spatial determinants of dyscalculia, some view it as a parietal lobe disorder (Benson and Weir, 1972). Many argue that given the heterogeneity of dyscalculic manifestations, it is of nonspecific localization (Cohn, 1961, 1968; Luria, 1973, 1980; Levin, 1979). Nevertheless, there have been attempts to delineate dysgraphic types with implications for localization. One such effort is that of Luria (1973, 1980) who distinguishes between parieto-occipital disturbances of spatial operations and concepts (strephosymbolia, finger agnosia, maintenance of the idea of numbers but loss of their meaning as symbols, as in reading "316" as "3-1-6"); left temporal lobe disturbances of the ability to do oral arithmetic in the context of intact written arithmetic; and frontal lobe disturbances in which simple calculations can be performed but major difficulty is encountered with complex calculation.

Despite the great similarity of their above-mentioned classificatory efforts, which divide disorders due to aphasia, spatial disorganization, and memory deficits, Johnson and Myklebust (1967) and Benson and Weir (1972) indicate they are not in agreement with each other about localization. Johnson and Myklebust regard dyscalculias of aphasic origin to be left (dominant) hemisphere problems. This is in contrast to those attributable to spatial disorganization which are thought to be right (nondominant) hemisphere disorders, and those related to memory which are not necessarily readily associated with any specific area of difficulty. Benson and Weir do not make these distinctions but rather emphasize the prevalence of parietal pathology of the dominant hemisphere.

Thus, several frequently mentioned types of neuropsychologically based learning disorders, or learning disabilities, have been delineated. We have generally eschewed the postulation of subtypes or syndromes except where they bear direct pragmatic relevance to remedial treatment. Too often such syndromal classifications defeat the essential process of careful attention to individual variations manifested by each child.

Chapter 7

Treatment in Relation to the Diagnostic Spectrum

In line with the book's major thrust, this chapter will explore the multiple treatment possibilities which derive from a careful and integrative consideration of the sources of learning disorder. Fundamental is the notion that one need not choose between an intervention aimed exclusively at neuropsychological or psychodynamic factors.

It is entirely possible for a child with a learning disorder of psychogenic etiology to be unimpaired neuropsychologically. However, the converse cannot be as readily concluded. Neuropsychologically impaired children frequently develop psychodynamic elaborations of their difficulties, particularly when they remain undiagnosed for lengthy periods of time. They may be especially prone to conflicts since there has been interference with ego development. As Vereecken (1965) wrote:

> [In such children,] anxieties and psychodynamic conflict [have] such deep influences on . . . ego functions because [they are] not yet cathected with stable and sufficiently neutralized energies . . . it explains in part why psychodynamic factors have such disastrous effects in cases of organic damage or general immaturity. . . . The same psychodynamic factors play

a much weaker role when the ego is well structured and when
its functions are cathected with enough neutralized energy
[p. 553].

Neuropsychological dysfunction and its psychological elaboration
exist side by side and exert mutual influences upon each other in the
developing child. Furthermore, psychodynamic conflicts and neuropsychological disorder may simultaneously use the same channels of expression (Betlheim and Hartmann, 1924; Rappaport,
1961). Conflicts may also develop secondary to parents' and
teachers' reactions to the child's disability (Blanchard, 1946).

Therefore, given the complexity of the clinical possibilities
these patients present, several considerations govern selection of a
treatment modality or combination of modalities. In this discussion
emphasis will be placed upon treatment for children which must in
some way address neuropsychological contributions to problems in
learning, since a familiarity with indications for psychoanalytically
oriented psychotherapy and psychoanalysis is assumed, and since
so much has been written on the psychotherapy of children with
psychogenic learning disorders. In one sense establishment of the
appropriate form of treatment involves locating the point on the
proposed spectrum of diagnostic possibilities (chapter 2) at which a
particular patient may be said to belong. To do so, a series of
branching and interrelated questions must be asked of the array of
data elicited in the consultative process described in chapter 4.

The most fundamental question is whether a neuropsychological basis for the learning disorder has been discovered. If so, the
nature of this dysfunction—the degree of severity and pervasiveness of the deficits—must be delineated. Branching off from this
are two paths of inquiry which are not truly separable but are here
distinguished for heuristic purposes. One relates to the deficits'
academic consequences and the other to their implications for the
child's overall development.

Which academic functions are involved, if any? Can the child
be helped to compensate for deficits with special, individualized
approaches to his array of areas of deficit and intactness through
remediation, or does he simply need extra help and repetition,
namely, tutoring? In addition, or alternatively, are the affected
areas unresponsive to efforts at treatment but rather demanding of
environmental accommodation?

Do the particular neuropsychological manifestations diagnosed impact upon aspects of ego development and object relations other than learning? Are they now problems in their own right which require attention in conjunction with or in addition to the effect they have had upon processes of learning? The point in the child's life at which the diagnosis of neuropsychological dysfunction was made is important in this regard. If this diagnosis took place well into the school years, how have the deficits previously been understood by the child, his parents, teachers, and peers. Have they developed symbolic meanings and/or been recruited to salient neurotic conflicts so that they are now intrapsychic problems in and of themselves? Are the affected areas ones of special parental investment? How distressing is the discovery of neuropsychological dysfunction to the child's parents? Will intervention which is primarily focused upon the child be adequate to address their reactions, or will knowledge of such dysfunction seriously threaten either the family equilibrium or the personal equilibrium of mother or father because of its symbolic meaning?

When learning disorders are of primary psychogenic origin in the absence of neuropsychological dysfunction, psychotherapy or psychoanalysis is almost invariably essential. Tutoring may be needed to make up for gaps without which further academic progress is impossible. If the child's parents have a central, albeit unconscious stake, in the child's academic difficulty, family therapy and/or individual psychotherapy or psychoanalysis for them may be required as well.

When the disorder is of primary neuropsychological etiology without significant psychological elaboration, remediation and/or environmental alteration is essential, along with clarification of the nature of the disorder for the child and his parents and teachers.[1] It sometimes happens that the type of neuropsychological deficits which the child displays are not central to ego functioning, but rather are circumscribed and thus discovered only once academic requirements bring them to light. Given several conditions, the child with circumscribed deficits does not require psychotherapy

[1]There are also cases in which pharmacotherapy (Baldwin, 1965; Forman, 1975; Schain, 1977) or behavior therapy (Werry and Wolfersheim, 1967) are crucial. While these are not the subject of this book, case 8, Brad, in this chapter illustrates the combination of psychotherapy, remediation, and pharmacotherapy. The above-cited articles are several of many on this subject.

in addition to remediation, but instead clarification and sometimes environmental adaptation of academic and familial demands: the deficits are diagnosed early enough, they are not profound, the child's parents are able to be sensitive to the child's feelings related to these areas of incapacity, and there is no dovetailing of deficit and special investment in that function by parents which would lead to profound disappointment. However, the remedial therapist must be carefully attuned to the possibilities that subsequent academic frustrations will eventuate in reactive psychological problems requiring psychotherapeutic intervention, or that already existing psychological difficulties which did not become apparent in the consultation will surface later. Parents must be alerted to these possibilities as well.

Remediation is also required for children with learning disorders which are admixtures of psychogenic and neuropsychological contributions. In the case of this group of disorders, whether remediation is accompanied by psychotherapy[2] depends upon the degree to which the disorder has become interwoven with or the nidus for psychodynamic conflict and self-esteem problems. When, as noted above, either or both parents have serious difficulty accepting the nature of the disorder they may require psychotherapy or psychoanalysis in their own rights.

Learning disorders due to intellectual limitations in the absence of neuropsychological dysfunction require, above all, clarification for the patient and his parents and teachers. The clinician's assessment of family members during the consultation, as well as the nature of their reactions to this explanation of the child's learning "disorder," will help to make the clinical judgment of whether psychological intervention for the child and/or his parents is

---

[2]The issue of whether dual interventions should be undertaken by one or two professionals is a complex one, adequate discussion of which is beyond the scope of this book. Suffice it to say that in our opinion there are some valid indications for a combined intervention by the same therapist. A major indication for this is the highly constricted and guarded child whose motivation for psychotherapy can only be elicited with the promise of reduced humiliation at school by virtue of help with his learning difficulties. Only when he is given something concrete can he permit a rudimentary exploration of his feelings and fantasies. In some cases such a combined treatment may be a preparation for more intensive psychotherapy rather than a substitute. Despite the advantages of combining psychotherapeutic and remedial approaches in a case such as the above, we recognize both the resulting dilution of each intervention and the complication of therapists' roles which are in so many respects different (see case 3, Matthew, p. 327).

needed to integrate the reality of his intellectual limitations. Remediation is not indicated in such cases and indeed may foster magical fantasies of repair. However, tutoring may aid learning in some instances in that it provides the child with additional time and repetition.

The complexities of the above questions about learning disorders and some approaches to answering them will be explored in case illustrations of a variety of interventions. First, however, the nature of remedial principles and procedures will be explicated in some detail since it is assumed that the reader has little or no familiarity with them. With this background, the indications for and treatment process of the following interventions will be presented as they unfolded in our three major cases and in work with another child not yet introduced, Brad: psychoanalytically oriented psychotherapy without remediation in a neurotic child without neuropsychological dysfunction (Noah, case 1); psychoanalysis concurrent with special educational intervention in the school setting in a borderline child with neuropsychological dysfunction (Daniel, case 2); psychoanalytically oriented psychotherapy concomitant with remediation by the same therapist in a child with neuropsychological dysfunction who evidenced a reactive depression to his learning disability (Matthew, case 3); and modified psychoanalytically informed psychotherapy after termination of which followed a period of remediation in an ego deviant child with neuropsychological dysfunction (Brad, case 8).

In so doing it is hoped that the profound importance of the psychoanalytic perspective on these patients will be conveyed as well as the essential nature of flexibility and specificity in considering additional modalities. These are sometimes conceptualized as alternatives to psychotherapy or psychoanalysis, but more frequently as accompanying interventions.

REMEDIAL PRINCIPLES AND PROCEDURES[3]

The ideas and procedures presented here reflect the belief that what is needed in the teaching of learning disabled children is less

---

[3]This section is not meant to be a manual of remediation. Instead its purpose is to illustrate some basic principles and possible procedures for approaching common disorders. Should the reader wish to implement these techniques, he is encouraged to contact one of the authors for further discussion of their application in specific individual cases.

emphasis upon finding—and training or retraining—a *theoretical* deficiency and more stress on defining those physical and mental skills necessary for negotiating real-life situations. Such a pragmatic delineation of abilities and disabilities in a given child necessarily precedes the conception of teaching programs geared to the development of those specific skills. Rather than sometimes elusive perceptual or cognitive skills, those addressed are basic to everyday functioning: reading, spelling, arithmetic, self-care in feeding and grooming, orienting oneself in time and space, understanding other people and making oneself understood, and remembering specific things. Copying diamonds, drawing angulated lines, solving coding tasks, and drawing pictures of people are regarded as important only insofar as the processes required for these functions also interfere with the practical problems of life. The major aim of addressing the practical problems of living nevertheless encompasses an appreciation of neuropsychological problems to the extent that these problems interfere with the tasks to be acquired.

This approach is taken not because such underlying processes are ignored, but because there is not the luxury of time to hope for theoretically implied generalizations. When a child needs to learn to make a bed, a real bed is used rather than embarking on a program for the development of fine and gross motor skills. Letters and numbers, rather than circles, squares, and triangles are employed in teaching the shape discrimination necessary for reading. The purpose of such an approach is twofold: psychological and theoretical. When a child is failing to master tasks his peers handle with ease, the more rapidly one improves his capacity for mastery of those tasks, the more adequate his self-image becomes. From the child's point of view, he is intelligent or unintelligent relative to what he can or cannot do as he looks about and compares himself with his peers. Therefore, it is critical to the child's developing self-image to acquire specific skills as early as possible. Whether a child can be taught concepts is questionable. When concepts are acquired they are a function of generalization from a series of operations; such an acquisition is not entirely an internal process but somewhat independent of what is taught. A teacher can organize materials and sequence various operations in order to increase the likelihood of a concept being developed by the child, but essentially it is operations that are taught.

A good example of the difference between concepts and operations exists in the current curriculum for the "New Math." Children are offered a different vocabulary from that taught in more traditional mathematics with the aim of maximizing conceptual ability. They learn to manipulate visual representations concordant with this vocabulary and different number systems. That they are in fact learning new concepts, which will facilitate the development of arithmetic skills using only a base 10 number system, is somewhat questionable. For some children all that will be learned is a series of impractical operations; for others, concepts will develop. Unfortunately, the children who learn a series of impractical operations will not necessarily develop concepts and may not manage to learn basic skills, that is, number facts in addition, subtraction, and multiplication.

To repeat: remediation is here conceptualized as a process by which those tasks the child needs to learn are broken down into discrete units and presented in ways that will, it is hoped, circumvent the difficulty the child has previously experienced in learning them. Some methods for an array of the more frequently seen problems in learning will now be explicated. An exhaustive presentation of all aspects of remediation, or of all remedial approaches to all difficulties, is neither possible nor desirable since, as stated in chapter 2, there are no methods which have utility for all children. Rather, this description of remedial principles and procedures is meant to illustrate a general approach, one guided by several intermeshing principles.

One is the task analytic method described in chapters 1 and 4—the idea that steps will be simplified as far as possible into "building blocks." Also crucial are the beliefs that alternative pathways (i.e., circumventing rather than "exercising" areas of dysfunction) to the goal must be constructed and that the needs of the individual child at all times dictate the goals and methods used. This last statement requires special emphasis. All too often in remediation the child himself is left out of the process and procedures. The clinician's use of a remedial technique must always carry with it the understanding that if it fails, the onus must be on the procedure rather than the child. In other words, the approach to remediation must be experimental; hypotheses must be tested and discarded if necessary and new ones instituted in an effort to account for discrepancies in the data.

The procedures presented here are ones which both illustrate these general principles particularly well and have been effective in helping many but not all children. More esoteric remedial approaches, for instance, those for dysnomic or dyspraxic disorders, will not be discussed because they neither exemplify additional principles nor have widespread application.

The principles, processes, and procedures that will be discussed are also all dependent upon a one-to-one involvement of learner and teacher. While this may seem economically inefficient, it is nevertheless most effective in helping such children learn and in allowing the teacher to observe processes of task solution. Such observation is essential to identification of the nature of errors and the necessary mediators that sometimes result in subtle corrections in procedure that may be crucial as one moves from step to step.

Two Major Principles of Remediation: Shunting and Fading

To discuss the principles of remediation one should recognize that these *principles*, applicable to all children, are not meant to be interpreted as universal remedial *procedures*. It invariably happens that a principle, when translated into a procedure, needs major modification. Nonetheless, two major principles are always used: "shunting" and "fading." A shunt is the intermeshing process by which a desired response is elicited via an alternate pathway when it has been impossible to elicit it through the ordinary route because of a breakdown in the functional system. Fading is the removal of unnecessary stimuli and responses so that only the desired response to the critical stimuli is left.

For example, a dyslexic child frequently presents an inability to produce the correct sound for a vowel (e.g., "ă" for "a" when seen either in isolation or in the context of the word "cat"). The child, for whatever reason, is incapable of the cross-modal association involving visual and auditory material. Typically, such a child can be drilled with some temporary success, only to find his progress rapidly dissipating with lack of practice since he is without a technique to aid him in cross-modal association. The principle of the shunt, then, is to devise a means by which the child can always make the association via a route, no matter how ludicrous it may be. The desired response becomes possible in this way when it is impossible through the ordinary route because of a breakdown in the functional system. For example, in this kind of problem, the association between the letter (visual stimulus) and the sound (response) is strengthened when the letter is embedded in a picture. In this way the child is helped to recall a word from which he can extract the sound, thus the shunt. Graphically, it could be depicted as in Figure 7-1. The fading comes in when the child learns to extract the correct sound from the word he produces in response to the picture with the embedded letter. This process is more fully described below in the section on remediation of phonetic associative disorders.

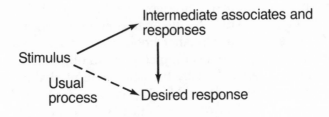

Figure 7-1

Procedures For Specific Disorders.

Phonetic associative disorders. One of the most common failures of young readers is the establishment of reliable auditory–visual arbitrary, and they are, in addition, flooded with multiple exceptions to the rules. Yet most children are not unduly dismayed by these exceptions, and whether or not they are taught phonetically, succeed in learning phonics. If a child does not learn phonics, he is unable to negotiate new words and is entirely dependent on a sight vocabulary. The failure to learn phonics is the failure to learn an arbitrary code; the problem, therefore, becomes one of making the code less arbitrary.

It can be puzzling that a child who names pictures and objects with no difficulty may nevertheless be unable to associate a sound, phoneme, with a letter, grapheme. When the child looks at an object or its representation in the picture form, he has built-in shunts. For instance, when the child sees a spoon or its representation and says "spoon," it may appear to be a simple visual–auditory association, although it is actually more. The spoon image not only triggers the auditory image producing the word, but it also sends nerve impulses to other parts of the brain. Thus, several images may be established—a kinesthetic image, a taste image, a tactile image, and the like—any or all of which may help in the production of the sound image. This may be the neurological substrate for what is meant by "meaning," that is, the varied and multiform associations produced in the brain after one sense modality is stimulated. The phoneme–grapheme association, on the other hand, relies entirely on auditory–visual associations. If such associations are disordered and there are no alternate pathways to be used, the grapheme is essentially meaningless.

The procedures here considered capitalize on bringing into play those alternate pathways giving meaning, so to speak, to each letter. Children's initial alphabet books show a letter written in capital and in lower case near a picture of an object whose name begins with that letter. Usually the name is printed also. Why an "A," for example, should stand for "apple" is completely baffling for the child except that someone indicates this is so. Which of the many letters printed on that page is an "A" is also baffling. Children with association disorders will fail to make the connection between the scratches of lines and the well-known objects. Since there is no inherent connection, it remains arbitrary.

The procedure thus involves establishing an essential connection between letter and sound. Each letter is embedded in a picture of a well-known object so that if the letter were to be removed from the picture the object would not be identifiable. The letter is part of the object.

To illustrate:

(apple),   (cat),   (pencil).

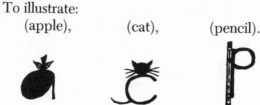

Appropriate pictures for each letter the child does not know are arrived at in collaboration with the child, thus increasing the likelihood of a strong association. Each "picture" is then put on one side of an index card with the corresponding letter on the other side.

The first step is to have the child name the picture, usually an easy task. He is not to say the name of the letter. The second step is to have the child guess the picture when only the partial cue, the letter, is shown. Ultimately, the whole picture is faded out. The child is asked to "make a guess," therefore, avoiding issues of right and wrong. If the child does not "guess" the picture immediately, it is shown to him. The third step involves fading part of the response. Children are taught to say the first part of the name and to simply think the last part. One leaves the actual pictures available on the reverse side of the card in the event the child forgets the name of the object when looking at the letter. The process the child goes through at the end may be characterized as follows: he looks at a letter, recalls the picture of the object via perceptual completion, the object is named, and the sounds of the name are divided into a voiced first part and a thought-of second part. Using stimuli like these and the procedure described, there has been no difficulty establishing firm associations for the whole alphabet as long as there is no evidence of a significant dysnomia.

Once the phonics are learned the exceptions to the rules have to be taught. Special attention has to be drawn to the vowels which, when in combination with another vowel, are usually sounded by their name, the long vowel sound, rather than by the previously learned short vowel sound; thus, for example,

$$IE = I, OA = O, EA = E, EE = E.$$

This is usually taught as one rule; the silent e rule is not singled out as a special case. That is, children are taught to look for the number of vowels in the word and to respond with the first vowel name if there are two, or with the short vowel sound if there is one. Some children do better, however, learning each letter combination as a separate case. Then embedded pictures are used and the procedure described above is employed.

For instance,

$$ai$$

for "chair." This can be used for teaching any letter combination, whether it be vowel–vowel, consonant–vowel, vowel–consonant, or consonant–consonant. *Remedial Reading Drills* (Hegge, Kirk, and Kirk, 1969), a series of word lists encompassing all phonetic possibilities, is a helpful tool for practice with the child.

Blending disorders. Sound blending is that part of the reading process which involves the child's taking two or more distinct
sounds and merging them so that one smoothly articulated
sequence is heard. It is a process which involves smoothly functioning fine motor control of the vocal musculature as well as accurate
auditory perception. Children can have difficulty with reading
because they have not learned how to blend sounds. They may be
able to correctly perform all the other required steps—to identify
the letters and attach the appropriate sounds to them in the proper
sequence—but they may nevertheless be unable to produce the
correct word because they cannot blend.

While this is a relatively rare condition, when it exists its impact
upon reading is profound. Its successful remediation may produce
dramatic results. The problem of blending sounds independent of
letters is approached without letters present because it is unclear
whether failures in sound blending are due to poor auditory perceptual abilities or to conceptual failures, that is, the child simply does
not understand the task. The remedial process involves four steps,
the child at first having only to make simple differentiations and
ultimately to make his own blends.

In the first step, the teacher, using a list of sounds and sound
blends the child has already mastered (e.g., "r-o, ro"; "a-b, ab")
always says the "two" separate sounds first and the blended sounds
second. The child has to "guess" which is the "one" (i.e., the
blended) sound and say it. For example, if the teacher says "r-o, ro,"
then the child says "ro." If the child has difficulty deciding which is
the "one" sound, the teacher can accentuate this distinction by
tapping as the "two" sounds and the blended sound are presented.
The teacher taps each time a single sound is presented (one tap each
for "r" and "o," two taps in all) and, followed by a pause, one tap for
the blended sound. This is maintained in the procedure and slowly
faded so that the child becomes less dependent upon it in making
the discrimination.

The second step involves randomizing the order of presentation such that the cue sound is sometimes given first (e.g., "ro,"
"r-o"). This is an essential step to insure that the child does not
develop a response set, always saying the last thing he has heard.
This is an approach which would in the first step always result in the
correct response or guess. This is done until the task seems well
learned, by some preestablished criterion of success, for example,
85 percent correct.

In the third step, all terms are presented in the same order, the "two" sounds followed by the "one" sound. The child still selects the "one" sound, reporting his guess. The difference between this step and the first is that now it has been established that the child can actually perform the task without relying on a response set. This step is essentially a bridge, albeit a critical one, to the fourth step.

At the last step, the child must guess what the teacher is going to say after the teacher has said the "two" sounds. In other words, the child, not the teacher, will be making the blend. In using this procedure, it is important that a sufficiently long list of sounds is employed so that the child does not learn all of the list by rote. In this last step, if there is any question about whether the child has really learned the task, the teacher can introduce new and unfamiliar sounds. If the child can anticipate what the teacher will say, then he has learned to blend.

Language-based sequential disorders: Numerical and temporal organization. The theoretical basis for the methods to be discussed derives in part from the works of Piaget (1969) and Luria (1973). Mental operations in normal children develop from sensorimotor operations. As mental faculties become more efficient, the underlying sensorimotor processes are not as evident, and in fact usually abate. Many mental skills seem quite automatic to the adult, although in the process of becoming automatic they require language mediation. For example, when an adult is asked the sum of 3 and 2 he can produce the answer as quickly as a calculator. The information is accessible without resort to counting. Young children, however, always seem to need objects or fingers as aids. As the frequency of doing sums increases, the reliance on counting diminishes and certain combinations of numbers become automatic. Children with dissociated sensorimotor and verbal functions need to refer to concrete counting of objects in doing sums. The automatic quality of simple sums never seems to develop.

In order to eliminate counting and in order to develop other concepts of sequence, the child is taught a sensorimotor schema on which serial organization can be based. Further, he is provided with the language constructs that help mediate sensorimotor and mental processes. The successive transformations are diagrammed in Table 7-1.

Teaching of these sequential organizational skills is crucial because, aside from correcting the child in time and along the

Table 7-1
Successive Transformations from Nominative to Sensorimotor to Mental Operations

Transformations	Synonyms		Use
I. Nominative	Front ↓	Back ↓	Stable body anchor
II. Motor	In Front	In Back	Transformation from nominative to sensorimotor
III. Verbal Motor	Before	After	For all serial organization
IV. Mental Systems of Serial Organization			
A. Number	Before ↓	After ↓	
1. Quantity	{ Less Smaller	{ More Bigger	
2. Arithmetic Operations	Minus	Plus	
B. Time	Before ↓	After ↓	
1. Clock Reading	Before	After	
2. Days of Week	Yesterday / Day before yesterday	Tomorrow / Day after tomorrow	
3. Months	Last Month	Next Month	
4. Seasons	Last	Next	

number line, the newly acquired structures are directly applicable to learning simple arithmetic, especially in helping orient the child in the spatial arrangement of numbers and in learning the procedural steps in handling different mathematical operations. One should regard sequential organization as the elemental building block upon which all future learning of these arithmetic operations is built. Children with disorganization in sequencing often need further special procedures for deciding how to write two-digit numbers, learning which of the digits in a number is to be carried in simple addition, how to borrow in subtraction, where to place numbers in multiplication, and to organize the sequence of steps in division. The understanding of the terms "before" and "after" in both their temporal and spatial meanings is necessary in all of these operations. Children who do not have serious sequential confusion or language problems which result in confusion over sequential-spatial terms—"before," "after," "less," "greater," and the like —do not require the following remedial intervention. They are provided with a means of making number facts automatic without reliance on counting (see pp. 299–306).

The approach begins with terms with which the child is usually familiar: the "front" and "back" of his body. These nominative terms are given directional meaning by having the child walk and point in response to the commands "walk in front," "walk in back." The command is slowly changed by associating the terms "before" with "in front" and "after" with "in back". These two terms "before" and "after" become the foundation for all subsequent mental systems of serial organization.

Through association the child eventually learns that "before" means the same as "less" or "smaller" for quantity concepts, "minus" in arithmetic operations, "yesterday" for the days of the week, and "last" for the months and seasons of the year. Similarly, the child learns that "after" means the same as "more" or "bigger" for quantity concepts, "plus" in arithmetic operations, "tomorrow" for the days of the week, and "next" for the months and seasons of the year.

Frequently children do not understand that "point in front" refers to the space before them. They respond to the nominative meaning of "front" and point to their chest. Therefore, one has to demonstrate what it is that one wants when asking the child to point and to walk. The phrases "in front" and "in back" then become organizers for movement in space. In order to assure that the child attends to body and not room cues he is rotated in space several times during these instructions.

Table 7-2 shows successive transformations from nominative to sensorimotor to mental operations specific to the number system. In step 1 the child is asked for the name of the appropriate part of

Table 7-2
Successive Transformation from Nominative to
Sensorimotor to Mental Operations of the Number System

Process	Stimuli		Response	
	Auditory	Visual	Motor	Verbal
	1. Touch child's chest (or back). What part of your body is this?	Hand on child's chest (or back)	— —	My front (my back)
First Synonym Introduced	2. Point in front (in back)	— —	Pointing	— —
	3. Walk in front (in back)	— —	Pointing & walking	— —
Second Synonym Introduced	4. Walk in front, before (or in back, after)	— —	Pointing & walking	— —
Auditory Fading Introduced	5. Walk before (in front faded)	— —	Pointing & walking	— —
	6. Walk before (or after)	Aligned figures	Pointing & walking	— —
	7. Walk before 9 (child standing at figure 9)	Aligned figures & numerals	Pointing & walking	Before 9 is 8
Visual Fading Begins	8. Walk before 6	Aligned figures. Numerals face down	Point, walk. Check verbal response (looking at overturned numeral)	Before 6 is 5
Rotation of Figures and Child's Body	9. What number is before 10?	Aligned figures. Numerals face up	Point before (left) walking laterally	Before 10 is 9
Visual Fading Continues	10. What number is before 6?	Aligned figures. Numerals face down	Point, walking laterally. Check verbal response	Before 6 is 5

Table 7-2 (continued)

| Process | Stimuli | | Response | |
	Auditory	Visual	Motor	Verbal
Motor Fading	11. What number is before 11?	Figures removed. Numerals face down	Pointing. No walking. Check verbal response	Before 11 is 10
	12. What number is before 11?	No visual stimuli	No motor response required.	10

his body. In steps 2 and 3 the first synonym is introduced changing the naming response to a directional response in the form of both pointing and walking. At step 4 the second synonym is introduced. The word "before" is associated with the phrase "in front". In step 5, fading begins; that is the elimination of the irrelevant phrase "in front". The responses to all of these changes in commands remain the same, that is, the child always points and walks.

The next stage requires the child to generalize the directional terms from his own body to other figures. Toward this end he aligns models of people on a table, all facing in the same direction. Models of people can be very simple, the minimum requirements being that they be full people with a readily identifiable front and back (see Figure 7-2).

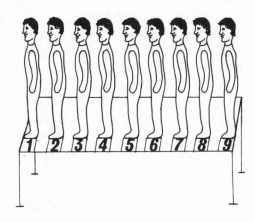

Figure 7-2

The same process is used for teaching the child how to respond to the word "after" such that "after" becomes associated with "behind" and the child walks "behind–after" instead of "in front–before."

In the early stages of teaching, it is crucial that he face in the same direction as these models and that the models be spaced sufficiently far apart that the child in walking one step be near only one figure. Next to each figure is a printed numeral. When the child walks "in front" or "before" he walks toward the lower end of the number series. Conversely, when he is asked to walk "after" he will walk backwards toward the higher end of the number series.

In step 6 he is given practice in walking "before" and "after" along the aligned figures. For steps 7 through 12, the verbal stimuli in this table are sample test items used after teaching has taken place. The teaching process itself involves having the child go through the whole number series from 1–12 for "after" instruction and from 12–1 for "before" instructions. For example, between steps 6 and 7 the following teaching procedure would have taken place: the child stands at 12, points, walks forward one step, and reads the new number while saying, "Before 12 is 11." He then points, takes another step, reads the new number and says, "Before 11 is 10," and so on. Until step 11, pointing and walking through the number series is required. Successive fading of stimuli occurs through step 11 and successive fading of responses occurs at steps 11 and 12.

At step 8 the numerals are face down, requiring the child to rely on memory. A checking procedure is incorporated by reference to the cards. At step 9 the numerals may be returned to face-up position, as the child is rotated in space facing the figures. In this step he is required to walk laterally. He now has to image the forward and backward motion of his own body along a left to right continuum. If returning numerals to their face-up position in step 9 is necessary, then in step 10 the numerals are returned to their face down position.

At step 11 the figures are removed, requiring internalization of directional cues to movement. At step 12 all visual cues are removed and motor responses are inhibited, rendering the whole procedure mental. The linear arrangement of numbers 1–12 is now converted to a circular one in preparation for clock reading.

Having the child construct the clock in order to focus on the direction that the figures face is crucial for later recall of direction after the figures have been removed. The child now learns to move "before" and "after" numbers in a circular pattern and, in addition, now moves past 12 to 1. Procedures similar to those used for the number system are employed for clock reading. Fading of both visual cues and motor responses takes place.

The teaching of minute reading, that is, that one is supposed to say "five" when looking at "1" on a clock, "ten" when looking at a "2," and the like, is relatively simple as is the procedure for recognizing the "before" and "after" sides of a clock. More difficult to teach is the decision about the position of the hour hand when it is between two numbers. The reason for this difficulty is that the referent changes from the number series itself, to an object (hour hand). The cues for making the decision remain the same, the "front" and "back" of the figures. The child stands between the two numbers on either side of the hour hand. The front of one figure and the back of another appear in the visual field. In response to the question, "What number is the hour hand before?" he picks the number that corresponds to the figure whose face (front) he sees, in this case, 6. In response to the question, "What number is the hour hand after?" he picks the number that corresponds to the figure whose back he sees. Eventually these figures are removed and the child is required to remember the direction of orientation of the figures in order to make appropriate responses to these questions.

All the elements for telling time have been taught in isolation: on which side of the clock the hour hand is, the minute equivalent to the numerals on the face of the clock, and the relative position of the hour hand when it is between two numerals. The last step is the teaching of clock reading when all of these elements are presented together. A binary decision process is incorporated in this final stage.

Figure 7-3 shows the verbal formula for this decision. The child goes through the following procedures for each of the tasks. The days of the week are taught linearly in the same fashion as number sequencing. The figures are aligned and word cards of the days are placed near each figure. "Before" and "after" are the initial terms used and are subsequently made synonymous, in terms of motor movements, with "yesterday" and "tomorrow." Both the visual stimuli (i.e., cards and figures) and motor responses (i.e., walking and pointing) are gradually faded. One can often note the use of the child's thumbs, remnants of earlier gross motor associations. The procedure for the "day before yesterday" involves two steps forward, one for "before" and one for "yesterday"; the procedure for the "day after tomorrow" involves two steps backward, one for "after" and one for "tomorrow." Similar instructions are used for the months of the year.

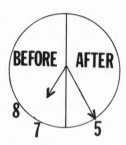

1. The minute hand is on the *after* side so I have to pick the *after* number.	1. The minute hand is on the *before* side so I have to pick the *before* number.
2. The hour hand is *before* 8 and *after* 7.	2. The hour hand is *after* 4 and *before* 5.
3. (Therefore) *after* 7.	3. (Therefore) *before* 5.
4. How much *after* 7?	4. How much *before* 5?
5. 25 *after* 7.	5. 20 *before* 5.

Figure 7-3
Verbal Formulae for Deciding the Time to Read

It is sometimes seen that a child who has learned all these operations still cannot decide which of two multidigited numbers is larger and which is smaller, although he can do this task for single-digit numbers after being trained as described. Explanations such as "the second number from the right means the tens' place" and "the third is the hundreds' place" are incomprehensible to him. How does one decide which of two numbers, for example, 839 and 26, is larger? The process is so automatic that the tendency is to think one simply reads the numbers off and knows that anything in the hundreds is more than a number not in the hundreds. However, it can be done by first counting and then deciding. Because a child is able to decide which of two single-digit numbers is larger, a number such as 839 is placed on three index cards, one digit to a card, and the number 26 on two index cards. To obviate attention to the numerals the child can be taught to turn the five cards upside down and to count the number of cards. He is then instructed to decide which is larger, to replace the cards, and read off that number. Once this is learned, a further contingency is introduced: "What do you do when the number of cards in each number is equal?" The child is instructed in such a circumstance to turn over the "before" or left-side card of each number, decide which is larger, and then replace all upside-down cards. The third contingency is when these first cards are equal in value. He is instructed to go to the next card of each number. Ultimately, he may be able to perform these tasks with pencil and paper and look as if he is doing exactly what anyone else does in making such decisions. The shunt here involves the use of sensorimotor schema for eventual mental operations.

One may appropriately ask whether children taught in this manner ever develop sequential concepts identical to those of other children. The answer is an auxiliary question: what is meant by a concept? A concept is a theoretical construct which a person has if he can do a series of tasks thought to require that concept. Suppose a concept is chosen and all the possible ways of testing whether an individual indeed possesses it are identified. Now suppose a particular individual is taught to perform on all the tasks identified. If the subject has not generalized from one task to another but has learned all the possible tests of the concept, that individual would be indistinguishable from others who did generalize and, for all practical purposes, could get along as well as the generalizer, at least in regard to that one concept. When a child fails to develop a generalization from operations, then the educator's task is simply to teach more operations. The development of a concept can be potentiated by organizing materials and operations in such a way as to increase the likelihood of the concept developing. But conceptualizations are not essential for all kinds of learning. If a child is taught something which is at the least important to him in various life situations, it is hoped that he will make generalizations, or something like generalizations, from what he is taught.

Disorders of writing: Reversals. Disorders of writing due to dyspraxic or constructional problems (i.e., the inability to produce the appropriate lines), will not be discussed here. These are more basic disorders less frequently encountered in practice. Rather, we will consider letter reversals that occur past a developmental stage at which they are supposed to have corrected themselves. These disorders, contrary to what is typically thought, seem rarely to be associated with visual perceptual difficulties but more often involve a failure in integration of language mediators associated with motor acts or in the development of reliable kinesthetic images. The child who reverses when asked to solve true perceptual discrimination tasks often has little difficulty. He can say that a forward five, "5," and a backward five, "ƨ ," are different, but he may not be able to tell which is correct. Or he may be able to tell which is correct when presented with both but reverses when presented with a blank piece of paper on which to write. The fact that he reverses indicates that he has all the perceptual elements available as visual images but that his motor acts are not congruent with these images. This is especially true and graphically seen in older children who erase their reversed letters.

It is helpful to have the labels "left" and "right" available for this process, as well as for other spatial events. A visual cue, for example, a mole on one hand or fingernail polish on a finger of one hand, is typically useful in aiding the child with this discrimination.

To begin, one must note how the child constructs each of his reversed letters and numbers. Some children start from the top while others start from the bottom of the figure. Most children, although they may vary their starting place between letters or numbers, do begin in the same place for a particular letter or number. Thus, a child who begins a "2" from the top and an "S" from the bottom usually does so routinely. Having mapped out where each reversed figure is started, it is a simple matter to require that figure to be drawn at the edge of the paper so that it cannot be reversed. For example, if the child starts an S from the top, one places a dot at the extreme right edge of the paper so that he cannot move his pencil to the right without going off the paper (see Figure 7-4). It is further stipulated for the child that "S's" always start "over here" or "on the right side" of the paper. Exercises for all the right-sided letters and numbers can be introduced with a dot moving toward the center of the page along a drawn-in margin. The field to the right of the margin is "out of bounds" and, if need be, colored in. The left-sided letters and numbers, that is, those that have to begin at the left edge in order that they not be reversed, are similarly taught; this is the shunt. Fading enters as one literally fades the visual cues, making the drawn-in margin lighter and lighter until it is perhaps one dot and the out-of-bounds area lighter and lighter if it had been colored in. It is important during such exercises that the child be given the language elements (such as those described above) necessary for remembering which group starts at the left and which at the right. When he is then faced with a blank piece of paper and has to draw a previously reversed figure in the center of the page, he need make only quick reference to the side of the page he originally learned to associate with that figure.

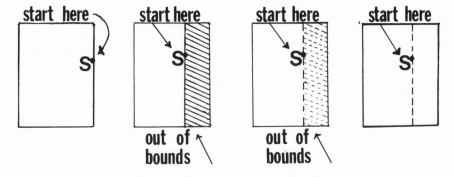

Figure 7-4

Dysgraphia.   Unfortunately, this disorder is one which offers few successful remedial possibilities. While there are some remedial strategies that can be employed, they are typically effective only with very bright children who are extremely ambitious, since the work is demanding and frustrating. The more typical approach to dysgraphic problems is one which permits the child to experience some relief. Parents are educated as to what dysgraphia is, and are helped to communicate with the school to lessen demands on the child in his particular area of difficulty. A remedial therapist or psychologist is available to the school to serve an educative function since most schools and educators are not acquainted with dysgraphia, in contrast with dyslexia.

To enable parents to better deal with schools, letters (or consultation on writing letters) are provided. Examples of such communications follow. One is written by a parent of a bright 9 1/2-year-old boy describing his son's difficulty:

To Carl's Teachers:

This letter is an attempt to clarify a very confusing problem which Carl has with his schoolwork and his ability to demonstrate his learning capacity. Carl is dysgraphic and this presents a rather perplexing and easily misunderstood condition. This problem lends itself to much confusion for Carl's teachers, his parents, and, perhaps above all, sometimes Carl himself.

Dysgraphia is a condition which is defined as a difficulty or inability to express ideas by means of writing or written symbols. It can be present congenitally at birth or develop later in life as a result of various neurological disorders.

Before I attempt to describe what dysgraphia is like, let me describe what it is not. It has nothing to do with intelligence, verbal ability, mathematical ability, etc. Carl has a verbal IQ of 130 (98th percentile), a Performance IQ of 111 (79th percentile) and a Full Scale IQ of 123 (94th percentile). His highest scores on subtests are in Information, Arithmetic, and Vocabulary. The 19-point difference between Verbal and Performance IQ suggests uneven development and Verbal IQ is often the more accurate predictor of actual ability. Dysgraphia is not dyslexia. Dyslexia is an impairment of the ability to read or to understand what one reads silently or aloud, independent of any speech defect. Children who are dyslexic often have dysgraphic problems as well. If you have trouble reading, you will have trouble writing. Carl has no problem at all with reading. He is an avid reader and soaks up information like a sponge. His dysgraphia is a "pure" writing problem, present most likely as a congenital difficulty. Dysgraphia is not a "motor" problem. Carl has no difficulty at all with the movement of his hands, fingers, etc., or his ability to write letters or words.

What then is Carl's dysgraphia like? He has great difficulty in getting his ideas onto the written page. Since this has nothing to do with his ability to write, the written page means the typewritten page also. The difficulty comes in complex tasks and is therefore very confusing to the observer. For instance, he may be able to spell very well in his head. He may also be able to spell a list of words perfectly by writing them down. However, when he is trying to write a sentence and express a more complicated synthesis of words he will have difficulty. The difficulty is not with the ability to express the ideas or concepts. He can speak them clearly, articulately, and often creatively. The difficulty is purely with getting the sentence to the written page. An analogy would be that although you may be able to easily juggle a single ball up and down in the air with your right hand, if you attempted it while trying to simultaneously do the same thing with your left hand while standing on one leg and spinning a hoop on the other leg, you might drop the ball from your right hand. Thus, Carl's written sentences are confusing, with words left out, misspelled, etc. The misspelling has nothing to do with his ability to spell and is inconsistent and therefore open to misinterpretation as being the product of carelessness. Often very simple words are spelled wrong such as: the = "he," off = "of," could = "chould." Carl has problems with written mathematics. Thus he can tell you that 75 plus 8 is 83 but on the written page it may come out:

$$\begin{array}{r} 75 \\ + \ 8 \\ \hline 163 \end{array}$$

This is arrived at by $8 + 5 = 13$, carry the $1, 8 + 7 = 15$ plus the $1 = 16$.

It can be mind boggling to see this in action. While doing multiplication flash cards with him recently he verbally was arriving at answers as follows: "9 times 7 is 10 times 7, 70, minus 7, equals 63. 8 times 4 is 2 times 8, 16, plus 2 times 8, 16, equals 32." While all of this was going on I saw his written answers on the back of the card which had reversed 3s and 5s written down. Another interesting example of this is that if you observe Carl writing 14 you will see him write the 4 first, then the 1 to the left of the 4. That is his method of correcting his tendency to wind up writing "four-teen" equals 4-1 (41), just as you write "thirty-two" equals 3-2 (32).

Can Carl write? Can practice make things better? The answers are yes and perhaps. But the analogy is as follows. If you are right-handed, can you copy a sentence with your left hand while looking through a mirror? Would it involve inordinate amounts of time, energy, and patience and would you soon get very turned off to the task especially if you were constantly being reminded that you were sloppy even after you had put in all that effort? The answer is yes. Would all that effort take energy away from the task of writing a creative sentence? The answer is yes. Would you, being aware of your capability of thought and inability to express it on paper and your inability to get the reward of success instead of the punishment of failure, become depressed, uninterested in school, and disorganized in your study habits? The answer is yes. Dysgraphic children often wind up by age 12 or 13 refusing to go to school.

All of this raises numerous questions for you as Carl's teachers as well as for Carl and his parents. We would like to pursue those questions at meetings with you throughout the year.

Sincerely,

Two additional types of letters outline the special educational needs a dysgraphic child might have. The second is clearly more dramatic and meant to shock. It has been observed that many children, particularly adolescents, languish in school for years with this disorder. This "shock" letter is, therefore, designed to alert people to the problems the child presents. It is a good position from which to begin bargaining with an intransigent school that will not make accommodations to a child's disorder.

To Whom It May Concern:

Dysgraphia is a condition which is defined as a difficulty or inability to express ideas by means of written symbols. Treatment for Dysgraphia requires the services of a trained professional.

Educating a student with Dysgraphia requires only modest accommodation and understanding on the part of the school. Thus, a mainstream secondary school, deciding that an applicant is otherwise worthy, can with assurance enroll the candidate in the regular curriculum.

The underlying premise of accommodation and understanding is to provide maximum relief from requirements to write with a minimum of deviation from the usual program. Explicitly, no punitive consequences or grade reduction for errors in spelling and punctuation should accrue. Because of the arduous nature of the task of writing, whenever possible, as in book reports or lengthy essays, etc., the student should be permitted to taperecord the material, have the tape transcribed, and have the finished product accepted as his own work. Finally, special accommodations, if still necessary, are readily available in college years.

Sincerely,

To Whom It May Concern:

The treatment for dysgraphia is relief.

All compositions (book reports, etc.) should be dictated into a taperecorder or to a scribe who does the writing (a parent, a friend, a secretary). The school should accept the scribe's copy or the taperecording as the *finished* product. To have the child rewrite does *nothing* educationally. Spelling tests should be eliminated if such testing still goes on. For written tests the child should be provided with a proctor (teacher, trusted student) to whom answers are dictated. Foreign language study other than a "Berlitz-type" of education (i.e., vocal) should be avoided. In short, with regard to written productions, the youngster should be treated as one would a person who is blind or who has no hands. Any assignments requiring writing, rewriting, typing, etc., should be regarded as equivalent to someone requiring a cerebral-palsied child to satisfy the usual gym requirements.

In the event someone inadvertently requires writing, no punitive consequences for spelling errors, punctuation, "sloppiness," etc., should accrue. No grading should be based on written performance. Teachers each year may have to be educated about the problem and special accommodations may have to be made in college years.

If need be I will make myself available to the educational staff for further explanation.

Sincerely,

Although it is important to run interference, as it were, for the child in school, a select group of dysgraphic children can benefit from remediation: those who are motivated to undertake a time-consuming, long-term, and frustrating process encompassing three types of approaches. In the first the child learns to say words phonetically, or "funny," and then to spell what he hears; this, of course, requires intact phonetic skills. To ensure that this is the case, time is spent periodically and repetitively with phonetic dictation. For example, if the teacher says the sound "ow," then the child must be able to write either "ou" or "ow." When a word is said phonetically, it frequently bears little resemblance to its correct pronunciation (e.g., *beach* is pronounced *be-ach*, *cough* is pronounced *co-ugh*, and *laugh* is pronounced *la-ugh*). This clearly requires the child to keep track of large amounts of material and fairly complex transformations. A typical way to begin this approach is with spelling lists two grades below the child's grade level from which the unfamiliar words are culled. Considerable effort is required as teacher and child go through 50 words at a clip finding those the child does not know. Interestingly, it is often the more difficult or longer words that present less difficulty. Other lists such as "one hundred spelling demons" or homonyms may also be useful (see Tables 7-3 and 7–4).

TABLE 7-3
One Hundred Spelling Demons

ache	friend	shoes
again	grammar	since
always	guess	some
among	half	straight
answer	having	sugar
any	hear	sure
been	heard	tear
beginning	here	their
believe	hoarse	there
blue	hour	they
break	instead	through
built	just	though
business	knew	tired
busy	know	tonight
buy	laid	too
can't	loose	trouble
choose	lose	truly
color	making	Tuesday
coming	many	two
cough	meant	used
could	minute	very
country	much	wear
dear	none	Wednesday
doctor	often	week
does	once	where
done	piece	whether
don't	raise	which
early	road	whole
easy	ready	women
enough	said	won't
every	says	would
February	seems	write
forty	separate	writing
from		wrote

Table 7-4
Homonyms

break	whole	beet
brake	hole	beat
creek	capitol	cellar
creak	capital	seller
board	peek	bin
bored	peak	been
cell	where	hall
sell	wear	haul
course	here	fur
coarse	hear	fir
reed	to	ade
read	too	aid
	two	
		borough
steel	won	burro
steal	one	burrow
real	see	eight
reel	sea	ate
hi	deer	so
high	dear	sew
I	bear	no
eye	bare	know
flower	laid	mane
flour	layed	main
tee	leak	cent
tea	leek	sent
week	pier	threw
weak	peer	through

(Continued)

Table 4
Homonyms (continued)

wood	lead	new
would	led	knew
weather	plain	pear
whether	plane	pair
rap	sail	which
wrap	sale	witch
steak	grown	him
stake	groan	hymn
by	horse	flyer
buy	hoarse	flier
bye		
herd	hour	sum
heard	our	some

Words that continue to present difficulty after this approach can sometimes be taught through a kind of mnemonic device. The child is taught a sentence that will somehow aid him in remembering how to spell the word in question. For instance, the mnemonic sentence for "sleeve" might be "I have three e's up my sleeve." One child who was unable to distinguish between "course" and "coarse" using phonetic pronunciation learned to differentiate them using several sentences: for "coarse" he used, "My coat is coarse" and for "course," he used, "The tour is on course." This naturally relied upon his ability to spell "coat" and "tour."

A last resort for teaching phonetics involves a process similar to the embedded alphabet. This technique is generally effective, but slow and laborious. Pictures that incorporate and somehow demonstrate the word are drawn. The child then uses them to recall the spelling of the word; thus he recalls line structure, rather than a sequence of letters. For example, "holy" is represented as:

"Camel" can be represented as:

One of the values of these approaches is that they teach something specific, as well as general. Once the bright and motivated child learns the principle of each of these three techniques he can generate his own phonetic pronunciations, his own sentences, or his own pictures.

Arithmetic disorders. A child with an arithmetic disorder usually presents with difficulties that fall in two broad areas: one is a difficulty in retaining number facts, the other includes difficulties in maintaining the proper sequence of steps in solving an operation, sometimes, but not necessarily, in conjunction with mastering the spatial aspects of the problem. For example, carrying involves not only a sequence of discrete steps but also judgments about which numbers to put where.

Number Facts. The first remedial emphasis falls upon teaching number facts. Addition comes first, followed by subtraction, multiplication, and division, in that order. Each set of number facts is approached in a step-by-step method; the child has to learn each step before moving on to the next one. The amount of information to be learned at any one step is thus controlled and kept manageable. The set of possible number combinations is broken down into a series of rules, eventually covering all but a few of the number combinations. The goal is for the child to know the facts without finger counting; the shunt (i.e. the rule), always serves as a means for the child to arrive at the correct answer without having to count on his fingers. Finger counting tends to result in errors as well as being slow and tedious. While there is nothing wrong in principle with finger counting, it is simply not very successful.

While the rules presented here are complex and may seem to be more difficult than learning number facts by simple association, this is not the case for some children with arithmetic disorders. They have demonstrated an inability to retain number facts by drill and thus require a process by which any number fact can be recalled. The rules discussed here contribute to that process by which a child does not have to rely upon arbitrary associations. The association becomes meaningful and is, therefore, more easily recalled.

The child is presented with each rule, and all the examples of that rule are written in red on index cards. He employs the rule to aim at the correct answer as quickly as possible. As the first rule is learned with sufficient speed and total accuracy, its set of cards is converted to another color and set aside except for occasional practice. A new rule is introduced on another set of cards written in red. This rule is practiced independently until it too is learned with sufficient speed and complete accuracy. Once accuracy and speed are achieved, the two sets of cards are combined and mixed. As the child reaches the point where all examples of both sets are responded to correctly and speedily, then the cards are all converted to the same color and a third rule is introduced. This procedure is followed for each individual rule within each set of rules until the child has two full sets of cards containing all the possible number combinations. The cards written in red—or whichever discrimination color is selected—can be given to the child as tangible proof of what he has learned. It should be noted that some children tend to learn these number facts rather concretely and will not necessarily generalize from

$$\begin{array}{r} 2 \\ + 5 \\ \hline \end{array} \quad \text{to} \quad \begin{array}{r} 5 \\ + 2 \\ \hline \end{array} \quad \text{or from} \quad \begin{array}{r} 8 \\ \times 3 \\ \hline \end{array} \quad \text{to} \quad \begin{array}{r} 3 \\ \times 8 \\ \hline \end{array}$$

Cards with both possible configurations will be needed for children who do not generalize from one to the other. Care should also be taken that the examples be presented vertically rather than horizontally, for example,

$$\begin{array}{r} 5 \\ + 2 \\ \hline \end{array} \quad \text{not} \quad 5 + 2 =.$$

Children who have spatial or lateralization problems may not generalize correctly from the horizontal to the vertical format.

What follows is a discussion of the set of rules for addition, subtraction, multiplication, and division. While no reference will be made to the above general procedure, it must be remembered that it is a principle aspect of the remedial process. The rules discussed below should be presented using these principles. Some children seem to take to the "tricks" while others fight them. It goes without saying that those who fight them do not do as well.

ADDITION.   Addition facts are broken down into the following set of rules:

1. + 0 rule—any number plus 0 is itself;

2. + 1 rule—any number plus 1 is the one after it on the number line;

3. Double rule—the doubles are taught; for some reason, children tend to learn these quickly, even though there is no rule here to follow and memorization is required. Note that 0 + 0 and 1 + 1 do not have to be included since they are already learned;

4. + 9 rule—for any number plus 9, find the number that is not 9, go back one from (or before) that number, put a 1 in front of it and that is the answer. For example, to solve

$$\begin{array}{r} 9 \\ + 3 \\ \hline \end{array},$$

the number that is not 9 is 3, one back from it is 2, putting a 1 in front of it makes 12. Some children are helped by encouraging them to picture filling the loop of the 9 with the number before 3 and putting a 1 in front of it. Therefore,

5. $+8$ rule—this is the same as the $+9$ rule except that the child goes back two numbers. He can be encouraged to visualize counting backwards in the loops of the 8 and putting a 1 in front of the second number. Therefore,

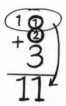

6. Good neighbor rule—if two numbers are next to each other along the number line, find the smaller of the two, double it, and add 1 to that number. For example, to solve

$$\begin{array}{r} 7 \\ +\ 6 \end{array},$$

the smaller number, 6, doubled is 12, add 1 (or count one more) is 13;

7. The missing number rule—if two numbers are separated by one other number along the number line, find the missing number, double it, and that is the answer. For example, to solve

$$\begin{array}{r} 6 \\ +\ 4 \end{array},$$

the missing number 5, when doubled, is 10;

8. The last step involves learning the few combinations remaining. These can be learned by rote by most children. If not, then rules 6 and 7 can be applied to them using a number line. With a number line of 0 to 9, the child puts his right finger on the larger number and his left finger on the smaller one and starts moving his fingers symmetrically toward each other, number by number. He must stop when there is no number in between or when there is one number in between. If there are no numbers in between, then he applies the good neighbor rule to the number under his finger. If there is one number in between, then he applies the missing number rule. For example, to solve

$$\begin{array}{r} 7 \\ +\ 3 \end{array},$$

as seen in Figure 7-5, there is one number, 5, in between his fingers after he has moved them one step; the missing number rule is applied such that 5 is doubled to 10.

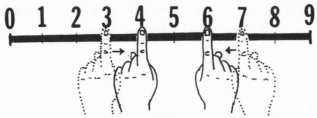

Figure 7-5

SUBTRACTION. Children with difficulty learning number facts have the most trouble with subtraction. There are few rules, or "tricks," that can be taught. While a child may identify $5 + 4$ as a manifestation of a rule, that same child does not so readily identify $5 - 4$ as such. Some of the rules used are:

1. $- 0$ rule—any number minus zero is itself;

2. $- 1$ rule—any number minus 1 is the one before it on the number line. To solve $9 - 1$, the number before 9 is 8;

3. Identity rule—any number minus itself is 0;

4. $- 9$ rule—this applies only to the teen numbers, but other possibilities are already covered by the previous rules. For a teen number minus 9, add the two numbers of the teen number together for the answer. To compute

$$\begin{array}{r} 17 \\ - 9 \end{array},$$

the answer is $1 + 7 = 8$;

5. $- 8$ rule—this is the same as the $- 9$ rule but when one adds the two numbers of the teen number together, one must also add one more. To subtract

$$\begin{array}{r} 13 \\ - 8 \end{array},$$

$1 + 3 = 4$, then $4 + 1 = 5$.

A missing number rule and a good neighbor rule can be taught in subtraction, but again, children tend to have difficulty identifying and using them reliably. Some counting is generally needed. With that, however, children should be taught to count up rather than down, as they are taught in school, since it makes for less confusion. Presented with $9 - 3$, for example, the child counts with 4 being his first step and 9 being the last step, thus there are six steps.

In working with subtraction, it is often helpful to have the child convert a problem into something that is meaningful to him. For instance, one boy when faced with

$$\begin{array}{r} 5 \\ -\ 4 \end{array},$$

would simply stare. If one said to him, "If you had five cookies and somebody took four, how many would you have left?" he readily said, "One." The process became one of getting him to make that statement to himself.

MULTIPLICATION.   Multiplication facts present some special problems but are generally learned fairly rapidly. Again, each rule is begun only after the previous rule has been fully learned and the steps followed are those steps outlined above. The multiplication facts are taught through the 11s only. Twelves tables are not taught since they are rarely used. Although 10s and 11s are also used infrequently, they are taught because they are easily learned and the child feels a sense of competence in having mastered "my elevenses." The rules are:

1. × 0 rule—any number multiplied by 0 is 0;
2. × 1 rule—any number multiplied by 1 is itself;
3. Double rule—any number multiplied by 2 is the same as the double rule in addition. For example, 8×2 is the same as $8 + 8$;
4. × 10 rule—for a number times 10, put zero after it;
5. × 11 rule—for a number times 11, write the number twice;
6. × 9 rule—this rule involves a trick using the hands. The hands are placed palms down on the table and each finger, including the thumb, is numbered beginning on the left and moving to the right, as in Figure 7-6. For example, to compute 9×6, the 6 finger is put down. The number of fingers to the left of that finger becomes

Figure 7-6
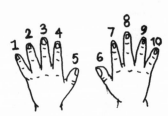

the "tens" ($5 \times 10 = 50$) and the number of fingers to the right of that finger becomes the "ones" ($4 \times 1 = 4$). The two are written in that order, or "put together" to make 54. Perhaps more simply stated, the number of fingers to the left becomes the first number of a two-place number (5 $\times$) and the number of fingers to the right becomes the second number of that two-place number (5 4);

7. The bridge—this rule also involves a trick with the hands. It is good for any number 6 or more, up to and including 10, multiplied by any number 6 or more, up to and including 10. For example, to compute $6 \times 6, 6 \times 7, 6 \times 8, 7 \times 7, 7 \times 8, 8 \times 8$, the hands are held in front, palms facing inward with the thumbs up. Each finger is assigned a number as shown in Figure 7-7. To multiply 6 $\times$

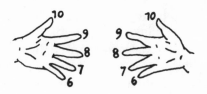

Figure 7-7

8, the 6 finger of one hand is touched to the 8 finger of the other hand (Figure 7-8). The two fingers touching and all these below (the darkened fingers)—as the thumbs are pointing up—are each worth 10. If there are four fingers, that makes 40. The number of fingers (4) on the left hand above the touching finger is then multiplied by the number of fingers (2) above the touching finger on the right hand, thus $4 \times 2 = 8$. That product is added to the earlier one for the answer ($40 + 8 = 48$);

Figure 7-8

8. $\times$ 3 rule—the child is taught to count by 3s. The child learns in three groups: 3 — 6 — 9 are learned in one week, 12 — 15 —18 are learned the next week, and 21 — 24 — 27 are learned the following week. Another method is to teach the child to count aloud, emphasizing strongly every third number, eventually fading all but every third number;

9. × 4 rule—the child is taught to count by 4s as in the ×3 rule; and

10. × 5 rule—the child, if he does not already know how, learns to count by 5s. Note that he must learn only $5 \times 5, 5 \times 6, 5 \times 7,$ 5×8.

With that, the multiplication number facts should be mastered.

DIVISION.   Division is not taught as a series of facts but as a process. Short division is not permitted since performing an operation "in the head" presents great difficulties for these children. Instead, the teacher insists that all steps be written down.

For numbers divided by 2, 3, or 5, the child counts by 2, 3, or 5 until he reaches the number that is the dividend. For 2s, the child can be encouraged to think of the doubles. For example, to compute "2 into 16," he is asked, "What number times 2 is the dividend?" In general, however, these children have difficulty reversing a process, thus making it difficult for them to recall multiplication facts for use in division. Nevertheless, for a number divided by 6, 7, or 8, one hopes those multiplication tables are remembered well enough. Extra work to render these sufficiently automatic is frequently required. For a number divided by 4, the child can either count by 4s or divide by 2 twice. For example, to divide 4 $\overline{|16}$, the child first computes 2 $\overline{|16}$, arriving at an answer of 8. He then divides 2 $\overline{|8}$, arriving at the answer of 4, which is the solution to 4 $\overline{|16}$ For a number divided by 9, if the dividend is only a two-digit number, the answer is the first digit plus 1. For example, to calculate 9 $\overline{|54}$ the first digit, 5, is added to 1, making 6. For a longer dividend this same approach is attempted; if it does not work the child tries one number lower. In dividing 9 $\overline{|516}$, he tries 6 but finds it is too large, so he tries 5 which is effective.

Spatial and Right-Left Problems.   Children whose learning disabilities affect their arithmetic performance frequently have difficulty with the spatial and/or lateralization requirements of visually presented arithmetic. These problems call, essentially, for some alteration in the manner in which the problem is presented and in which the child orients himself to the problem.

For instance, adding columns of numbers can present significant problems to a child who has difficulty maintaining the distinction between left and right. Numbers from neighboring columns can easily be incorporated into the column he is adding. The aid here—or the shunt—may be twofold. First, using graph paper and then, if necessary, the drawing of vertical lines (either darker or in another color) through the columns to separate them. Fading can occur, if need be, as the child gradually lightens the line until it becomes nearly imperceptible. At that point it can probably be eliminated. It is also essential that the child always begin on the right and work toward the left. This is a confusing state of affairs for a child who has trouble with such decisions and has always worked left to right in reading and written work.

This same child often encounters difficulty with the process of borrowing and carrying, being uncertain which number to carry, or when and from what to borrow. It is important for this child that the procedures or operations be taught without reference to concepts. To teach carrying, it is first important to make sure the child has no difficulty with number writing, particularly with the teen numbers. Often teen numbers are written with the digits reversed or in the order in which they are heard. For example, the child has learned that to write "forty-three," one writes the digits in the order of hearing them: forty = "4," three = "3." Using this method, however, results in errors when writing teen numbers. For example, "fourteen" becomes "four = 4," "teen = 1" or "41." The child needs to be cued to the need for a different approach so that he can begin to recognize how to correct such errors. Of course, any number writing problem of this sort will result in errors in carrying problems; the wrong number will be carried. The child is then taught to put one number in one place and another number in another place, or to write the number in a "funny way." For instance, instead of writing "32," he must learn to write something more on the order of 3

2.

Learning the operation of borrowing can present great difficulty because so many spatial and left–right decisions are required. For instance, in subtracting the child must first decide which number to subtract, whether it is possible to subtract and, if not, then from which number to "borrow." Again, as in carrying, these steps are all taught operationally, with no reference to the underlying concepts. No reference to "the 10s place," for instance, is ever made. The child must learn to be able to decide whether he can subtract; that is, does he have to borrow? For some children, this is accomplished by presenting pages of single-column subtractions. The child's first task is simply to state whether he can or cannot subtract, based on whether the top number is larger than the bottom number. If it is larger, he can subtract; if it is smaller, he cannot. The next step involves the presentation of subtraction examples all of which involve borrowing. The child must go through a series of rather rote behaviors: crossing out the number "on that side," writing down the number one less, putting a 1 next to the original number and, finally, subtracting. The task is eventually rendered more complicated by the introduction of problems in which no borrowing is required, so the child must decide whether or not carrying is necessary. There is essentially no fading here. The shunt is the process by which one arrives at the correct solution. It is a "shunt" around typically confusing discussions of "one's" place and other more conceptual, and not very explanatory, terms.

Multiple-digit multiplication also presents an array of complicated spatial demands, for example, ascertaining which number to multiply by which other number, which number to carry, and when and where to write the numbers that have been produced through multiplication. This can all be done in a step-by-step manner, much as with borrowing in subtraction. However, a "device" known as the "grating method" (Newman, 1956) circumvents this problem for children with spatial disorders affecting arithmetic. The "grating method" involves multiplying with a matrix and thus few spatial decisions are required. For example, to multiply

$$\frac{\begin{array}{r} 426 \\ \times\,628 \end{array}}{}\,,$$

a 3×3 matrix is established as in Figure 7-9. This can be greatly simplified for the child by having a rubber stamp made with the matrix and diagonal lines included. The child must then multiply within the matrix, that is, $6 \times 8, 2 \times 8, 4 \times 8, 6 \times 2, 2 \times 2, 4 \times 2$, and so on, placing the products as shown in Figure 7-10. The child must then add the products within the diagonals (as encircled in Figure 7-11), starting with the one in the lower right-hand corner, the 8. When numbers need to be carried, as in adding the contents of the next diagonal ($2 + 4 + 6 = 12$), the 1s column is put below the diagonal and the 10s column carried to the subsequent diagonal. For example, the 2 from the 12 is put beneath the second diagonal and the 1 is carried over to the next diagonal which encompasses $3 + 2 + 0 + 8 + 3$, as seen in Figure 7-11. The final product is then read in the direction of the arrows in Figure 7-11, resulting in the answer 267,528.

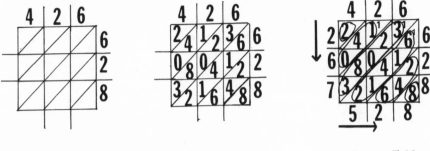

Figure 7-9   Figure 7-10   Figure 7-11

Children with various cognitive problems, particularly difficulty with lateralization, are often confused when required to arrange numbers in columns. Instead of aligning numbers on the right they may align them on the left, or not at all (see Figure 7-12).

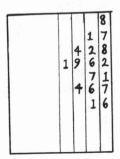

Figure 7-12

This kind of difficulty can be handled by having the child draw vertical columns which end at the right edge of the paper. The child must keep the numbers in columns such that there is no more than one number for each column and the last digit in the column is placed at the edge of the paper, as in Figure 7-13. Gradually, the lines designating columns are faded out.

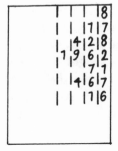

Figure 7-13

In this discussion of remedial approaches for a variety of problems in reading, writing, spelling, and arithmetic, the goal has been not simply to present ways of remediating but rather to illustrate general principles which should underlie any remedial approach. Emphasis has been on the training of specific skills rather than on abstract goals. The principles of shunting and fading are used to facilitate the skills becoming integral to the child's repertoire. The shunt provides a means for the child to arrive at the correct response; the fading of the shunt enables the child to produce the correct response in a way that is *apparently* no different from that of the next child. Furthermore, any particular effort should always be experimental; hypotheses are tested and discarded if necessary. The onus for failure must be on the method not the child, if remediation is to be truly different from the milieu in which the child has already experienced his learning disability. It is the responsibility of the remediator to find a way to teach that which has not yet been learned.

CASE MATERIAL

Case 1: Noah, A Learning Disorder of Primary Psychogenic Etiology: Psychoanalytically Oriented Psychotherapy Without Remediation

As will be recalled, Noah was an 8-year-old boy who suffered from an eye tic and a general preoccupation with his "yucky eyeballs." After two consultations, the second of which revealed no neuropsychological component to his poor school performance, his parents finally consented to the recommendation that Noah required psychotherapy for neurotic conflicts surrounding learning. He was treated in three times weekly psychoanalytically oriented psychotherapy for a period of 15 months and then seen twice a week for several months at his parents' insistence, although against the advice of his psychiatrist, Dr. Farber. He initially appeared as a thin, depressed 9 1/2-year-old boy who spoke easily after overcoming his initial shyness. His concerns were his fears at night, particularly of spiders, and some uncomfortable feelings that he would get in his body but could not clearly describe. He easily reported his frightening dreams, and within the first week of therapy admitted to frightening visual, probably hypnagogic, phenomena when he awakened from a dream in the middle of the night. He showed an almost obsessive curiosity which was subsequently better understood to have its roots in his wishing to see and know more about sexuality and sexual anatomy. He also reported a voice inside his head that warned him it would be "the end" if he told too much about what he thought. He blurted out to his mother during the first week of therapy, "I'm half crazy!"

By inviting Noah to try to understand that his blinking was related to a conflict about seeing, and by being accepting of as well as reassuring about his sharing the things he felt made him "crazy," it was relatively easy to move gradually with him to a better psychodynamic understanding of his conflicts. Furthermore, they could be linked to his need to avoid overwhelming anxiety by not learning and seeming not to know. For instance, through a series of drawings over a period of many months, his fear of "yucky" spiders was understood in terms of primal scene experiences and fantasies. He drew two multilegged, hairy creatures, supposedly spiders, which he labeled Adam and Eve. After he told the therapist that he had sneaked down the hall to peek in his parents' room, to watch and listen for them at night, Dr. Farber suggested that the figures drawn with all the appendages might be like what a boy would see if two grownups were embraced in a clasp with legs and arms intertwined. Noah confirmed this notion and expressed great interest in another series of pictures he drew of hairy insects with pointy stingers. It was not long before he was drawing pictures of his version of what the stingers went into, namely "berginas." These vaginas were threatening dentate organs that elicited both disgust and terror in him. He was familiar with feminine sexual anatomy through having seen his younger sister, but he invested the female genital with frightening aggressiveness. Later on in therapy, he reported a memory of having peeked through the wall of a summer bungalow to witness his mother sitting astride the toilet, separating her labia as if inserting something into herself.

Concurrently the therapist was able to help Noah discuss his father's medical condition and to recover some memories associated with the illness and neurosurgery. It was clear that he had a great deal of knowledge about this, despite his parents' intense denial that their son could know much about it. In addition, suggestions of primal scene exposure were confirmed in sessions with Noah's parents, who admitted quite readily that it was "highly possible" that he had seen them in sexual intercourse. They discovered him in their bed one night during foreplay, "unaware" that he had come in previously.

The psychotherapeutic work led to a lessening of parental punitiveness, a better understanding of the psychodynamic aspects of Noah's learning avoidance, by all parties, and a better resolution of the conflictual aspects of seeing, knowing, and learning on the part of the patient. Not surprisingly, school became more conflict-free, studies became less invested with threat and were, therefore, avoided less. Noah's academic performance and study habits improved significantly after about a year, at which point his parents insisted upon diminishing the frequency of the treatment from three to two times weekly. Ultimately the therapy was discontinued by Noah's parents who were in many ways threatened by change in him. In Dr. Farber's opinion, several important issues remained unresolved, most particularly Noah's intense regressive sibling rivalry. Nevertheless Noah did seem to have achieved a substantial and stable improvement in academic performance.

Case 2: Daniel, a Learning Disorder Based on an Admixture of Psychogenic and Neuropsychological Contributions: Psychoanalysis[4] Concurrent with Remediation Followed by Special Educational Intervention in the School Setting

It will be remembered that Daniel was a 7-year-old boy who demonstrated remarkable social adeptness with adults, side

---

[4]This is a treatment in which the analyst considered an analytic process to have developed. Some colleagues who have reviewed the material were impressed with the meaningfulness of the treatment for the patient but considered it a psychoanalytically oriented psychotherapy. They felt that the primary mode of therapeutic action was the analyst's function as a reparative object rather than a provider of insight through interpretation. While this is an important distinction, it is not central to the purpose of including Daniel's case in this book. His case illustrates the intermeshing of psychological and neuropsychological contributions to a learning disorder. Because he was properly evaluated a treatment plan evolved which included several interventions which complemented each other rather than competing or conflicting.

by side with massive anxiety when interacting with peers and separating from his mother. He was referred for psycho-analysis as well as further psychological testing to assess the possibility of a neuropsychological contribution to his poor school performance. Indeed difficulties in short-term sequential memory, sequential organization, time orientation, reading, and spelling were diagnosed.

Daniel was seen in treatment for 3 1/2 years by Dr. Loni. An attempt will be made to convey the process of this treatment as it interwove with remedial and educational interventions and academic progress. Dr. Loni's role in these aspects of the patient's life will be highlighted since an unusually active, yet harmonious and balanced, attention was devoted to them. In addition, the ways in which Dr. Loni's appreciation of Daniel's neuropsychological deficits colored her thinking about and work with him will be delineated.

The most striking fact of the initial months of the treatment was Daniel's thrust for a relationship with Dr. Loni. During the first few weeks he asked such questions as, "Did you sit in that chair? Do others use that couch? Some don't want to leave, do they?" He quickly grasped Dr. Loni's inquiring stance, saying "I know you'll say, 'I wonder why you do that.' "

Three prominent themes at the outset were his general anxiety, his separation anxiety, and his birth fantasies. These were expressed in play, albeit sometimes with a narrow gap between symbolization and impulse activity. Anal play included calling disks "doodies" and using a Play-Doh machine to form long "stools." In the midst of this play, he often ran from the office to have a bowel movement or drink some water. Anal themes were interwoven with separation and birth fantasies, for example, when he buried a rubber band in a mass of clay and then serially sliced the emerging clay in search of the rubber band. Other similar play involved repetitively, and supposedly secretively, hiding and sliding one door behind another. Daniel also used a combination lock to attach Dr. Loni's purse to his belt or the lock to circles of clay. Less prominent were oedipal conflicts which, when expressed, were in the context of a power struggle. With a "Play-Doh Fuzzy Pumper" he "grew" hair and a beard on a father mold.

Speaking for himself and the father, he enacted a dialogue in which the father did not want a haircut and Daniel insisted, saying "Sorry, Mister, you have to have it." At this early stage of the treatment several resistances were observed. Daniel might feign unawareness, for example, as Dr. Loni interpreted, "Yesterday you also had to have a bowel movement as we talked about your hiding a rubber band in the Play-Doh" or, in relation to his play with the lock, "It feels good to know you can hook us together." Alternatively, when anxious, Daniel might say with mild irritation, "Let's not talk about this," or revert to less organized, aggressive play. In general Daniel expressed joyous pleasure about coming to his hours, and after the first two sessions was able to separate and spontaneously run up to Dr. Loni's office. He clearly stated, "I bet some kids never want to go from here."

During the second six months of treatment, Daniel dealt with a wide range of conflicts and developmental issues. These included separation–individuation and merger, reality testing of wishful fantasies and impulsivity, birth fantasies, castration anxiety, and primal scene preoccupations. He creatively utilized games, original activity patterns, materials from home, and nondeliberate facets of the office—construction in the building and sliding doors in the office—as vehicles to expose and explore these conflicts with Dr. Loni. For example, he piled pillows behind a sliding door, raised them behind the doors to a high shelf, and then either forcibly ejected them or directed Dr. Loni to open the door and let them fall out spontaneously. Several sessions were spent throwing a single dart at different targets in the room. Daniel imaginatively altered this game slightly. In so doing he struggled with the boundaries of the treatment situation and his own problems with wishes, impulse control, and separation without loss of constancy as he enunciated where and what could be a target. At other times he sat near or beside Dr. Loni and hid a dart demanding that she search for it. He then requested that she hide it and he retrieve it. He was also involved with which of the papers, pads, and the like he could go through or move and which not, evidencing a need to recall the exact pattern from session to session. Lastly he devised a game in which he "castrated" and "impregnated" baseball figures on a dart board with a little screw-hook, additional sensorimotor matrices for exploring issues of birth, separation–individuation, and the primal scene. Dr. Loni's interventions frequently consisted of questions or observations, for example, "I wonder what that boy did that makes him get the hook," or "You enjoy giving it to them. I wonder if you feel that way toward children at school or on the bus." While Daniel rarely responded directly, Dr. Loni felt that he grasped her meaning and that such understanding facilitated his active absorption in his play.

Daniel's father was seen only occasionally during this period of treatment. While loving and tender, he was often quite awkward as a father. His own profound disappointment in his son, his disinclination for altering his life patterns to accommodate Daniel's needs, and his skeptical views of psychotherapy were gently addressed. This did result in his ability to engage in more anxiety-free, age-appropriate activity with Daniel. Dr. Loni felt she related well to both parents. She was able to work effectively with Daniel's mother, despite mother's pathological desires for a seductive symbiotic relationship with Daniel and her mistrustful fear of loss of her son through his alliance with the therapist. Compassionate restraint and psychodynamic understanding of her situation facilitated her reporting of behaviors and attitudes toward Daniel which she knew to be ill-advised. For example, she slept in bed half-naked with Daniel and explained, "As my mother felt toward me, I feel toward him. He is a guest in my home and can leave if he dislikes my rules." Dr. Loni felt that Daniel's mother struggled to be an effective parent, despite her inner psychopathology.

At this stage, the school's access to Dr. Loni, which was requested and appreciated by both parents, was essential for multiple reasons. Daniel attended a select private school for normal, extremely bright children whose staff were a bit awed by his psychological presentation. Furthermore, a mutually hostile relationship had developed between Daniel's mother and school personnel, such that much of the communication typically conducted by parents could not effectively be accomplished. Daniel was apprised of all school contacts. In Dr. Loni's view he did not regard her involvement as unusual, since the initial referral was put in motion by the school psychologist. Dr. Loni felt Daniel was comfortable with the idea of her familiarity with his teachers and school progress; he was equally comfortable as she gradually curtailed her involvement as his mother was able to assume her parental functions in communicating with the school.

Dr. Loni had frequent phone conversations with the school psychologist and Daniel's teacher during the first few months of treatment. The school psychologist worked with her as an intermediary to Daniel's teachers who had to deal with his emerging disruptive behavior, for example, sticking another child with a thumbtack and having a tantrum. There were also direct calls from his teachers to Dr. Loni as they tried to find an optimal educational approach. In addition Dr. Loni initiated calls to Daniel's teachers to discuss his educational progress. Four months into treatment, and as a result of the testing evaluation, a remediation therapist was introduced. Dr. Loni spoke with her several times. The school felt free to call Dr. Loni when they were concerned, for example, about how to deal with the sudden death of a librarian of whom Daniel was fond and with not allowing him to go on a particular trip he wanted to join because he would become too anxious and frightened.

This work notwithstanding, all concerned—Dr. Loni, Daniel's parents, his teachers, and the school psychologist—had the expectation that a change of school would be effected by the following year. Daniel's parents consulted with Dr. Hirsch, the psychologist who retested him at the beginning of the treatment, in an effort to select a school geared to the needs of children with neuropsychological dysfunction and mild to moderate emotional difficulties. Daniel's parents were realistic in considering the advisability of sending their son to such a school rather than the high-powered academic atmosphere in which he had been floundering, even with the benefits of psychological and remedial intervention. Therefore, this referral was accomplished without difficulty in discussion with Dr. Loni.

During the first year of treatment, Daniel developed from a total nonparticipant into a child who played with peers, albeit possessively and rigidly. He was able to learn, attend gym and field trips, despite some episodes of aggressive and sexual impulsivity, for example, grabbing at other boys' genitalia. He was able to join a neighborhood junior bowling league which reflected a major shift in his capacity to tolerate separation from his mother, diminished anxiety with peers and enhanced frustration tolerance for failure.

An awareness of Daniel's neuropsychological deficits also suggested areas requiring further history development with his parents (e.g., information regarding his time concepts and his capacity to absorb new situations) and lent an additional perspective in understanding his play and style of interaction. Clearly Daniel had a remarkable awareness of himself which he could share only later in treatment. He knew of his deficits before the adults in his life had gained this awareness. Already he felt self-conscious and tried to conceal what he regarded as his weaknesses. He would not wear a Mickey Mouse watch because, "People would ask me the time and I could only read a few numbers." Or he told his mother, "Don't tell me I'm going to visit someone so suddenly. I need time to get used to these things." As treatment progressed, he increasingly alerted his mother to his special needs. While this reflected in part his awareness of her pathology, it was also a manifestation of the deliberate, rather than spontaneous, attention the child with neuropsychological dysfunction may pay to himself—a specific type of observing ego.

During the second year of treatment, when Daniel was 8 to 9 years old, he was able to master many of his anxieties about separation–individuation. Concomitantly, therapeutic work with Daniel was facilitated by his mother's resumption of her own psychotherapy.

The main mode of communication in sessions continued to be play, with Daniel showing creativity and an ability to maintain continuity between sessions. For example, he played with a Velcro "baseball" mitt used to catch Velcro Ping-Pong balls in an effort to see the minimal amount of surface area needed to sustain contact. Daniel brought in helium balloons for several sessions, tying small objects to the string to "gauge" the weight needed to hold the balloon down, and the weight which could be lifted by the balloon. Daniel seemed to register interpretations that these games related to his questions about how much he could be separate from his mother without losing her, but consistent with his pattern of resistance he was disinclined to discuss these issues directly. Dr. Loni pointed out such avoidance, saying, for example, "You seem to have so much fun with the balloons and balls, yet when I try to talk about them you stop playing. I wonder what is so upsetting to you about it." Typically

Daniel responded by growling, stomping around the room, or trying to dismiss such an observation, as if it were "crazy."

Despite such manifestations of resistance, Daniel seemed to regard his sessions with Dr. Loni as a unique opportunity to deal with painful feelings and experiences. His strong attachment was expressed in statements to his teacher that Dr. Loni was a "special friend I discuss my problems with." Once during a two-week interruption Daniel's mother responded to Dr. Loni's "abandonment" by asking her son if he wanted to stop coming. He replied, "No, I think I still have problems to discuss with her." A move of Dr. Loni's office to a newly constructed wing of the same building became a focus for expression of issues of separation and attachment to Dr. Loni. One day he ran out to his mother saying, "We're having the rug cleaned and moved."

Daniel also began to work on his capacity for controlled drive discharge and his excessive fear of aggression. Related to this a predominant theme in the hours was his mother's phallic-intrusiveness. Daniel worked to contain his affective experience of his mother and to develop inner controls as a wedge between impulse and behavior. Exploration of his need to leave sessions to go to the bathroom with all its various meanings—to control anxiety, anger, excitement, to communicate via acting out, as well as to avoid communication and to achieve distance when he experienced Dr. Loni as intrusive—proved a fruitful arena.

In some respects Dr. Loni felt she served as an object in relationship to whom Daniel was presented with new possibilities. In contrast to his mother, Dr. Loni and the structure of the treatment situation afforded an experience of reliability, constancy, and acceptance. Furthermore, Daniel had the opportunity to be alone in the presence of another; he rarely directly engaged Dr. Loni in his play but more often approached sessions by bursting into the room, not to cling to Dr. Loni, but rather to get to what he was doing, working in front of her. He contrasted this to his experience of his mother to whom he said about the prospect of activity, "I want to make it when you're not there because when you're there it's never my thing." Daniel seemed to regard his hours as a place to deal with conflict areas and anxiety, with Dr. Loni and the atmosphere associated with her serving as a catalyst for such expression. Dr. Loni felt that the predominant tone was one of Daniel working in front of her, rather than showing off for her. However, Dr. Loni never felt that Daniel attempted to use his relationship with her against his mother but instead viewed her as siding with him against his own pathology.

At the same time there were expressions of anger toward Dr. Loni. For example, Daniel occasionally dropped things out of her second-story office, and messed up or put things in places other than the ones in which they belonged. He seemed to experience as intrusive Dr. Loni's attempts to bring in pieces of reality with which he did not wish to deal. His anger might be expressed, for example, in jabbing a puppet or blackening a drawing of a figure. Interpretations of these displaced expressions of anger were typically neither confirmed nor disconfirmed overtly, although Dr. Loni felt that Daniel integrated them.

A fair amount of work was done with Daniel's mother in terms of her potential to overidentify with Daniel and to overreact to his aggression and thrust for autonomy. Her own therapy at that time was indispensable to this work. Both parents' basically benevolent wishes for Daniel and their mutual respect and concern for him were indeed useful assets.

Daniel's improvement was reflected in his greater capacity to learn and share his skills enthusiastically with his parents and his enhanced and less anxiety-dominated object relations. For example, he went trick-or-treating when previously he had refused to go even to his own door to let other children in. Furthermore, he evidenced a thrust toward more developmentally appropriate masculine activities, for example, a bowling league on Saturdays and an after-school group.

During this year Daniel began to attend a small, special school for children with normal intelligence who have psychological problems and neurospychologically based learning difficulties. All students attending this school had simultaneously to be in psychotherapy. Initially, Dr. Loni visited the school and met for a conference with the teachers and principal. This laid the groundwork for her understanding of their plans, teaching methodology, and goals for their students. Furthermore, this contact with school staff facilitated future informal phone conversations; actually few were necessary the first year and none took place in Daniel's last year of treatment. The principal called once, after Daniel had a major panic-rage outburst in the context of his mother picking him up late, to seek advice and reassurance on how the situation had been handled. Occasional discussions were held with Daniel's teachers, which all but ceased as his mother was more successfully able to assume her parental role in bringing teachers' comments to Dr. Loni's attention. At the year's end, Daniel's teachers reported, "He had much better impulse control this year and you can see him mastering himself." This school with one teacher for five to six students was ideal for Daniel who thrived educationally and developed his capacities for socialization.

During the third year of the treatment, when Daniel was 9 to 10 years of age, he continued to work through his problems of differentiating himself from his mother without panic or disorganization, more comfortably tolerating his impulses and affects, continuing the developmental processes seen earlier, and beginning to deal with the issue of termination as a positive, non-panic-inducing, autonomous step. He continued his reliance upon play as a mode of communication, but also engaged in more overt verbal expression of some of his concerns and conflicts. There was rarely spontaneous or direct discussion of problems in school or with his parents or peers. However, when early in the year he got a new puppy named Jack, Daniel used it to displace and project his feelings about separation, aggression, and vulnerability. Many sessions were spent exploring his ambivalence toward Jack, his interpretation of Jack's feelings, his anger toward Jack, and his plans for Jack's growth, training, and modification of his omnipotent strivings. Daniel was afraid that his puppy would cry inconsolably. Regarding his aggressive impulses, he said, "He's not bad 'cause he's mischievous."

Developmentally, Daniel became solidly entrenched in latency. For instance, he often told jokes and did tricks, turning passive into active in a nonthreatening manner. At times he brought a taperecorder, playing meaningful and favorite tapes. Similarly, he was able to tolerate his expression of aggression. He and two 10-year-old friends scouted out caterpillars and eradicated them, an adventure which he enthusiastically shared with Dr. Loni.

There was also evidence of ego growth and reality testing in Daniel's emerging ability to set limits for his parents and assume the maternal role to foster development where his mother lacked the capacity. He urged his mother to stay out of the bathroom when he used it and would only go to the pediatrician's bathroom with his father. One night when he was apparently ready to give up his night light, his mother found this note under the switch in his bathroom: "Do not put this on." At the same time his attunement to his need for ego support was manifested by his cautioning his mother, when she precipitously arranged for him to sleep out, "It's too sudden, I need time to get used to these things." His observing ego and integration of his past were reflected in his compassion and perceptiveness with his peers. When one schoolmate cried before school, Daniel said empathically, "He can't come in. He's afraid to leave his mother as I was." Once while he and Dr. Loni were sitting together in a dark area in the office he said, "I used to be afraid of going blind. Lots of kids have gotten over a lot of worries." He seemed to feel more confident about the permanence of things and persons and to be less preoccupied with balancing relationships with more than one person at a time. This was seen for instance in the fact that whereas he used to make three photocopies of pictures—one each for mother, father, and Dr. Loni—he now made none, saying, "I'll keep it, we don't need a copy." Daniel also evidenced less fear of what he might discover about himself and tended to experience safety—and sometimes even excitement—in the course of self-exploration. With his enhanced reflective faculties, he began to work through his previous idealization of Dr. Loni. Attempting to flesh out the "real person" she was, he would say, "I know you'll say, I wonder why that comes up.'" Daniel shared his disapproval of Dr. Loni's sloppy handwriting and commented on her vocal mannerisms.

Work with Daniel's father was mostly to support his relationship with Daniel, to foster his pride in Daniel's growth, and to empathize with his unrealistic and age-inappropriate wishes for his son, for example, to sit and read encyclopedias with him. Daniel's mother's psychopathology still posed problems for him. However, he was better able to understand her and modulate his responses to her. When he played the game of Old Maid he worked extra hard to avoid getting the Old Maid, commenting, "I avoid getting the Old Maid. I didn't want to have to take care of her."

Before the summer break mother spoke of her sense that

termination could take place within the next year, the timing of which seemed reasonable to Dr. Loni. During this third year of analysis no direct school contacts by Dr. Loni were necessary. Indeed, Daniel's mother now took pride in her role as liaison between school staff and Dr. Loni. Daniel continued to learn, had pleasurable relationships with his friends, and no longer suffered from panic states. It was felt that a psychological reevaluation by Dr. Hirsch would be useful at this time to corroborate clinical impressions of improvement and to monitor the state of his learning disability. Findings at the age of 9 years, 3 months were as follows:

Tests Administered:

Wechsler Intelligence Scale for Children-Revised (WISC-R)
Illinois Test of Psycholinguistic Abilities: Auditory & Visual
    Sequential Memory; Sound Blending (only)
Wide Range Achievement Test (WRAT)
Benton Test of Visual Retention
Raven Progressive Matrices
Rorschach
Thematic Apperception Test (TAT)
Purdue Pegboard
Motor Tests (Rapid Alternating Movements, Thumb Wiggling,
    Apraxias)
Laterality Tests
Figure Drawings & Most Horrible & Most Pleasant Concepts
Time Orientation
Finger Agnosia & Graphesthesia

The previous clinical signs of separation anxiety, pain in being given tasks to do, and his "old man" look and gait have all disappeared. Hyperacusis is still present but is not debilitating. Although Daniel did not "like" me after our first encounter when he was 7½, he participated quite willingly and with some eagerness in all aspects of testing, showing no negative transference reactions. The structured tests were still more pleasurable than the projective tests.

General Findings

Intelligence: On the WISC-R, Daniel obtained a Verbal IQ of 109 (73rd percentile), a Performance IQ of 101 (53rd percentile), and a Full Scale IQ of 105 (63rd percentile). Below are the scaled scores:

Information	9	Picture Completion	8
Similarities	17	Picture Arrangement	11
Arithmetic	10	Block Design	13
Vocabulary	12	Object Assembly	7
Comprehension	10	Coding	12
(Digit Span)	(8)	(Mazes)	(10)

The scores are consistent with the last evaluation. Abstract reasoning has improved as has Coding. Vocabulary often shows a drop in dyslexic children. The IQs are relatively stable suggesting expectable intellectual growth.

Rather than feeling devastated by failure, Daniel works diligently and shows no signs of cognitive disruption from lack of success. There is a resigned quality when he fails and an acceptance of my explanation that the task was for older children. At times he would laugh while having a hard time.

Achievement: On the WRAT, Daniel obtained a reading Grade of 4.5 (55th percentile), a Spelling Grade of 2.9 (18th percentile), and an Arithmetic Grade of 2.7 (10th percentile).

Qualitatively, reading has improved dramatically and is done rather easily. The quality of his efforts suggests a well-compensated dyslexic condition. Phonics have been learned well and word attack skills are present. He had been taught and has learned superbly. Spelling is still dysgraphic and will probably remain so. My experience with dysgraphic children is that they grow up to be dysgraphic adults. His written stories exemplify the problem: "going to cil her soon going into the rom he cild her pee cos he wonted to" and "a prsun opning the dore closet (closed) dore closet dore." Words which should be automatic are not: address = "main stritt," father's name = "richert." Simple high frequency words are misspelled: make = "mack" and say = "saye." The lack of improvement in spelling is not uncommon in disabled children; relief may be needed in the high school years.

Mathematics has shown little or no improvement and should be attended to immediately. His score has dropped from the average to the deficit range.

Part Functions

Perception: On the Raven, a test of visual–perceptual development, Daniel scored at the 90th percentile, ruling out a disorder in this area. Clinically and from the Blending test, there is no evidence of auditory imperception. Somatosensory tests revealed neither finger agnosia nor difficulties with graphesthesia tests.

Motor: Fine finger speed and dexterity are excellent. Gross motor coordination is intact. Rapid alternating movements were done well and no synkinesia was noted. All tests for dyspraxia (eye, tongue, verbal, facial, and constructional) were negative.

Laterality: Daniel has a dominant right hand and foot, and left eye. The terms "left" and "right" were reversed on himself and no rotation principle is present for extracorporeal judgments. A left to right orientation is present for lexic and nonlexic material.

Time Orientation: Daniel can read and construct a clock accurately. The days and associated concepts are known. The month series has not been learned yet.

Memory: Short-term visual spatial memory is in the deficit range. Short-term auditory-sequential memory is at age 8-8 and short-term visual–sequential memory is 5-1.

Language: There were no dysphasic phenomena noted throughout testing. The terms "before" and "after" are understood spatially and temporally. Automatic, responsive, and spontaneous speech are intact. Numbers are read, written, and aligned accurately. Autotopagnosia tests were negative. (He now easily counts backwards.)

To summarize the above, Daniel's general cognitive and intellectual growth have proceeded apace. He is still learning disabled and will suffer the effects of a dysgraphia. Reading has improved dramatically, but arithmetic has not. The findings are still consistent with a diagnosis of minimal cerebral dysfunction with probable left temporal involvement: left–right disorientation, dysgraphia (dyseidetic type), short-term memory impairment.

Personality

The most impressive change on the Rorschach is the control over emotions and the nondisruption from depressive mood swings. Daniel could tolerate taking the test in one session and was able to give many reality-oriented popular responses. There is rather good integration of emotional stimulation. Deteriorative responses are absent. The breaks in reality testing, regressive or peculiar thought are all absent.

Daniel's best defenses now are avoidance, constriction, and inhibition of fantasy, all of which work quite successfully to keep anxiety under control. He becomes disgruntled and mildly angry when asked to express fantasy, all as a means of coping and keeping his thoughts under control.

Daniel's self-image is one of being somewhat defective, but he is beginning to find areas of competence and success. His ego is therefore in a stage of beginning consolidation instead of being totally inundated as it was earlier. Because he has made these gains I would suggest he continue with therapy.

Thus psychological evaluation bore out clinical impressions of improvement with the exception of poor progress in mathematics. Both Dr. Hirsch and Daniel's mother conveyed these findings to school staff, who admitted they had erred in not sufficiently attending to this area of his functioning. Daniel, having been one of the best in the class was "helping others" but not adequately profiting from instruction himself.

Both of Daniel's parents were pleased to receive confirmation of the changes they had noted in their son. While their deferential attitude toward professional authority was sustained—in the sense that they cooperatively followed recommendations—this was not a case of false deference. They seemed to be genuinely appreciative of the effectiveness of the combined interventions of treatment and remediation, followed by special school instruction. Dr. Hirsch noted that Daniel's mother was far more relaxed in her role as a mother and his father exuded a feeling of pride in his son.

During the fourth year of his treatment, Daniel, aged 10 to 11 years, continued his ego growth and consolidation as he solidly mastered the tasks of latency and began to manifest definite early adolescent trends. While issues of termination were prominent for over eight months, Daniel continued to utilize Dr. Loni to more firmly differentiate his sense of self from the earlier mother–son fusion so evident in his presenting separation anxiety and so clearly promoted by his mother's psychopathology.

In the fall the frequency of sessions was diminished from four to three times a week at Daniel's request because of difficulties in scheduling lessons in Hebrew, piano, and sessions. Dr. Loni felt that the process could effectively be continued at this frequency. Daniel's progress could be measured by his more realistic integration of mother's separateness and her pathology. As he once said, "She may be my mother but I don't have her mind." In a monthly session, his mother related a conversation she had with Daniel which beautifully illustrated his ability to assume greater responsibility in the mother–son relationship. He asked his mother, "Do you undress when you make love?" She answered, "Sometimes I do and sometimes he takes it off." Daniel reacted to this too graphic response by saying, "Let's not talk about it, it's too embarrassing." Then mother asked Dr. Loni, "Does this mean a limit in what Daniel will talk with me about? Before there was no limit. Now will he go to friends?" An attempt was made to help her feel she would always be his mother, although he would reach out in new ways and she would express her feelings for him in different ways.

The clinical impression was that the age appropriateness of the themes expressed by Daniel, the state of his ego develop-ment, his self-reflective capacity within the sessions, and his less idealized and more accurate perception of Dr. Loni indicated the timeliness of termination. These were consistent with the expansion of his socialization and the alleviation of symptoms: panic outbursts over separation and frustration, rituals over dirty or once-touched food, and school inhibitions. Daniel planned a birthday party complete with hand-made invitations and two different seating plans tailored to each guest's strengths and preferences, which culminated in a successful experience. He did well at school according to his report card and mother–teacher conferences and there was no need for Dr. Loni to have contacts with his teacher during the last 18 months of the treatment.

Daniel occasionally returned to a play mode seen much earlier in the treatment, musing over his former "motives" and their contrast with his current ones. For example, three years before he took a screwlike ring and dug it into the eyes of figures on a cardboard box. Now he looked at the box, found the screw, and soliloquized, "Those were good old times. I really pulled the shit out of him. Now I'm not trying to kill him." He commented on classmates who had problems he "used to have": "We have a new kid in class who is really mental. He's smart but just can't control himself."

Several months before termination, Daniel remarked that his mother asked him if he wished to set a date or to stop right away, "dead turkey." The slip was his, as his mother had said "cold turkey." The meaning of the slip was explored as he played with a Rubic puzzle cube. Suddenly he rushed outside to get a piece of paper with the solution, which was interpreted as a parallel to being totally on your own, "dead turkey."

In one of the last sessions he brought a complicated multi-function watch and asked Dr. Loni to help set one of the dates. He noted how helpful she was and wondered what he would have done without her. Encouraged to analyze this further, he decided he would have taken it back to the store or to a jewelry shop. In another session he brought in a blender he and his mother had just bought and explained he wanted Dr. Loni to help him unwrap it and try it out. Then he told her all the things he and his mother would try to do with it. It was felt to be an indication of the reduced friction between Daniel and his mother, his expectation of growth and comfort in his relationship with her, and his ability to control her intrusive tendencies, and his reactions to them, without insisting she leave the kitchen. As further evidence of his capacities for reflection and internalization of the treatment process, he made paper airplanes, named one for himself and another for Dr. Loni, and launched them in a race. He then said, "Winning won't be which one gets the farthest but how they do in the flight!"

Daniel felt he would prefer to terminate without a follow-up appointment in the fall; he would call if it were necessary. He called Dr. Loni's service one week after the last session. When she returned his call he told her he had started day camp and loved it. There was no subsequent contact.

In conclusion, the treatment was considered to be very successful by Dr. Loni, Daniel, and his parents, who seemed to be deeply satisfied, proud, and accepting of their son. Furthermore, there appeared to be adequate resolution of the most intrusive aspects of his mother's pathology.

Case 3: Matthew, a Depressive Reaction to a Learning Disorder of Primary Neuropsychological Etiology: Psychoanalytically Oriented Psychotherapy Concomitant With Remediation by the Same Therapist

It may be recalled that Matthew was a 5 1/2-year-old boy who was a "blank wall" to both his parents and teachers. He presented a puzzling combination of charm and boisterous hyperactivity—"leading others in the wrong direction"—with a capacity to calmly involve himself in work. Upon completion of a consultation with Dr. Trilling, a clinical psychologist with neuropsychological expertise, psychotherapy was recommended. Matthew's difficulties in learning were regarded as part of a neurotic constellation of conflicts over oedipal strivings and anxiety about

castration, loss, and separation. The few positive neuropsychological findings were regarded as equivocal at his age, possibly
"immaturities" which, however, required monitoring.

Matthew was seen twice a week and his parents were seen
by the same therapist on an intermittent basis, as needed. The
therapy began with Matthew's genuine joy upon being back at
Dr. Trilling's office. He carefully reexplored the room and
commented how good it was to see his "good buddy" again. With
the beginning of treatment his behavior difficulties diminished
precipitously at home and at school. The "honeymoon" had
begun. Matthew was very invested in therapy. He tried to understand what it was all about, as reflected in his insistent and
provocative questions about who the therapist was and why he
said such "funny" things. At the same time a lot of energy was
devoted to concealing his internal life. He flitted from activity to
activity or, as Dr. Trilling tried to make an interpretive comment,
Matthew began yelling, talked over his voice, or said, "That's
disgusting." Matthew objected most strenuously to interventions
aimed at unearthing the impact of the trauma of his circumcision
at age 4 with which he was obviously preoccupied. He drew
pictures of fires and saved numerous people from burning cars
only to have them lose their lives on the way to the hospital.
People and monsters were drawn with marked disfigurements or
other types of impairment.

The therapeutic work moved slowly until, after some six
months in treatment, Matthew reproduced Godzilla, in the midst
of much frenzy and gutteral noise, with a phallus nearly identical
to one he had drawn during testing. Dr. Trilling interpreted that
Matthew must often remember the time in the hospital when he
saw his bloody penis, that the memory must frighten him, and
that he must be trying to forget it and to make sure it will never
happen again. Matthew's body visibly relaxed as he slumped
onto the floor and put his head on the therapist's knee. The next
session Matthew brought a note from his mother saying that,
"Despite a big blow-up and regression in his behavior over the
weekend, Matthew has become much more affectionate and less
argumentative." Thus it was felt that a crucial determinant of
Matthew's learning and behavior problems had been identified
and could effectively be worked through.

However, frantic phone calls from Matthew's teacher
began as spring approached. He was making satisfactory prog-

ress in arithmetic but not in reading and spelling. He was no longer a behavior problem but either would not or could not do the work in these subjects. In a conference between the teacher and therapist it emerged that Matthew had trouble containing himself when faced with too many demands. A program of gradually increased work demands was established, but, again, the anticipated academic progress did not take place.

As Matthew continued not to learn, he began to enter his therapy sessions looking increasingly depressed. He complained of hating school, his teacher, and the other children. Interpretations geared toward clarifying his rage at being placed in a helpless position were fruitless. As Matthew yelled one day that this was "stupid stuff," Dr. Trilling heard him in a new way; perhaps this was not simply an expression of resistance.

Work with Matthew's parents during this period was critical, not only as a means of monitoring what was happening at home but also in assessing the progress of the treatment. Essentially his parents had come to believe that Matthew was a learning disabled child before Dr. Trilling had done so. They made known to him their wishes that he address himself to this aspect of Matthew, whether or not it represented only an immaturity. As this was discussed and Dr. Trilling registered the child's and parents' sense of hopelessness, a joint decision was made immediately to begin remediation to offer Matthew its benefits prior to his return to school. A trial of remediation would be instituted for the summer only. If it proved successful, in the fall Matthew's parents would work with the school to place Matthew in a learning disabilities program in which he would receive remedial instruction for 30 minutes a day, thus freeing the treatment to return to its original goals.

It was the end of the school year and an agreement was made with Matthew that he would try to work with Dr. Trilling on reading, after a grace period of three weeks in which to discuss this new intrusion into what had been a place with relatively few demands. Matthew agreed, but only half-heartedly. It was clear that he had very little hope.

Matthew's depression did not lift with the end of the academic year. He seemed defeated and broken in a profound way, which was especially troubling given his former vibrant and engaging manner. Now he was sad and smoldering with anger. Dr. Trilling approached the session in which the remedial work was to begin with some trepidation. Using the above-delineated method of teaching phonic associates he quickly involved Matthew in the work. Matthew, who knew only 10 when he arrived, left the session knowing almost all phonic associates. By the end of the third session Matthew knew all 26. He had begun to read at home, demonstrating some interest in sounding out the spelling of words. While this was in itself no mean accomplishment, what was most impressive was the change in Matthew's affect. He continually beamed from ear to ear. Although he had always been a bit of a peacock, he now walked with a new and more pronounced strut. His parents reported that he seemed more "grown up and responsible," changes which thrilled them.

Dr. Trilling had finally recognized that Matthew indeed had a learning disability and treated him as such. The original psychodynamic formulation of his anxiety and difficulty in controlling and modulating his affects and behavior was not modified. However, what had additionally seemed like the acute emergence of a serious depression could now be understood as a depressive reaction to perception of actual neuropsychological deficits with a resulting loss of self-esteem. In fact the reality of a defect may well have been elaborated in fantasy as a castration. Treatment of his neuropsychological difficulties eventuated in a rapid lifting of the depression.

Combined therapeutic and remedial work with Matthew resulted in some difficulty. Dr. Trilling thought it fortunate that the remedial work could ultimately be done in school separately from the psychotherapy. Introducing remediation constituted a modification that produced some distortion and confusion in the treatment. Whereas previously Matthew's fantasies that the therapist was highly demanding of performance could be explored interpretively, now they were to some degree actualized. The reduction of Matthew's tension as he saw he could do the remedial tasks was almost visible. He felt relieved that he would not have to disappoint, be angry at, or refuse to perform for Dr. Trilling in this area. This constellation of feelings and behaviors contributed to his difficulty at school. Attempting to find some balance between the reality aspects of remedial work and the interpretation of fantasies, conflicts, and transference manifestations that had little to do with reality considerations was difficult. Introducing reality, in the form of remediation, into an ongoing therapy was complicated but also useful in this case, although only when approached with much care and caution.

Since a comprehensive delineation of the course of psychotherapy is beyond the scope of this presentation, suffice it to say that as termination approached, Matthew had made huge strides in understanding himself and the way in which he managed his inner world. He had become much better at integrating the blows to his esteem at school both because he learned a better method of dealing with rage and continued to receive special remedial instruction which enabled him to perform on par with his peers—albeit using a different route to arrive at solutions. Matthew was 8 years old and the "immaturities" had not cleared up. He was a learning disabled child but one who was at long last learning.

Case 8: Brad, a Learning Disorder of Mixed Neuropsychological and Psychodynamic Etiology: Modified Psychoanalytically Informed Psychotherapy Followed by a Period of Remediation

Brad, a 6-year, 11-month-old boy, was referred to Dr. Ginsberg, a psychoanalytically oriented clinical psychologist with expertise in diagnosis of neuropsychological difficulties, by another psychologist with comparable training. Brad's mother contacted the first psychologist because of her son's recent periods of "enormous" sadness and concern with losing treasured objects. She and Brad's father had divorced two years earlier, although father kept in close and regular contact with Brad. Marital difficulties characterized by "loaded silences" predated the separation by many years. Brad's father had several manic-depressive episodes requiring hospitalization, the first just prior to Brad's birth.

Several features of the early history were remarkable. Brad had suffered seizures since birth which were never adequately controlled, although medical attention was sought at age 3. Three early hospitalizations were for observation of seizures. Brad did not acquire language until 4 years of age. There were suggestions that parental neglect may also have contributed to this prolonged period when the seizures were not controlled. Brad's father reported that he was the major caretaker in the early years since Brad's mother was absent a great deal of the time due to intense pursuit of her career.

An extensive evaluation by the first psychologist—including clinical interviews and psychodiagnostic testing—beginning when Brad was 6 years, 3 months, revealed an intertwining of psychodynamic and neuropsychological factors. Test findings depicted Brad as a child with an array of neuropsychological deficits, difficulties with affect modulation and object relations, in part secondary to his language disturbance, as well as concerns about his body boundaries and potential threats to his safety. There was no evidence of a thought disorder or serious disturbance in reality testing. In addition, his behavior was thought to be too well organized and directed to suggest severe internal ego disorganization and early difficulties with differentiation.

While Brad's Full Scale, Verbal, and Performance IQs placed him in the Low Average range of intellectual functioning, there was considerable variability. His best performance was on tests of abstract verbal and nonverbal conceptualization, discrimination of and attention to visual detail and nonsequential memory. Gross motor coordination was excellent and in contrast to deficits in fine graphomotor coordination, for example, in handwriting and copying designs. Particular difficulty emerged on tasks involving sequential concepts and/or sequential memory. This was true whether materials were verbal (e.g., repeating sentences from memory with words in proper order), spatial (e.g., matching correct color pegs with a series of animals as dictated by a sequential key), visual (e.g., remembering the order of visual stimuli placed sequentially), or temporal (grasping sequential time and number concepts, e.g., yesterday, tomorrow, before, after). Confused word order was one of a series of deficits in expressive and receptive language, including a dysnomia and syntactic problems. An example was Brad's statement, "You don't cut bigger scissors with your hair," when he meant to say, "You don't cut your hair with bigger scissors." Related to the above sequential difficulties were Brad's right-left confusion with regard to his own body, faulty discrimination between similar but different visual stimuli such as "b" and "d," and his tendency to read or write a word from right to left.

Clinically Brad presented as an endearing, physically sturdy

6 1/2-year-old boy who made too ready contact with strangers, for example, asking unfamiliar women, "Do you have a vagina?" He similarly greeted the first therapist with a barrage of questions about his childhood, current living arrangements, and the like. These were seen as efforts both to establish sequential order and to relate interpersonally in a language-disordered child who relies upon overlearned automatic phrases regardless of context. Being alone in the presence of another was difficult for Brad who sought to fill the silence. Brad's affect was also found to be too flat, stereotyped and, at times, inappropriate. Intense, insufficiently controlled feelings occasionally flooded him, resulting in "affect storms."

A recommendation for "intensive psychotherapy, combining remedial, cognitive approaches with work around interpersonal and affective difficulties" was made. Treatment had just begun with the same therapist, when the patient's family planned a move which made continuation difficult; therefore, a referral was made to Dr. Ginsberg. The sudden, unplanned circumstances under which work began with the second therapist was only one loss in a past and future series.

When Brad's mother consulted with Dr. Ginsberg, her stated reason was vague: "I thought it was time to get him checked out." In part, this reflected a characterologically casual style. It also exemplified a lack of empathy and attachment to this child from early in his life. A great sense of relief was expressed at having finally learned in the evaluation that Brad "senses things differently" but is not "retarded" and that "there will be a place for him in the normal world." As his father expressed it, what they had learned was akin to a "Eureka!" experience. With little affect, mother catalogued multiple recent losses to which she attributed Brad's sadness: at first his father through separation and divorce, but most recently his home and that of his father when both parents almost simultaneously moved to a major city from a small town; mother's best friend who died at this same period; the family cat which, allegedly unaccustomed to heights, fell out of their apartment window; the previous therapist and a teacher of three years. Also new was both the absence of seizures and discussion of this phenomenon with Brad who asked, "Do you die when you have a seizure?"

Upon first meeting, Brad appeared more disturbed than the

referring therapist's description of him had led her to expect. With obvious expressive language problems, he conveyed intense concerns about the stability of the environment (Would the wind blow the building down?), important persons (Did the previous therapist die? Would the current therapist die if he threw her out the window?), the intactness of his own body and those of others (Would the therapist's ear bleed if he touched her earring?), and differentiation between self and others (How come the therapist smiled when he did?). Evident in such questions were fears of the destructiveness of his own rage, as well as the danger to himself of others' rage. He was hyperalert to differences between the current office and that of the previous therapist and insisted upon purchasing and repetitively playing for several months a game associated with the previous therapist. While his mother was available to meet with the therapist for consultation, she rarely accompanied Brad to his twice weekly appointments. Indeed Brad rarely arrived with the same adult.

Given this presentation, initial treatment goals were aimed at structuring Brad's environment and parental responses to him and at helping his parents, particularly his mother, to empathically appreciate his needs for reliability and predictability and his sense of frustration in expressing himself. Plans for psychoeducational intervention were postponed until a time when Brad was subject to less anxiety. However, several aids were introduced to address time sequential difficulties as well as fears of object loss. Brad was encouraged to indicate appointments for several months hence by placing stickers on a calendar, which was consulted regularly. Objects in the office were kept in place as much as possible. Mother was advised to delineate in advance the day's and week's events, when feasible.

After two months of treatment, a massively stressful coincidence of events overwhelmed Brad's ego, resulting in a transiently psychotic disorganization. In a single week, the therapist was away, Brad's mother accepted an out-of-town job on short notice, his father had a manic episode requiring hospitalization, and a recently hired maid had a paranoid psychotic episode resulting in her hospitalization. This episode reportedly centered around Brad's then frequent teasing threat to "throw her out the window." Dr. Ginsberg returned from her one-week absence to find Brad frankly bizarre and subject to anxiety of panic proportions. Fantasies of omnipotent self-sufficiency based on oral incorporative modes represented attempts at repair. Standing on a table, Brad would announce that he was Popeye, Superman, or the Statue of Liberty. He spoke of "the womb of a tire" and asked, "If I put my stomach in you and swallow you, what would happen?" Most poignant was his repeated plea, "Where can you buy a Mommy?" While these in part reflected expressive language difficulties, Brad also had a thought disorder.

Interpretation of his guilty sense of having caused the maid's illness, and of how frightened and angry he must have felt at being all alone with her, only served to mount his panic. The use of the calendar, which had previously bound anxiety, now led to its increase as Brad focused on its "end." He was unable to find comfort in by now well-known games, particularly the one associated with the previous therapist, because they too would end. Indeed he became ingenious at devising ways to avoid "the end." Feeling responsible for and terrified of the maid's illness, Brad began to have difficulty remaining in the office alone with Dr. Ginsberg, as if fearful of precipitating another catastrophic response. He frequently recited the story of "The Lion Who Roared," shaking the whole forest. Previous concerns about damage and destruction were understandably heightened. It was as if Brad, who had already been largely deprived of the corrective externalization of omnipotent, magical fantasies made possible by language (Katan, 1961), now had his development of reality testing further compromised by a reality which too often echoed his fantasies.

Brad's mother was informed at this time of the severity of her son's difficulties which, although evident at home, were largely denied or minimized. She was urged to make herself far more reliably available to him, at least for several months, a part of which was to accompany him to and participate in sessions. The major aim was to interpret for mother Brad's communications of neediness.

A period followed in which Brad angrily demanded obedience to and even mind reading of his wishes. When Dr. Ginsberg or his mother were out of tune with his needs or unable to understand him, he could be explosive. At moments of high excitation, he frequently resorted to an upper torso "quiver" that closely replicated descriptions he had been given of seizures. However, these were not accompanied by loss of consciousness and were clearly intentional efforts at drive and affect control.

This ultimately gave way to experimentation with more daring physical activities in what he gradually began to find a trusting and reliable environment. A bicycle left in the office provided a major arena for such experimentation. Seated on it he increasingly suspended his balance, which also involved an infantile rocking sensation, from which he fell into Dr. Ginsberg's arms over and over again, his whole body molding to hers. This also provided the experience of a finely attuned maternal figure. While rocking, Brad was able for the first time to express his sadness about being unable to do many of the things his classmates could do and about the teasing he suffered for this. Concurrently, referral to a school for emotionally and neuropsychologically handicapped children was in progress; separation-individuation issues emerged. As if having been deprived of experiences of mirroring or contagion of affect within the normal reciprocity of the mother–infant matrix, he would ask, "How come you smile or laugh when I do?" Bits of imitative behavior appeared. Brad arrived wearing a necklace he associated with the therapist or used a gesture of his mother's in a stilted fashion.

Brad's grandiose defensive responses to fears of overwhelming danger and unfulfilled neediness slowly became available to interpretation. Mother was less frightened of his affect storms and better able to help him in containing them, both physically and through words. This coincided with Brad's development of some areas of true competence in athletics, beginning friendships based on these activities, improved language capacities, and a greater ability to admit to not knowing and, therefore, to engage in learning. In his favor, Brad had an intense drive for mastery and perseverance, unlike the typically poor frustration tolerance of language-disordered children described by De Hirsch (1975).

In the third year, the treatment far more closely approximated a traditional interpretive approach. Oedipal competitive strivings were paramount in the transference and in relation to family members. Brad had been able to weather the remarriages of both parents, a series of separations, both expected (Dr. Ginsberg's vacations) and unexpected (his mother's hospitalization for a physical ailment and the sudden departure of a teacher). Remedial work was subsequently planned.

There was certainly sufficient genetic and psychodynamic material to account for Brad's symptoms and ego deficits, even in the absence of his documented seizure disorder and array of neuropsychological deficits. However, what is of interest in this case is the convergence of neuropsychological and psychodynamic factors and their similar routes of expression. Brad's concern with sameness and order may be construed variously as an effort to ward off overwhelming experiences both of object loss—which reverberated with an earlier vulnerability due to disturbances in establishment of object constancy—and of the environment changing with transient losses of consciousness during years of insufficiently controlled seizures. These had particular impact in a child who largely lacked the structuring possibilities of language for connecting discrete but sequentially related events and reassuring the return of important objects. Brad's voluntary "quiver" may be conceptualized both as a mock seizure in which passivity is turned into activity and an effort at containment of frightening affect states which have not been adequately controlled by the maternal object or by language.

However, to offer psychodynamic formulations for Brad's difficulties in sequencing and right-left spatial orientation—for example, as a global disorientation in time and space related to unresolved symbiotic issues and insufficient structuring of experience by mother—would be to deprive him of the full range of necessary interventions. Mastery of these building blocks central to higher cortical academic functions required remedial treatment. Nor could Dr. Ginsberg dispense with psychoanalytic technical and theoretical concepts. Both traditional approaches and remediation were crucial to effective work with this patient.

Chapter 8

Summary and Further Considerations

We have conveyed the complexity of etiological possibilities that require consideration in diagnostic and therapeutic work with learning disordered children and adolescents, and illustrated some of the disadvantages of favoring one possibility over another, a favoritism that serves as an obstacle to maximally open-minded investigation of the individual patient's clinical realities. In our opinion a less than comprehensive diagnostic process (as delineated in chapter 4) represents at least a subtle form of favoritism, for which there is no convincing clinical justification. Illustrations of several of the many possible oversights that may ensue from a partial evaluation were provided in chapter 5. When an evaluation reveals neuropsychological dysfunction of sufficient magnitude to account for a patient's disorder in learning, this is not an indication for ending the evaluation; such a set of findings does not rule out the existence of parallel and/or interweaving psychodynamic and ego structural contributions. Conversely, when a careful psychoanalytic or psychoanalytically-oriented consultation yields a compelling formulation of psychological factors eventuating in a learning inhibition, this does not eliminate the possibility of significant accompanying or intermeshing neuropsychological dysfunction. The developmental impact of variations in one's "equipment," or disturbances thereof, upon psychic structure formation was highlighted long ago by Freud (1923) and Hartmann (1950) and elaborated more recently most notably by Weil (1961, 1970, 1971, 1977, 1978). It is surprising then that an integrative consideration of neuropsychological dysfunction and its psychological sequelae so rarely finds expression in clinical reports of learning disordered patients. For heuristic purposes, some possible effects of disorders in isolated neuropsychological functions upon the development of the ego and object relations are delineated in chapter 1. Chapter 6 reports some of the common cognitive disorders associated with neuropsychological dysfunctions. The diagnostic spectrum proposed in chapter 2 illustrates the array of possible discrete etiological determinants of learning disorders as well as their combinations.

Allowance for complexity in the determination of learning disorders necessarily entails a flexible approach to consideration of treatment approaches. The approach (or approaches) selected derives from the diagnostic conclusion that a child's disorder primarily reflects (1) unresolved dynamic conflict in the absence of neuropsychological dysfunction, (2) the effects of neuropsychological dysfunction on the development of ego functions and object relations as well as on learning, or (3) the existence of neuropsychological dysfunction that has not significantly affected aspects of the child's development other than learning. The need to consider multiple treatment possibilities has been emphasized in chapter 7. Controversies and distinctions among remedial, tutorial and other educational interventions which are probably less familiar to analysts and psychoanalytically-oriented clinicians in general have been discussed.

Despite its considerable length, many significant questions are beyond the scope of this book. Perhaps they will be the subject of future communications and research. We also hope to inspire interest on our readers' parts in some of these questions as they further consider or reconsider their own patients from an integrative perspective.

Although we have confined our remarks and clinical material to child and adolescent patients, an integrative approach is no less applicable to adults. It is illuminating to see the frequently intense reactions among parents of neuropsychologically-impaired children, who themselves had undiagnosed and therefore untreated learning disabilities, when they are informed of their child's difficulty. The psychic residua of such a condition linger long beyond its academic consequences in the form of painful and often distorted ways of viewing one's self and important others. On an unconscious level parents with learning disabilities relive and repeat with their children conflicts and attitudes related to their own deficits. Most often adults are referred for the kind of comprehensive diagnostic testing assessment we recommend when their professional functioning is seriously compromised. It is not uncommon for such people to complain of a sense of incapacity in performing selected responsibilities at work or at home. However, such complaints are also sometimes heard from patients in psychoanalysis or psychotherapy who do not suffer from difficulties in work. Closing one's mind to the possibility that an undiagnosed form of neuropsychological dysfunction may be at play, because there are sufficient psychodynamic contributions to account for professional difficulties, may be a disservice to the patient. One might well overlook the need for remediation as well as salient foci of psychotherapeutic work; a disorder that remains undiagnosed for the better part of a lifetime is highly likely to take on psychological elaborations contributing, for example, to a sense of defect that is generalized well beyond the actual scope of the neuropsychological dysfunction. The discovery of a neuropsychological contribution may be a crucial aspect of the reconstruction of childhood experiences. Even if the patient has spontaneously found compensatory means of dealing with academic demands, the existence of disordered cognitive functions may have subtle sequelae for the development of the ego and object relations, the very material with which one is concerned in psychoanalysis. If this diagnosis is not made (or ruled out for that matter), such interrelationships or investments in believing one's self to be "defective" cannot fully be understood. Kakfa's (1984) case illustrates the impact of such a discovery.

Other questions may be divided into those primarily concerned with diagnosis and those primarily pertinent to treatment. In the diagnostic realm, a chapter could easily be devoted to the special issues and patterns of diagnosis in the preschool and early elementary years. Some of the tests included in our comprehensive battery are inapplicable to younger children and consequently require supplementation by a series of informal tasks. Furthermore, interpretation of what must be regarded as equivocal findings at this young age requires special comment. Although such findings are not definitive, one can venture an opinion as to the likelihood of their having an enduring effect. From a different perspective, the subject of neuropsychological dysfunction of no consequence deserves more attention than it could be given in this book. To illustrate, a child may evidence dysfunction in spatial orientation that apparently has no current consequences for his academic functioning. Thus he may not be considered learning disabled. Nonetheless his parents should be alerted to the possibility of later sequelae of this dysfunction, for example, difficulties in geometry or biology, as well as current nonacademic sequelae: problems in following geographical directions, playing board games and the like. A far more in-depth contribution remains to be made concerning the projective test manifestations of neuropsychologically-impaired children, about which we could offer only broad statements. This is a subject to which the child testing literature has devoted little attention. Yet another subject, which might usefully be clarified, is the nature of distinctions among the various types of professionals who perform diagnostic testing; differences in the batteries they are trained and licensed to administer and the scope of their capacity to maintain an integrative perspective would be of particular importance to the clinician confronted with a previous evaluation or the need to make a future referral.

In the realm of treatment many significant issues deserve further consideration. It would be of great interest to develop case studies of the impact of various kinds of neuropsychological dysfunction upon the child's ability to make use of the treatment situation in general and interpretation in particular. This might lead toward a more appropriate individualized approach to the introduction of modifications and prevent what we consider to be the incorrect overgeneralization, sometimes found in the literature, that children with such dysfunction cannot profit from a psychoanalytically oriented interpretive approach. In this regard, special attention remains to be given to the needs of language-impaired children. Another fascinating area for study is the effect on the treatment process of late diagnosis of neuropsychological dysfunction. This would pertain to cases in which this possible source of learning disorder was initially overlooked and subsequently considered and confirmed at an advanced stage of treatment and/or an advanced point in the patient's academic career. Does this "discovery" in any significant way alter the therapeutic course and/or the child's or adolescent's self-experience? Related to this is the subject of technique in conveying diagnostic test findings to a child or adolescent: to what extent to share diagnostic conclusions with him and in what manner to translate findings into concepts that can be grasped. A related therapeutic issue that does not appear in any form in the existing literature is that of the impact of a learning disability (or neuropsychological dysfunction without academic consequence) upon siblings who do not themselves suffer from neuropsychological dysfunction. We would anticipate that there might be a psychological equivalent of the "survivor syndrome" in children or adolescents who had "escaped" the ill fate of their siblings. Furthermore, the unaffected siblings would be likely to experience some confusion about the nature of their affected sibling's disorders and, in that sense, profit from efforts at education and clarification. At the very least this is an important area for research.

Another subject deserving of explanation, which was not highlighted by any of the major cases in this book, is that of special problems in the collaboration of psychotherapist and remediator or tutor. While their goals and techniques are distinct in most respects, one possible complication is that of the split transference. Technical considerations in managing this clinical situation could valuably be explored. As already noted, with some rare exceptions, we generally do not believe it to be profitable for the same person to work with a patient psychotherapeutically and remedially or tutorially. However, this is an opinion with which not all clinicians would concur. Clinical studies of the advantages and disadvantages of each approach would be very useful in establishing more empirically-based guidelines for various kinds of cases. A similar set of issues surrounds the learning disordered or disabled child's need for any other kind of intervention, such as those of the psychopharmacologist or neurologist.

This sketch of questions for further thought and research is by no means exhaustive. If we have catalyzed curiosity about these or other issues and expanded our readers' perspectives on their learning disordered patients, we will consider our effort in writing this book well rewarded.

References

Abraham, K. (1924), The influence of oral eroticism in character formation and contributions to the theory of the anal character. *Selected Papers*. London: Hogarth Press, 1965, pp. 393–406.

Abrams, A. L. (1968), Delayed irregular maturation versus minimal brain injury: Recommendations for a change in current nomenclature. *Clin. Ped.*, 7:344–349.

Adams, R. M., Kocsis, J., & Estes, R. E. (1974), Soft neurological signs in learning-disabled children and controls. *Amer. J. Dis. Child.*, 128:614–618.

Adamson, W. C., & Adamson, K. K., Eds. (1979), *A Handbook for Specific Learning Disabilities*. New York: Gardner Press.

Albert, M. L. (1979), Alexia. In: *Clinical Neuropsychology*, ed. K. M. Heilman & E. Valenstein. New York: Oxford University Press, pp. 59–91.

Ames, L. B. (1968), Learning disabilities: The developmental point of view. In: *Progress in Learning Disabilities*, Vol. 1, ed. H. R. Myklebust. New York: Grune & Stratton, pp. 39–74.

———— Metraux, R. W., Rodell, J. L., & Walker, R. N. (1974), *Child Rorschach Responses*. New York: Brunner/Mazel.

Anderson, R. P. (1966), Physiologic considerations in learning: The tactual mode. In: *Learning Disorders*, Vol. 2, ed. J. Hellmuth. Seattle, WA: Special Child Publications, pp. 97–112.

Anthony, E. J. (1973), A psychodynamic model of minimal brain dysfunction. *Ann. NY Acad. Sci.*, 205:52–60.

Arnold, E. (1976), MBD: A hydraulic parfait model. *Dis. Nerv. Syst.*, 37:171–173.

Baker, H. J., & Leland, B. (1967), *Detroit Tests of Learning Aptitude*. Indianapolis: Bobbs-Merrill.

Baldwin, R. W. (1965), The treatment of behavior disorders with medication. In: *Children with Learning Problems: Readings in a Devel-*

opmental-Interaction Approach, ed. S. G. Sapir & A. C. Nitzburg. New York: Brunner/Mazel, 1973, pp. 648–659.

Bannantyne, A. (1971), *Language, Reading and Learning Disabilities.* Springfield, IL: Charles C Thomas.

Basso, A., Taborelli, A., & Vignolo, L. A. (1978), Dissociated disorders of speaking and writing in aphasia. *J. Neurol. Neuro-sur., Psychiat.*, 41 6:556–563.

Bateman, B. D. (1968), *Interpretation of the 1961 Illinois Test of Psycholinguistic Abilities.* Seattle, WA: Special Child Publications.

———— (1972), Educational implications of minimal brain dysfunction. In: *Children with Learning Problems: Readings in a Developmental-Interaction Approach*, ed. S. G. Sapir & A. C. Nitzburg. New York: Brunner/Mazel, 1973, pp. 674–681.

Beck, S. J., Beck, A. G., Levitt, E. E., & Molish, H. B. (1961), *Rorschach's Test: Basic Processes.* New York: Grune & Stratton.

Bellak, L. (1979), Psychiatric aspects of minimal brain dysfunction in adults: Their ego function assessment. In: *Psychiatric Aspects of Minimal Brain Dysfunction in Adults*, ed. L. Bellak. New York: Grune & Stratton, pp. 73–101.

———— Adelman, C. (1960), The children's apperception test (CAT). In: *Projective Techniques with Children*, ed. A. I. Rabin & M. R. Haworth. New York: Grune & Stratton, pp. 62–94.

Bender, L. (1945), Organic brain conditions producing behavior disturbances. In: *Modern Trends in Child Psychiatry*, eds. N. D. C. Lewis & B. L. Pacella. New York: International Universities Press, pp. 155–192.

———— (1946), *Bender Visual Motor Gestalt Test.* New York: The Psychological Corporation.

———— (1956), *Psychopathology of Children with Organic Brain Disorders.* Springfield, IL: Charles C Thomas.

———— (1958), Problems in conceptualization and communication in children with developmental alexia. In: *Children with Learning Problems: Readings in a Developmental-Interaction Approach*, eds. S. G. Sapir & A. C. Nitzburg. New York: Brunner/Mazel, 1973, pp. 528–548.

Benson, D. F., & Geschwind, N. (1970), Developmental Gerstmann syndrome. *Neurol.*, 20:293–298.

———— Weir, W. F. (1972), Acalculia: Acquired anarithmetria. *Cortex*, 8:465–472.

Benton, A. L. (1963), *The Revised Visual Retention Test.* New York: The Psychological Corporation.

———— (1973), Minimal brain dysfunction from a neuropsychological point of view. *Ann. NY Acad. Sci.*, 205:29–37.

———— (1975), Developmental dyslexia: Neurological aspects. In: *Advances in Neurology*, Vol. 7, ed. W. J. Friedlander. New York: Raven Press, pp. 1–47.

_____ (1977), Reflections on the Gerstmann syndrome. *Brain and Lang.*, 4:45–62.

_____ (1979a), Body schema disturbances: Finger agnosia and right-left discrimination. In: *Clinical Neuropsychology*, ed. K. M. Heilman & E. Valenstein. New York: Oxford University Press, pp. 141–158.

_____ (1979b), Visuoperceptive, visuospatial, and visuoconstructive disorders. In: *Clinical Neuropsychology*, ed. K. M. Heilman & E. Valenstein. New York: Oxford University Press, pp. 186–232.

_____ (1980), The neuropsychology of facial recognition. *Amer. Psychol.*, 35:176–186.

Berger, M., & Kennedy, H. (1975), Pseudobackwardness in children; Maternal attitudes as an etiological factor. *The Psychoanalytic Study of the Child*, 30:279–306. New Haven, CT: Yale University Press.

_____ Yules, W., & Rutter, M. (1975), Attainment and adjustment in two geographical areas: The prevalence of specific reading retardation. *Brit. J. Psychiat.*, 126:510–519.

Bergman, P., & Escalona, S. K. (1949), Unusual sensitivities in very young children. *The Psychoanalytic Study of the Child*, 3/4:333–352. New York: International Universities Press.

Betlheim, S., & Hartmann, H. (1924), On parapraxes in the Korsakow psychosis. In: *Organization and Pathology of Thought*, ed. D. Rapaport. New York: Columbia University Press, 1951, pp. 288–307.

Bettelheim, B., & Zelan, K. (1981), *On Learning to Read: The Child's Fascination with Meaning*. New York: Alfred Knopf.

Birch, H. G. (ed.) (1964), *Brain Damage in Children*. Baltimore, MD: Williams & Wilkins.

_____ Lefford, A. (1964), Two strategies for studying perception in brain-damaged children. In: *Children with Learning Problems: Readings in a Developmental-Interaction Approach*, ed. S. G. Sapir & A. C. Nitzburg. New York: Brunner/Mazel, 1973, pp. 335–349.

Black, W. F. (1974), The word explosion in learning disabilities: A notation of literature trends, 1962–1972. *J. Learn. Dis.*, 7:323–325.

Blanchard, P. (1946), Psychoanalytic contributions to the problems of reading disabilities. *The Psychoanalytic Study of the Child*, 2:163–187. New York: International Universities Press.

Blank, M., & Bridger, W. H. (1966), Deficiencies in verbal labeling in retarded readers. *Amer. J. Orthopsychiat.*, 36:840–847.

Boder, E. (1971a), Developmental dyslexia: A diagnostic screening procedure based on three characteristic patterns of reading and spelling. In: *Learning Disorders*, Vol. 4, ed. B. Bateman. Seattle, WA: Special Child Publications, pp. 297–343.

_____ (1971b), Developmental dyslexia: Prevailing diagnostic concepts and a new diagnostic approach. In: *Progress in Learning Disabilities*, Vol. 2, ed. H. R. Myklebust. New York: Grune & Stratton, pp. 293–321.

————— (1973), Developmental dyslexia: A diagnostic approach based on three atypical reading-spelling patterns. *Dev. Med. Child Neurol.*, 15:663–687.

Bogen, J. E. (1969), The other side of the brain I: Dysgraphia and dyscopia following cerebral commisurotomy. *Bull. LA Neurol. Soc.*, 34:73–105.

Bornstein, B. (1930), Zür Psychogenese der Pseudodebilitat. *Internat. J. Psycho-Anal.*, 16:378–399.

Boshes, B., & Myklebust, H. R. (1964), A neurological and behavioral study of children with learning disorders. *Neurol.*, 4:7–12.

Breuer, J., & Freud, S. (1893–1895), Studies in Hysteria. *Standard Edition*, 2. London: Hogarth Press, 1964.

Bruininks, H. (1978), *Bruininks-Oseretsky Test of Motor Proficiency*. Circle Pines, MN: American Guidance Service.

Burgemeister, B. B. (1962), *Psychological Techniques in Neurological Diagnosis*. New York: Harper & Row.

Buxbaum, E. (1964), The parents' role in the etiology of learning disabilities. *The Psychoanalytic Study of the Child*, 19:421–447. New York: International Universities Press.

Cantwell, D. P., & Baker, L. (1980), Children with communication disorders. *J. Amer. Acad. Child. Psychiat.*, 19:579–591.

————— Forness, S. R. (1982), Editorial on learning disorders. *J. Amer. Acad. Child Psychiat.*, 21:417–419.

Carter, S., & Gold, A. P. (1973), The nervous system: Diagnosis of neurologic disease. In: *Children with Learning Problems: Readings in a Developmental-Interaction Approach*, ed. S. G. Sapir & A. C. Nitzburg. New York: Brunner/Mazel, pp. 569–585.

Chalfant, J. C., & Flathouse, V. E. (1971), Auditory and visual learning. In: *Progress in Learning Disabilities*, Vol. 2, ed. H. R. Myklebust. New York: Grune & Stratton, pp. 252–292.

Chess, S. (1969), *An Introduction to Child Psychiatry*. New York: Grune & Stratton.

Clements, S. D. (1966a), *Minimal Brain Dysfunction in Children*. NINDS Monograph No. 3, U.S. Public Health Service Publication No. 1415, Washington, DC: Government Printing Office. U.S. Department of Health, Education and Welfare, Bethesda, MD.

————— (1966b), The child with minimal brain dysfunction: A multidisciplinary catalyst. *Lancet*, 86:121–123.

Cohen, D. H. (1972), *The Learning Child*. New York: Random House.

Cohen, R. L. (1979a), History taking. In: *Basic Handbook of Child Psychiatry*, Vol. 1, ed. J. D. Noshpitz. New York: Basic Books, pp. 493–500.

————— (1979b), The developmental interview. In: *Basic Handbook of Child Psychiatry*, Vol. 1, ed. J. D. Noshpitz. New York: Basic Books, pp. 500–504.

————— (1979c), Examination in the pre-school and school-age child. In:

Basic Handbook of Child Psychiatry, Vol. 1, ed. J. D. Noshpitz. New York: Basic Books, pp. 529–547.

———— (1979d), Special considerations in the examination of adolescents. In: *Basic Handbook of Child Psychiatry*, Vol. 1, ed. J. D. Noshpitz. New York: Basic Books, pp. 547–550.

Cohn, R. (1961), Dyscalculia. *Arch. Neurol.*, 4:301–307.

———— (1964), The neurological study of children with learning disabilities. *Except. Child.*, 3:179–185.

———— (1968), Developmental dyscalculia. *Ped. Clin. N. Amer.*, 15:651–668.

Connolly, A. J., Nachtman, W., & Pritchett, E. M. (1976), *Key Math Diagnostic Arithmetic Test*. Circle Pines, MN: American Guidance Service.

Connolly, C. (1971), Social and emotional factors in learning disabilities. In: *Progress in Learning Disabilities*, Vol. 2, ed. H. R. Myklebust. New York: Grune & Stratton, pp. 151–178.

Critchley, M. (1968), Isolation of the specific dyslexic. In: *Dyslexia*, ed. A. Keeny & V. Keeny. St. Louis: Mosby, pp. 17–20.

———— (1970), *The Dyslexic Child*. Springfield, IL: Charles C Thomas.

———— Critchley, E. A. (1978), *Dyslexia Defined*. London: William Heinemann Medical Books.

De Hirsch, K. (1952), Specific dyslexia or strephosymbolia. *Folia Phoniat.*, 4:231–248.

———— (1963), Concepts related to normal reading processes and their application to reading pathology. *J. Genet. Psychol.*, 102:277–285.

———— (1965), The concept of plasticity and language disabilities. In: *Children with Learning Problems: Reading in a Developmental-Interaction Approach*, ed. S. G. Sapir & A. C. Nitzburg. New York: Brunner/Mazel, 1973, pp. 477–484.

———— (1975), Language deficits in children with developmental lags. *The Psychoanalytic Study of the Child*, 30:95–126. New Haven, CT: Yale University Press.

Delacato, C. H. (1963), *Diagnosis and Treatment of Speech and Reading Problems*. Springfield, IL: Charles C Thomas.

Denckla, M. B. (1977), Minimal brain dysfunction and dyslexia: Beyond diagnosis by exclusion. In: *Topics in Child Neurology*, ed. M. E. Blaw, I. Rapin, & M. Kinsbourne. Englewood Cliffs, NJ: Spectrum, pp. 243–261.

———— (1979), Childhood learning disabilities. In: *Clinical Neuropsychology*, ed. K. Heilman & E. Valenstein. New York: Oxford University Press, pp. 535–573.

———— Rudel, R. G., & Broman, M. (1981), Tests that discriminate between dyslexic and other learning-disabled boys. *Brain and Lang.*, 13:118–129.

Denhoff, E. (1973), Natural life history of children with M.B.D. *Ann. NY Acad. Sci.*, 205:188–205.

Dennis, M. (1979), Neuropsychological assessment. In: *Basic Handbook of Child Psychiatry*, Vol. 1: ed. J. D. Call, J. D. Noshpitz, R. L. Cohen, & I. N. Berlin. New York: Basic Books, pp. 574–582.

Doris, J., & Solnit, A. (1963), Treatment of children with brain damage and associated school problems. *J. Amer. Acad. Child Psychiat.*, 2:618–635.

Dunn, L., & Markwardt, F., Jr. (1970), *Peabody Individual Achievement Test*. Circle Pines, MN: American Guidance Service.

Durrell, D. D. (1955), *Durrell Analysis of Reading Difficulty*. New York: Harcourt, Brace & World.

Dykman, R. A., Ackerman, P. T., Clements, S. D., & Peters, J. E. (1971), Specific learning disabilities: An attention deficit syndrome. In: *Progress in Learning Disabilities*. Vol. 2, ed. H. R. Myklebust. New York: Grune & Stratton, pp. 56–93.

Eisenberg, L. (1964), Behavioral manifestations of cerebral damage. In: *Brain Damage in Children: The Biological and Social Aspects*, ed. H. G. Birch. Baltimore, MD: Williams & Wilkins, pp. 61–73.

————— (1975), Psychiatric aspects of language disability. In: *Reading, Perception and Language*, ed. D. Duane & M. Rawson. Baltimore, MD: York Press, pp. 215–229.

Elliott, L., Halliday, R., & Callaway, E. (1978), Brain event related potentials: Contributions to research in learning disabilities. In: *Progress In Learning Disabilities*, Vol. 4, ed. H. R. Myklebust. New York: Grune & Stratton, pp. 121–144.

Exner, J. E., Jr. & Weiner, I. B. (1982), *The Rorschach: A Comprehensive System*, Vol. 3. New York: John Wiley.

Farnham-Diggory, S. (1980), Learning disabilities: A view from cognitive science. *J. Amer. Acad. Child Psychiat.*, 19:570–578.

Fenichel, O. (1937), The scoptophilic instinct and identification. *Internat. J. Psycho-Anal.*, 18:6–34.

Fernald, G. (1943), *Remedial Techniques in Basic School Subjects*. New York: McGraw-Hill.

Festinger, L. (1957), *A Theory of Cognitive Dissonance*. Evanston, IL: Row, Peterson.

Filskov, S. B., & Boll, T. J., Eds. (1981), *Handbook of Clinical Neuropsychology*. New York: John Wiley.

Flappan, D., & Neubauer, P. B. (1975), *Assessment of Early Child Development*. New York: Jason Aronson.

Forman, P. M. (1975), Pharmacological intervention. In: *Progress in Learning Disabilities*, Vol. 3, ed. H. R. Myklebust. New York: Grune & Stratton, pp. 151–177.

Forness, S. R. (1982), Diagnosing dyslexia: A note on the need for ecological assessment. *Amer. J. Dis. Child*, 136:794–799.

Fraiberg, S. (1968), Parallel and divergent patterns in blind and sighted infants. *The Psychoanalytic Study of the Child*, 23:264–300. New York: International Universities Press.

Freeman, T. (1974), Childhood psychopathology and psychotic phenomena in adults. *Brit. J. Psychiat.* 142:556–563.

Freud, A. (1963), The concept of developmental lines. *The Psychoanalytic Study of the Child*, 18:245–265. New York: International Universities Press.

———— (1970), The symptomatology of childhood. A preliminary attempt at classification. *The Psychoanalytic Study of the Child*, 25:19–44. New York: International Universities Press.

Freud, S. (1916–1917), Introductory lectures on psychoanalysis, Part III. *Standard Edition*, 16:243–463. London: Hogarth Press, 1964.

———— (1923), The ego and the id. *Standard Edition*, 19:12–66. London: Hogarth Press, 1964.

———— (1926), Inhibitions, symptoms and anxiety. *Standard Edition*, 20:87–174. London: Hogarth Press, 1964.

Fries, M. E. (1944), Psychosomatic relationships between mother and infant. *Psychosom. Med.*, 6:159–162.

———— Lewi, B. (1938), Interrelated factors in development. *Amer. J. Orthopsychiat.* 8:726–752.

Frostig, M. (1964), *The Marianne Frostig Development Test of Visual Perception*. Palo Alto: Consulting Psychologists.

———— (1968), Education for children with learning disabilities. In: *Progress in Learning Disabilities*, Vol. 1, ed. H. R. Myklebust. New York: Grune & Stratton, pp. 234–266.

———— Horne, D. (1965), An approach to the treatment of children with learning disorders. In: *Learning Disorders*, Vol. 1, ed. J. Hellmuth. Seattle, WA: Special Child Publications, pp. 291–305.

———— Orpet, R. E. (1972), Cognitive theories and diagnostic procedures for children with learning difficulties. In: *Manual of Child Psychopathology*, ed. B. B. Wolman. New York: McGraw-Hill, pp. 820–843.

Gardner, R. A. (1968), Psychogenic problems of brain-injured children and their parents. *J. Amer. Acad. Child Psychiat.*, 7:471–491.

———— (1973), Psychotherapy of the psychogenic problems secondary to minimal brain dysfunction. *Internat. J. Child Psychother.*, 2:224–256.

———— (1979), *The Objective Diagnosis of Minimal Brain Dysfunction*. Cresskill, NJ: Creative Therapeutics.

———— (1980), Minimal brain dysfunction. In: *Child Development in Normality and Psychopathology*, ed. J. R. Bemporad. New York: Brunner/Mazel, pp. 269–304.

Gates, A. I., McKillop, A. S., & Horowitz, E. C. (1981), *Gates–McKillop-Horowitz Reading Diagnostic Test*. New York: Teachers College Press.

Gerstmann, J. (1940), Syndrome of finger agnosia, disorientation for right and left, agraphia, and acalculia. *Arch. Neurol. Psychiat.*, 44:398–408.

Geschwind, N. (1968), Neurological foundations of language. In: *Progress in Learning Disabilities*, Vol. 1, ed. H. R. Myklebust. New York: Grune & Stratton, pp. 182–198.

————— Kaplan, E. (1962), A human cerebral disconnection syndrome. *Neurol.*, 12:675–685.

Giffin, M. (1968), The role of child psychiatry in learning disabilities. In: *Progress in Learning Disabilities*, Vol. 1, ed. H. R. Myklebust. New York: Grune & Stratton, pp. 75–97.

Gilmore, J. V., & Gilmore, E. C. (1968), *Gilmore Oral Reading Test*. New York: Harcourt, Brace & World.

Gittelman, R. (1980), Indications for the use of stimulant treatment in learning disorders. *J. Amer. Acad. Child Psychiat.*, 19:623–636.

Glasser, A. J., & Zimmerman, I. L. (1967), *Clinical Interpretation of the Wechsler Intelligence Scale for Children*. New York: Grune & Stratton.

Glover, E. (1925), Notes on oral character formation. *Internat. J. Psycho-Anal.*, 6:131–154.

Golden, C. J. (1978), *Diagnosis and Rehabilitation in Clinical Neuropsychology*. Springfield, IL: Charles C Thomas.

Gomez, M. R. (1967), Minimal brain dysfunction (maximal neurologic confusion). *Clin. Ped.*, 6:589–591.

Goodman, J. D., & Sours, J. A. (1967), *The Child Mental Status Examination*. New York: Basic Books.

Gottesman, R., Belmont, I., & Kaminer, R. (1976), Admission and follow-up status of reading disabled children referred to a medical clinic. *Annual Progress in Child Psychiatry and Child Development*, ed. S. Chess & A. Thomas. pp. 301–315.

Gray, W. S. (1963), *Gray Oral Reading Tests*. Indianapolis: Bobbs-Merrill.

Greenacre, P. (1941), The predisposition to anxiety. *Psychoanal. Quart.*, 10:66–94.

Greenspan, S. I. (1979), Principles of intensive psychotherapy of neurotic adults with minimal brain dysfunction. In: *Psychiatric Aspects of Minimal Brain Dysfunction in Adults*, ed. L. Bellak. New York: Grune & Stratton, pp. 161–175.

Gross, M. B., & Wilson, W. C. (1974), *Minimal Brain Dysfunction*. New York: Brunner/Mazel.

Guthrie, J. T. (1977), Principles of instruction: A critique of Johnson's "Remedial approaches to dyslexia." In: *Dyslexia: An Appraisal of Current Knowledge*, ed. A. L. Benton & D. Pearl. New York: Oxford University Press, pp. 423–433.

————— Seifert, M. (1978), Education for children with reading disabilities. In: *Progress in Learning Disabilities*, Vol. 4, ed. H. R. Myklebust. New York: Grune & Stratton, pp. 223–255.

Hagin, R. A. (1973), Models of intervention with learning disabilities: Ephemeral and otherwise. *School Psychol. Monog.*, 8:1–24.

_____ Silver, A. (1977), Learning disability: Definition, diagnosis, and prevention. *NY Univ. Ed. Quart.*, 8:9–15.

_____ _____ Beecher, R. (1978), TEACH: Learning tasks for the prevention of learning disabilities. *J. Learn. Dis.*, 11:445–449.

_____ _____ Kreeger, H. (1976), *TEACH: Learning Tasks for the Prevention of Learning Disability*. New York: Walker.

Halpern, F. (1953), *A Clinical Approach to Children's Rorschachs*. New York: Grune & Stratton.

Hammer, E. F. (1960), The house-tree-person (HTP) drawings as a projective technique with children. In: *Projective Techniques with Children*, eds. A. I. Rabin & M. R. Haworth. New York: Grune & Stratton, pp. 258–272.

Harris, I. D. (1966), *Emotional Blocks to Learning*. New York: Free Press of Glencoe.

Hartmann, H. (1950), Comments on the psychoanalytic theory of the ego. In: *Essays on Ego Psychology: Selected Problems in Psychoanalytic Theory*. New York: International Universities Press, 1964, pp. 113–141.

Hartocollis, P. (1968), The syndrome of minimal brain dysfunction in young adult patients. *Bull. Menn. Clin.*, 32:102–114.

_____ (1979), Minimal brain dysfunction in young adults. In: *Psychiatric Aspects of Minimal Brain Dysfunction in Adults*, ed. L. Bellak. New York: Grune & Stratton, pp. 103–112.

Harway, V. T. (1979), Psychoeducational assessment. In: *Basic Handbook of Child Psychiatry*, eds. J. D. Call, J. D. Noshpitz, R. L. Cohen, & I. N. Berlin. New York: Basic Books, pp. 583–592.

Hegge, T. G., Kirk, S. A., & Kirk, W. D. (1969), *Remedial Reading Drills*. Ann Arbor, MI: George Wahr Publishing.

Heilman, K. M. (1978), Language and the brain: Relationship of localization of language function to the acquisition and loss of various aspects of language. *Education and the Brain*, Seventy-seventh Yearbook of the National Society for the Study of Education. Chicago: University of Chicago Press, pp. 143–168.

Heinicke, C. M. (1972), Learning disturbances in childhood. In: *Manual of Child Psychopathology*, ed. B. B. Wolman. New York: McGraw-Hill, pp. 662–705.

_____ (1980), Continuity and discontinuity of task orientation. *J. Amer. Acad. Child Psychiat.*, 19:637–653.

Hellman, I. (1954), Some observations on mothers of children with intellectual inhibitions. *The Psychoanalytic Study of the Child*, 9:259–273. New York: International Universities Press.

Hertz, M. R. (1960), The Rorschach in adolescence. In: *Projective Techniques with Children*, ed. A. I. Rabin & M. R. Haworth. New York: Grune & Stratton, pp. 29–60.

Hodges, K., McKnew, D., Cytryn, L., Stern, L., & Kline, J. (1982), The child assessment schedule (CAS) diagnostic interview: A report on reliability and validity. *J. Amer. Acad. Child Psychiat.*, 21:468–473.

Hoffer, W. (1952), The mutual influences in the development of ego and id: Earliest stages. *The Psychoanalytic Study of the Child*, 7:31–41. New York: International Universities Press.

Hynd, G. W., & Obrzut, J. E., Eds. (1981), *Neuropsychological Assessment and the School-Age Child*. New York: Grune & Stratton.

Ingram, I., Mason, A., & Blackburn, I. (1970), A retrospective study of 82 children with reading disability. *Dev. Med. Child Neurol.*, 12:271–281.

Ingram, T. (1973), Soft signs. *Dev. Med. Child Neurol.*, 15:527–530.

Jansky, J. J. (1980), Specific learning disabilities: A clinical view. In: *Child Development in Normality and Psychopathology*, ed. J. R. Bemporad. New York: Brunner/Mazel, pp. 305–336.

Jarvis, V. (1958), Clinical observations on the visual problem in reading disability. *The Psychoanalytic Study of the Child*, 13:451–470. New York: International Universities Press.

Jastak, J. F., & Jastak, S. (1978), *Wide Range Achievement Test*. Wilmington, DE: Jastak Associates.

John, E. R., Kamel, B. Z., Corning, W. C., Easton, P., Brown, D., Ahn, H., John, M., Harmony, T., Prichep, L., Toro, A., Gerson, I., Bartlett, F., Thatcher, R., Kaye, H., Valdes, J., & Schwartz, E. (1977), Neurometrics. *Science*, 196:1393–1410.

Johnson, D. S., & Myklebust, H. R. (1967), *Learning Disabilities: Educational Principles and Practices*. New York: Grune & Stratton.

Kafka, E. (1984), Cognitive difficulties in psychoanalysis. *Psychoanal. Quart.*, 53:533–550.

Kagan, J. (1960), Thematic apperception techniques with children. In: *Projective Techniques with Children*, ed. A. I. Rabin & M. R. Haworth. New York: Grune & Stratton, pp. 105–129.

Katan, A. (1961), Some thoughts about the role of verbalization in early childhood. *The Psychoanalytic Study of the Child*, 16:184–188. New York: International Universities Press.

Kaufman, A. S. (1979), *Intelligence Testing with the WISC-R*. New York: John Wiley.

Kaye, S. (1982), Psychoanalytic perspectives on learning disability. *J. Contemp. Psychother.*, 13:83–93.

Kennard, M. (1960), Value of equivocal signs in neurological diagnosis. *Neurol.*, 10:753–764.

Kephart, N. C. (1960), *The Slow Learner in the Classroom*. Columbus, OH: Charles E. Merrill.

——— (1968), Development sequences. In: *Readings in a Developmental-Interaction Approach*, ed. S. G. Sapir & A. C. Nitzburg. New York: Brunner/Mazel, 1973, pp. 318–334.

Kernberg, O. (1975), The diagnosis of borderline conditions in adolescence. In: *Adolescent Psychiatry*, Vol. 6; ed. S. Feinstein & P. L. Giovacchini. Chicago: University of Chicago Press, pp. 298–319.

Kinsbourne, M. (1968), Developmental Gerstmann syndrome. *Ped. Clin. N. Amer.*, 15:771–778.

———— (1973a), Minimal brain dysfunction as a neuro-developmental lag. *Ann. NY Acad. Sci.*, 205:268–273.

———— (1973b), Diagnosis and treatment: School problems. *Pediatrics*, 52:697–710.

———— (1979), Principles of the neurological examination. In: *Basic Handbook of Child Psychiatry*, Vol. 1, ed. J. D. Call, J. D. Noshpitz, R. L. Cohen, & I. N. Berlin. New York: Basic Books, pp. 568–574.

———— Caplan, P. J. (1979), *Children's Learning and Attention Problems*. Boston: Little, Brown.

———— Warrington, E. K. (1963), The developmental Gerstmann syndrome. *Arch. Neurol.*, 8:490–501.

———— ———— (1966), Developmental factors in reading and writing backwardness. In: *The Disabled Reader: Education of the Dyslexic Child*, ed. J. Money. Baltimore, MD: Johns Hopkins Press, pp. 59–71.

Kirk, S. A., McCarthy, J. J., & Kirk, W. D. (1968), *Illinois Test of Psycho-linguistic Abilities*. Urbana: University of Illinois Press.

Klein, E. (1949), Psychoanalytic aspects of school problems. *The Psychoanalytic Study of the Child*, 3/4:369–390. New York: International Universities Press.

Klein, G. S. (1951), The personal world through perception. In: *Perception*, ed. R. R. Blake & G. V. Ramsey. New York: Ronald Press, pp. 328–355.

———— (1954), Need and recognition. In: *Nebraska Symposium on Motivation*, ed. M. R. Jones. Lincoln: University of Nebraska Press, pp. 224–274.

———— (1970), *Perception, Motives, and Personality*. New York: Alfred Knopf.

Klein, M. (1931), A contribution to the theory of intellectual inhibitions. *Internat. J. Psycho-Anal.*, 12:206–218.

Klopfer, B., Ainsworth, M., Klopfer, W. G., & Holt, R. R. (1954), *Developments in Rorschach Technique*, Vol. 1. Yonkers, NY: World Book.

———— Davidson, H. H. (1962), *Rorschach Technique: An Introductory Manual*. New York: Harcourt, Brace & World.

Klueur, R. (1971), Mental abilities and disorders of learning. In: *Progress in Learning Disabilities*, Vol. 2, ed. H. R. Myklebust. New York: Grune & Stratton, pp. 196–212.

Koppitz, E. M. (1964), *The Bender Gestalt Test for Young Children*, Vol. 2. New York: Grune & Stratton.

———— (1968), *Psychological Evaluation of Children's Human Figure*

Drawings. New York: Grune & Stratton.

Kuhn, T. S. (1962), *The Structure of Scientific Revolutions.* Chicago: University of Chicago Press.

Levin, H. S. (1979), The acalculias. In: *Clinical Neuropsychology,* eds. K. M. Heilman & E. Valenstein. New York: Oxford University Press, pp. 128–140.

Levitt, E. E., & Truuma, A. (1972), *The Rorschach Technique with Children and Adolescents.* New York: Grune & Stratton.

Lezak, M. (1976), *Neuropsychological Assessment.* New York: Oxford University Press.

Liss, E. (1955), Motivations in learning. *The Psychoanalytic Study of the Child,* 10:100–116. New York: International Universities Press.

Luria, A. R. (1973), *The Working Brain.* New York: Basic Books.

———— (1980), *Higher Cortical Functions in Man.* New York: Basic Books.

———— Tzvetkova, L. S. (1968), The re-education of brain-damaged patients and its psychopedagogical applications. In: *Learning Disorders,* Vol. 3, ed. J. Hellmuth. Seattle, WA: Special Child Publications, pp. 137–154.

Machover, K. (1960), Sex differences in the development pattern of children as seen in human figure drawings. In: *Projective Techniques with Children,* eds. A. I. Rabin & M. R. Haworth. New York: Grune & Stratton, pp. 238–257.

Magnussen, M. G. (1979), Psychometric and projective techniques. In: *Basic Handbook of Child Psychiatry,* Vol. 1, ed. J. D. Call, J. D. Noshpitz, R. L. Cohen, & I. N. Berlin. New York: Basic Books, pp. 553–568.

Mahler, M. S. (1942), Pseudoimbecility; a magic cap of invincibility. *Psychoanal. Quart.,* 11:149–164.

Marcie, P., & Hécaen, H. (1979), Agraphia: Writing disorder associated with unilateral cortical lesion. In: *Clinical Neuropsychology,* ed. K. M. Heilman & E. Valenstein. New York: Oxford University Press, pp. 92–127.

Mattick, I., & Murphy, L. B. (1971), Cognitive disturbances in young children. In: *Children with Learning Problems: Readings in a Developmental-Interaction Approach,* ed. S. G. Sapir & A. C. Nitzburg. New York: Brunner/Mazel, 1973, pp. 415–460.

Mattis, S. (1979), Dyslexia syndromes: A working hypothesis that works. In: *Dyslexia: An Appraisal of Current Knowledge,* ed. A. L. Benton & D. Pearl. New York: Oxford University Press, pp. 43–58.

———— French, J., & Rapin, I. (1975), Dyslexia in children and young adults: Three independent neuropsychological syndromes. *Dev. Med. Child Neurol.,* 17:150–163.

McGrady, A. J., Jr. (1968), Language pathology and learning disabilities. In: *Progress in Learning Disabilities.* Vol. 1, ed. H. R. Myklebust. New York: Grune & Stratton, pp. 199–233.

Meier, J. H. (1976), *Developmental and Learning Disabilities: Evaluation, Management and Prevention in Children*. Baltimore, MD: University Park Press.

Millman, I. K., & Canter, S. M. (1972), Language disturbances in normal and pathological development: Comparisons and practical considerations. *The Psychoanalytic Study of the Child*, 11:243–254. New York: International Universities Press.

Moore, W. T. (1975), The impact of surgery on boys. *The Psychoanalytic Study of the Child*, 30:529–549. New Haven, CT: Yale University Press.

Mundy, J. (1972), The use of projective techniques with children. In: *Manual of Child Psychopathology*, ed. B. B. Wolman. New York: McGraw-Hill.

Murray, H. A. (1943), *Thematic Apperception Test*. Cambridge, MA: Harvard University Press.

Myklebust, H. R. (1964), Learning disorders—Psychoneurological disturbances in childhood. In: *Children with Learning Problems: Readings in a Developmental-Interaction Approach*, ed. S. G. Sapir & A. C. Nitzburg. New York: Brunner/Mazel, 1973, pp. 257–269.

———— Ed. (1968), *Progress in Learning Disabilities*, Vol. 1. New York: Grune & Stratton.

———— Ed. (1971), *Progress in Learning Disabilities*, Vol. 2. New York: Grune & Stratton.

———— (1975a), Nonverbal learning disabilities. In: *Progress in Learning Disabilities*, Vol. 3, ed. H. R. Myklebust. New York: Grune & Stratton, pp. 85–121.

———— Ed. (1975b), *Progress in Learning Disabilities*, Vol. 3. New York: Grune & Stratton.

———— Ed. (1978a), *Progress in Learning Disabilities*, Vol. 4. New York: Grune & Stratton.

———— (1978b), Toward a science of dyslexiology. In: *Progress in Learning Disabilities*, Vol. 4, ed. H. R. Myklebust. New York: Grune & Stratton, pp. 1–39.

———— Ed. (1983), *Progress in Learning Disabilities*, Vol. 5. New York: Grune & Stratton.

———— Bannochie, M. N., & Kellen, J. R. (1971), Learning disabilities and cognitive processes. In: *Progress in Learning Disabilities*, Vol. 2, ed. H. R. Myklebust. New York: Grune & Stratton, pp. 213–251.

Nelville, D. (1966), The intellectual characteristics of severely retarded readers and implications for teaching techniques. In: *Learning Disorders*, Vol. 2, ed. J. Hellmuth. Seattle, WA: Special Child Publications, pp. 283–294.

Newman, C. J., Dember, C. F., & Krug, O. (1973), He can but he won't; A psychodynamic study of so-called gifted underachievers. *The Psychoanalytic Study of the Child*, 28:83–129. New Haven, CT: Yale University Press.

Newman, J. Ed. (1956), *The World of Mathematics*, Vol. 1. New York: Simon & Schuster.

New York University Medical Center, Department of Psychiatry (undated), *The Neurometric Evaluation Service* (brochure). New York: New York University Medical Center.

Ochroch, R. (1981), The case for the "case" manager. In: *The Diagnosis and Treatment of Minimal Brain Dysfunction in Children: A Clinical Approach*, ed. R. Ochroch. New York: Human Sciences Press, pp. 127–135.

Ong, B. H. (1968), The pediatrician's role in learning disabilities. In: *Progress in Learning Disabilities*, Vol. 1, ed. H. R. Myklebust. New York: Grune & Stratton, pp. 98–112.

Opperman, J. (1978), Tutoring: The remediation of cognitive and academic deficits by individual instruction. In: *Child Analysis and Therapy*, ed. J. Glenn. New York: Jason Aronson, pp. 495–528.

Orton, S. T. (1937), *Reading, Writing, and Speech Problems in Children*. New York: W. W. Norton.

Ozer, M. N., & Richardson, H. B. (1974), The diagnostic evaluation of children with learning problems: A "process" approach. *J. Learn. Disab.*, 7:30–34.

Pearson, G. H. J. (1952), A survey of learning difficulties in children. *The Psychoanalytic Study of the Child*, 7:322–386. New York: International Universities Press.

Peters, J. E., Roming, J. S., & Dykman, R. A. (1975), A special neurological examination of children with learning disabilities. *Dev. Med. Child Neurol.*, 175:63–78.

Piaget, J. (1954), *The Construction of Reality in the Child*. New York: Basic Books.

———— (1969), *The Child's Conception of the World*. Totowa, NJ: Littlefield, Adams.

Pihl, R. O. (1975), Learning disabilities: Intervention programs in the schools. In: *Progress in Learning Disabilities*, Vol. 3, ed. H. R. Myklebust. New York: Grune & Stratton, pp. 19–48.

Pine, F. (1980), On phase-characteristic pathology of the school-age child: Disturbances of personality development and organization (borderline conditions) of learning, and of behavior. In: *The Course of Life: Psychoanalytic Contributions Toward Understanding Personality Development*, Vol. 2, ed. S. J. Greenspan & G. H. Pollock. Washington, DC: Government Printing Office, pp. 165–203.

Plank, E. N., & Plank, R. (1954), Emotional components in arithmetical learning as seen through autobiographies. *The Psychoanalytic Study of the Child*, 9:274–293. New York: International Universities Press.

Poeck, K., & Orgass, B. (1966), Gerstmann's syndrome and aphasia. *Cortex*, 2:421–437.

Rabinovitch, R. D. (1968), Reading problems in children: Definitions and classification. In: *Dyslexia: Diagnosis and Treatment of Reading Disorders*, eds. A. Keeney & V. Keeney. St. Louis: Mosby, pp. 1–10.

———— (1972), Dyslexia: Psychiatric considerations. In: *Reading Disability: Progress and Research Needs in Dyslexia*, ed. J. Money. Baltimore, MD: Johns Hopkins Press, pp. 73–79.

———— Drew, A. L., DeJong, R. N., Ingram, W. & Withey, L. (1954), A research approach to reading retardation. *Research Publication of the Association of Nervous and Mental Diseases*, 34:363–387.

Rangell, L. (1972), Aggression, Oedipus and historical perspective. *Internat. J. Psycho-Anal.*, 53:3–11.

Rapaport, D., Gill, M. M., & Schafer, R. (1968), *Diagnostic Psychological Testing*. New York: International Universities Press.

Rappaport, S. R. (1961), Behavior disorder and ego development in a brain-injured child. *The Psychoanalytic Study of the Child*, 16:423–450. New York: International Universities Press.

———— (1964), The brain damage syndrome. In: *Children with Learning Problems: Readings in a Developmental-Interaction Approach*, eds. S. G. Sapir & A. C. Nitzburg. New York: Brunner/Mazel, 1973, pp. 252–256.

Raven, J. C. (1965), *The Coloured Progressive Matrices*. London: H. K. Lewis.

Rie, H. E., & Rie, E. D. (1980), *Handbook of Minimal Brain Dysfunctions*. New York: John Wiley.

Rorschach, H. (1948), *Rorschach Psychodiagnostic Plates*. New York: Grune & Stratton.

Ross, A. O. (1976), *Psychological Aspects of Learning Disabilities and Reading Disorders*. New York: McGraw-Hill.

Roswell, F. G. & Natchez, G. (1977), *Reading Disability, A Human Approach to Learning*. New York: Basic Books.

Rothstein, A. (1982), Learning disorders: An integrative perspective on diagnosis. *J. Amer. Acad. Child Psychiat.*, 21:420–426.

Rourke, B. P. (1975), Minimal brain dysfunction: Is diagnosis necessary? Paper presented at the meeting of the American Psychological Association, Chicago, August.

———— (1978), Reading, spelling, arithmetic disabilities: A neuropsychologic perspective. In: *Progress in Learning Disabilities*, Vol. 4, ed. H. R. Myklebust. New York: Grune & Stratton, pp. 97–120.

———— (1981), Neuropsychological assessment of children with learning disabilities. In: *Handbook of Clinical Neuropsychology*, ed. S. B. Filskov & T. J. Boll. New York: John Wiley, pp. 453–478.

———— Bakker, D. J., Fisk, J. L., & Strang, J. D. (1983), *Child Neuropsychology: An Introduction to Theory, Research and Clinical Practice*. New York: Guilford Press.

Rubenstein, B. O., Falick, M. L., Levitt, M., & Eckstein, R. (1959), Learning problems; learning impotence, a suggested diagnostic category. *Amer. J. Orthopsychiat.*, 29:315–323.

Rubin, E. Z. (1971), Cognitive dysfunction and emotional disorders. In: *Progress in Learning Disabilities*, Vol. 2, ed. H. R. Myklebust. New York: Grune & Stratton, pp. 179–195.

Rudel, R. G. (1980), Learning disability: Diagnosis by exclusion and discrepancy. *J. Amer. Acad. Child Psychiat.*, 19:547–569.

Rutter, M. (1979), Prevalence and types of dyslexia. In: *Dyslexia: An Appraisal of Current Knowledge*, ed. A. L. Benton & D. Pearl. New York: Oxford University Press, pp. 3–28.

––––––– Graham, P., & Yule, W. (1970), *A Neuropsychiatric Study in Childhood*, Clin. Div. Med. No. 35/36. London: William Heinemann.

Santostefano, S. (1978), *A Biodevelopmental Approach to Clinical Child Psychology*. New York: John Wiley.

––––––– (1980), Cognition in personality and the treatment process. *The Psychoanalytic Study of the Child*, 35:41–66. New Haven, CT: Yale University Press.

Sapir, S. G. (1973), Learning disability and deficit centered classroom training. In: *Children with Learning Problems: Readings in a Developmental-Interaction Approach*, ed. S. G. Sapir & A. C. Nitzburg. New York: Brunner/Mazel, 1973, pp. 660–672.

––––––– Nitzburg, A. C. Eds. (1973), *Children with Learning Problems: Readings in a Developmental-Interaction Approach*. New York: Brunner/Mazel.

––––––– Wilson, B. (1978), *A Professional's Guide to Working with the Learning Disabled Child*. New York: Brunner/Mazel.

Sarvis, M. A. (1960), Psychiatric implications of temporal lobe damage. *The Psychoanalytic Study of the Child*, 15:454–481. New York: International Universities Press.

Satz, P., Taylor, H. G., Friel, J., & Fletcher, J. M. (1978), Some developmental and predictive precursors of reading disabilities: A six year follow-up. In: *Dyslexia: An Appraisal of Current Knowledge*, ed. A. L. Benton & D. Pearl. New York: Oxford University Press, pp. 315–347.

Schain (1977), *Neurology of Childhood Learning Disorders*. Baltimore, MD: Williams & Wilkins.

Schilder, P. (1944), Congenital alexia and its relation to optic perception. *J. Genet. Psychol.*, 65:67–88.

Schmitt, B. D. (1975), The minimal brain dysfunction myth. *Amer. J. Dis. Child.*, 129:1313–1318.

Shaffer, D. (1978), "Soft" neurological signs and later psychiatric disorder— A review. *J. Child Psychol. Psychiat.*, 19:63–65.

Silver, A. A., & Hagin, R. A. (1960), Specific reading disability: Delineation of the syndrome and relationship to cerebral dominance. *Comprehensive Psychiat.*, 1:126–134.

_____ _____ (1964), Specific reading disability: Follow-up studies. *Amer. J. Orthopsychiat.*, 34:95–102.

_____ _____ (1980), Profile of a first grade; A basis for preventive psychiatry. In: *Child Development in Normality and Pathology*, ed. J. R. Bemporad. New York: Brunner/Mazel, pp. 645–674.

_____ _____ Hersh, M. (1967), Reading disability: Teaching through stimulation of deficit perceptual areas. *Amer. J. Orthopsychiat.*, 37:744–752.

_____ _____ De Vito, E., Kreeger, H., & Scully, E. (1976), A search battery for scanning kindergarten children for potential learning disability. *J. Amer. Acad. Child Psychiat.*, 15:224–239.

Silver, L. B. (1971), A proposed view on the etiology of the neurological learning disability syndrome. *J. Learn. Disab.*, 4:123–133.

_____ (1974a), Emotional and social problems of children with developmental disabilities. In: *Handbook on Learning Disabilities*, ed. R. E. Weber. Englewood Cliffs, NJ: Prentice-Hall, pp. 97–120.

_____ (1974b), Emotional and social problems of the family with a child who has developmental disabilities. In: *Handbook on Learning Disabilities*, ed. R. E. Weber. Englewood Cliffs, NJ: Prentice-Hall, pp. 121–130.

_____ (1975), Acceptable and controversial approaches to treating the child with learning disabilities. *Pediatrics*, 55:406–415.

_____ (1976), The playroom diagnostic evaluation of children with neurologically based learning disabilities. *J. Amer. Acad. Child Psychiat.*, 15:240–256.

_____ (1979), The minimal brain dysfunction syndrome. In: *Basic Handbook of Child Psychiatry*, Vol. 2, ed. J. D. Noshpitz. New York: Basic Books, pp. 416–439.

Silverman, J. S., Fite, M. W., & Mosher, M. M. (1959), Learning problems: Clinical findings in reading disability children—Special cases of intellectual inhibition. *Amer. J. Orthopsychiat.*, 29:298–314.

Silverman, M. A. (1976), The diagnosis of minimal brain dysfunction in the preschool child. In: *Mental Health in Children*, Vol. 2, ed. D. V. Siva Sankar. Westbury, NY: PJD Publications, pp. 221–301.

Slade, P. & Russell, G. (1971), Developmental dyscalculia: A brief report on four cases. *Psychol. Med.*, 1:292–298.

Smith, S. L. (1979), *No Easy Answers: The Learning Disabled Child at Home and at School*. Cambridge, MA: Winthrop.

Sours, J. A. (1978), An analytically oriented approach to the diagnostic evaluation. In: *Child Analysis and Therapy*, ed. J. Glenn. New York: Jason Aronson, pp. 597–613.

Spreen, O., & Benton, A. L. (1969), *Neurosensory Center Comprehensive Examination for Aphasia*. Canada: Neuropsychology Laboratory Department of Psychology, University of Victoria.

Sprince, M. P. (1967), The psychoanalytic handling of pseudo-stupidity and grossly abnormal behavior in a highly intelligent boy. In: *The Child Analyst at Work*, ed. E. R. Geleerd. New York: International Universities Press, pp. 85–114.

Staver, N. (1953), The child's learning difficulty as related to the emotional problems of the mother. *Amer. J. Orthopsychiat.*, 23:131–141.

Stevens, D. A., Boydstun, J. A., Dykman, R. A., Peters, J. E., & Sinton, D. W. (1967), Presumed minimal brain dysfunction in children. *Arch. Gen. Psychiat.*, 16:281–285.

Stone, L. (1954), The widening scope of indications for psychoanalysis. *J. Amer. Psychoanal. Assn.*, 2:567–594.

Strachey, J. (1930), Some unconscious factors in reading. *Internat. J. Psycho-Anal.*, 11:322–331.

Strauss, A. A., & Kephart, N. C. (1955), *Psychopathology and Education of the Brain Injured Child*, Vol. 2. New York: Grune & Stratton.

———— & Lehtinen, L. (1947), *Psychopathology and Education of the Brain Injured Child*, Vol. 1. New York: Grune & Stratton.

Strother, C. R. (1972), Minimal cerebral dysfunction: An historical overview. In: *Children with Learning Problems: Readings in a Developmental-Interaction Approach*, ed. S. G. Sapir & A. C. Nitzburg. New York: Brunner/Mazel, pp. 173–186.

Thompson, L. J. (1974), Learning disabilities: An overview. In: *Annual Progress in Child Psychiatry and Child Development*, Part IV, ed. S. Chess & A. Thomas. New York: Brunner/Mazel, pp. 166–181.

Tiffin, J. (1948), *Purdue Pegboard Test*. Lafayette, IN: Purdue Research Foundation.

Torgesen, J. (1975), Problems and prospects in the study of learning disabilities. *Review of Child Development Research*, Vol. 5, pp. 385–439.

Towbin, A. (1971), Organic causes of minimal brain dysfunction: Perinatal origin of minimal cerebral lesions. *J. Amer. Med. Assn.*, 217:1207–1214.

Vellutino, F. R. (1977), Alternative conceptualizations of dyslexia: Evidence in support of a verbal deficit hypothesis. *Harvard Educ. Rev.*, 47:334–354.

Vereecken, P. (1965), Inhibition of ego functions and the psychoanalytic theory of acalculia. *The Psychoanalytic Study of the Child*, 20:535–566. New York: International Universities Press.

Voeller, K. (1981), A proposed extended behavioral, cognitive, and sensorimotor pediatric neurological examination. In: *The Diagnosis and Treatment of Minimal Brain Dysfunction in Children: A Clinical Approach*, ed. R. Ochroch. New York: Human Sciences Press, pp. 65–90.

Vuckovich, D. M. (1968), Pediatric neurology and learning disabilities. In: *Progress in Learning Disabilities*, Vol. 1, ed. H. R. Myklebust. New York: Grune & Stratton, pp. 16–38.

Waelder, R. (1930), The principle of multiple function. *Psychoanal. Quart.*, 5:45–62, 1936.

Waldhorn, H. F. (1960), Assessment of analyzability: Technical and theoretical observations. *Psychoanal. Quart.*, 29:478–506.

Wechsler, D. (1974), *Wechsler Intelligence Scale for Children—Revised.* New York: The Psychological Corporation.

Weil, A. P. (1961), Psychopathic personality and organic behavior disorders—Different diagnostic and prognostic considerations. *Comp. Psychiat.*, 2:83–95.

———— (1970), The basic core. *The Psychoanalytic Study of the Child*, 25:422–460. New York: International Universities Press.

———— (1971), Children with minimal brain dysfunction. *Psychosoc. Process*, 1:80–97.

———— (1977), Learning disturbances with special consideration of dyslexia. *Issues Child Ment. Hlth.*, 5:52–66.

———— (1978), Maturational variations and genetic-dynamic issues. *J. Amer. Psychoanal. Assn.*, 26:461–491.

Wender, P. H. (1971), *Minimal Brain Dysfunction in Children.* New York: John Wiley.

Wepman, J. M. (1972), Auditory imperception: A perceptual–conceptual developmental construct. In: *Manual of Child Psychopathology*, ed. B. B. Wolman. New York: McGraw-Hill, pp. 653–661.

———— (1973), *Auditory Discrimination Test.* Beverly Hills, CA: Western Psychological Services.

Werry, J. (1968), Studies on the hyperactive child: An empirical analysis of the minimal brain dysfunction syndrome. *Arch. Gen. Psychiat.*, 19: 9–16.

———— (1972), Organic factors. In: *Psychopathological Disorders in Childhood*, ed. H. C. Quay & J. Werry. New York: John Wiley, pp. 90–133.

———— Aman, M. G. (1976), The reliability and diagnostic validity of the physical and neurological examination for soft signs (PANESS). *J. Aut. Child. Schizophr.*, 6:253–263.

———— Wolfersheim, J. P. (1967), Behavior therapy with children: A broad overview. *J. Amer. Acad. Child Psychiat.*, 6:346–370.

Whorf, B. L. (1956), *Language, Thought and Reality: Selected Writings of Benjamin Lee Whorf.* New York: John Wiley.

Wong, B. (1979a), The role of theory in learning disabilities research; Part I. An analysis of problems. *J. Learn. Disab.*, 12:585–595.

———— (1979b), The role of theory in learning disabilities research; Part II. A selective review of current theories of learning and reading disabilities. *J. Learn. Disab.*, 12:649–658.

Woodcock, R. A. (1973), *Woodcock Reading Mastery Test.* Circle Pines, MN: American Guidance Service.

Zentall, S. (1981), Specific learning disabilities: Communication and language process disturbances. In: *The Diagnosis and Treatment of Minimal Brain Dysfunction in Children: A Clinical Approach*, ed. R. Ochroch. New York: Human Sciences Press, pp. 180–193.

Zigmund, N. (1977), Remediation of dyslexia: A discussion. In: *Dyslexia: An Appraisal of Current Knowledge*, ed. A. L. Benton & D. Pearl. New York: Oxford University Press, pp. 435–449.

Name Index

Subject Index